A DOCUMENTARY HISTORY OF THE MEXICAN AMERICANS

A
DOCUMENTARY
HISTORY
OF THE
MEXICAN
AMERICANS

EDITED BY WAYNE MOQUIN
WITH CHARLES VAN DOREN

Introduction by Feliciano Rivera
Consulting Editor

PRAEGER PUBLISHERS
New York • Washington • London

The editors wish to express their gratitude for permission to reprint material from the following sources:

Academy of American Franciscan History for a selection from Chapter 28, from *Writings of Junipero Serra*, copyright 1955 by Academy of American Franciscan History.

American Council for Nationalities Service for "Pachucos in the Making," by George I. Sanchez, from *Common Ground*, Autumn 1943, copyright 1943 by Common Council for American Unity. Also for "The Mexican American: A National Concern—Program for Action," by Ernesto Galarza, from *Common Ground*, Summer 1949, copyright 1949 by Common Council for American Unity.

John Howell—Books for "Father Fray Alonso Giraldo de Terreros, President of the Mission of San Saba, to his Excellency the Marques de las Amarillas, Viceroy of New Spain," from *The San Saba Papers: A Documentary Account of the Founding and Destruction of San Saba Mission*. Also for "Father Jose Senan to Viceroy the Marques de Branciforte, Mexico City, May 14, 1796," from *The Letters of Jose Senan, O.F.M., Mission San Buenaventure, 1796–1823*.

Institute of Jesuit History of Loyola University of Chicago for "The Texas Missions in 1785," from *Mid-America*, January 1940.

Carey McWilliams for "Getting Rid of the Mexican," by Carey McWilliams, from *American Mercury*, March 1933.

The Reporter Magazine Company and Arnold Mayer for "The Grapes of Wrath, Vintage 1961," by Arnold Mayer, from *The Reporter*, February 2, 1961, copyright 1961 by The Reporter Magazine Company.

The University of New Mexico for "Letter from Don Diego de Vargas to the Conde de Galve," El Paso, January 12, 1693," from *Coronado Cuarto Centennial Publications, 1540–1940*, Vol. X, copyright 1940 by The University of New Mexico Press. Also for "Petitions of Benavides Regarding Tribute and Personal Service by the Indians," from *Coronado Cuarto Centennial Publications, 1540–1940*, Vol. IV, copyright 1945 by The University of New Mexico Press. Also for "Don Juan de Oñate to the Viceroy of New Spain, March 2, 1599," from *Don Juan de Oñate: Colonizer of New Mexico, 1595–1628*, copyright 1953 by The University of New Mexico Press.

The H. W. Wilson Company for "The Chicano Movement," by Ysidro Ramon Macias, from the March 1970 issue of the *Wilson Library Bulletin*, Copyright © 1970 by The H. W. Wilson Company.

PRAEGER PUBLISHERS
111 Fourth Avenue, New York, N.Y. 10003, U.S.A.
5, Cromwell Place, London S.W.7, England

Published in the United States of America in 1971
by Praeger Publishers, Inc.

Second printing, 1971

© 1971 by Praeger Publishers, Inc.

All rights reserved

Library of Congress Catalog Card Number: 78–101671

JUN 7 '72
Printed in the United States of America

CONTENTS

SECTIONS OF ILLUSTRATIONS FOLLOW PAGES 178 AND 338.

EDITORS' PREFACE

A book of this kind must depend on the efforts and expert knowledge of many persons. This is particularly so when the subject, as in this case, is relatively new and untried. The Mexican Americans have a long history on this continent and in this country, but their presence here and their achievements have not been appreciated and understood so extensively as those of other groups that have neither been here so long nor done so much. Take, for example, the question "When did American colonial history begin?" The traditional answer would be 1607, or even 1620—and the answerer would have mental images of Pilgrims landing at Plymouth Rock or of John Smith landing at Jamestown. In fact, however, the first enduring colony in an area that later became part of the United States was founded in New Mexico in the sixteenth century. Or take the question "When did American colonial history end?" The traditional answer, again, would be 1776, when the British colonies declared their independence from the mother country. But a much larger portion of the present United States—the entire Southwest, into which the thirteen Atlantic Coast colonies would fit several times over—did not declare *its* independence from *its* mother country (Spain) until 1821. And much of this territory did not become part of the United States until the conclusion of the Mexican War, in 1848.

The editors, therefore, wish to express their deep gratitude for the history lessons that they had to take from several scholars who had preceded them in their researches. First and foremost of these is Professor Feliciano Rivera of the history department of San Jose State College, San Jose, California. The editors began by asking Professor Rivera to serve simply as a consultant, but his knowledge was so great, and his advice, comments, and just plain conversation so valuable, that they ended up by asking his permission to list him as consulting editor of the volume. He very graciously consented. It is particularly important, therefore, to say that, although many of the merits of this book are owing to him, its defects and errors— if there are such—should be counted against the other editors.

A large number of historical and literary works were consulted in the preparation of the volume: state and regional histories, ethnic studies, novels, short stories, poems, and the like. Three books were especially helpful; the editors recommend them for any who wish to go more deeply into the subject. Paul Horgan's *Great River: The Rio Grande in North American History* (Volume 1, *The Indians and Spain*; Volume 2, *Mexico and the United States*) are essential for the background and interpretation of the early period and were mined for the first two chapters in the present book. For the modern period, two books were consulted more than any others. *The Spanish Americans of New Mexico*, by Nancie L. González, proved useful on many occasions. And Stan Steiner's recent best seller, *La Raza: The Mexican Americans*, is an unfailingly authoritative source of information, at the same time that it is fascinating reading.

The editors also wish to express their gratitude for the cooperation and generosity of the following institutions from which selections reprinted here were obtained: the Bancroft Library of the University of California at Berkeley; the Zimmerman Library of the University of New Mexico in Albuquerque; the Wilson Library of the University of Minnesota; and the Henry E. Huntington Library in San Marino, California. Acknowledgments to copyright holders for permission to reprint certain selections are listed in another place.

Finally, the editors wish to thank Dorothy J. Anderson for her patient help in preparing the manuscript of the book. Her contribution went far beyond what both she and they anticipated, and without her the book would have been later and worse.

Chicago, 1970   WAYNE MOQUIN
                                                       CHARLES VAN DOREN

INTRODUCTION

The sixty-five readings in this volume highlight the long and varied career of "La Raza"— the Mexican Americans. Their history, even within the geographical confines of the present United States, stretches back over four centuries. That makes them the second oldest component of American society. Only the Indians were here before them.

This documentary history of a people presents them in the changing circumstances of their past and present. It lets them speak for themselves, as well as letting outsiders talk about them. And it gives some indication of the historical settings through which they have passed. The readings are presented in chronological order from 1536 to 1970 and are divided into five chapters that illustrate markedly different epochs in the story of the Mexican Americans.

The background for most of the material in this book is the American Southwest: New Mexico, Texas, Colorado, California, and Arizona. The Southwest is where the American component of La Raza has always lived. Until 1848, all of this region constituted the northern provinces of Mexico.

The selections are divided into five chapters, which correspond, albeit somewhat arbitrarily, to fairly precise historical periods for the Mexican Americans. The first chapter deals with events during the long period of Spanish rule, ending in 1821. This was the era of the origins of La Raza, of the encounter between Spain and the Indian in the New World.

The second chapter covers the short period during which Mexico held sway over the Southwest. This chapter does not begin in 1821, the year in which Spain's rule came to an end, but rather in 1810. 1810 was the year in which the call for revolution went forth in Mexico. The years between 1810 and 1821 are counted as part of the Mexican era for several reasons. Mexico was in an almost continual state of turmoil and constitutional crisis from 1810 on. It was during this decade that the United States began to look forward seriously to acquiring the North American continent all the way to the Pacific. Mexico, internally divided, was, altogether knowingly or not, on the defensive against the expansionist tendencies of its neighbor to the north. Also during this time, Mexico—first under Spain's authority, then on its own—unwillingly planted the seeds that would sprout into a full-blown Texas Revolution in 1835. The United States was not unaware, from as early as 1810, of the weaknesses of the Interior Provinces of New Spain in terms of military defenses, lack of developed resources, and paucity of population. Finally, this decade of 1810 to 1821 saw the first substantial "Anglo" incursions into the Southwest. Attitudes were thus shaped that would be decisive for the relationship between the two peoples following the Mexican War.

The third chapter covers the period—from 1849 to 1910—of the Anglo-American take-over of the Southwest and the integration of the region into the society and economy of the United States. During these sixty years, Eastern capital was invested to revitalize the area, railroads were built, and thousands of Anglos and immigrants arrived to take up residence. Population was first attracted to places where quick and easy wealth seemed likely from the gold or silver mines. However, as the decades wore on, more and more thousands took up the land for farming or for the raising of cattle and sheep. With this Anglo conquest, the Mexican Americans began to find themselves a minority, and frequently an exploited minority relegated to second-class citizenship in their own homeland. It was during these post–Civil War years that the Mexican Americans became a "forgotten people," as later authors were to describe them.

The 1890's saw the beginning of a migration from Mexico into the United States that increased greatly after 1910, when revolution again broke out south of the border. This immigration is one of the main subjects of the fourth chapter, covering the years from 1911 to 1939. For the first time, during this period, both Mexicans and Mexican Americans began to move out of the Southwest into the industrial cities and the agricultural areas of the North. However, the economic and social progress made by La Raza continued to be minimal, because the Mexican Americans were still treated as a "foreign" enclave within American society.

The fifth chapter, covering the period from 1940 to the present, deals with the reawakening of La Raza, with its renewed confidence in the values of its heritage, its language, and its cultural contributions, and with its intense determination to take its rightful place in a pluralistic American society. Crucial to this new outlook for the Mexican Americans were the transition during and after World War II to an economy of abundance and an upsurge in the demands of all disadvantaged groups for fuller participation in the national life. The Mexican Americans pressed for social acceptance, civil and political rights, decent education, and expanded economic opportunities. In other words, La Raza began to desire, and to demand, citizenship in the fullest sense.

Such are the times and places of La Raza. But what of La Raza itself? To whom does the term refer? The word literally means "the race," but it would be better translated as "our people" or "my people." Although the term is basically ethnic in reference, La Raza itself is not solely an ethnic entity. It denotes a spirit of belonging and a sense of common destiny. In fact, it may be affirmed that La

Raza is not *one* thing of any kind. It is a plurality of ethnic groups and of interests, a fact that is equally true but rarely recognized about every ethnic component of American society.

The difficulties involved in the attempt to unitize La Raza are evident as soon as we try to name the people that make it up. There are several names to choose from: Spanish-American, Latin American, Mexican, and (most recently) Chicanos. Nor is it just that we are given a variety from which to make a random selection. The name preferred will depend on geography, age, and ethnic background. For instance, the members of La Raza in New Mexico seem to prefer the term Spanish-American, while those in California opt for Mexican American (without a hyphen). Descendants of the colonial Spaniards with no admixture of Indian blood prefer the name Hispano. The younger generation has revived Chicano, once considered derogatory, while members of the older generation, remembering its former meaning, shy away from it. The difficulties have been compounded in the last few years by those Mexican Americans who want to welcome all Spanish-speaking Americans into the fold. This would mean including the many Puerto Ricans and Cubans who have come to the United States largely since 1940. The point, of course, is that the larger the organized Spanish-speaking minority is, the more political and economic pressure it can bring to bear on the problems that confront it.

The editors of this book have adopted the term Mexican Americans, for they consider it the most precise verbal description of the people with whom these readings are concerned. The editors concede the arguments, historical, cultural, and ethnic, in favor of other terms, but they feel that it would have been historically inaccurate to use any other, even La Raza, consistently. In fact, no current term can be carried back through the centuries without at least some distortion. Nor can any historical name be carried forward with much greater success.

Settling on a name does not solve all the problems. The Mexican American of today is the product of a racial, cultural, and linguistic mingling that took place over three centuries. Mexican Americans can be purely Spanish, purely Indian, or a mixture of the two; but the racial factor is not the predominant one, although it is complicated enough when one considers the number of Indian nations with whom the Spaniards intermixed. The cultural and linguistic factors, rather, have created La Raza's life style, a collage of Spanish and Indian traditions permeated by the language of the former.

Not only were the Mexican Americans of the past ethnically divided; they were also riven by class divisions. Spain founded in the New World what was basically a feudal society. The civil rulers, the military leaders, and the clergy were mostly native Spaniards. The Spanish colonists gradually assumed the role of a lesser nobility; while the Indians gradually emerged as serfs, slaves, or peons. After the Anglo conquest, these distinctions were softened, but they did not disappear. There are still vestiges of class division apparent within La Raza. In addition, many members of Mexican-American communities are moved by interests other than ethnic ties. This is a natural tendency, and has been true for most immigrant peoples who came to America as well as among the Indians who were here already. The attractions of wealth, social position, and educational attainment have been nearly as significant among Mexican Americans as the equally alluring "will o' the wisp" of ethnic loyalty.

The people with whom the readings in this volume deal, the Mexican Americans, are either native born or immigrant and live for the most part in the Southwestern states. They dwell mostly in urban centers today, a complete reversal of the situation that obtained as late as 1940. Their attitudes, problems, interests, and economic potential are as diversified as those of any segment of American society. However, it remains true that most of them are poor, and that large numbers are ill fitted to play a significant role in contemporary society by virtue of educational and cultural deprivation. Moreover and at the same time, no group has become more aware of its problems, or of the obstacles placed in the way of solving them by society at large, as the Mexican American. If La Raza is obstreperous or militant today, it is only because it has finally come to understand the American dream. And, understanding it at last, the people of La Raza wonder why it cannot also be theirs.

FELICIANO RIVERA
Consulting Editor

San Jose, California
June, 1970

Part One

THE HISPANO-
INDIAN SYNTHESIS,
1536–1809

A vast crescent of largely arid land stretches from Southeast Texas to Southern California. Within it, in addition to the portions of those two states, lie New Mexico, Arizona, and parts of Colorado, Utah, and Nevada. Here it was that American history began nearly three quarters of a century before Jamestown was settled. Here stands the oldest state capital in the nation—Santa Fe—founded in 1610. And it was here, and in Old Mexico, that La Raza had its origins. That blending and overlapping of races, cultures, and life styles, which occurred when Spain encountered the Indian tribes of Mexico and the Southwest, took place in the nearly 275 years covered by the readings in this chapter.

Spain was the first European colonizing power to come to the New World. Largely through ignorance of geography, it was granted for its domain most of the Western Hemisphere by dint of a papal edict. Like other colonizing nations, Spain came to stay, and like the others, it laid down a thoroughgoing mercantilist policy with regard to its new-found possessions. Exploitation was the rule—not the only rule, to be sure, but the overriding one. And there was much to be exploited in Mexico and Peru—almost unbelievable wealth to be had for the taking.

But there was also a marked difference between Spain's policies and the practices of the English, Dutch, Swedes, and French in

North America. This lay in the relationship of Spaniard and Indian. In no other case was there a merger of the two peoples as there was in Mexico and the Spanish Southwest. Ethnically, of course, it was not a total merger, for there were Hispanos who had no Indian blood and pure Indians who became Spanish-speaking (and acting) Mexicans. Instead, it was the encounter itself that was different. For the British colonists, the aborigines were obstacles to be overcome on the frontier. Spain did not drive the tribes out and put them on reservations. Instead, it surrounded the Indians with religion, culture, societal attitudes and customs, and in turn took much from them on the same basis. Spaniards and Indians incorporated each other in the many decades from Cabeza de Vaca's wanderings until Mexico declared for independence.

This is not to suggest that all went smoothly between the two races. The opposite is true. Between Spaniards and Indians occurred every kind of human viciousness, barbarity, cruelty, even genocide. The brutalities chronicled by the Spaniards themselves are almost too appalling to be believed, had we not the events of our own century to convince us.

Spain came to the New World with the Cross in one hand and the Crown in the other—the two majesties of church and state, supposedly two powers equally involved in each other, ministering to each other, and dealing with the natives on an equal footing. For Spain, more than any Catholic vestige of the old Roman Empire, was both a church and a state. But with humankind, theory and practice often go their separate ways, and so it was with Spain's colonial policy. The church, in the persons of the friars, came to call the Indians to the Kingdom of God. The state came to gather wealth, to build a kingdom, and to gratify the avaricious desires of thousands of Spaniards for whom the mother country offered few rewards.

The Indian, of course, found himself caught between the coeval majesties. Was he a soul to be saved or a beast of burden to be worked until he dropped? Was he a human, little lower than the angels, or a base animal whose existence mattered not at all, except that he be useful? Torn between the two, the Indian was never wholly Christianized, nor was he ever brutalized out of existence. But he was at the center of the conflict that raged intermittently between the "two majesties" until Spain was expelled from the New World.

The situation, of course, was not really black and white. The friars were not always completely solicitous of the natives' welfare; nor did the civil power consistently grind the poor aborigines under its heels. Right and wrong were much more evenly apportioned between the two authorities. But it was nevertheless normally the case that edicts went out from Spain at the behest of the clergy to treat the Indians in a humane way, only to be disregarded by the civil power on this side of the Atlantic.

We must be more or less confined in this chapter to the Southwest, to what is today New Mexico, Arizona, California, and Texas, and most of all to New Mexico, for that was the heartland of the synthesis. New Mexico was settled first—in 1598—and remained the pivotal Mexican province in the north for most of the period. Texas was settled only after 1700 and then never more than halfheartedly.

By the end of the Spanish era, there were only four villages of any consequence, with a total population of perhaps 2,000. California was not colonized until 1769, by which time Spain had only a half century left in North America. Arizona was hardly bothered with at all, save for the missions among the Indians. It is in New Mexico alone that the continuity of Spanish colonial history is visible, down to the Mexican Revolution.

Spain's venture north of old Mexico was essentially a search for wealth, primarily for gold and silver. There had been so much to plunder in the lands of the Aztecs, Mayas, and Incas, why should there not be more to be had for the taking up north? Rumor had it that somewhere in that unknown region stood Cíbola—the Seven Cities of Gold containing wealth surpassing all the dreams of Spanish greed. And, of course, most Indians that the Spaniards met in the north were only too glad to confirm such rumors. "Más allá," they said. "Farther on." Just keep going, they meant, but please don't stay here. And so the Spaniards kept going. Coronado first, in his vain quest from 1540 to 1542; then other expeditions, official and legal or otherwise, until finally it was decided to plant a colony in 1598 in what would be called New Mexico, in the valley of the Rio del Norte (now the Rio Grande). Even after the colony was planted, the search went on, at least for a time. The founder of New Mexico, Don Juan de Oñate, traveled east and west looking for what everyone felt had to be out there somewhere. But it was not out there; and so the colony settled down to the business of making a living off the land, along with converting—and plundering—the Indians.

Life was never easy for these settlers at the fringe of civilization, but it was always eventful. The Plains Indians—thoroughly unconvertible, it seemed—would periodically swoop in for devastating raids. And there was the ceaseless bickering between civil and ecclesiastical officials to occupy the minds of the faithful and bewilder the native population. Slowly this bewilderment turned to contempt, distrust, and, finally, open rebellion. The Pueblo Revolt of 1680 was the most successful attempt ever staged by Indians in North America to drive the white man away (if we except the mysterious disappearance of the colony at Roanoke, Virginia). The Spaniards were driven completely out of New Mexico, taking refuge in El Paso until the reconquest thirteen years later.

Once New Mexico was resettled, Spain could look in other directions for additional colonies. But the later days of expansion were marked not so much by the quest for gold as by fears of intrusion by other European powers. It was the proximity of a French colony in east Texas that drew Spain there early in the eighteenth century. It was a similar threat of Russian adventuring on the Pacific Coast that led to the founding of the California province in 1769.

The Texas enterprise never really prospered until the Mexican period, when citizens of the United States began arriving there by the thousands. Under Spain, Texas was nearly abandoned once the French threat was removed by the transfer of the Louisiana Territory to Spain following the Seven Years' War. California, remotest of all the provinces from Mexico City, did prosper. In time it became a nearly self-sufficient, virtually independent colony. These good results derived from the energetic devotion of the Franciscan missioners to temporal as well as spiritual matters, for California was exclusively a mission colony. True, there were military presidios and civil pueblos there, but they were intended for the defense and maintenance of the twenty-one missions.

Much that makes up the Southwest today had a beginning during Spanish rule: the mining, the sheep- and cattle-raising, the irrigation projects, and the planting of orchards and vineyards. Once it was accepted that there was no gold or silver to be picked up from the ground, Spaniards and Indians together worked to wrest whatever living could be made from the arid lands. And it was this very fact that kept the region so lightly populated. Spain's mineral discoveries in the Southwest were meager, compared to the gold and silver bonanzas that would be uncovered after 1846, and there was therefore no incentive for Spaniards to flock there in great numbers. Had they done so, the history of the region would have been very different. For one thing, La Raza might have had a country of its own.

THE CAPTIVITY OF ALVAR NUNEZ CABEZA DE VACA

[In February, 1528, an expedition consisting of 400 men led by Pánfilo de Narváez set sail from Cuba for the mouth of the Rio de las Palmas—the Rio Grande. The intent was to explore the region and colonize it for the King of Spain. But, driven off course by spring storms, most of the men landed on the west coast of Florida. They changed their plan and decided to proceed overland with their leader to their destination, while the ships would sail ahead and meet them there. The two parties never encountered each other again, and the ships finally sailed off to Mexico after giving up the search. The land party met with complete disaster through storm, starvation, or Indian captivity. Only four men survived to appear seven years later in Mexico City to tell an amazing tale of captivity and travels among the Indians in the region from Florida to Texas. These survivors were Alvar Núñez Cabeza de Vaca, Alonso de Castillo Maldonado, Andrés Dorantes de Carrança, and a Moorish slave named Estebanico. In 1536, the four finally made their escape from the Indians and reached Mexico, where, on May 8, they were found by fellow Spaniards and taken to the capital. The report they made of their adventures to the Viceroy of New Spain convinced him there was great wealth to be had in the lands north of Mexico—wealth that would fill even the bottomless coffers of Spain and, incidentally, enrich some colonial officers. The selection reprinted here is a twentieth-century rendering, by Haniel Long, of what Cabeza de Vaca might well have wanted to say to the King of Spain. In Mr. Long's words, "My account of Núñez is not the account he sent the King, apart of course from the actual facts. But I believe it to be the account he wished to send the King. I preserve the core of the narrative, . . . and I try to show what, quite plainly, was happening to the spirit of the man."]

From Haniel Long, *The Power Within Us*. New York: Duell, Sloane and Pearce, 1944.

This is the tale of what men can and cannot do when they must do something or die. We built nine open boats. During the weeks it required, some of us went with scant food, and those whose palates allowed it devoured the horses.

Our 580 men had become 400 when at last we set sail and left behind us the Indian marksmen and the snakes, neither of which in Florida err when they strike.

Day after day tide and wind washed us out to sea and then washed us in to land, along a dazzling and uncertain coast. From thirst, and from the exposure to the frightful sun, our 400 became 40.

Who knows what was lost in these boats? Another Magellan, another Camões, another Cervantes, another St. John of the Cross . . .

While we were subjects of your Majesty, we had everything life offers, and now we had nothing. To understand what it means to have nothing one must have nothing. No clothing against the weather might appear the worst. But for us poor skeletons who survived it, it was not.

The worst lay in parting little by little with the thoughts that clothe the soul of a European, and most of all of the idea that a man attains strength through dirk and dagger, and serving in your Majesty's guard. We had to surrender such fantasies till our inward nakedness was the nakedness of an unborn babe, starting life anew in a womb of sensations which in themselves can mysteriously nourish. Several years went by before I could relax in that living plexus for which even now I have no name; but only when at last I relaxed, could I see the possibilities of a life in which to be deprived of Europe was not to be deprived of too much. . . .

In April the Indians went down to the sea taking us with them; for a whole month we ate the blackberries of the sand dunes. The Indians danced incessantly. They asked us to cure their sick. When we said we did not know how to cure, they withheld our food from us. We began to watch the procedure of their medicine men. It seemed to us both irreligious and uninstructed. Besides, we found the notion of healing Indians somewhat repellent, as your Majesty will understand. But we had to heal them or die. So we prayed for strength. We prayed on bended knees and in an agony of hunger. Then over each ailing Indian we made the sign of the Cross, and recited the Ave Maria and a Pater Noster. To our amazement the ailing said they were well. And not only they but the whole tribe went without food so that we might have it. Yet so great was the lack of food for us all, it seemed impossible that life could last.

Truly, it was to our amazement that the ailing said they were well. Being Europeans, we thought we had given away to doctors and priests our ability to heal. But here it was, still in our possession, even if we had only Indians to exercise it upon. It was ours after all, we were more than we had thought we were.

I am putting my words together for whatever intelligence there may be in the world. There is no other reality among men than this intelligence; Sire, it is greatly to your glory that you can incarnate it.

To be more than I thought I was—a sensation utterly new to me . . .

Starvation, nakedness, slavery: sensations utterly new to me, also . . . The last of my fellow Spaniards on the island dies . . . Nothing to eat after the sea roots sprouted but the blackberries of the sand dunes. Nothing to protect me from the attack of the terrible frost, or the terrible sun. No one who knew my language . . . And it endured for months, for years maybe . . . Everyone I saw was as starved as I was. The human body emaciated, the lean cheek, the burning eye—the ribs showing, each rib distinct—the taut skin, the weak loins, the shrunken haunch and pap. In the whole world there can be no poverty like the poverty of these people. I could not stand it. I ran away . . .

At this time, as I remember it, I began to think of Indians as fellow human beings. If I introduce this idea it is to prepare your Majesty for other ideas which came to me later, in consequence. . . .

One day I heard someone calling me by name, "Alvar Nuñez, Alvar Nuñez!" It was Alonso del Castillo, one of the captains of the expedition. He said that Pámfilo's barge had drifted ashore among unfriendly Indians, and left of its occupants were only himself and Captain Andrés Dorantes, and Dorantes' blackamoor, Estevanico. We hid ourselves in a thicket and laid our plans.

That summer, when the coast tribes came together for the summer orgies, we four made good our escape westward.

Thus our 580 had become 400, our 400, forty, and our forty, four. . . .

Indians came bringing five persons shriveled and paralyzed and very ill. Each of the five offered Castillo silently his bows and arrows. Castillo prayed, we with him; in the morning the five were cured . . .

Indians came from many places. But Castillo was always afraid his sins would interfere with his working miracles. The Indians turned to me. I told Castillo it was no moment for indulging the idea of being sinful, and then I followed the Indians to their ranch. The dying man was dead; Dorantes and I found him with eyes upturned, and no pulse. I removed the mat that covered him and prayed. At last the something in me like a membrane broke, and I was confident the old man would rise up again. As he did. During the night the natives came to tell us he had talked, eaten and walked about. They gave us many presents, and we left them the happiest people on earth, for they had given away their very best. . . .

Months went by as in a dream. The nerve of vision no longer rendered plausible that European world of which we had been a part. That world grew fantastic, and fantastic our countrymen there. We ourselves were only too real. From lack of clothing we had big sores and deep skin fissures on our backs and shoulders, and it hurt us to carry the hides we slept in. And it hurt us to find firewood among the cactus. My thighs and arms bled so much I stood it only by remembering—and yet whom or what did I remember? Was it a Person—was it a quality of life—was it an emotion? Was it even a remembering, was it not perhaps a listening? . . .

I said to Andrés, "If we reach Spain I shall petition His Majesty to return me to this land, with a troop of soldiers. And I shall teach the world how to conquer by gentleness, not by slaughter." "Why then a troop of soldiers?" asked Dorantes, smiling. "Soldiers look for Indian girls and gold." "Perhaps I could teach them otherwise." "They would kill you, or tie you to a tree and leave you. What a dunce you are, Alvar Nuñez!"

"And what will *you* do if we reach Spain again?" I asked Andrés. "It will be enough to reach Mexico," he answered. "I may look about for a rich widow, and spend the rest of my life as a rancher." "I could not care for such a life," I said. "To each his adventure," replied Andrés. . . .

At last we found a sign of our countrymen—what through months and years we had been praying for. On the neck of an Indian a little silver buckle from a sword belt, with a horseshoe nail sewed inside it. . . . We questioned him. He said that men with beards like ours had come from heaven to that river; that they had horses, lances, and swords, and had lanced two Indians.

The country grew more and more doleful. The natives had fled to the mountains, leaving their fields. The land was fertile and full of streams, but the people were wan. They told us our countrymen had burned all the villages, taking with them half the men and all the women and children . . .

Then a day when Indians said that on the night before they had watched the Christians from behind some trees. They saw them take along many persons in chains.

Our countrymen, these slave catchers, were startled when they saw us approaching. Yet almost with their first words they began to recite their troubles. For many days they had been unable to find Indians to capture. They did not know what to do, and were on the point of starvation. The idea of enslaving our Indians occurred to them in due course, and they were vexed at us for preventing it. They had their interpreter make a fine speech. He told our Indians that we were as a matter of fact Christians too, but had gone astray for a long while, and were people of no luck and little heart. But the Christians on horseback were real Christians, and the lords of the land to be obeyed and served. Our Indians considered this point of view. They answered that the real Christians apparently lied, that we could not possibly be Christians. For we appeared out of sunrise, they out of sunset; we cured the sick, while they killed even the healthy; we went naked and barefoot, while they wore clothes, and rode horseback and stuck people with lances; we asked for nothing and gave away all we were given, while they never gave anybody anything and had no other aim than to steal.

Your Majesty will remember my indignation in my first narrative that Christians should be so wicked, especially such as had the advantages of being your subjects. I did not at the time understand the true source of my indignation. I do now, and I will explain it. In facing these marauders I was compelled to face the Spanish gentleman I myself had been eight years before. It was not easy to think of it. Andrés and Alonso agreed that it was not easy. What, your Majesty, is so melancholy as to confront one's former unthinking and unfeeling self?

It was many days before I could endure the touch of clothing, many a night before I could sleep in a bed.

Shoes were the worst. In the Spanish settlements I dared not go barefoot, for provincials are the most easily shocked of Spaniards. I had not valued enough the pressure of earth on my naked feet while permitted that refreshment.

At first I did not notice other ways in which our ancient civilization was affecting me. Yet soon I observed a certain reluctance in me to do good to others. I would say to myself, "Need I exert what is left of me, I who have undergone tortures in an open boat and every privation and humiliation among the Indians, when there are strong healthy men about me, fresh from Holy Church and from school, who know their Christian duty?" We Europeans all talk this way to ourselves. It has become second nature to us. Each nobleman and alcalde and villager is an avenue that leads us to this way of talking; we can admit it privately, your Majesty, can we not? If a man need a cloak, we do not give it to him if we have our wits about us; nor are we to be caught stretching out our finger in aid of a miserable woman. Someone else will do it, we say. Our communal life dries up our milk: we are barren as the fields of Castile. We regard our native land as a power which acts of itself, and relieves us each of exertion. While with them I thought only about doing the Indians good. But back among my fellow countrymen, I had to be on my guard not to do them positive harm. If one lives where all suffer and starve, one acts on one's own impulse to help. But where plenty abounds, we surrender our generosity, believing that our country replaces us each and several. This is not so, and indeed a delusion. On the contrary the power of maintaining life in others lives within each of us, and from each of us does it recede when unused. It is a concentrated power. If you are not acquainted with it, your Majesty can have no inkling of what it is like, what it portends, or the ways in which it slips from one. In the name of God, your Majesty, farewell.

A SEARCH FOR THE SEVEN CITIES OF CIBOLA

[Suspicions of enormous wealth in the unexplored areas north of Mexico were confirmed in August, 1539, by reports brought back to Mexico City by Fray Marcos de Niza. Fray Marcos had been sent out the previous March, accompanied by Estebanico—Stephen—one of Cabeza de Vaca's companions in captivity, and a number of Indians. The small party was to make a reconnaissance trip through the Southwest, and they journeyed into present-day New Mexico and Arizona, Stephen going on ahead and sending back reports of what he found. Stephen was killed by the Zuñi Indians, and Fray Marcos hurriedly returned to Mexico City after glimpsing, though only from a distance, the city of Cíbola. At the capital, he rendered an account of the things he had seen and heard about to the Viceroy and other officials of New Spain. It is true that Fray Marcos embellished his narrative somewhat, repeating, as true, rumors passed on to him by various Indians and by Stephen himself, but it is not to be wondered at that he believed the Indians, for he was convinced of their truthfulness on the basis of his own dealings with them. Fray Marcos neither invented the tale of the cities of gold, nor did he give way to gross exaggeration. It took only a little encouragement for his hearers to be persuaded of what they had pretty much determined to believe anyway—that vast, untapped wealth lay in the regions to the north. Based on such a hope, the ill-fated Coronado expedition scoured the whole territory in search of gold from 1540 to 1542, and future expeditions would always be sure that somewhere—if only they could find them—were the seven cities of gold. This selection reprints the opening paragraphs of Fray Marcos's *Relación* of 1539, detailing the early reports of the seven cities.]

From "Fray Marcos de Niza and His Discovery of the Seven Cities of Cíbola," by Percy M. Baldwin, in: *New Mexico Historical Review*, April 1926.

With the aid and favor of the most holy Virgin Mary, our Lady, and of our seraphic father St. Francis, I, Fray Marcos de Niza, a professed religious of the order of St. Francis, in fulfillment of the instructions above given of the most illustrious lord Don Antonio de Mendoza, viceroy and governor for H[is]. M[ajesty]. of New Spain, left the town of San Miguel, in the province of Culiacan, on Friday, March 7th, 1539. I took with me as companion Friar Honoratus and also Stephen of Dorantes, a negro, and certain Indians, which the said Lord Viceroy bought for the purpose and set at liberty. They were delivered to me by Francisco de Coronado, governor of New Galicia, along with many other Indians from Petatlan and from the village of Cuchillo, situated about fifty leagues from the said town. All these came to the valley of Culiacan, manifesting great joy, because it had been certified to them that the Indians were free, the said governor having sent in advance to acquaint them of their freedom and to tell them that it was the desire and command of H. M. that they should not be enslaved nor made war upon nor badly treated.

With this company as stated, I took my way towards the town of Petatlan, receiving much hospitality and presents of food, roses and other such things; besides which, at all the stopping-places where there were no people, huts were constructed for me of mats and branches. In this town of Petatlan I stayed three days, because my companion Friar Honoratus fell sick. I found it advisable to leave him there and, conformably with the instructions given to me, I followed the way in which I was guided, though unworthy, by the Holy Ghost. There went with me Stephen Dorantes, the negro, some of the freed Indians and many people of that country. I was received everywhere I went with much hospitality and rejoicing and with triumphal arches. The inhabitants also gave me what food they had, which was little, because they said it had not rained for three years, and because the Indians of that territory think more of hiding than of growing crops, for fear of the Christians of the town of San Miguel, who up to that time were accustomed to make war upon and enslave them. On all this road, which would be about 25 or 30 leagues beyond Petatlan, I did not see anything worthy of being set down here, except that there came to me some Indians from the island visited by the Marquess of Valle, and who informed me that it was really an island and not, as some think, part of the mainland. I saw that they passed to and from the mainland on rafts and that the distance between the island and the mainland might be half a sea league, rather more or less. Likewise there came to see me Indians from another larger and more distant island, by whom I was told that there were thirty other small islands, inhabited, but with poor food excepting two, which they said had maize. These Indians wore suspended from their necks many shells of the kind which contain pearls; I showed them a pearl which I carried for sample and they told me that there were some in the islands, but I did not see any.

I took my way over a desert for four days and there went with me some Indians from the islands mentioned as well as from the villages which I left behind, and at the end of the desert I found some other Indians, who were astonished to see me, as they had no news of Christians, having no traffic with the people on the other side of the desert. These Indians made me very welcome, giving me plenty of food, and they endeavored to touch my clothes, calling me *Sayota*, which means in their language "man from heaven." I made them understand, the best I could by my interpreters, the content of my instructions, namely, the knowledge of Our Lord in heaven and of H. M. on earth. And always, by all the means that I could, I sought to learn about a country with numerous towns and a people of a higher culture than those I was encountering, but I had no news except that they told me that in the country beyond, four or five days' journey thence, where the chains of mountains ended, there was an extensive and level open tract, in which they told me there were many and very large towns inhabited by a people clothed with cotton. When I showed them some metals which I was carrying, in order to take account of the metals of the country, they took a piece of gold and told me that there were vessels of it among the people of the region and that they wear certain articles of that metal suspended from their noses and ears, and that they had some little blades of it, with which they scrape and relieve themselves of sweat. But as this tract lies inland and my intention was to stay near the coast, I determined to leave it till my return, because then I would be able to see it better. And so I marched three days through a country inhabited by the same people, by whom I was received in the same manner as by those I had already passed. I came to a medium-sized town named Vacapa, where they made me a great welcome and gave me much food, of which they had plenty, as the whole land is irrigated. From this town to the sea is forty leagues. As I found myself so far away from the sea, and as it was two days before Passion Sunday, I determined to stay there until Easter, to inform myself concerning the islands of which I said above that I had news. So I sent Indian messengers to the sea, by three ways, whom I charged to bring back to me people from the coast and from some of the islands, that I might inform myself concerning them. In another direction I sent Stephen Dorantes, the negro, whom I instructed to take the route towards the north for fifty or sixty leagues to see if by that way he might obtain an account of any important thing such as we were seeking. I agreed with him that if he had any news of a populous, rich and important country he should not continue further but should return in person or send me Indians with a certain signal which we arranged, namely, that if it were something of medium importance, he should send me a white cross of a hand's breadth, if it were something of great importance, he should send me one of two hands' breadth, while if it were bigger and better than New Spain, he should send me a great cross. And so the said negro Stephen departed from me on Passion Sunday after dinner, whilst I stayed in the town, which I say is called Vacapa.

In four day's time there came messengers from Stephen with a very great cross, as high as a man, and they told me on Stephen's behalf that I should immediately come and follow him, because he had met people who gave him an account of the greatest country in the world, and that he had Indians who had been there, of whom he sent me one. This man told me so many wonderful things about the country, that I forebore to believe them until I should have seen them or should have more certitude of the matter. He told me that it was thirty days' journey from where Stephen was staying to the first city of the country, which was named Cíbola. As it appears to me to be worth while to put in this paper what this Indian, whom Stephen sent me, said, concerning the country, I will do so. He asserted that in the first province there were seven very great cities, all under one lord, that the houses, constructed of stone and lime, were large, that the smallest were of one storey with a terrace above, that there were others of two and three storeys, whilst that of the lord had four, and all were joined under his rule. He said that the doorways of the principal houses were much ornamented with turquoises, of which there was a great abundance, and that the people of those cities went very well clothed. He told me many other particulars, not only of the seven cities but of other provinces beyond them, each one of which he said was much bigger than that of the seven cities.

THE CALIFORNIA VOYAGE OF JUAN RODRIGUEZ CABRILLO

[The Spaniards were hardly established in Mexico under Cortés before they fanned out in all directions to gather information on other territories and to search for wealth comparable to that of the Aztecs. By 1533, the peninsula of Lower California had been discovered, and further interest in the northern reaches developed when Cabeza de Vaca told of his wanderings among the Indians from Florida to Texas and when Fray Marcos returned to Mexico with his news of the seven cities of Cíbola. There was also a persistent hope of finding the elusive Strait of Anian, the short water-passage from Europe to the Far East. In June, 1542, a small expedition captained by Juan Rodríguez Cabrillo sailed from Puerto de Navidad in Mexico to explore the coast of California. His party sailed north along the coast in two small ships, stopping at many points to land and converse with the Indians of the region. They probably sailed farther north than the San Francisco Bay area but never sighted it. On the return trip, Cabrillo died of injuries received in a fall, but the ships finally made it back to Mexico, after numerous difficulties, on April 14, 1543, ten months after their departure. A short portion of the diary of the voyage covering the weeks from September 23 to October 17, 1542, is reprinted here. The Spaniards reported seen by the Indians were almost certainly members of Coronado's party nearing the end of two years' vain search for the cities of gold.]

From "Relation of the Voyage of Juan Rodríguez Cabrillo, 1542–1543," in: *Spanish Exploration in the Southwest, 1542–1706*, Herbert Eugene Bolton, ed., New York, 1916, pages 13–39.

On Saturday, the 23d of said month [September], they left said port of San Mateo and sailed along the coast until the Monday following, when they must have gone about eighteen leagues. They saw very beautiful valleys and groves, and country both level and rough, but no Indians were seen.

On the following Tuesday and Wednesday they sailed along the coast about eight leagues, passing by some three islands completely denuded of soil. One of them is larger than the others. It is about two leagues in circumference and affords shelter from the west winds. They are three leagues from the mainland, and are in thirty-four degrees. They called them Islas Desiertas (Desert Islands). This day great smokes were seen on the land. The country appears to be good and has large valleys, and in the interior there are high mountains.

On the following Thursday they went about six leagues along a coast running north-northwest, and discovered a port, closed and very good, which they named San Miguel [San Diego Bay]. It is in thirty-four and one-third degrees. Having cast anchor in it, they went ashore where there were people. Three of them waited, but all the rest fled. To these three they gave some presents and they said by signs that in the interior men like the Spaniards had passed. They gave signs of great fear. On the night of this day they went ashore from the ships to fish with a net, and it appears that here there were some Indians, and that they began to shoot at them with arrows and wounded three men.

Next day in the morning they went with the boat farther into the port, which is large, and brought two boys, who understood nothing but signs. They gave them both shirts and sent them away immediately.

Next day in the morning three adult Indians came to the ships and said by signs that in the interior men like us were travelling about, bearded, clothed, and armed like those of the ships. They made signs that they carried crossbows and swords; and they made gestures with the right arm as if they were throwing lances, and ran around as if they were on horseback. They made signs that they were killing many native Indians, and that for this reason they were afraid. These people are comely and large. They go about covered with skins of animals. While they were in this port a heavy storm occurred, but since the port is good they did not feel it at all. It was a violent storm from the west-southwest and the south-southwest. This is the first storm which they have experienced. They remained in this port until the following Tuesday. The people here called the Christians Guacamal.

On the following Tuesday, the 3d of the month of October, they departed from this port of San Miguel, and on Wednesday, Thursday, and Friday, they held their course a matter of eighteen leagues along the coast, where they saw many valleys and plains, and many smokes, and mountains in the interior. At nightfall they were near some islands which are some seven leagues from the mainland, but because the wind went down they could not reach them that night.

At daybreak on Saturday, the 7th of the month of October, they were at the islands which they named San Salvador [San Clemente] and La Vitoria [Santa Catalina]. They anchored at one of them and went ashore with the boat to see if there were people; and when the boat came near, a great number of Indians emerged from the bushes and grass, shouting, dancing, and making signs that they should land. As they saw that the women were fleeing from the boats they made signs that they should not be afraid. Immediately they were reassured, and laid their bows and arrows on the ground and launched in the water a good canoe which held eight or ten Indians, and came to the ships. They gave them beads and other articles, with which they were pleased, and then they returned. Afterward the Spaniards went ashore, and they, the Indian women, and all felt very secure. Here an old Indian made signs to them that men like the Spaniards, clothed and bearded, were going about on the mainland. They remained on this island only till midday.

On the following Sunday, the 8th of said month, they drew near to the mainland in a large bay which they called Bay of Los Fumos, (Bay of the Smokes) [Santa Monica], because of the many smokes which they saw on it. Here they held a colloquy with some Indians whom they captured in a canoe, and who made signs that toward the north there were Spaniards like them. This bay is in thirty-five degrees and is a good port, and the country is good, with many valleys, plains, and groves.

On the following Monday, the 9th of the said month of October, they left the Bay of Los Fuegos (the Fires), and sailed this day some six leagues, anchoring in a large bay. From here they departed the next day, Tuesday, and sailed some eight leagues along a coast running from northwest to southeast. We saw on the land a pueblo of Indians close to the sea, the houses being large like those of New Spain. They anchored in front of a very large valley on the coast. Here there came to the ships many very good canoes, each of which held twelve or thirteen Indians; they told them of Christians who were going about in the interior. The coast runs from northwest to southeast. Here they gave them some presents, with which they were greatly pleased. They indicated by signs that in seven days they could go to where the Spaniards were, and Juan Rodriguez decided to send two Spaniards into the interior. They also indicated that there was a great river. With these Indians they sent a letter at a venture to the Christians. They named this town the Pueblo of Las Canoas [San Buena-Ventura]. The Indians dress in skins of animals; they are fishermen and eat raw fish; they were eating *maguey* also. This pueblo is in thirty-five and one-third degrees. The interior of the country is a very fine valley; and they made signs that in that valley there was much maize and abundant food. Behind the valley appear some very high mountains and very broken country. They call the Christians Taquimine. Here they took possession and here they remained until Friday, the 13th day of said month.

On Friday, the 13th of said month of October, they left the pueblo of Las Canoas to continue their voyage, and sailed this day six or seven leagues, passing along the shores of two large islands. Each of them must be four leagues long, and they must be about four leagues from the mainland. They are uninhabited, because they have no water, but they have good ports. The coast of the mainland trends to the west-northwest. It is a country of many savannahs and groves. On the following Saturday they continued on their course, but made no more than two leagues, anchoring in front of a magnificent valley densely populated, with level land, and many groves. Here came canoes with fish to barter; the Indians were very friendly.

On the following Sunday, the 15th day of the said month, they continued on their course along the coast for about ten leagues; all the way there were many canoes, for the whole coast is very densely populated; and many Indians kept boarding the ships. They pointed out the pueblos and told us their names. They are Xuco, Bis, Sopono, Alloc, Xabaagua, Xocotoc, Potoltuc, Nacbuc, Quelqueme, Misinagua, Misesopano, Elquis, Coloc, Mugu, Xagua, Anacbuc, Partocac, Susuquey, Quanmu, Gua, Asimu, Aguin, Casalic, Tucumu, and Incpupu.

All these pueblos are between the first pueblo of Las Canoas, which is called Xucu, and this point. They are in a very good country, with fine plains and many groves and savannahs. The Indians go dressed in skins. They said that in the interior there were many pueblos, and much maize three days' journey from there. They call maize Oep. They also said that there were many cows; these they call Cae. They also told us of people bearded and clothed.

This day they passed along the shore of a large island which must be fifteen leagues long. They said it was very densely populated and that there were the following pueblos: Niquipos, Maxul, Xugua, Nitel, Macamo, and Nimitapal. They called this island San Lucas. From here to the pueblo of Las Canoas it must be about eighteen leagues. The island must be about six leagues from the mainland.

On Monday, the 16th of the said month, sailing along the coast, they made about four leagues, and cast anchor in the afternoon in front of two pueblos. All this day, likewise, many canoes came with the ships and made signs that farther on there were canoes much larger.

On the following Tuesday, the 17th of the said month, they made three leagues, with favorable winds. Many canoes went with the ships from daybreak, and the captain kept giving them many presents. All this coast which they have passed is very thickly settled. The Indians brought for them many sardines, fresh and very good. They say that in the interior there are many pueblos and abundant food. They ate no maize. They were dressed in skins, and wore their hair very long and tied up with long strings interwoven with the hair, there being attached to the strings many gewgaws of flint, bone, and wood. The country appears to be very fine.

A CONDEMNATION
OF SPAIN'S
INDIAN POLICY

[Bartolmé de las Casas, "Apostle of the Indies," was the most uncompromising opponent of Spain's colonial Indian policy. He recognized the wide gap between the announced noble intention of converting the Indians to Christianity and the actual brutality and slavery that the Spaniards adopted to further their own avaricious goals and to fill the treasury in Spain. Las Casas had a good deal of first-hand experience in the colonies, as missionary and as bishop, and, from his observations of cruelty toward the Indians, he was able to prevail upon the government in Spain to promulgate laws in 1542 limiting the right of colonists to tribute and service from the natives. Unfortunately, such well-intentioned legislation went largely unheeded in the New World, and, on both sides of the ocean, Las Casas made some very bitter enemies for daring to tell all the world how Spain treated its Indian subjects. Reprinted below is the introduction and opening section of his *Very Brief Account of the Destruction of the Indies*, written in 1540 and published in Séville in 1552. This tract is the most celebrated of his attacks on colonial Indian policy.]

From "The Brevissima Relacion," in: Frances A. MacNutt, *Bartholomew De Las Casas*. New York, 1909. Appendix I.

As I have fifty, or more, years of experience in those countries, I have therefore been considering the evils, I have seen committed, the injuries, losses, and misfortunes, such as it would not have been thought could be done by man; such kingdoms, so many, and so large, or to speak better, that most vast and new world of the Indies, conceded and confided by God and his Church to the Kings of Castile, that they should rule and govern it; that they should convert it, and should prosper it temporally, and spiritually.

When some of their particular actions are made known to Your Highness, it will not be possible to forbear supplicating His Majesty with importunate insistence, that he should not concede nor permit that which the tyrants have invented, pursued, and put into execution, calling it Conquests; which if permitted, will be repeated; because these acts in themselves, done against those pacific, humble, and mild Indian people, who offend none, are iniquitous, tyrannous, condemned and cursed by every natural, divine, and human law.

So as not to keep criminal silence concerning the ruin of numberless souls and bodies that these persons cause, I have decided to print some, though very few, of the innumerable instances I have collected in the past and can relate with truth, in order that Your Highness may read them with greater facility.

Although the Archbishop of Toledo, Your Highness' Preceptor, when Bishop of Cartagena, asked me for them and presented them to Your Highness, nevertheless, because of the long journeys by sea and land Your Highness has made, and of the continual royal occupations, it may be that Your Highness either has not read them or has already forgotten them.

The daring and unreasonable cupidity of those who count it as nothing to unjustly shed such an immense quantity of human blood, and to deprive those enormous countries of their natural inhabitants and possessors, by slaying millions of people and stealing incomparable treasures, increase every day; and they insist by various means and under various feigned pretexts, that the said Conquests are permitted, without violation of the natural and divine law, and, in consequence, without most grievous mortal sin, worthy of terrible and eternal punishment. I therefore esteemed it right to furnish Your Highness with this very brief summary of a very long history that could and ought to be composed, of the massacres and devastation that have taken place.

I supplicate Your Highness to receive and read it with the clemency, and royal benignity he usually shows to his creatures, and servants, who desire to serve solely for the public good and for the prosperity of the State.

Having seen and understood the monstrous injustice done to these innocent people in destroying and outraging them, without cause or just motive, but out of avarice alone, and the ambition of those who design such villainous operations, may Your Highness be pleased to supplicate and efficaciously persuade His Majesty to forbid such harmful and detestable practices to those who seek license for them: may he silence this infernal demand for ever, with so much terror, that from this time forward there shall be no one so audacious as to dare but to name it.

This—Most High Lord—is most fitting and necessary to do, that God may prosper, preserve and render blessed, both temporally and spiritually, all the State of the royal crown of Castile.   Amen.

The Indies were discovered in the year fourteen hundred and ninety-two. The year following, Spanish Christians went to inhabit them, so that it is since forty-nine years that numbers of Spaniards have gone there: and the first land, that they invaded to inhabit, was the large and most delightful Isle of Hispaniola, which has a circumference of six hundred leagues.

There are numberless other islands, and very large ones, all around on every side, that were all—and we have seen it—as inhabited and full of their native Indian peoples as any country in the world.

Of the continent, the nearest part of which is more than two hundred and fifty leagues distant from this Island, more than ten thousand leagues of maritime coast have been discovered, and more is discovered every day; all that has been discovered up to the year forty-nine is full of people, like a hive of bees, so that it seems as though God had placed all, or the greater part of the entire human race in these countries.

God has created all these numberless people to be quite the simplest, without malice or duplicity, most obedient, most faithful to their natural Lords, and to the Christians, whom they serve; the most humble, most patient, most peaceful, and calm, without strife nor tumults; not wrangling, nor querulous, as free from uproar, hate and desire of revenge, as any in the world.

They are likewise the most delicate people, weak and of feeble constitution, and less than any other can they bear fatigue, and they very easily die of whatsoever infirmity; so much so, that not even the sons of our Princes and of nobles, brought up in royal and gentle life, are more delicate than they; although there are among them such as are of the peasant class. They are also a very poor people, who of worldly goods possess little, nor wish to possess: and they are therefore neither proud, nor ambitious, nor avaricious.

Their food is so poor, that it would seem that of the Holy Fathers in the desert was not scantier nor less pleasing. Their way of dressing is usually to go naked, covering the private parts; and at most they cover themselves with a cotton cover, which would be about equal to one and a half or two ells square of cloth. Their beds are of matting, and they mostly sleep in certain things like hanging nets, called in the language of Hispaniola *hamacas*.

They are likewise of a clean, unspoiled, and vivacious intellect, very capable, and receptive to every good doctrine; most prompt to accept our Holy Catholic Faith, to be endowed with virtuous customs; and they have as little difficulty with such things as any people created by God in the world.

Once they have begun to learn of matters pertaining to faith, they are so importunate to know them, and in frequenting the sacraments and divine service of the Church, that to tell the truth, the clergy have need to be endowed of God with the gift of pre-eminent patience to bear with them: and finally, I have heard many lay Spaniards frequently say many years ago, (unable to deny the goodness of those they saw) certainly these people were the most blessed of the earth, had they only knowledge of God.

Among these gentle sheep, gifted by their Maker with the above qualities, the Spaniards entered as soon as they knew them, like wolves, tigers, and lions which had been starving for many days, and since forty years they have done nothing else; nor do they otherwise at the present day, than outrage, slay, afflict, torment, and destroy them with strange and new, and divers kinds of cruelty, never before seen, nor heard of, nor read of, of which some few will be told below: to such extremes has this gone that, whereas there were more than three million souls, whom we saw in His-paniola, there are to-day, not two hundred of the native population left.

The island of Cuba is almost as long as the distance from Vallado-lid to Rome; it is now almost entirely deserted. The islands of San Juan [Porto Rico], and Jamaica, very large and happy and pleasing islands, are both desolate. The Lucaya Isles lie near Hispaniola and Cuba to the north and number more than sixty, including those that are called the Giants, and other large and small Islands; the poorest of these, which is more fertile, and pleasing than the King's garden in Seville, is the healthiest country in the world, and con-tained more than five hundred thousand souls, but to-day there remains not even a single creature. All were killed in transporting them, to Hispaniola, because it was seen that the native population there was disappearing.

A ship went three years later to look for the people that had been left after the gathering in, because a good Christian was moved by compassion to convert and win those that were found to Christ; only eleven persons, whom I saw, were found.

More than thirty other islands, about the Isle of San Juan, are destroyed and depopulated, for the same reason. All these islands cover more than two thousand leagues of land, entirely depopulated and deserted.

We are assured that our Spaniards, with their cruelty and ex-ecrable works, have depopulated and made desolate the great con-tinent, and that more than ten Kingdoms, larger than all Spain, counting Aragon and Portugal, and twice as much territory as from Seville to Jerusalem (which is more than two thousand leagues), although formerly full of people, are now deserted.

We give as a real and true reckoning, that in the said forty years, more than twelve million persons, men, women, and children, have perished unjustly and through tyranny, by the infernal deeds and tyranny of the Christians; and I truly believe, nor think I am deceived, that it is more than fifteen.

Two ordinary and principal methods have the self-styled Christians, who have gone there, employed in extirpating these miserable nations and removing them from the face of the earth. The one, by unjust, cruel and tyrannous wars. The other, by slaying all those, who might aspire to, or sigh for, or think of liberty, or to escape from the torments that they suffer, such as all the native Lords, and adult men; for generally, they leave none alive in the wars, except the young men and the women, whom they oppress with the hardest, most horrible, and roughest servitude, to which either man or beast, can ever be put. To these two ways of infernal tyranny, all the many and divers other ways, which are numberless, of exterminating these people, are reduced, resolved, or sub-ordered according to kind.

The reason why the Christians have killed and destroyed such infinite numbers of souls, is solely because they have made gold their ultimate aim, seeking to load themselves with riches in the shortest time and to mount by high steps, disproportioned to their condition: namely by their insatiable avarice and ambition, the greatest, that could be on the earth. These lands, being so happy and so rich, and the people so humble, so patient, and so easily subjugated, they have had no more respect, nor consideration nor have they taken more account of them (I speak with truth of what I have seen during all the aforementioned time) than—I will not say of animals, for would to God they had considered and treated them as animals—but as even less than the dung in the streets.

In this way have they cared for their lives—and for their souls: and therefore, all the millions above mentioned have died without faith, and without sacraments. And it is a publicly known truth, admitted, and confessed by all, even by the tyrants and homicides themselves, that the Indians throughout the Indies never did any harm to the Christians: they even esteemed them as coming from heaven, until they and their neighbours had suffered the same many evils, thefts, deaths, violence and visitations at their hands.

CIVILIZING THE INDIANS

[The following royal order on colonial Indian policy was promulgated on May 26, 1570. It is one of many instances of the Spanish desire to obtain a controlled, submissive, and dependent Indian population. Given the two-pronged goal of colonization—wealth and the conversion of the natives—such orders were not entirely unaltruistic; but, in the end, humane intent normally gave way to ruthless exploitation and slavery. This particular order affected the province of Nueva Galicia in western Mexico.]

The King. To our *oidores, alcaldes mayores* [judges and magistrates] of the Audiencia of the province of Nueva Galicia: Juan de la Peña, in the name of the council of justice and government of the city of Guadalajara, has made a report to me saying that because the Indian inhabitants of the province are not gathered into towns where they may have political government, much harm is done and many difficulties arise in their conversion and indoctrination, and they are

From "Royal Order commanding that the Indians of Nueva Galicia be gathered into towns where they may live under an organized government," in: Charles Wilson Hackett, ed., *Historical Documents Relating to New Mexico, Nueva Vizcaya, and Approaches Thereto, to 1773.* Collected by Adolph F. A. Bandelier and Fanny Bandelier. Washington, D.C., 1923. Vol. I, pages 101–103.

not taught to live under the control and ordered system conducive to their salvation and welfare. For, scattered as they are over the mountains and deserts, the religious are unable to go everywhere to visit them; moreover, the Indians began to flee for the purpose of preventing interference with their manner and custom of life, and of securing better opportunities to assault, rob, and kill both Spaniards and peaceful Indians on the highways as they had repeatedly done. De la Peña supplicated me to order as a remedy for this that the Indians of that province who are wandering about in the mountains should be gathered together and made to live in established towns where they might have political organization for their better instruction in the things of the faith, and not be allowed to live as they do in the mountains and out-of-the-way places, because of the difficulties which would result. The plan suggested has been discussed by the members of our Council of the Indies, who considered how much benefit to the Indians would accrue from it; I have therefore approved it, and do now command you to issue orders and instructions for gathering the Indians of that province who are wandering in the mountains into towns where they may live in a civilized manner and have their organized government, that they may better communicate with each other, have order and system in their living, be more advantageously converted and indoctrinated, and escape the dangers and difficulties which may attend the opposite mode of living in the mountains and deserts. Whatever you may do in this matter above your ordinary obligation we shall accept as service to us, and you will report to us how this order is complied with and executed. *Dated at El Carpio, May 26, 1570*
I THE KING.

JUAN DE ONATE'S SETTLEMENT OF NEW MEXICO

[The signal failure of the Coronado expedition of 1540–42 to find great wealth north of the Rio Grande dampened Spanish enthusiasm for those regions for several decades. Prior to actual settlement, the only notable attempts to explore the area were made from 1581 to 1583 by two separate groups. The first was led by Agustín Rodríguez and Francisco Chamuscado, the second by Antonio de Espejo. Between them, they explored nearly all of Arizona and New Mexico and visited all of the major pueblos. But it was not until 1595 that a colonizing expedition, under the leadership of Juan de Oñate, was commissioned by the King of Spain. Oñate was a wealthy and influential Spaniard whose family had long been active in the conquest and exploitation of Mexico for the crown. Following many delays, Oñate's party finally set out in February, 1598. On April 30, he took possession of New Mexico in the name of the King of Spain, and a capital city, San Juan de los Caballeros, was laid out about twenty-five miles north of present-day Santa Fe. Oñate remained in his post as governor of New Mexico for ten years. In 1608, he was removed from office and brought to trial on a number of charges of maladministration, chief of which was cruelty to the Indians. But his prime fault was very likely his failure, shared with his predecessors, to find great new accessions of wealth for Spain. This selection reprints part of Oñate's report to the Viceroy of New Spain on March 2, 1599, concerning the new colony.]

From "Don Juan de Oñate to the Viceroy of New Spain, March 2, 1599," in: George P. Hammond and Agapito Rey, eds., *Don Juan de Oñate, Colonizer of New Mexico 1595–1628.* Albuquerque, 1953. Pages 480–488.

From the Nombre de Dios river I last wrote to your lordship and gave an account of my departure and of the discovery of a wagon road to the Río del Norte [Rio Grande], and the reassuring hopes I held of the success of my trip. God (may He always be praised) willed that these hopes should be rewarded for His service and for that of his majesty, and that no other lands in the Indies should surpass them, judging solely by what I have seen and by reliable information, some of which was almost verified by what persons in my army saw. I do not include in this account the great towns and wealth which the natives claim that there are in the west, nor the certainty of pearls in the South sea, judging by the many pearl shells that the Indians possess, nor do I mention the numerous peoples who tell of the origin of these rivers and of the Dios, which is a tributary, called the Seven Caves, of the Río del Norte, but only the provinces that I have seen and traversed, and the people of this eastern part, the Apaches, the nation of Cocoyes, and many others who in this region and neighborhood are found every day, as I will particularly tell in this letter. I wish to begin by giving your lordship an account of this matter, because it is the first since I left New Spain.

I have, then, discovered and inspected to date the following provinces: the province of the Tziguis, which one passes on the way from New Spain; the province of the Xumanas; the province of the Chiguas, which we Spaniards call Puaray; the province of the Cheres; the province of Tzia; the province of the Emmes; the province of the Teguas; the province of the Picuríes; the province of the Taos; the province of the Peccos; the province of Abbó and the Salines; the province of Tzuñi; and the province of Mohoce. These last two are at some distance to the west of the others. This is where I have now discovered the rich lodes, as set forth in the papers that your lordship will see. I was not able to work or exploit them because of the death of my maese de campo, Don Juan de Zaldívar, and the need to remedy the situation resulting therefrom, which I finished late last month; nor was I able to carry out my trip to the South sea, which was what brought me to the said provinces, having left my army at this province of the Teguas, from where I am writing at present.

Here and in the other above-mentioned provinces there must be, being conservative in my reckoning, sixty thousand Indians, with towns like ours and with houses built around rectangular plazas.

They have no streets. At the pueblos where there are many plazas or large houses, they are joined by narrow passageways between the buildings. Where there are fewer people, the houses are two and three storeys high, of an estado and a half each, or an estado and a third, but there are some houses and even entire pueblos with four, five, six, and seven storeys.

The dress of the Indians consists of cotton or agave blankets, well decorated, white or black; it is very good clothing. Others dress in buffalo skins, of which there is a great abundance. These furs have a beautiful wool; I am sending you some samples of what they make of it. This land is plentiful in meat of the buffalo, sheep with huge antlers, and native turkeys. At Mohoce and Zuñi there is game of all kinds. There are many wild animals and beasts: lions, bears, tigers, wolves, penicas [?], ferrets, porcupines, and others. The natives tan and use their skins. To the west there are bees and very white honey, of which I am sending a sample. Their corn and vegetables, and their salines, are the best and largest to be found anywhere in the world.

There is great abundance and variety of ores; those I mentioned above are very rich. Some discovered around here do not seem so, although we have hardly started to examine the many things that there are. There are fine grape vines, rivers, and woods with many oak and some cork trees; there are also fruits, melons, grapes, watermelons, Castilian plums, capulins, piñon, acorns, native nuts, *coralejo*, which is a delicate fruit, and other wild plants: There are also many fine fish in this Río del·Norte and other streams. From the metals that we find here, we can obtain all colors and the finest.

The people are as a rule of good disposition, generally of the color of those of New Spain, and almost the same in customs, dress, grinding of meal, food, dances, songs, and in many other respects. This is not true of their languages, which here are numerous and different from those in Mexico. Their religion consists in worshiping of idols, of which they have many; in their temples they worship them in their own way with fire, painted reeds, feathers, and general offerings of almost everything: little animals, birds, vegetables, etc. Their government is one of complete freedom, for although they have some chieftains they obey them badly and in very few matters.

We have seen other nations, such as the Querechos or Vaqueros, who live among the Cíbola cattle in tents of tanned hides. The Apaches, some of whom we also saw, are extremely numerous. Although I was told that they lived in rancherías, in recent days I have learned that they live in pueblos the same as the people here. They have a pueblo eighteen leagues from here with fifteen plazas. They are a people that has not yet publicly rendered obedience to his majesty, as I had the other provinces do, which cost us much labor, diligence, and care, traveling long distances with arms on our shoulders, with much watching and wariness. Because of failure to exercise as much caution as was necessary, my maese de campo and twelve companions were killed at a fortress pueblo named

Acoma, which must have contained three thousand Indians, more or less. In punishment of their wickedness and treason to his majesty, to whom they had previously rendered obedience in a public ceremony, and as a warning to the others, I razed and burned their pueblo in a manner that your lordship will see by the legal proceedings of this trial. I have seen all of these provinces with my own eyes.

There is another nation, the Cocoyes, a very numerous people who dwell in jacal huts and who farm. I have detailed information of them and of the large settlements at the source of the Río del Norte, and of those to the northwest and west and toward the South sea. From that sea I have obtained pearl-bearing shells of unusual size, and news of the certainty that there are an infinite number of them along the coast of this land. There is at my camp an individual from the eastern region, an Indian interpreter who came with Humaña and who has been at a pueblo of the Vaqueros, which is nine leagues long and two wide and which has streets and jacal houses. It is situated in the midst of the multitudes of Cíbola cattle. The latter are so numerous that my sargento mayor who hunted them and procured a supply of skins, meat, fat, and tallow, affirms that in one short trip he saw more of them than there are of our cattle on the ranches of Rodrigo del Río, Saluago, and Gerónimo López, all put together, which are famous in those parts.

It would be an endless story to attempt to describe in detail each one of the many things that are found there. All I can say is that with God's help I am going to see them all and give more pacified worlds, new and conquered, to his majesty, greater than the good Marquis [Hernan Cortés] gave him, despite his having done so much, if your lordship but gives me the succor, favor, and aid that I expect from such a hand. Even though I confess that I was disheartened when I left that land in such disfavor—and a depressed spirit in disfavor often loses hope and despairs of success—still I have not lost hope nor shall I ever lose hope of receiving greater favors at the hands of your lordship, especially in matters of such great service to his majesty. In order that your lordship may be inclined to grant them to me I beg you to take into consideration the great increase of the royal crown and his majesty's revenues and their future expansion from such numerous and diverse sources. Each one promises great returns. I emphasize only the following four, omitting the others as commonplace and well known.

First, the great wealth that the mineral lodes have begun to reveal, and the large number of them in the land, from which royal fifths and other benefits will be derived.

Second, the certainty of the nearness of the South sea, whose trade with Peru, New Spain, and China should not be underestimated, for with the passing of time it will be the source of profitable and continuous customs revenues because of its proximity to China and that land [New Spain?]. What I consider important in this respect is the trade in pearls, the report of which is so reliable, as I have stated, and we have seen their shells here with our own eyes.

Third, the increase in vassals and tributes, together with the increase in revenue, whereby the prestige and power of our king is also augmented, if that is possible.

Fourth, the wealth from the rich salines and the mountains of rich sulphur, of which there is more than in any other province. Salt is a universal article of commerce among these savages and a part of their common food. They even eat it alone or suck it just as we do sugar.

These four things seem reserved for his majesty alone. I omit the founding of the numerous republics, the many offices, their quittances, vacancies, appointments, etc., and the wealth from the wool and skins of the buffalo, as well as many obvious resources and the suitability of the land for wines and oil.

I know, Illustrious Sir, that if your lordship, with your great prudence, magnanimity, and nobility, will give consideration to these things of such honor, interest, and value, everything will prosper and dispel the dark clouds of my disgrace. Therefore, I humbly beg and entreat you, since it is of such importance to the service of God and his majesty, to send me all the help possible, both to colonize and pacify. Your lordship with your favor will give spirit, warmth, and life to the maintenance, growth, and development of this land through the preaching of the holy gospel and the founding of this government, and by granting permission and favor to everyone, opening the doors wide to them to come here and if necessary even ordering them to come and serve their king in a cause of such honor and usefulness and in a land of such abundance and of so many different sources of wealth. I describe them thus, for even though we have seen much, we have not even begun, in view of how much there is to see and enjoy. Even if more than five hundred men should come, they would all be needed, especially married men, who are the solid rock on which to build a lasting new nation; of such noble persons there is an abundance in New Spain.

THE CONFLICT OF
CHURCH AND STATE
IN NEW MEXICO

[The rule of Spain in the New World was both ecclesiastical and political, and the history of Spanish New Mexico shows almost unrelieved combat between these "two majesties," as they were called. While both majesties accepted the other's authority, they vied for control of the colony's destiny, and the focal point of that control was, of course, the Indian. The Indian did not necessarily benefit from the attentions of either civil or religious leaders. Charges and countercharges were sent to the Viceroy of New Spain by the mutually hostile governors and Franciscan friars of the colony. The governors accused the priests of getting rich off the labor of Indians and hampering the development of the colony. The friars berated the governing officials for encouraging the Indians to relapse into paganism and for making slaves of them. Strife and intrigue mounted during the first half of the seventeenth century, until, by 1645, the colony was in a virtual state of civil war. Although the crisis passed, tensions remained until they were overshadowed by the Pueblo Revolt of 1680. The foremost result of the civil-religious strife was the undermining of Spanish authority among the Indians.

The two selections below represent the opposing sides in the conflict between the two majesties in New Mexico. The first reading is a petition by Alonso de Benavides to the King of Spain, probably written late in 1630 or early in 1631. Benavides had been custodian of the missions in New Mexico from 1626 until late 1629. He re-

From 1. "Petitions of Benavides Regarding Tribute and Personal Service by the Indians," in: Frederick W. Hodge, George P. Hammond, and Agapito Rey, eds., *Fray Alonso de Benavides, Revised Memorial of 1634*. Albuquerque, 1945. Pages 168–177.

2. Charles W. Hackett, ed., *Historical Documents Relating to New Mexico, Nueva Vizcaya, and Approaches Thereto, to 1773*. Collected by Adolph F. A. Bandelier and Fanny Bandelier. Washington, D.C., 1937. Vol. III, pages 66–74.

turned to Spain in the summer of 1630. The second reading is part
of a report to the Viceroy of New Spain by the *cabildo*, or town
council, of Santa Fe, dated February 21, 1639.]

1. PETITION OF ALONSO DE BENAVIDES REGARDING TRIBUTE AND PERSONAL SERVICE BY THE INDIANS

Through royal decrees it is ordered that no tributes or personal
services be imposed on the Indians of New Mexico until after they
have been baptized. Before any can be levied against them, the
governor of the province and the custodian must notify the viceroy
and the royal audiencia of Mexico stating the reasons why they
should be imposed, this is to be done by the viceroy himself and the
royal audiencia, and in no other way. At present everything is done
in just the opposite manner; even before the pueblos are converted,
the governor himself gives them out in encomienda without notifying the custodian or the viceroy. Even before they are converted and
baptized, when they are only pacified, they [Spaniards] constrain
them to pay tribute and to do personal service, taking them far
from their pueblos and treating them badly. As a result, the heathen
Indians who have not yet been converted or even pacified say that
they do not want to become converted, or even pacified, that they
do not want to become Christians, in order not to pay tribute or
serve. They have even been sent to be sold as slaves in New Spain,
as was the practice. They escape these and other abuses as long
as they remain free and do not become Christians.

Wherefore your Majesty is entreated to order, under severe pen-
alties, that the Indians of New Mexico be not given in encomienda
by the governors of New Mexico until five years after the whole
pueblo has been baptized, and in order to be given in encomienda,
the said governor and the custodian there must notify the viceroy
and the audiencia, reporting that the five years have passed, so that
they may be authorized to do it; that the encomenderos of the said
pueblos should have no other power or rights over the pueblos and
Indians than the tribute owed them; that the Indians must remain
always as tributary vassals of your Majesty, in whose name they
pay the tribute to their encomenderos, without owing them any
more obligations than to those who are not encomenderos; that
neither the encomenderos nor any other Spaniards be allowed to
live in their pueblos without the consent of the Indians themselves;
that they may not have houses in the pueblos for their employment

or other gain; but which they cause much harm to the pueblos and the Indians.

Likewise, it has been established by the first governors of New Mexico, and is being continued by order of the viceroy that each house pay a tribute consisting of a cotton blanket, the best of which are about a yard and a half square, and a fanega of corn. This is understood to be for each house and not for each Indian, even though many Indian families live in such houses. It often happens that the pueblos increase or decrease in houses, or, if one tumbles down, its dwellers move to that of their relatives, and none of these pay tribute, except for the house in which they live. This works against the increase in houses, as tribute is collected as soon as the owners occupy them.

The encomenderos compel the Indians whose houses may have fallen down, or which they may have lost for other reasons, to pay tribute, even though they live in someone else's house. It is requested of your Majesty that the Indians of New Mexico do not pay tribute by the person, but by the house, as has always been done; that, as the encomendero is ready to receive the tribute of houses added to their pueblos, he should also be ready to lose and cease taking tribute from abandoned houses, even though the owners live in someone else's house.

It is requested that the Indians who, of their own will, move to live in other pueblos, being free, as they are, must not be hindered by their encomenderos, the governors, or other persons; that they may live freely in whatever pueblo they wish, and that, after they have established residence there for one year and a day, they become taxpapers at the place like the others of the same pueblo to the encomendero with whom they live. For the Indians suffer much harm when, if they do not get along with the encomendero in a pueblo where they do not find as good facilities for their work and farming as in some other one, they are forced to live there for the accommodation of the encomendero, whether they like it or not. If they have this freedom, the encomenderos will help and accord good treatment to their tributary Indians so that they will not leave their pueblos and their tributes diminish.

It is requested that all the caciques, chief captains, governors, alcaldes, and fiscales of the churches, on account of the big tasks they perform for the republic and the service of your Majesty, be exempt from tribute and personal service while they hold these offices. They are so busy in their offices that even their planted fields are cared for by others, as they are unable to do it themselves. The native lords and chieftains resent very much that they are compelled to pay tribute. Likewise, all the Indians who are choir singers and assistants in the churches are free only from personal service, but not from tribute, because of their regular attendance in church and in the schools.

It is requested that the Spanish governors be forbidden to issue warrants or permits to take Indian boys or girls from the pueblos on the pretext that they are orphans, and take them to serve permanently in the houses of the Spaniards where they remain as slaves. As a matter of fact, the orphans are well cared for at the homes of their grandparents or other relatives where they are brought up as if they were their own children. In case there should be any one without a home, the governor should not issue warrants without the consent of the ecclesiastical minister, who lives alone with the Indians and knows their needs and relieves them as much as he is able. This must be done so that the destitute Indian orphans may live freely with their relatives. The governors often take from the Spaniards some Indians who are serving the Spaniards well, in order to keep them for themselves. They take them without compensation, or, in payment, give them a permit to go to the pueblos to look for other boys and girls and to take them by force.

It is requested that the Indians taken in wars, whatever their nation, may not be given as slaves or sentenced to personal service outside of New Mexico, as is prescribed by royal decrees. On the contrary, they should be placed in convents of the friars or in houses of Spaniards or Indians of exemplary conduct so that they may be taught our holy Catholic faith with all kindness in order that they may become Christians. If any of them should run away they will tell the people of their nations of the good treatment accorded them and they will become inclined to our life and religion. This assignment to a convent may not be in the nature of a sale, transfer, or any other material consideration or period of time, but simply as an act of charity to instruct and convert them, which is the only purpose for which we have gone there. They must always be free in their lands, as they are often taken in wars and on other occasions, placed with an individual for many years who then transfers them to another individual for a consideration for the remainder of the time the assignment is to last. This is often done by the governors through a third party, and under this pretext they take many Indians, both men and women, to Mexico and other places to be sold.

It is requested that the Spanish governors be forbidden from depriving any native Indian chief of his post or authority, because of the fact that the Indians greatly resent seeing their leaders and chieftains mistreated.

It is requested that the grants of lands which the governors may make to Spaniards both for grazing and farming shall conform to the royal ordinances; that to make grants the adjacent Indians and pueblos must be notified, and the proposal must be announced for a period of thirty days at the time of mass on holidays with the aid of the ecclesiastical minister so that these grants may not be to the detriment of the Indians and their lands be taken from them. These grants are made secretly so that when the poor Indians want to return to their lands the Spaniards are already in possession of them, and from there they expand and add to their lands more than was given to them. They force the Indians, by evil treatment and by losses to their cattle, to abandon their lands and to leave their possessions to the Spaniards.

It is requested that the governors, since your Majesty gives them a salary of two thousand ducats a year for their support, shall obey the royal cedulas, by which they are ordered not to have farms or cattle ranches, even on the pretext that they are for the maintenance of their houses, as they are given a salary for that. This will prevent them from taking the best lands that the Indians have for their fields and from depriving the adjacent Spaniards of help to develop their lands. And in order to send their cattle to New Spain to sell, they rob the land of the cattle which are so desirable for increasing its welfare and permanence. In addition, in order to care for the cattle, they send along the best Indians of the land who then are left stranded because the distance is so great, and they find themselves unable to return to their country and homes. With their connivance others, too, send out cattle, and in particular female cattle, whereby the land is impoverished.

One of the main reasons for the unrest in that land of New Mexico is the desire of the governor that there be no other judge or tribunal than his; that the custodian, who is the one who administers ecclesiastical justice there, does not do or execute anything in the matters of the church without the intervention and authority of the governor. In particular, if any one seeks the protection of the church for any reason, the governor says that it can only be done by his authority, the consultation of the ecclesiastical judge being unnecessary. Many serious disaffections ensue over upholding these and other prerogatives, the country being so far away, and the conversions are disturbed and even hindered. To bring this about the governors issue proclamations, telling the people not to obey the friars in anything, except that those who want to may hear mass, that the friars have no other powers, that the governor alone is the one who has authority as a judge there. In order to avoid all this, your Majesty is entreated to grant that primitive church, now that it is established according to its principles, that whoever takes refuge in a church or cemetery in New Mexico be fully respected and protected, even in cases where this is not granted to others. This will afford some protection and relief to the helpless Spaniards who live there as in a walled prison. If they are deprived of the protection of the church, they will have no means of defending themselves against the tyranny of many governors. And the Indans, when they see this, will conceive a greater respect and veneration for the church. Because of such absolute power of the governors there, many people desist from going to colonize at their own expense.

The privilege that your Majesty has granted this land provides that whoever has served there at his own expense for a period of five years be declared *hijodalgo* and be entitled to hold encomiendas in those pueblos. The governors often take away these encomiendas and give them to those who came with them, thereby keeping them for themselves during the time they remain there, thus depriving many Spaniards and their children who have served for many years of their due reward. May your Majesty be pleased to order that no one can be granted an encomienda or be in charge of one until he has served the said five years in that land as is prescribed, and also that in all cases the natives, sons of the founders and the conquistadores, be preferred, in order that in this way many may be encouraged to go to settle in that land at their own expense, whereby your Majesty will be greatly benefited.

It is requested that whoever founds establishments of mines, farms, or cattle ranches anywhere along the road from the valley of Santa Bárbara to the Rio del Norte be thereby favored and protected in their occupancy, and that they be exempt for twenty years from the payment of any royal fifth, tribute, *alcabala*, or any other assessment; that they be given, in the name of your Majesty, the mercury they need in the same manner as other miners.

It is requested that if anyone should wish to found at his own cost a town at the pass of the Rio del Norte, which is midway to New Mexico, royal authorities and powers should be sent to the viceroy of Mexico to agree with him as to the privileges that might be granted to him and that he might demand. That pass is extremely important, both for keeping open that trail and for the conversion of the many savage nations in that region. Your Majesty would be greatly benefited by the foundation of such a town and by the production of the mines and farms that may be established there. The same terms should be arranged for anyone who should like to settle at the bay of the Espíritu Santo river, which is situated across from Havana, on the coast that borders New Mexico on the east between Florida and Tampico.

It is provided and established in New Mexico that, because the trip is so long and difficult—it requires a whole year to make it— every three years, at the cost of your Majesty, there be brought from Mexico everything that is needed both for the founding of new churches at the conversions and for the vestments of the friars, their ministers. As this is handled by the royal officials, no matter how much we may ask for this aid, they do not give it every three years, but it reaches New Mexico at the end of six or seven years. Since this aid is furnished in limited quantity for three years only, the friars endure so much difficulty and privation that lately mass has been said only on holidays for lack of wine, which is furnished in three-year shipments, as it is sent either through bidding or through agents and is paid for from the accounts of your Majesty at excessive prices.

In this connection there are other strange details that cannot be put in writing. We take to New Mexico things of little value, and your Majesty pays for them as if they were the best in the world.

This would not happen if the goods had been entrusted to the friars who are to receive them, and if they themselves were in charge of buying the goods. Thus your Majesty would save a good many ducats in these expenses, and those conversions would receive this help punctually every three years, and even every year in the following manner:

Let anyone examine the royal books in which are recorded the expenses of your Majesty in the last supply service and deduct respectively what a missionary friar in New Mexico costs your Majesty each year, including all the expenses from the time he leaves Mexico with the wagons which your Majesty maintains for this purpose. By giving this quantity in reales each year in Mexico and Zacatecas and having on the first trip the wagons fully equipped as usual, we would save your Majesty from four to six thousand pesos every three years, which you spend in the upkeep of the said wagons; from then on we will manage them and keep them up. In this manner we shall have our provisions every three years or oftener, and we ourselves will buy to our satisfaction the goods that are needed in those conversions. We will buy much cheaper, and with the same amount we would maintain the people in charge of the wagons. So, without your Majesty spending a single additional penny more than now, we would save the great cost of the upkeep of the wagons, and the conversions would be provisioned on time.

There is another way whereby we could be punctually provisioned and at much less cost to your Majesty. This would be by giving us the stipend or aid in the same manner that it is given to the Jesuit fathers in the conversions of Sinaloa, which are less than two hundred leagues from Mexico, and in a country at peace and with better climate. We are four hundred leagues away, in a severe climate, in a walled prison, in a country at war. Since greater work deserves greater reward, we receive the same amount that is given and spent on the said fathers, which is three hundred fifty pesos in reales each year for each minister. The first year they serve in the mission, they are given all that is necessary in the way of sacred vestments. Thus, computing all that is spent on a missionary friar in New Mexico per year and what is spent for one in Sinaloa, the royal books will show that we spend much more in New Mexico because of the manner in which it is used. This means that we would save your Majesty more than one-fourth of the cost. On this matter it is not possible to write everything that would rebound to the benefit of all.

I beseech the king, our lord, in the name of all New Mexico and in behalf of the friars, Spaniards, and natives, to please order that a cedula be issued stating that you consider yourself well served by everyone and instructing the governors to accord good treatment and maintain good relations with such loyal vassals in order that they may put a stop to the ill treatment they often inflict on their adjacent Spaniards and Indians, and the bad relations they maintain with the friars, whom all the Catholic kings have honored so much in royal cedulas. This would encourage everyone to go ahead and outdo himself in the service of the two Majesties.

2. COMPLAINTS OF THE TOWN COUNCIL OF SANTA FE AGAINST THE MISSIONARIES

Most Excellent Sir: In the past year of 1637 and in that of 1638, in the month of October, this *cabildo* gave account to your Excellency of the affairs of these provinces, transmitting some papers in which are set forth to your Excellency the justification and necessity with which this *cabildo* asks for the remedy made necessary by the excessive annoyance and disturbances against the royal jurisdiction from which this commonwealth and the governors and other magistrates are suffering, a thing not to be remedied with the power and forces of this land, for they are so few and so poor that no remedy is to be had except from the powerful hand of his Majesty and that of your Excellency in his royal name. Therefore matters go each day from bad to worse, so that we cannot live or remain in this land, if indeed the events themselves do not make an end of us and of this new church. This, Sir, is no exaggeration, but rather it is very incompletely stated in the reports, for it is not possible to express in writing what we are suffering or to give account of all that happens, although it is a consolation to know that your Excellency, with your Christian zeal, will learn of it from the despatches that have been sent to your Excellency and from that which is now drawn up by our captain-general and this *cabildo*.

The cause, Sir, is that the inhabitants are few, poor, and have little knowledge of business affairs or of anything except arms, while the religious are many and enjoy rich profits, acquired from the labor of the natives and the poverty of the Spaniards. These profits were neither asked for nor given as alms but [acquired] from private dealings and contracts, and since these [ecclesiastics] are all of the same religious Order they are all-powerful, which only serves to produce more disturbances. They deprive us of the confession and [other] ministrations, and as they have the ecclesiastical jurisdiction, with commissions from the Holy Inquisition and the Cruzada, and administration of the holy sacraments, this land has no recourse to their superiors or to any other Order, nor clergy to whom to appeal. As a result they are so powerful that, from the quiet and comfort of their cells and *doctrinas* they so disturb and afflict the land that they keep it in a continual martyrdom. By the authority of a paper sent by the custodian to his religious, they withold and deny the holy sacraments and refuse to receive confessions, as they do often in Lent and are now doing; and those who wish to make confession have to go in search of the custodian fifteen or twenty leagues from here among the Indians where he lives.

The commissary of the Holy Inquisition conducts himself in a similar manner, summoning the inhabitants to the place where he lives, which is thirty leagues away from this villa, in which he has never resided, although it is the capital. He says that it is for the business of the Holy Inquisition, although it is really to annoy us, and to show his power and authority. When edicts are read in this church he places at the side of the gospel stand, close to the main altar, a canopy so large that it covers and hides from view a part of the altar-piece. Seated under it are the said commissary, and two other commissaries who are here also—so that our poor citizens may not lack judges—as well as a secretary and other officials, such as the *alguacil mayor*, the notary, and the person who carries the standard of the faith; all wear habits given them by the said commissary, and the religious put on embroidered robes over those of their Order of Saint Francis. On the other side are seated the commissary of the Santa Cruzada, with an equal number of companions in office and the same officials—treasurer, *alguacil*, and notary. Meanwhile, on the doors of the church there are posted more excommunications than bulls. . . .

May your Excellency also consider for the love of God, that the bulls are not of any interest to his Majesty, for they do not amount to a hundred pesos. They are simply [designed] to put arms in the hands of the religious to disturb and annoy this commonwealth and the natives newly converted to our holy faith. To prevent [the residents] from holding or establishing farms, under the excuse of protecting the maize-fields of the Indians they find sufficient reason for interfering with the Spanish inhabitants, even though the latter settle two or three leagues away from the Indian pueblos. This is not on account of their cattle and sheep, for they keep them in their pueblos in greater numbers than those of the Spanish inhabitants. When they [the religious] can do no more they even burn the farms, as they have done in some cases, as must have been made known to your Excellency by the despatch of General Francisco Martínez de Baeza. In order to disturb the country still more, the commissary of the Cruzada came to this villa to direct excommunications against the magistrate [*justicia*] at a time when our captain-general was calling the inhabitants to arms to go out to meet the enemy, who were coming against the frontiers, all of which created more confusion in the midst of that occasioned by the coming of the enemy, and compelled this *cabildo* to make the requisitions that your Excellency will see in despatch of our captain-general. At the same time some *autos* are transmitted which were drawn up with the said commissary for the purpose of requesting him to obey and execute an order of the Santa Cruzada in which it is commanded that no funds shall be collected by the Cruzada except those that proceed from the bull. He refused to execute the order.

Your Excellency will understand from all this how they are seizing power and what this land will suffer, for by such exactions on property bought in order to have collections made through the Cruzada (as was that of a friend of the commissary's, Don Francisco de la Mora, former governor here), communities richer than this in property and in people would be impoverished and destroyed. Let your Excellency consider, for the love of God, that this is a very poor land, with few people, and that the measures were taken in passion and with great harshness; and furthermore, your Excellency, the bull of the Cruzada was granted for war against the heathen, and those now serving in the war enjoy the benefits of the bull without its being proclaimed. Since we are in this land, usually without any salary, with our arms in hand in the presence of the enemy, pouring out our blood in the defense of this new church and extending our holy Catholic faith in these provinces, what reason is there that the said bull should be published and we should have to accept it? We humbly beg and pray your Excellency to do us the favor to order that this be looked to, and to relieve us of this very heavy yoke, in view of the little or no profit that it will bring his Majesty, and the great good that will come from exercising his clemency and love for his vassals. . . .

Finally, most Excellent Sir, the religious are proceeding in such a free and unbridled way that they do not neglect any human means of persecuting us, which they do by making use of divine worship and the holy sacraments, as at present, when they have taken from us and denied and are now denying the confession to this entire community, including our captain-general and the other magistrates, as will be made known to your Excellency by the *autos* that have been drawn up concerning it and the statement of the father *guardián* of this town which is transmitted herewith. Thus, Sir, may your Excellency consider, for the love of God, in what state this commonwealth will be, without confession or ministration of the holy sacraments, when Lent and holy week pass without our receiving them. In what land inhabited by Christians and subjects of his Majesty has such a thing ever been done or known as is being done and has been done here? It will have been made known to your Excellency by the dispatch of General Francisco Martínez de Baeza. The same thing happened in the time of General Don Juan de Eulate, and on other occasions when they did not wish to confess any one except those to whom they gave and who signed cedulas against the governors. Indeed, they did not confess Governor Francisco Martínez himself until he had given them a cedula against himself in favor of the religious.

Since there is no recourse here, as your Excellency is more than four hundred leagues away, nor are there priests of any other Order, or clergymen, and since there were many uncomforted and afflicted souls—which is the thing most to be considered—some cedulas were given to the religious, for such is the power of force in these affairs. And as the land is to-day oppressed with this harshness, the people are crying out and clamoring to God and to your Excellency that you will, for the love of God, order that these grave outrages shall be remedied, and that you will be pleased to send at once the *procurador* with your Excellency's favor and succor, for we are now awaiting him, without confessing ourselves. Until his return our governor and this *cabildo* will guarantee, as they do, that no difficulty shall occur that cannot be mended without great trouble and expense to his Majesty. All are so desperate that among other things they say: "How can it be permitted that the religious shall sell the sacraments for false reports and cedulas!" May your Excellency, for the love of God, be the father and protector of this poor and afflicted land, take pity upon its troubles, and order that the *procurador* shall be sent at once; and let the measures that your Excellency may order be gratis, for in no other way will the favor that your Excellency does us be effective, as this *cabildo* has no property of its own and we are extremely poor.

For this reason there never reached these provinces an order which your Excellency sent directing that his Majesty's carts should go under the governor's orders, for it was hidden and did not come, as has happened with other despatches. One of the great annoyances that the religious inflict upon the inhabitants is in preventing them from having farms on which to raise a few cattle to support themselves, saying that they damage the Indians' cornfields, although they are two or three leagues away from the pueblos. The reason for their opposition cannot be on account of their cattle and sheep, which they keep within the pueblos in large numbers, for each religious has from one to two thousand sheep, while few inhabitants have as many as five hundred [each] and most of them have no more than a hundred; and those who live in this town have neither farms nor cattle. Inasmuch as his Majesty supports the religious, it is right, your Excellency, that they shall not raise cattle, and that those that they now have shall be given and divided among the poor, for they [the cattle] are the progeny of those his Majesty placed in these provinces when the land was first settled. The same should be done with the horses that all of them have—as many as twenty, thirty, and forty apiece—for there are many soldiers so poor that through their inability to buy horses and arms they are incapable of serving his Majesty. In this way a great deal of trouble would be saved the Indians, for they are now occupied in guarding the cattle and horses and the very large fields of wheat and corn that they plant [for the religious] as well as the vegetable gardens and orchards, and the stables where they keep three or four saddle horses very daintily, for they are quite valuable and are taken to be sold in New Spain. In these and other similar services, such as porters, men and women cooks, wood-choppers, and millers, more than thirty or forty Indians are constantly employed, their pueblos consisting of from fifty to sixty houses. The worst thing, most excellent Sir, is that the religious hold most of the arms that there are in the country, for they have armor for the horses, leather jackets, swords, arquebuses, and pistols, and these arms are not for fighting the enemy, as they do not do that, but for the inhabitants and for holding juntas, as they have just been doing. We therefore pray that your Excellency will order that the arms shall be placed in these royal houses in the possession of the governors, so they may be given out in time of need, for there are none in the storehouse. . . .

It is very important, most excellent Sir, for the correction of these disorders on the part of the religious, that your Excellency shall order that Father Fray Juan de Vidania, present *guardián* of this town, shall be sent as custodian, for he will reform these disorders, as he is a very devoted Franciscan religious, virtuous, and of exemplary life, who possesses no qualities except those that are to be desired in a good prelate. He is modest, courteous, and gets along well with the justices and citizens, and has always given conscientious ministration, preaching to us in the accepted manner, as ought to be done, by proclaiming only the holy gospel and good doctrine, without employing angry and discourteous words and refrences to their special business and quarrels, as other religious are in the habit of doing. As a result he has been snubbed and affronted on all occasions by the others and by his prelate, which is sufficient proof of his virtue. And, Sir, let not the office of custodian be bestowed upon one of three or four of those older religious who had a part in the imprisonment of the governor and captain-general, Don Pedro de Peralta, and who have maintained the quarrels and disturbances in this land, making of it a state matter, in consequence of which they have not only not been chastised, but have instead been rewarded with offices.

As a result of all this the governors desire to quit this office as soon as they enter it, for it is of no benefit to them but rather an expense, as the land is so poor and they cannot serve his Majesty as they would wish because of the small force of soldiers and arms (as has been said). There is nothing but quarrels and more quarrels with the religious, and the governors have to resist vituperations and depositions, the religious thrusting themselves into their jurisdiction without the right to make use of it or to administer justice as it should be done; and so we have learned that the present governor has petitioned your Excellency to send him a successor. It is our duty to inform your Excellency that our captain-general has withstood these difficulties with great courage, and that he has also served his Majesty to greater advantage than have his predecessors, as must have been made known to your Excellency by the punitive expeditions and discoveries that he has made, overcoming obstacles and not permitting quarrels or envy to stop him, holding and keeping the citizens and soldiers in peace and jutice. We therefore entreat your Excellency, as earnestly as we can, to be pleased to keep him in this office, for it will be a great consolation and relief in the troubles and afflictions from which we are suffering, and very important to his Majesty's service.

THE LOSS AND RECONQUEST OF NEW MEXICO

[The Pueblo Revolt of 1680 in New Mexico was the most successful (albeit temporary) Indian uprising ever to occur on the North American continent. By the end of 1680, the Indians had rid themselves entirely of their Spanish overlords. The causes of the revolt were many, but chief among them were the divisions of the colony owing to the incessant strife between civil and religious leaders. The Indians came to despise both sides, and they eventually felt strong enough to challenge their role. Of course, the very fact of being forced to adopt an alien civilization and a new religion was also a grating experience for many of the Pueblo tribes. The revolt itself was planned over a five-year period by medicine men and chiefs of the northern pueblos, led by one Popé, a medicine man from San Juan. Word of the coming revolt leaked out to Governor Antonio de Otermín four days before its scheduled outbreak on August 13. Knowing this, the Indians began hostilities immediately. About 400 Spanish residents were killed in the first onslaught, and nearly all of the land from Taos south to Isleta was devastated. The populace at Santa Fe was forced south, along with a contingent of refugees under the lieutenant governor at Isleta, and all eventually retired to the tiny trading post of El Paso on the Rio Grande. The reconquest of New Mexico was not completed for thirteen years, but it was virtually a bloodless event. Once the Spaniards were overthrown, the Indians fell into disunity, and Popé's rule was found to be as oppressive as

From 1. "Letter from the Governor and Captain-general, Don Antonio de Otermín, from New Mexico [September 8, 1680]," in: Charles W. Hackett, ed., *Historical Documents Relating to New Mexico, Nueva Vizcaya, and Approaches Thereto, to 1773*. Collected by Adolph F. A. Bandelier and Fanny Bandelier. Washington, D.C., 1937. Vol. III, pages 327–335.

2. "Letter from Don Diego de Vargas to The Conde de Galve, El Paso, January 12, 1693," in: J. Manuel Espinosa, ed. and translator, *First Expedition of Vargas into New Mexico, 1692*. Albuquerque, 1940. Pages 278–289.

that of the Spanish governors. Under the generalship of Don Diego de Vargas Zapata Luján Ponce de León, a small force of Spaniards and loyal Indians left El Paso on August 21, 1692. By the end of the year, twenty-three pueblos had been restored to Spanish allegiance, and, in September, 1693, a party of 800 settlers began the recoloniza-tion. The selections printed below tell of the beginning and end of the Pueblo Revolt. The first reading is a letter from Governor Otermín, dated September 8, 1680, to Fray Francisco de Ayeta, tell-ing of the start of hostilities. The second reading is from a letter from Don Diego de Vargas to the Viceroy, El Conde de Galve, dated January 12, 1693, summing up the reconquest and assessing pros-pects for New Mexico's immediate future.]

1. THE REVOLT OF THE PUEBLO INDIANS, 1680

My very reverend father, Sir, and friend, most beloved Fray Fran-cisco de Ayeta: The time has come when, with tears in my eyes and deep sorrow in my heart, I commence to give an account of the lamentable tragedy, such as has never before happened in the world, which has occurred in this miserable kingdom and holy *custodia*, His Divine Majesty having thus permitted it because of my grievous sins. Before beginning my narration I desire, as one obligated and grateful, to give your reverence the thanks due for the demonstrations of affection and kindness which you have given in your solicitude in ascertaining and inquiring for definite notices about both my life and those of the rest in this miserable kingdom, in the midst of persistent reports which had been circulated of the deaths of myself and the others, and for sparing neither any kind of effort nor large expenditures. For this only Heaven can reward your reverence, though I do not doubt that his Majesty (may God keep him) will do so.

After I sent my last letter to your reverence by the *maese de campo*, Pedro de Leyba, while the necessary things were being made ready alike for the escort and in the way of provisions, for the most expeditious despatch of the returning carts and their guards, as your reverence had enjoined me, I received information that a plot for a general uprising of the Christian Indians was being formed and was spreading rapidly. This was wholly contrary to the existing peace and tranquillity in this miserable kingdom, not only among the Spaniards and natives, but even on the part of the heathen enemy, for it had been a long time since they had done us any considerable damage. It was my misfortunte that I learned of it on the eve of the day set for the beginning of the said uprising, and though I immediately, at that instant, notified the lieutenant-general on the lower river and 'l t' e other *alcaldes mayores*—so that they could take every care and precaution against whatever might occur, and so that they cou d make every effort to guard and protect the religious ministers and the temples—the cunning and cleverness of the rebels were such, and so great, that my efforts were of little avail. To this was added a certain degree of negligence by reason of the [report of the] uprising not having been given entire credence, as is apparent from the ease with which they captured and killed both those who were escorting some of the religious, as well as some citizens in their houses, and, particularly, in the efforts that they made to prevent my orders to the lieutenant-general passing through. This was the place where most of the forces of the kingdom were, and from which I could expect some help, but of three orders which I sent to the said lieutenant-general, not one reached his hands. The first messanger was killed and the others did not pass beyond Santo Domingo, because of their having encountered on the road the certain notice of the deaths of the religious who were in that convent, and of the *alcalde mayor*, some other guards, and six more Spaniards whom they captured on that road. Added to this is the situation of this kingdom which, as your reverence is aware, makes it so easy for the said [Indian] alcaldes to carry out their evil designs, for it is entirely composed of *estancias*, quite distant from one another.

On the eve [of the day] of the glorious San Lorenzo, having received notice of the said rebellion from the governors of Pecos and Tanos, [who said] that two Indians had left the Theguas, and particularly the pueblo of Thesuque, to which they belonged, to notify them to come and join the revolt, and that they [the governors] came to tell me of it and of how they were unwilling to participate in such wickedness and treason, saying that they now regarded the Spaniards as their brothers, I thanked them for their kindness in giving the notice, and told them to go to their pueblos and remain quiet. I busied myself immediately in giving the said orders which I mentioned to your reverence, and on the following morning as I was about to go to mass there arrived Pedro Hidalgo, who had gone to the pueblo of Thesuque, accompanying Father Fray Juan Pio, who went there to say mass. He told me. that the Indians of the said pueblo had killed the said Father Fray Pio and that he himself had escaped miraculously. [He told me also] that the said Indians had retreated to the sierra with all the cattle and horses belonging to the convent, and with their own.

The receipt of this news left us all in the state that may be imagined. I immediately and instantly sent the *maese de campo*, Francisco Gómez, with a squadron of soldiers sufficient to investigate this case and also to attempt to extinguish the flame of the ruin already begun. He returned here on the same day, telling me that [the report] of the death of the said Fray Juan Pio was true. He said also that there had been killed that same morning Father Fray Tomás de Torres, *guardián* of Nambé, and his brother, with the latter's wife and a child, and another resident of Thaos, and also Father Fray Luis de Morales, *guardián* of San Ildefonso, and the family of Francisco de Anaya; and in Poxuaque Don Joseph de Goitia, Francisco Ximénez, his wife and family, and Doña Petronila de Salas with ten sons and daughters; and that they had robbed and profaned the convents and [had robbed] all the haciendas of those murdered and also all the horses and cattle of that jurisdiction and La Cañada.

Upon receiving this news I immediately notified the *alcalde mayor* of that district to assemble all the people in his house in a body, and told him to advise at once the *alcalde mayor* of Los Taos to do the same. On this same day I received notice that two members of a convoy had been killed in the pueblo of Santa Clara, six others having escaped by flight. Also at the same time the *sargento mayor*, Bernabe Márquez, sent to ask me for assistance, saying that he was surrounded and hard pressed by the Indians of the Queres and Tanos nations. Having sent the aid for which he asked me, and an order for those families of Los Cerrillos to come to the villa, I instantly arranged for all the people in it and its environs to retire to the *casas reales*. Believing that the uprising of the Tanos and Pecos might endanger the person of the reverend father custodian, I wrote him to set out at once for the villa, not feeling reassured even with the escort which the lieutenant took, at my orders, but when they arrived with the letter they found that the Indians had already killed the said father custodian; Father Fray Domingo de Vera; Father Fray Manuel-Tinoco, the minister *guardián* of San Marcos, who was there; and Father Fray Fernando de Velasco, *guardián* of Los Pecos, near the pueblo of Galisteo, he having escaped that far from the fury of the Pecos. The latter killed in that pueblo Fray Juan de la Pedrosa, two Spanish women, and three children. There died also at the hands of the said enemies in Galisteo Joseph Nieto, two sons of *Maestre de Campo* Leiba, Francisco de Anaya, the younger, who was with the escort, and the wives of *Maestre de Campo* Lieba and Joseph Nieto, with all their daughters and families. I also learned definitely on this day that there had died in the pueblo of Santo Domingo fathers Fray Juan de Talabán, Fray Francisco Antonio Lorenzana, and Fray Joseph de Montesdoca, and the *alcalde mayor*, Andrés de Peralta, together with the rest of the men who went as escort.

Seeing myself with notices of so many and such untimely deaths, and that not having received any word from the lieutenant-general was probably due to the fact that he was in the same exigency and confusion, or that the Indians had killed most of those on the lower river, and considering also that in the pueblo of Los Taos the fathers *guardianes* of that place and of the pueblo of Pecuries might be in danger, as well as the *alcalde mayor* and the residents of that valley, and that at all events it was the only place from which I could obtain any horses and cattle—for all these reasons I endeavored to send a relief of soldiers. Marching out for that purpose, they learned that in La Cañada, as in Los Taos and Pecuries, the Indians had risen in rebellion, joining the Apaches of the Achos nation. In Pecuries they had killed Francisco Blanco de la Vega, a *mulata* belonging to the *maese de campo*, Francisco Xavier, and a son of the said *mulata*. Shortly thereafter I learned that they also killed in the pueblo of Taos the father *guardián*, Fray Francisco de Mora, and Father Fray Mathías Rendón, the *guardián* of Pecuries, and Fray Antonio de Pro, and the *alcalde mayor*, as well as another fourteen or fifteen soldiers, along with all the families of the inhabitants of that valley, all of whom were together in the convent. Thereupon I sent an order to the *alcalde mayor*, Luis de Quintana, to come at once to the villa with all the people whom he had assembled in his house, so that, joined with those of us who were in the *casa reales*, we might endeavor to defend ourselves against the enemy's invasions. It was necessarily supposed that they would join all their forces to take our lives, as was seen later by experience.

On Tuesday, the thirteenth of the said month, at about nine o'clock in the morning, there came in sight of us in the suburb of Analco, in the cultivated field of the hermitage of San Miguel, and on the other side of the river of the villa, all the Indians of the Tanos and Pecos nations and the Querez of San Marcos, armed and giving war-whoops. As I learned that one of the Indians who was leading them was from the villa and had gone to join them shortly before, I sent some soldiers to summon him and tell him on my behalf that he could come to see me in entire safety, so that I might ascertain from him the purpose for which they were coming. Upon receiving this mesage he came to where I was, and, since he was known, as I say, I asked him how it was that he had gone crazy too—being an Indian who spoke our language, was so intelligent, and had lived all his life in the villa among the Spaniards, where I had placed such confidence in him—and was now coming as a leader of the Indian rebels. He replied to me that they had elected him as their captain, and that they were carrying two banners, one white and the other red, and that the white one signified peace and the red one war. Thus if we wished to choose the white it must be [upon our agreeing] to leave the country, and if we chose the red, we must perish, because the rebels were numerous and we were very few; there was no alternative, inasmuch as they had killed so many religious and Spaniards.

On hearing his reply, I spoke to him very persuasively, to the effect that he and the rest of his followers were Catholic Christians, [asking] how they expected to live without the religious; and said that even though they had committed so many atrocities, still there was a remedy, for if they would return to the obedience of his Majesty they would be pardoned; and that thus he should go back to his people and tell them in my name all that had been said to him, and persuade them to [agree to] it and to withdraw from where they were; and that he was to advise me of what they might reply. He came back from there after a short time, saying that his people asked that all classes of Indians who were in our power be given up to them, both those in the service of the Spaniards and those of the Mexican nation of that suburb of Analco. He demanded also that his wife and children be given up to him, and likewise that all the Apache men and women whom the Spaniards had captured in war [be turned over to them], inasmuch as some Apaches who were among them were asking for them. If these things were not done they would declare war immediately, and they were unwilling to leave the place where they were because they were awaiting the Taos, Pecuries, and Theguas nations, with whose aid they would destroy us.

Seeing his determination, and what they demanded of us, and especially the fact that it was untrue that there were any Apaches among them, because they were at war with all of them, and that these parleys were intended solely to obtain his wife and children and to gain time for the arrival of the other rebellious nations to join them and besiege us, and that during this time they were robbing and sacking what was in the said hermitage and the houses of the Mexicans, I told him (having given him all the preceding admonitions as a Christian and a Catholic) to return to his people and say to them that unless they immediately desisted from sacking the houses and dispersed, I would send to drive them away from there. Whereupon he went back, and his people received him with peals of bells and trumpets, giving loud shouts in sign of war.

With this, seeing after a short time that they not only did not cease the pillage but were advancing toward the villa with shamelessness and mockery, I ordered all the soldiers to go out and attack them until they succeeded in dislodging them from that place. Advancing for this purpose, they joined battle, killing some at the first encounter. Finding themselves repulsed, they took shelter and fortified themselves in the said hermitage and the houses of the Mexicans, from which they defended themselves a part of the day with the firearms that they had and with arrows. Having set fire to some of the houses in which they were, thus having them surrounded and at the point of perishing, there appeared on the road from Thesuque a band of the people whom they were awaiting, who were all the Teguas. Thus it was necessary to go to prevent these latter from passing on to the villa, because the *casas reales* were poorly defended; whereupon the said Tanos and Pecos fled to the mountains and the two parties joined together, sleeping that night in the sierra of the villa. Many of the rebels remained dead and wounded, and our men retired to the *casas reales* with one soldier killed and the *maese de campo*, Francisco Gómez, and some fourteen or fifteen soldiers wounded, to attend them and entrench and fortify ourselves as best we could.

On the morning of the following day, Wednesday, I saw the enemy come down all together from the sierra where they had slept, toward the villa. Mounting my horse, I went out with the few forces that I had to meet them, above the convent. The enemy saw me and halted, making ready to resist the attack. They took up a better position, gaining the eminence of some ravines and thick timber, and began to give war-whoops, as if daring me to attack them.

I paused thus for a short time, in battle formation, and the enemy turned aside from the eminence and went nearer the sierras, to gain the one which comes down behind the house of the *maese de campo*, Francisco Gómez. There they took up their position, and this day passed without our having any further engagements or skirmishes than had already occurred, we taking care that they should not throw themselves upon us and burn the church and the houses of the villa.

The next day, Thursday, the enemy obliged us to take the same step as on the day before of mounting on horseback in fighting formation. There were only some light skirmishes to prevent their burning and sacking some of the houses which were at a distance from the main part of the villa. I knew well enough that these dilatory tactics were to give time for the people of the other nations who were missing to join them in order to besiege and attempt to destroy us, but the height of the places in which they were, so favorable to them and on the contrary so unfavorable to us, made it impossible for us to go and drive them out before they should all be joined together.

On the next day, Friday, the nations of the Taos, Pecuries, Hemes, and Querez having assembled during the past night, when dawn came more than 2,500 Indians fell upon us in the villa, fortifying and entrenching themselves in all its houses and at the entrances of all the streets, and cutting off our water, which comes through the *arroyo* and the irrigation canal in front of the *casas reales*. They burned the holy temple and many houses in the villa. We had several skirmishes over possession of the water, but seeing that it was impossible to hold even this against them, and almost all the soldiers of the post being already wounded, I endeavored to fortify myself in the *casas reales* and to make a defense without leaving their walls. [The Indians were] so dexterous and so bold that they came to set fire to the doors of the fortified tower of Nuestra Señora de las Casas Reales, and, seeing such audacity, and the manifest risk that we ran of having the *casas reales* set on fire, I resolved to make a sally into the plaza of the said *casas reales* with all my available force of soldiers, without any protection, to attempt to prevent the fire which the enemy was trying to set. With this endeavor we fought the whole afternoon, and, since the enemy, as I said above, had fortified themselves and made embrasures in all the houses, and had plenty of arquebuses, powder, and balls. they did us much damage. Night overtook us thus and God was pleased

that they should desist somewhat from shooting us with arquebuses and arrows. We passed this night, like the rest, with much
care and watchfulness, and suffered greatly from thirst because of
the scarcity of water.

On the next day, Saturday, they began at dawn to press us harder
and more closely with gunshots, arrows, and stones, saying to us
that now we should not escape them, and that besides their own
numbers, they were expecting help from the Apaches whom they
had already summoned. They fatigued us greatly on this day, because all was fighting, and above all we suffered from thirst, as we
were already oppressed by it. At nightfall, because of the evident
peril in which we found ourselves by their gaining the two stations
where cannon were mounted, which we had at the doors of the
casas reales, aimed at the entrances of the streets, in order to bring
them inside it was necessary to assemble all the forces that I had
with me, because we realized that this was their [the Indians'] intention. Instantly all the said Indian rebels began a chant of victory
and raised war-whoops, burning all the houses of the villa, and
they kept us in this position the entire night, which I assure your
reverence was the most horrible that could be thought of or imagined, because the whole villa was a torch and everywhere were
war chants and shouts. What grieved us most were the dreadful
flames from the church and the scoffing and ridicule which the
wretched and miserable Indian rebels made of the sacred things,
intoning the alabado and the other prayers of the church with jeers.

Finding myself in this state, with the church and the villa burned,
and with the few horses, sheep, goats, and cattle which we had
without feed or water for so long that many had already died, and
the rest were about to do so, and with such a multitude of people,
most of them children and women, so that our numbers in all came
to about a thousand persons, perishing with thirst—for we had
nothing to drink during these two days except what had been kept
in some jars and pitchers that were in the casas reales—surrounded by such a wailing of women and children, with confusion
everywhere, I determined to take the resolution of going out in the
morning to fight with the enemy until dying or conquering. Considering that the best strength and armor were prayers to appease
the Divine wrath, though on the preceding days the poor women
had made them with fervor, that night I charged them to do so
increasingly, and told the father guardián and the other two religious to say mass for us at dawn, and exhort all alike to repentance
for their sins and to conformance with the Divine will, and to ab-
solve us from guilt and punishment. These things being done, all of
us who could mounted our horses, and the rest [went] on foot
with their arquebuses, and some Indians who were in our service
with their bows and arrows, and in the best order possible we
directed our course toward the house of the maese de campo, Francisco Xavier, which was the place where (apparently) there were
the most people and where they had been most active and boldest.

On coming out of the entrance to the street it was seen that there was a great number of Indians. They were attacked in force, and though they resisted the first charge bravely, finally they were put to flight, many of them being overtaken and killed. Then turning at once upon those who were in the streets leading to the convent, they also were put to flight with little resistance. The houses in the direction of the house of the said *maestre de campo*, Francisco Xavier, being still full of Indians who had taken refuge in them, and seeing that the enemy with the punishment and deaths that we had inflicted upon them in the first and second assaults were withdrawing toward the hills, giving us a little room, we laid siege to those who remained fortified in the said houses. Though they endeavored to defend themselves, and did so, seeing that they were being set afire and that they would be burned to death, those who remained alive surrendered and much was made of them. The deaths of both parties in this and the other encounters exceeded three hundred Indians.

Finding myself a little relieved by this miraculous event, though I had lost much blood from two arrow wounds which I had received in the face and from a remarkable gunshot wound in the chest on the day before, I immediately had water given to the cattle, the horses, and the people. Because we now found ourselves with very few provisions for so many people, and without hope of human aid, considering that our not having heard in so many days from the people on the lower river would be because of their all having been killed, like the others in the kingdom, or at least of their being or having been in dire straits, with the view of aiding them and joining with them into one body, so as to make the decisions most conducive to his Majesty's service, on the morning of the next day, Monday, I set out for La Isleta, where I judged the said comrades on the lower river would be. I trusted in Divine Providence, for I left without a crust of bread or a grain of wheat or maize, and with no other provision for the convoy of so many people except four hundred animals and two carts belonging to private persons, and, for food, a few sheep, goats, and cows.

In this manner, and with this fine provision, besides a few small ears of maize that we found in the fields, we went as far as the pueblo of La Alameda, where we learned from an old Indian whom we found in a maize-field that the lieutenant-general with all the residents of his jurisdictions had left some fourteen or fifteen days before to return to El Paso to meet the carts. This news made me very uneasy, alike because I could not be persuaded that he would have left without having news of me as well as of all the others in the kingdom, and because I feared that from his absence there would necessarily follow the abandonment of this kingdom. On hearing this news I acted at once, sending four soldiers to overtake the said lieutenant-general and the others who were following him, with orders that they were to halt wherever they should come up with them. Going in pursuit of them, they overtook them at the

place of Fray Cristóbal. The lieutenant-general, Alonso García, overtook me at the place of Las Nutrias, and a few days' march thereafter I encountered the *maese de campo*, Pedro de Leiba, with all
the people under his command, who were escorting these carts and
who came to ascertain whether or not we were dead, as your
reverence had charged him to do, and to find me, ahead of the
supply train. I was so short of provisions and of everything else
that at best I should have had a little maize for six days or so.

Thus, after God, the only succor and relief that we have rests with
your reverence and in your diligence. Wherefore, and in order that
your reverence may come immediately, because of the great importance to the service of God and the king of your reverence's
presence here, I am sending the said *maese de campo*, Pedro de
Leyba, with the rest of the men whom he brought so that he may
come as escort for your reverence and the carts or mule-train in
which we hope you will bring us some assistance of provisions.
Because of the haste which the case demands I do not write at
more length, and for the same reason I cannot make a report at
present concerning the above to the señor viceroy, because the
autos are not verified and there has been no opportunity to conclude them. I shall leave it until your reverence's arrival here. For
the rest I refer to the account which will be given to your reverence by the father secretary, Fray Buene Ventura de Berganza. I
am slowly overtaking the other party, which is sixteen leagues from
here, with the view of joining them and discussing whether or not
this miserable kingdom can be recovered. For this purpose I shall
not spare any means in the service of God and of his Majesty,
losing a thousand lives if I had them, as I have lost my estate and
part of my health, and shedding my blood for God. May He protect
me and permit me to see your reverence in this place at the head
of the relief. September 8, 1680. Your servant, countryman, and
friend kisses your reverence's hand. DON ANTONIO DE OTERMIN.

2. THE RECONQUEST OF NEW MEXICO, 1692

EXCELLENT SIR:
I scarcely arrived from my happy conquest, on the twentieth of
December last, when two hours later the courier arrived with the
answer to that which, with testimony of the records, I sent to your
Excellency from the villa of Santa Fe, notifying your Highness
through them and the letter of transmittal of what had been conquered up to the said day. A happy day, luck, and good fortune
were attained, your Excellency, through the impulse which, fer-
vently, spurred by the faith and as a loyal vassal of his Majesty,
led me to undertake the said enterprise, considering that it is a
region so large as to be a kingdom, all of which was in rebel hands
for the past twelve years, and only on the confines of which was it
known that they had been visited. For their safety, they were living
on the mesas, the approaches to which made it difficult to invade

them without their being assured of victory. All these conditions could have justly embarrassed me, but, realizing that the defense of my faith and my king were of greater importance, I scorned them and put into execution the said enterprise. . . .

I acknowledge the command and order of your Excellency, made in agreement with the real junta de hacienda, in which you say, order, and command that I should continue in the region. I wrote your Excellency, telling you that upon my return from subduing and conquering the Pecos, the Keres tribes living on various mesas, and the Jémez, I would make entry to the rock of Acoma and the provinces of Zuñi and Moqui, should I consider it possible for the horses to travel two hundred leagues. I answer that despite great obstacles, as attested in the records, I made the said entry which I had previously proposed to your Excellency with doubt; having also succeeded in obtaining some *almagre* earth, or vermilion, which is believed to contain quicksilver ore, and having made known the new route which might be used for transit from the said kingdom, for his Majesty, should it contain quicksilver. With great interest I embarked upon the discovery of the said route and crossing, and, having come out at the pueblo of Socorro on the tenth of December last, there was such continuous snow and ice that on the following day we found the river frozen over. And we found that to return to the said villa and its surrounding pueblos by this route would be a waste of time and unfruitful, for it entailed the danger of the enemy Apaches as well as their partisans in this region of El Paso. I decided to hasten there so that the inhabitants would have the defense and garrison of the arms of their presidio and in order that the horses might gain strength and recuperate in order that I might carry out your Excellency's orders.

With regard to the transportation of the families which may be found at this pueblo of El Paso, I decided to visit them in order to make a census list, which I am sending to your Excellency so that your Highness may have record of the exact number of children and other persons who are under the care of each family. Those who can be taken unburdened will go, trusting that your Excellency will take into consideration my report which I referred to in the letter of remission adjoined to the said census. As for the return of the inhabitants who have withdrawn and who live in the kingdoms of [New] Vizcaya and [New] Galicia, I have decided to go in person in order effectively to persuade them, for I shall endeavor to find those who are living in haciendas and known localities, and in the settlements, announcing your Excellency's order and command to the royal authorities, and with their assistance they also will be made known by the proclamation which I will have published. And I shall make known therein that all those who desire to come and colonize the said kingdom will be promised all that which is contained in your Excellency's order. I will enlist them all with their privileges, paying the expenses of those who are to be transported, not only to this pueblo of El Paso, but as far as the villa of Santa Fe. In order that your Excellency may be entirely without anxiety with regard to the said colonization, I shall at all costs set out from this pueblo of El Paso with both groups of settlers upon my return from the said kingdoms, providing that your Excellency, in view of this, will send me the necessary sum, in response to the same and with the same courier. He will find me at the camp of Sombrerete collecting the twelve thousand pesos which your Excellency has placed to my account, if it is not obtainable at Guadiana. For I shall also visit that place for the purpose of enlisting some people, as those obtained for these parts must be of good quality, campaigners and persons agile in the pursuit of this war. . . .

As for the settlement of the region, the soldiers needed for its presidio, its defense and safety, and that of the lives of the religious, I repeat to your Excellency my opinion that five hundred families are necessary for the settlement of the villa and the following districts, not counting the one hundred soldiers necessary for the presidio at the villa of Santa Fe.

While I was there I examined and appraised the land. And, nine days after its conquest, having taken the road to the pueblo of Galisteo, which is the wagon road, and having entered the pueblo of the Pecos tribe, I returned to the said villa by way of the short road through the mountains, which the said tribes travel on foot and on horseback. I then went to the pueblos of the Tegua and Tano tribes, continued to that of Picuríes, and from there to that of Taos. Having seen the said thirteen pueblos and inspected the character of their lands, pastures, water supply, and wood, I find that the only place adequate for the founding of the said villa is its existing site, setting it up and establishing it on this side [sic] of the arroyo where it overlooks and dominates the pueblo and stronghold occupied there by the Tegua and Tano tribes, which comprises what was formerly the major portion of the palace and royal houses of the governor, and those of the inhabitants of the said villa who left as a result of their rebellion. They have extended and raised the walls, and fortified them, so that the said pueblo is walled. Besides, in La Ciénega and its lowland, the waters gather from the surrounding mountains and mesas, and the said stronghold being near by, it is in the shade, and for that reason it is hidden from the sun in the morning, and in the afternoon it also is without the sun's rays. And, due to the climate and temperature of the said kingdom, which is extremely cold, cloudy, and abounding in water, with heavy frosts and ice, and due to its shade and thick fog and mists of known and evident detriment, the said place is unsatisfactory.

The favor granted to the said natives, which I promised them at the time of their conquest, is not prejudicial to the said colonists, rather it is to their interest to settle at the place where I established my encampment on the day of my entry there. It is located a musket shot distance away. Its land dominates and overlooks the said stronghold, the place having sufficient height so that the artillery may control and cause much respect from the enemy. Also the surrounding country is well supplied with wood, farm lands, and pastures. These can be reserved, setting aside and reserving from the entrance at Las Bocas along the road to Santo Domingo, a distance of seven leagues. And as for the pueblo of La Ciénega, which I found abandoned, if some Keres Indians should repopulate it, it will be with the *tasación* of five hundred varas, from the door of the church to the four cardinal points, and no more. Also with regard to the abandoned hacienda of El Alamo, to whomsover lays claim to it will be given the lands with limits, but without liability claims with regard to the said horses.

With regard to the abandoned hacienda which is located a distance of two leagues from there, beyond the arroyo or river called the Seco, also to its owner [*sic*], in the same manner, if he wishes to settle it, and the aforesaid length and distance, with its entrances and exits, will be reserved as the common land not only for the horses and mules of the inhabitants who settle there, but also for those of the soldiers of the presidio. And also, the said place should be settled because it has dry land, with very little gravel, and is clear, getting the sun all day, and enjoying the winds from every direction.

With regard to its settlers, as many as one hundred and fifty families may enter and settle the said villa, as well as the one hundred presidial soldiers, who may cover the land with their arms by being established at this central point which controls a distance of ninety leagues in the following manner: thirty-two long leagues to the pueblo of Taos, to the north, thirty leagues to the pueblos of the Jémez and the Keres of Sia, which are between the south and west, and thirty leagues to the pueblo of Isleta, which is to the west. At the said place they will be assured of having provisions, whether or not the weather is good, and should the population be augmented such that they will need additional sources of supply, the one hundred and fifty families may settle part of the land; for, the said kingdom having the protection of the arms of the presidio, many will decide to settle on the haciendas which they formerly had and which they abandoned at the time of the uprising. The number of those which are occupied will be shared with the families hailing from other parts.

It is my wish, with those with whom I enter, including the soldiers, that they should, first and foremost, personally build the church and holy temple, setting up in it before all else the patroness of the said kingdom and villa, who is the one that was saved from the ferocity of the savages, her title being Our Lady of the Conquest. And so, with the aid of the soldiers and settlers, the foundations will be laid and the walls of the holy temple raised, bringing at the same time, by means of the oxen that will be taken, the timber necessary. At the same time the said construction will be hastened, so that by our example the conquered will be moved to build gladly their churches in their pueblos, which I hope will be accomplished. . . .

With regard to the settlement at the pueblo of Taos, which is on the frontier, and the most distant one of the kingdom, where the Apaches continually make their entry, it will be necessary to place one hundred settlers there. This pueblo has a site even more favorable for settlement, because its valleys are very broad, and it has many arroyos, wood, and pastures, and the land is very fertile and will yield good crops and is very suitable for the raising of all types of livestock, large and small. The said number of settlers, backed by the strength of the arms of the presidio of the said villa, will make it impossible for the enemy easily to swoop down on the pueblos of the said tribes; and also those who rebuild and resettle their haciendas may live in safety, for on the way to this pueblo there are many abandoned sites which were pointed out to me and named by their previous owners.

At the pueblo of Pecos, a distance of eight leagues from Santa Fe, fifty families may be settled, for it is also an Apache frontier and is surrounded by very mountainous country, very adaptable to ambush. And so, if it is settled, and with the said arms at the said villa, it will be possible to prevent the thefts and deaths otherwise facilitated by easy entry. It is very fertile land, which responds with great abundance to all the types of seeds that are planted.

Between the pueblos of Santo Domingo and Cochití, the original inhabitants of this kingdom who so desire may settle, should the Indians of the Keres tribe not come down to occupy the said pueblos. Those of Cochití are living on the mesa and mountain of La Cieneguilla, a distance of four leagues away; and those of Santo Domingo are living on the mesa of the Cerro Colorado with the Keres Indians of Captain Malacate who were absent from their pueblo of Sia at the time General Don Domingo Jironza, my predecessor, burned it and captured those who escaped from fire and arms. And so the people of this Keres tribe are living on the said mesas, which are those of the said two pueblos and the one of Sia. From what they told me on the mesa of the Cerro Colorado, where they again have their pueblo, it is doubtful that they will return to resettle the one of Sia, which was burned by General Don Domingo. They said that they would not return to the pueblo for the additional reason that the land is nitrous, lacks sufficient water, is without wood, and is very sterile, and that if they should descend they would settle in the canyon between the pueblo of Sia and that of abandoned Santa Ana.

In the vicinity of this pueblo of Santa Ana, another fifty settlers may be established, because it has good lands and also because they are necessary to close the way to the enemy Apache; and so that the fathers who minister to the Keres Indians, and those of the Jémez tribe, may have the said settlers near by for their protection, and may, without fear of risking their lives, minister to them, punish them, and reprehend them as the case might be.

In the abandoned pueblo of Jémez, the walls of the church and most of the houses of the dwellings are standing, in which pueblo, should the Indians who are living on the mesa of the canyon remain there, one hundred residents can be settled. It has plenty of lands for planting and pastures, with water and very fertile, and the settlement of the said place would be very important because the Apaches make entry there, by virtue of which some of the Indians are rebellious in spirit and are our enemies.

From the hacienda of "La Angostura," two leagues from the pueblo of "La Angostura," that is, San Felipe, to the abandoned pueblo of Sandía, and one league from the abandoned pueblo of Puaray, at the said first one of Sandía Spaniards also may be settled. The walls of the church and some houses, although badly damaged, may be repaired. The lands are good, with their irrigation ditches. The said pueblos are on the camino real, and it would be very desirable to settle the region with another one hundred colonists, who will be able to live very comfortably and prosperously. It is a distance of twenty leagues from the said villa and will be of great value for the protection of the haciendas which extend from "Las Huertas."

At a distance of ten leagues, on the said camino real, on the other side of the river, there is situated the pueblo of Isleta, which is abandoned. The walls of the church are in good condition, as are most of the houses of the Indians of the Tegua nation who were withdrawn by General Don Antonio de Otermín when he made the entry in the year of 'eighty-one, at the expense of his Majesty, in the time of his Excellency, the viceroy, Conde de Paredes. The natives of the said tribe now live in some miserable huts in the pueblo of Isleta, in this district of El Paso, and so it will be desirable to restore them to their pueblo. They will be assured success in cultivating the fields which they plant at the pueblo, because the lands are extensive, in a good climate, and can be easily irrigated. And they will be protected if the said intervening haciendas called "Las Huertas" are settled, along with those extending from Las Barrancas, and those toward the abandoned pueblos of Alamillo and Sevilleta, whose natives are scattered and restless, and with the settlement of the said haciendas and the pueblo referred to, it will be possible to restore them to their pueblos.

Continuing a distance of ten leagues, Socorro is found, which may be settled with the Indians who at present occupy this one of Socorro in this district of El Paso, and they may be joined by the Piros, who are few, and who live in the pueblo of Senecú in this district, for it is a vast and fertile land; it has its irrigation ditches, and some of the walls of the convent are in good condition. Senecú, which the Piros occupied previously, a distance of ten leagues away, should not be settled because the river has damaged the land, and furthermore it is on a frontier infested with many Apaches. If it is the wish of some to settle the abandoned haciendas, it will be useful for the protection of the said Indians, and it will also prepare the way for the filling in and occupying of the land. The above is only the form in which the settlement should be made, in order that the natives of the said tribes, aware of the neighboring settlers and of the armed strength of the presidio, may be kept in submission, and so that our holy faith may be spread among them, and their children may join it with full obedience, and the missionaries, their teachers of Christian doctrine, may not find themselves alone and afraid to teach them, as I repeat, the doctrines of our holy faith.

As for the natives of the rock of Acoma, since they are a distance of twenty-four leagues from Isleta, and also those of the province of Zuñi, they may be left as they are. But as for those of the province of Moqui, in case the said vermilion earth is found not to contain quicksilver ore, it is my opinion that they should be removed from their pueblos to the abandoned ones of Alamillo and Sevilleta and the region between them, for in this way they will be safe and their missionaries will have control over them, for otherwise they would undergo great risk.

EUSEBIO KINO'S WORK IN THE SOUTHWEST

[The Jesuit Eusebio Kino was, by vocation, a missionary to the Indians and, by disposition, an explorer and cartographer. It was he who first brought Spanish civilization successfully to southern Arizona and lower California. He lived among the Pima Indians from 1687 until his death in 1711 and explored the Southwest extensively during that time. He was the first to make known the accurate geography of the region on the basis of actual travels; perhaps most notable among his achievements was the conclusive demonstration that California was not an island. The area in which Kino worked was called the Pimería Alta, today southern Arizona and northern Sonora. He himself claimed to have made nearly forty expeditions throughout the Southwest in all directions from his mission, and his many maps of the region were widely circulated in Europe, especially his famous 1705 map entitled "A Land Passage to California." Three chapters from Kino's memoirs are reprinted here. The first deals with his assertions about California, the second and third with his proper vocation—the conversion of the Indians.]

CHAPTER VIII. COGENT REASONS AND CLEAR ARGUMENTS WHICH ESTABLISH THE CERTAINTY OF THE LAND PASSAGE TO CALIFORNIA

In case there should be some incredulous persons or someone ignorant of it, the continuity of these lands with California would be rendered certain and proved by the seven following convincing reasons or arguments:

From Herbert E. Bolton, *Kino's Historical Memoir of Pimería Alta, 1683–1711.* Cleveland, 1919. Vol. I, pages 351–354, 357–362.

1st. Because thus I saw it on October 9, 1698, from the neighboring high mountain of Santa Clara. And again in March of the past year, 1701, we saw this connection and passage by land to California, in the company of Father Rector Juan María de Salvatierra, for his Reverence came with ten soldiers and other persons to see this demonstrated, since some had contradicted us.

2d. Because in four other journeys inland which I have made, travelling fifty leagues to the northwest of the said hill of Santa Clara, which is near to and to the eastward of the arm and head of the Sea of California, and afterwards in going ten leagues more to the westward, along the Rio Grande, to where it unites with the Colorado River, and from this confluence forty leagues more to the southwest, along the same Colorado River to its mouth, no Sea of California has been found or seen, for it does not rise higher than barely to the latitude of thirty-two degrees. Hence it is plainly to be inferred that Drake, besides many other modern cosmographers, in their various printed maps, with notable discredit to cosmography, deceive themselves as well as others, by extending this sea, or arm, or strait of the Sea of California from thirty-two to forty-six degrees, making it thereby an island, and the largest in the world, whereas it is not an island but a peninsula.

3d. Because in this journey inland when I was saying mass on March 11 at the above-mentioned mouth of the Colorado River, in company with Father Rector Manuel Gonzales, the sun rose above more than thirty leagues of sea, at the head of this California arm or gulf. At the same time, from the same estuary we saw to the westward thirty leagues more of continuous land, as many more to the south and southwest, and many more to the north, northwest, and northeast. Therefore, this sea does not extend to the north.

4th. Because the natives nearest to that estuary, Quiquimas as well as Cutganes and Coanopas, both this time and on other occasions, gave us various blue shells which are found only on the opposite coast and on the other, or South Sea, where the ship from China comes. And they gave us this time some little pots which shortly before they had brought from that opposite coast, travelling ten leagues from the west by continuous land.

5th. Because these natives and others who came to see us from far to the southwest gave us various reports of the fathers of our Company, telling us that they wore our costumes and vestments, and that they lived down there to the southward with the other Spaniards at Loreto Concho, where the Guimies and Edues, or Laimones Indians obtained their food, and where Father Rector Juan María de Salvatierra and others were. And I having purposely asked them if those Guimies and Edues Indians down there planted maize, and what foods they lived on, they answered us that they did not plant maize nor beans, etc., but that their food was game, the deer, the hare, the mountain goat, the *pitajaya*, the *tuna*, the *mescal*, and other wild fruits, and that the Indians to the westward had blue shells, all being things and reports which it was plain to me were true, since I was there and lived with those Indians seventeen years ago.

6th. Because now in this journey inland and on other occasions I have found various things—little trees, fruit, incense, etc.—all species which are peculiar to California alone, and samples of which I bring, to celebrate with the incense, by the favor of heaven, this Easter and Holy Week, and to place five good grains of incense in the Paschal candle. Moreover, near this estuary we already have found some words of the Guimia language which I learned there, while missionary and rector of that mission of California, although unworthy, in the two trienniums of Fathers Provincial Bernardo Pardo and Luys del Canto, from the year 1681 to that of 1685.

7th. Because the ancient maps with good reason showed California as a peninsula and not as an island, as well as some modern ones, among them the universal map of my Father master of mathematics in the University of Ingolstadt, which is in my possession. He dedicated it to our Father San Ygnacio and to San Francisco Xavier, with this inscription: *de Universo Terrarum Orbe Opime Meritis* [To the well-deserving of the whole world].

And if some hostile and obstinate persons should maintain that some Quiquima Indians say that farther west the sea still extends to the northwest, these Quiquimas speak of the other sea, on the opposite coast, and not of this our Sea of California, of which, as some call it Red Sea, we may say, because we have found this passage, *Aparuit terra arida, et in Mari Rubro via sine inpedimento* [Dry land appeared and in the Red Sea a road without hindrance], as says the Church on August 8, on the day of the saints who have the Gospel: *Euntes in mundum universum. Predicate Evangelium omni creaturæ* [Go into all the world and preach the gospel to every creature]. . . .

CHAPTER X. TEMPORAL MEANS FOR THESE NEW CONVERSIONS AND FOR THE TOTAL REDUCTION OF THIS NORTH AMERICA, WHICH HITHERTO HAS BEEN UNKNOWN

I. First, there are already many cattle, sheep and goats, and horses; for, although in the past year I have given more than seven hundred cattle to the four fathers who entered this Pimería, I have for the other new conversions and missions which by the favor of heaven it may be desired to establish, more than three thousand five hundred more cattle; and some of them are already far inland, ninety leagues from here, and by the divine grace they can pass with ease to the Californias, Upper and Lower, as a certain important person is pleased to name them, the latter being in twenty-six and the former in thirty and more degrees of latitude.

II. There are in this very fertile and rich Pimería, which already has five missions with five fathers, many fields of wheat, maize, beans, etc; and produces all sorts of vegetables, garden products, and fruit trees, as in Europe. There are already vines for Castilian wine for the missions, a watermill, pack trains, fields, oxen, lands, level roads, beautiful rivers, abundant pasturage, good timbers for buildings, and mineral lands.

III. Of these new nations almost all are composed of industrious, docile, affable, and very friendly Indians; and only in some remote parts are there some Indians somewhat more barbarous and un-civilized, because of never having seen civilized people in all their lives.

IV. The temperature of these lands, which extend from thirty degrees of latitude to thirty-one, thirty-two, thirty-three, thirty-four, etc., is similar to that of Mexico and the better part of Europe, without excessive heat or excessive cold.

V. With these means and with these new conversions it will be possible to trade by sea and land with other near-by and remote provinces, nations, and kingdoms, with Sonora, Hyaqui, Cinaloa, Culiacan, with all New Galicia, with New Biscay, with Moqui, with New Mexico, which will be able to come to join hands with these provinces of Sonora, and even with New France.

CHAPTER XI. ADVANTAGES WHICH MAY RESULT FROM THESE NEW CONVERSIONS TO THE BENEFIT OF ALL THIS UNKNOWN NORTH AMERICA

I. First, with these new conversions the Catholic dominion of the royal crown of our very Catholic monarch Philip V, God preserve him, and our holy Roman Catholic Faith, will be extended.

II. Very extensive new lands, nations, rivers, seas, and people of this North America which hitherto have been unknown will be discovered and won; and, besides, thereby these Christian provinces will be more protected, safer, and more quiet.

III. Thereby will be removed the great errors and falsehoods imposed upon us by those who have delineated this North America with feigned things which do not exist, such as a crowned king whom they carried on a golden litter; a lake of quicksilver, and another of gold; a walled city with towers, etc.; the Kingdom of Axa; the pearls, amber, and corals of the Rio del Tizon, the Rio del Coral, and the Rio de Aganguchi, which they represent as emptying into this sea of California in thirty-five or thirty-six degrees, although this sea does not extend to that latitude; likewise the error of the Seven Cities, which some represent. Although at present they do not exist, ten years ago we saw some great houses at different places near the Rio Grande, whose structures, now fallen, indicate that they did exist a long time ago; and it is very possible that from them issued the people of Monte Suma, when they went to found the great City of Mexico.

IV. Since Father Mariano reprehends with reason those feigned grandeurs and riches, in particular when they wish to attribute them to the account of the Adelantado of New Mexico, Don Juan de Oñate, we shall be able to make drawings and true cosmographic maps of all these new lands and nations, of this passage by land to California, as well as of the very large volumed, fertile, and very populous rivers which empty into the head of this sea, and of the harbors and bays of the opposite coast and Sea of the South, of Gran Quivira, of Gran Teguayo, and of the neighboring Apachería, Moqui, etc. And as your Reverence, in the journey inland made two years ago with Señor Lieutenant Juan Mateo Manje, Father Francisco Gonzalvo, and me, which in going and returning was more than two hundred leagues, found these Pima nations, with some Opas and Cocomaricopas, already reduced to our friendship, so now the Yumas, Coanopas, Cutganes, Quiquimas, and many others to the north, northwest, and west are reduced, in this terra firma as well as in the neighboring California Alta; all of which lands combined are as large as all of Europe, and of the same climate and temperature.

Moreover, by the north, northeast, and east, can be found a road to Europe shorter by half than the one which we now use by way of Mexico and Vera Cruz; as also by the northwest and west one shall be able to go in time by land even very near to Japan, Great China, and Tartary; for the Strait of Anian, which authors place with such a variety of opinions, probably has no more foundation in fact than had this arm of the sea with which for us they incorrectly delineated California as an island. That route to Japan and Great China can be found by way of Cape Mendozino, and by the land of Yesso [Alaska, perhaps], and by the land which they call Tierra de la Compañia, which by divine grace, with apostolic missionaries can become Land of the Company of Jesus.

V. The China ship can have a port call, as you have so much desired, on the opposite coast of California, where the many sick with scurvy which it is accustomed to bring will find relief. And it can have trade, very profitable for all, with the provinces of this Kingdom of New Biscay, for they told me seventeen years ago when I sailed in the Chinese ship from Matanchel to Acapulco that for a sheep they gladly gave an ivory tusk or a piece of China linen, which is usually forty *varas* [yards, approximately] long and which it is the custom to sell for a dollar a *vara*, because of the heavy freight charges entailed in carrying it by land from Mexico to these provinces of Sonora. And almost the same is true with respect to the other goods of this very rich Philippine galleon.

VI. We shall comply with what so Christianlike and so earnestly is charged upon us by the very Catholic *cédula* [certificate of instruction] of May [1]4, 1686, which the Royal Audiencia of Guadalajara gave me, inserted in a royal provision, when I was passing through that city on my return from California and coming to these new conversions. In that royal *cédula* his royal Majesty com-

mands that with respect to the most essential point of the new
conversions effort shall be made to make all haste possible as in a
matter of chief concern to his royal Majesty, and a matter of conscience to him, just as to those of us who live nearest, and that the
necessary expenses be not spared, because his royal Majesty recognizes that for all that is spent in those causes, so merciful, our Lord
always returns to his royal crown very abundant and well known
increase, which are the words of the royal *cédula*. And, indeed, we
very plainly see that at the very same time that his royal Majesty,
Don Carlos II, God preserve him, incurred the very great expense
of the three ships for the conversion of California through Admiral
Don Ysidro de Atondo y Antillon, there were discovered very near
to and opposite said conquest and conversion the great riches and
mines of the mining camps which are commonly called Los Frayles,
Alamos, and Guadalupe; and the day of our Lady of Sorrows, day
before yesterday, when I received the news of the six thousand
pesos which his royal Majesty Philip V, God preserve him, gave
to the new conversions of California, they gave me certain news of
the treasure and rich mines which have just been discovered near
here at Quisuani, Aygame, San Cosme, etc., and very near to the
new conversion or mission of San Francisco Xavier of the Pimas
Cocomacaques of Pimeria Baxa.

VII. In this way even with very great good fortune and profit
to ourselves, by divine grace, we will bring it about that, so many
souls being converted, *fiat unus pastor, et unum ovile*, and that all
will help us to praise our most merciful God through all the blessed
Eternity. All of which I commend very affectionately to the holy
sacrifices and to the paternal, holy protection of your Reverence,
whose life may our Lord preserve as I desire.

SPAIN'S PLANS TO CONVERT THE INDIANS OF TEXAS

[During the seventeenth century, several exploratory expeditions went out from New Mexico into Texas: in 1629, under Fray Juan de Salas; in 1650, under Hernando Martín and Diego del Castillo; in 1654, under Diego de Guadalajara; and, in 1683, under Juan Domínguez de Mendoza and Fray Nicolás López. At first, Spain's interest in Texas was the conversion of the Indians and the search for the wealth that Coronado might have missed. When no signs of wealth appeared, interest in the area lagged. But it was soon learned that the French had appeared in east Texas and were establishing themselves on the Gulf Coast at the mouth of the Mississippi. Between 1686 and 1693, Spain took a very active interest in Texas, making sure the French settlement was destroyed and initiating mission work among the natives. From 1693 until 1715, however, Texas was abandoned—out of fear of an Indian uprising—until further French consolidation in Louisiana drew Spain back into the region, this time to stay. In the fall of 1715, the Viceroy at Mexico City commissioned the founding of four missions among the Tejas Indians and sent out an expedition of sixty-five persons, including soldiers and missionaries. By 1730, there were in Texas, as a permanent counter to French incursion, four presidios and ten missions. The two leading settlements were San Antonio and Los Adaes. The letter reprinted below is concerned primarily with missionary activities among the Indians in Texas. Curiously enough, while reciting the history of Spanish interest in the colony, it fails to mention the significant motive of countering the threat of French colonization. The letter was written by Pedro de Rivera, a former inspector of the presidios in Texas, to the

From "Spain's Indian Policy in Texas," translated by J. Villasana Haggard, in: *Southwestern Historical Quarterly*, July 1942.

Viceroy, stating the reasons for forbidding the missionaries to use the military to facilitate conversions. The letter is dated June 10, 1730.]

In a letter dated the 8th of last month Reverend Father Fray Miguel Sevillano de Paredes stated that it was impossible for the missionaries to go to the rancherias of the wild Indians to recover from among them the Christian Indians who might have fled from the missions, to Christianize the wild Indians, and to urge them to assemble in groups for the reestablishment of missions which are to be erected on the San Marcos River without escorts of soldiers for their safety. The same statements are contained in the petition filed with Your Excellency by Reverend Father Fray Gabriel Vergara. In a decree dated the sixteenth of the afore-cited month, Your Excellency orders me to prepare a report on this matter, and I am doing so in the following manner:

During the times when our army has entered the province of Texas, it has always done so with the object of spreading the faith by preaching the Gospel. And the object of assembling them in missions has never been attained, although the reverend missionaries have done everything possible to their apostolic zeal. Inasmuch as all the tribes of that vast country live a free and licentious life, they have not desired to be subjected to the gentle yoke of the Church because on account of their depraved habits, it seemed heavy to them. And, if they are to be converted to our religion, their will cannot be coerced; and, therefore, force has not been used to attain those objects, as may be proved by the known facts.

In the year sixteen hundred eighty-eight Don Alonso de Leon, with two companies of soldiers, entered that province as far as the village of the Navidachos. Although those Indians were requested to assemble in the missions, they did not wish to do so despite the fact that the reverend missionaries, as their duties, endeavored to persuade them. Consequently, seeing the difficulties they were encountering, they withdrew without attaining their object. In the year sixteen hundred ninety-two Don Domingo Theran de los Rios entered as far as the Caudachos with the same instructions, but seeing the impossibility of the task, he withdrew without gaining any advantage.

The year seventeen hundred fifteen, for the just reasons existing at that time, the presidio of Texas was erected. And, although the missionaries made their greatest efforts by cajoling the Indians with presents as well as by demonstrations of their apostolic zeal, they were not able to persuade the Indians to assemble in the missions. The year seventeen hundred nineteen Don Martín de Alarcón entered [Texas] with fifty soldiers to re-enforce the garrisons of that province. He went as far as Los Adáes and left there two missionaries, and then he withdrew with the aforesaid soldiers to the place where the Presidio of San Antonio is now located, and which was erected at that time. At the same time the two missions now existing there were founded with the Indians of the Payayas, Aguastayas, and Mezquites, who were converted for fear of the Apaches. The year of seventeen hundred twenty-one the Marqués de San Miguel de Aguayo entered the aforesaid province with a numerous army. He re-enforced the Presidio of Los Adáes with one hundred men, and the one of La Bahía with ninety, and then he withdrew with the rest of the men, leaving those Indians in peace (as they have always been) but still refusing to assemble in villages in order not to be subjected by the missionaries, always living dispersed in their rancherias, as shown by later experience. These remarks show that none of the men that governed that province used the armed forces of his presidios to assemble the Indians in the missions, as proved by a statement submitted to me by Reverend Father Fray Gabriel de Vergara, when I passed by the mission where he was serving, and which is now in your superior office in a *cuaderno* of inquiries. It reads as follows:

I, Fray Gabriel de Bergar, member of the regular order of Our Lord of San Francisco, apostolic president of these three missions of the Province of Texas, pertaining to the College of Santa Cruz de Queretaro, appear before Your Lordship in due form, according to law, and state that I came to this province of Texas in the year [seventeen hundred] sixteen by order of the Duke of Linares, Viceroy of New Spain, with the object of converting its inhabitants to Evangelical law. Although they received us with joy and peace (a peace they still maintain), they have never cared to assemble in settlements where we might be able to separate them from their idolatry and acquaint them with Evangelical law. They are satisfied to live in their dwellings, a long distance from one another, so that in order to communicate with any of them, it is often necessary to travel four, six, and eight, and in places more than fifteen and twenty leagues, since their dwellings are so far distant from one another. Consequently, they cannot be taught the things necessary to the welfare of their souls. For the space of twelve years we have made several attempts to assemble the aforesaid Indians, insofar as we can consistently do so with our apostolic mission, but we have never had any success. We have noticed that none of the officers who have entered this province have been able to accomplish this object, either for lack of inclination or lack of means. And, in consideration of the great expense incurred by His Majesty without fruit, and to our great chagrin, in the year [seventeen hundred] twenty-four I decided to go to the capital of Mexico in person to inform the viceroy of the condition of this province, as I did by word of mouth, with much information, and also in writing. His reply was that Your Lordship would come here and make an inspection and determine whatever Your Lordship might deem advantageous to the service of His Majesty.

Consequently, I hereby beg Your Lordship to issue orders for these wild Indians to be assembled in settlements at points adequate to their maintenance, where they may be Christianized. If this is not done, the great expenses incurred by His Majesty are being wasted. The vicinity of San Antonio would seem to be adequate since excellent places are to be found, and many wild Indians who are willing to be converted and taught are living there. Please issue whatever orders Your Lordship may deem advantageous to the service of our king (may God guard him). Dated at this [mission] of La Purisima Concepción of the Province of Texas, on the eighth day of September, seventeen hundred twenty-seven.

FRAY GABRIEL DE VERGARA

It must be stated here that, if the army has not co-operated in compelling the wild Indians to live assembled in missions (which the fathers, doubtless have previously requested, as they do now), they have not done so probably because they have considered the matter with the reflection demanded by its gravity. They have probably seen at a glance the difficulty encountered by the fact that it would not be reasonable for the conversion of the wild Indians to be attained by force. Reverend Father Fray Gabriel, above cited, states in his appeal that His Majesty has ordered his officers to endeavor to convert and civilize the Indians, fugitives as well as new additions to the missions, but this royal order must be interpreted in practice only when no harm will come from its execution. The will of the Indians itself should prevail in this matter, as provided by Law One, Title Three, Book Six, page one hundred ninety-eight, Volume Two, of the New *Recopilación* of the Indies, which instructs the viceroys, presidents, and governors as to how they are to carry out the conversion of the wild Indians.

The missionaries were never given arms to assemble the wild Indians in missions, the opposite attitude was taken since that is desirable in order to preserve public peace in those distant [territories]. How, then, can I render an opinion favorable to the request of the father? Especially, when I bear in mind the fact that disturbances of the peace might ensue—a peace which at present is being preserved by the Indians—if changes were made in the established custom. Furthermore, we must wait until the wild Indians themselves, as a result of the good treatment they may receive, spontaneously, of their own free will, offer to be converted. This happened with the Indians of the Janos tribe, who remained assembled for eleven years in the place where they are living today without being baptized during that time until, compelled by the good treatment they received (and not by force), all of them became Catholics.

I do not mean to state that one missionary, with only one soldier to accompany him, should go to the rancherias of the wild Indians in order that, upon hearing his sermon and viewing his good example, they may be reduced to social life, although this is the best way to teach them. My proposal merely concerns dealing with the Indians of the large rancheria, which is made up of a large number of different tribes and because it has entered into an alliance with all the other tribes of that kingdom. And, since they are so proud, seeing themselves fully armed with muskets and with an abundance of food for their maintenance, if the missionaries should try to take from among them any Indian who has escaped from the missions and to this end they should go with an escort from the army of a presidio, they might be unwelcome to the Heruipiames, who are the ones in charge of the government of that—seemingly—republic. If they should look with disdain on the missionaries and the soldiers, the necessity for control would become acute, and once those tribes are aroused, much work would be required to reestablish peace and to preserve that province in a state of peace, as it is today. The officers who are governing it, therefore, need to exercise much prudence in any movement they may execute.

Returning to the escort needed by the fathers to enter the rancherias of the wild Indians who are wandering about, it will be important for this escort not to consist of more than two or three soldiers, which is a sufficient number to accompany them. And, if they are not concerned with any other duties save to accompany the missionary (as the chief duty to attain their objective), there will be no danger that the Indians will become more distrustful than they are and suspect that they are to be converted by force. Otherwise the spiritual conquest, which is aspired to, will not only be unattainable but much else will be ventured, and that kingdom might have to be abandoned.

It is true that the fathers, in their apostolic zeal, are endeavoring to effect the conversion of those wild Indians without any other interest than the salvation of their souls, but they have not taken into account the risks taken if the proper means are not chosen to attain the glorious success so ardently desired; and [they have not realized] that certain things can be obtained by art when they cannot be achieved by force.

This is all, Sire, that I can state with regard to this matter in compliance with your instructions. Nevertheless, since, for lack of wisdom, I may be in error in the opinion I have rendered, and if Your Excellency should so desire, this *expediente* should be forwarded to the Judge Advocate General of the War Department, who, with his well-known prudence, will set forth the most accurate opinion, or, whatever Your Excellency wishes may be done in the matter, for, as usual, that will be the best decision.

A MISSIONARY'S INDICTMENT OF PUBLIC OFFICIALS IN NEW MEXICO

[The fierce conflicts that raged between "the two majesties," the church and the state, in New Mexico prior to the Pueblo Revolt of 1680 were not renewed during the eighteenth century, at least not at the same level of intensity. This is not to say that abuses were corrected or that the Indians were any better treated than they had been before the revolt. Public officials still looked upon their offices as opportunities for gain and exploitation. Lack of open conflict probably indicated that Spanish officialdom was more thoroughly in control than it had been in the previous century, for the memory of the revolt was not lost among the colonists. Evidence of the extent to which public officials took advantage of the Indians and hindered the work of the missions is provided by this report from Fray Carlos Delgado on March 27, 1750, to Father Ximeno, custodian of the missions of New Mexico.]

From "Report made by Reverend Father Fray Carlos Delgado to our Reverend Father Ximeno concerning the abominable hostilities and tyrannies of the governors and alcaldes mayores toward the Indians, to the consternation of the custodia," in: Charles W. Hackett, ed., *Historical Documents Relating to New Mexico, Nueva Vizcaya, and Approaches Thereto, to 1773*. Collected by Adolph F. A. Bandelier and Fanny Bandelier. Washington, D.C., 1937. Vol. III, pages 425–430.

Very Reverend Father and our Minister Provincial: I, Fray Carlos José Delgado, preacher general, commissary, notary, and censor of the Holy Office, apostolic notary, and missionary in the *custodia* of the conversion of San Pablo of this province of El Santo Evangelio in the kingdom of New Mexico, appear before your reverence only for the purpose of lamenting before your paternal love the grave extortions that we, the ministers of these missions, are suffering, at the hands of the governors and alcaldes of that kingdom. I declare, that of the eleven governors and many *alcaldes mayores* whom I have known in the long period of forty years that I have served at the mission called San Agustín de la Isleta, most of them have hated, and do hate to the death, and insult and persecute the missionary religious, causing them all the troubles and annoyances that their passion dictates, without any other reason or fault than the opposition of the religious to the very serious injustices which the said governors and alcaldes inflict upon the helpless Indians recently received into the faith, so that the said converts shall not forsake our holy law and flee to the heathen, to take up anew their former idolatries. This is experienced every day, not without grave sorrow and heartfelt tears on the part of those evangelical sowers, who, on seeing that their work is wasted and that the fecund seed of their preaching to those souls is lost and bears no fruit, cry out to heaven and sorrowfully ask a remedy for this great evil. In order that your reverence's exalted understanding may regard as just the reasons which support the said missionaries in their opposition to the aforesaid extortions, even though it should be at the cost of their lives, and also in order that you may come to their aid with the measures best fitted for the total abolition of the said injuries and injustices, I shall specify them in the following manner:

The first annoyance with which the persons mentioned molest the Indians is to send agents every year (contrary to the royal ordinances, and especially to a decree of the most excellent señor, Don Francisco Fernández de la Cueva Henríquez, Duke of Albuquerque, and viceroy of New Spain, issued in this City of Mexico on May 18, 1709, whose content I present, the original being kept in the archive of the *custodia* mentioned) at the time of the harvest, to all the pueblos of the kingdom, under the pretext of buying maize for the support of their households, though most of it is really to be sold in the nearest villages. The said agents take from all the pueblos and missions eight hundred or a thousand *fanegas* [bushels], and compel the Indians to transport them to the place where the governor lives. Besides not paying them anything for the said transportation, they do not pay them for the maize at once, and when the date arrives which they have designated for the payment, if the maize is worth two pesos a *fanega* they give them only one. Even this amount is not in coin or in any article that can be useful to the Indians, but in baubles, such as *chuchumates*, which are glass beads, ill-made knives, relics, awls, and a few handfuls of common tobacco, the value of which does not amount even to a tenth part of what the maize is worth which they extract from them by force, and this even though as has been said, they pay them only half the proper price that is charged throughout the kingdom. From this manifest injustice two very serious evils result: first, the unhappy Indians are left without anything to eat for the greater part of the year; and second, in order not to perish of hunger they are forced to go to the mountains and hunt for game or to serve on the ranches or farms for their food alone, leaving the missions abandoned.

The second oppression that the Indians frequently suffer at the hands of the governors is being compelled arbitrarily and by force, for the small price of an awl or other similar trifle, to work on the buildings that they need, whatever they may be and whether they require little or much time. The Indians also are required to drive cattle as far as the villa of Chihuahua, which is more than two hundred leagues distant from the place where the governors live. They receive in payment for this service only a little ground corn, which they call *pinole*, and the Indian cattle drivers are compelled to pay for those [animals] that are lost or die for want of care or by any other accident. A pernicious evil arises from this cattle driving, for the Indians must abandon their families and leave their lands uncultivated, and, as a consequence, be dying of hunger during the greater part of the year.

The third oppression, and the most grievous and pernicious, from which originate innumerable evils and sins against God, and manifest injuries against the missionaries and Indians, is the wicked dissimulation of the governors in regard to the acts of the *alcaldes mayores*, for it is publicly known throughout the realm that when they give them their *varas*, or wands of office, they tell and advise them to make the Indians work without pity.

With such express license, your reverence can imagine how many disturbances will be caused by men who usually take the employment of *alcaldes mayores* solely for the purpose of advancing their own interests and acquiring property with which to make presents to the governors, so that the latter will countenance their unjust proceedings, even though they be denounced before them, and perhaps will even promote them in office. Every year they make the Indians weave four hundred blankets, or as many woolen sheets; they take from all the pueblos squads of thirty or forty Indians and work them the greater part of the year in planting maize and wheat, which they care for until it is placed in the granaries; they send them among the heathen Indians to trade indigo, knives, tobacco, and *chuchumates*, for cattle and for deer hides. Not even the women are exempt from this tyranny, for if the officials cannot make use of their work in any other way they compel them to spin almost all the wool needed for the said sheets and blankets. And the most lamentable thing about all this is that they recompense them for these tasks with only a handful of tobacco, which is divided among eighteen or twenty.

The most grievous thing for the heathen Indians is that the alcaldes and even some of the governors, mix with their wives and
daughters, often violating them, and this so openly that with a very
little effort the violation of their consorts comes to the knowledge
of the husbands, and as a result it often happens that they repudi-
ate their wives and will not receive them until the missionary
fathers labor to persuade them. The shameless way in which the
officials conduct themselves in this particular is proved by an occasion when a certain governor was in conversation with some missionaries, and an Indian woman came into their presence to charge
him with the rape of her daughter, and he, without changing countenance, ordered that she should be paid by merely giving her a
buffalo skin that he had at hand.

Yet all that I have hitherto related does not drive the Indians to
the limits of desperation or cause them to fall away from our holy
faith so much as when the said alcaldes compel them to deliver to
them a quantity of deer skins, lard, sheaves, [of grain], chickens,
and other things that their desires dictate, saying that they are for
the governors, who ask for them. The Indian has to submit to this
injustice, for they either take it from him without asking, or, if he
does not have what the alcaldes ask for or does not give it promptly
enough when he has it, he suffers either spoliation or punishment.

These punishments are so cruel and inhuman that sometimes for
a slight offence, sometimes because the Indian resists the outrages
that they inflict upon him, or sometimes because they are slow in
doing what the alcaldes order, they are put in jail for many days,
are confined in the stocks, or—and I cannot say it without tears—
the officials flog them so pitilessly that, their wrath not being ap-
peased by seeing them shed their blood, they inflict such deep scars
upon them that they remain for many years. It is a proof of this
second point that when I went among the heathen to reduce the
apostates there were among them some who, with an aggrieved air,
showed me their scars, thus giving me to understand that the reason
why they fled and did not return to the pale of the church was their
fear of these cruel punishments.

A further distressing proof of this practice is what was done in
the past year at El Paso by a captain to a Catholic Indian of the
Zuma nation, sacristan of the mission of El Real. A servant of the
captain of El Paso had hidden three ears of corn which he had
stolen from his master. The sacristan took them from him, and,
without any more proof or reason than having found him with them
in his hands, and because the said servant, to escape punishment,
said that the innocent Indian often stole corn from the granaries,
the said captain became so angered that, in violation of all natural
and divine laws, he ordered six soldiers to take the Indian out and
kill him in the fields.

They carried out the order, and when the unfortunate Zuma cried
aloud for confession they did not yield to his entreaties, but gave
him a violent death, perhaps being fearful that the missionary re-

ligious, whose duty it was to administer the holy sacrament to him, would prevent the execution of that unjust order, even though it might be at the cost of his life.

The outrage did not stop here, for when the Zuma Indians of the mission of El Real learned of the death of their countryman, they began to rise up, all crying out: "Why, since we are Christians, do they not permit us to confess at the hour of death? Let us flee to the mountains!" They did not flee, our father, either because the soldiers restrained them or because the fathers appealed to them. A still greater injury, however, arose from the remedy, for the governor having ordered a large troop of Zumas of both sexes to come to this city, simply because an Indian woman and two men were not able to travel as fast as the others, having crippled feet, the corporal who was leading them ordered them to be beheaded at a place called El Gallego, where he left the bodies unburied, to the intense grief of their companions and relatives, whose sorrow was not lessened on seeing that the said corporal and the rest of the escort robbed them of their little children in order to sell them as slaves in various places along the road.

Nor is it only the said alcaldes and governors that ill-treat the Indians in the manner described, but even the judges who enter to conduct the *residencias* of the alcaldes and governors who have completed their terms of office, inflict upon the Indians as much injury and hardship as may conduce to the advancement of their own interests and the success of their ambitious desires. It is public knowledge throughout the kingdom that such persons seek to conduct these *residencias* more for what they gain by unjust and violent spoliation of the Indians than for what they receive from the office that they exercise.

Finally, to such an extreme do the iniquities reach that are practiced against the Indians by governors and *alcaldes mayores*, as well as by the judges of *residencia*, that, losing patience and possessed by fear, they turn their backs to our holy mother, the Church, abandon their pueblos and missions, and flee to the heathen, there to worship the devil, and, most lamentable of all, to confirm in idolatries those who have never been illumined by the light of our holy faith, so that they will never give ear or credit to the preaching of the gospel. Because of all this, every day new conversions become more difficult, and the zealous missionaries who in the service of both Majesties are anxiously seeking the propagation of the gospel, most often see their work wasted and do [not] accomplish the purpose of their extended wanderings.

Although it cannot be denied that those barbarous nations are stiffnecked, yet there have been many instances where thousands of them have entered joyfully through the requisite door of the holy sacrament of baptism, and most of the apostates would return to the bosom of the Church if they did not fear, with such good reason, the punishments and extortions that I have already spoken of. They have told me this on most of the occasions when I have entered in fulfillment of my obligation to reduce apostates and convert the heathen. In the year 1742, when, at the cost of indescribable labor and hardships, I reduced four hundred and forty odd among apostates and heathen in the province of Moqui, innumerable souls would have come to the bosom of our holy Church had they not been deterred by the reason that I have stated.

Although the missionary religious ought to oppose themselves to these grave injuries and their pernicious consequences, they often do not do it; first, because they never succeed in attaining their purpose, but on the contrary are insulted, disrespected, and held to be disturbers of the peace; second, because the governors and alcaldes impute and charge them with crimes that they have never committed, which they proceed to prove with false witnesses whom they have suborned before the father custodian, and compel the latter to proceed against the religious whom they calumniate. And although the said custodians know very well that the denunciations are born of hatred, they proceed against the missionaries, changing them from one mission to another, in order to prevent the said governors from committing the excess of using their power to expel the missionaries from the kingdom, as has often happened; and also because, when the custodians do not agree to what the governors ask, the latter refuse to certify the allowance for the administration of the religious, which certification is necessary in order that the most excellent señor viceroy may issue the honorariums that his Majesty (whom may God preserve) assigns for the maintenance of the missionary religious. It has seemed to me that all that I have said ought to be presented before the charitable zeal of your reverence, so that, having it before you as father of those faithful sons, your apostolic missionaries, you may put into execution the means that your discretion may decide upon, with the purpose of ending this great abuse, of redeeming all those helpless people, and consoling your sorrowing sons. It is indisputable that whatever I have said is public, notorious, certain and true, as I swear *in verbo sacerdotis tacto pectore*, at this hospice of Santa Bárbara of the pueblo of Tlatelolco, on March 27, 1750. Our very reverend father, your humblest subject, Fray CARLOS JOSE DELGADO, who venerates you, places himself at your feet.

THE ABORTIVE EFFORT TO CONVERT THE APACHES OF TEXAS

[The Apache and Comanche Indians were the scourge of the Plains, with the Apaches providing a particular menace to Spain's sparsely-populated and frail Texas colony. For more than twenty years after 1730, the Spaniards sent out primitive expeditions to arrest the Indian depredators. By 1750, these patrols had been successful enough so that the Spanish officials looked forward to an era of peaceful coexistence and even mission work among the Apaches. The latter were sufficiently cooperative to petition for a mission station, which was established for them in 1757 on the San Sabá River near Comanche territory. The project was superintended by Fray Alonso Giraldo de Terreros, whose cousin Don Pedro Terreros had contributed the funds to found the mission. Unfortunately, the Apaches, mostly out of fear of their old enemy, the Comanches, refused to settle at the mission; and, in fact, the mission had no sooner been built than the Comanches swooped down and destroyed it in the "San Sabá Massacre" of March 16, 1758. Thus ended Spain's mission work among the Apaches of Texas. The letter reproduced below was written on February 13, 1758, by Fray Alonso, superintendent of the mission, to the Viceroy at Mexico City. He never got to make the trip of which he speaks, for he died in the massacre.]

From Lesley Byrd Simpson, ed., *The San Sabá Papers*, trans. by Paul D. Nathan. San Francisco, 1959. Pages 1–4.

Most Excellent Sir: The latest directive of your Excellency (dated September 28, last), concerning the subjugation of these miserable heathen Indians of the Apache Nation, sets up certain procedures that conform to my apostolic desire. I promise your Excellency that I shall persevere in the holy purpose for which this enterprise was undertaken. My fellow religious join me in the apostolic task of improving relations and friendly intercourse with these Gentiles, now that we are supported and justified by the superior authority of your Excellency, as shown in your said directive, and by the wise judgment of the honorable Ministers of your Captaincy General. As soon as I learned of this blessed good fortune and of your laudable support of our cause, it occurred to me that the sole and most effective means of accomplishing the pacification of the heathen was to continue persuading and catechizing their confused and irresolute wills.

In order to grasp our opportunities at the present time, and impelled by my strong desire to meet the obligations of my profession and the worthy injunctions of your Excellency, I took counsel, in the presence of the Visitor Commissary, the Reverend Father Fray Mariano de los Dolores, with my fellow religious of the Apostolic College of Santa Cruz de Querétaro who are serving in the Missions on the San Antonio River and the Río Grande del Norte. He attended for the purpose of considering the best and most desirable means of realizing certain objectives in the service of both Majesties.

He congratulated us all on having gained the sovereign protection of your Excellency and on the fact that the Auditor and the Fiscal of his Majesty's Court had likewise approved, with holy zeal, the conversion of the heathen. Such a conversion is sure to glorify the pious and Catholic desires of the King. At the same time his vassals in this region will obtain very substantial relief from their burdens and the advancement of their own interests.

Nothing we discussed was more important than the means of achieving our undertaking and the funds that have been spent on it, except the report that might be made to the wise understanding of your Excellency by Colonel Don Diego Ortiz Parrilla, present Commandant in this territory, in person, together with one of ourselves, always with the cooperation of the two Apostolic Colleges upon which we depend for the supervision of the territory. Because of our previous experience with the Indians, the means most conducive to their hoped-for subjugation became apparent. In no other way can the proper explanation of such an arduous enterprise be communicated, nor its importance duly emphasized.

These thoughts of ours were submitted to the Colonel, who strongly supported them, for with his extraordinary talent he had helped formulate them in accordance with the approved plans. It was not in his power, however, to decide upon a journey to visit your Excellency without appropriate permission. We decided only that he should offer to make it whenever the superior will of your Excellency should so determine.

On this premise, Most Excellent Sir, I, on my own account, and in the name of all our religious, appeal to the benignity of your Excellency for approval, and to your well-known diligence in the service of both Majesties, praying for your approbation and consent, so that Colonel Don Diego Ortiz Parrilla and one of ourselves may proceed to your court with all the speed the situation requires. I assure your Excellency that we shall conform to your good wishes and those of the established government, which customarily listens to all that has been done for the benefit of the natives and the King's servants who, for so many years, in misfortune and hardship, have dwelt in the regions of the north. No other means is so well suited to the clarification of these projects, and the favorable consideration and decision of your Excellency, than a report made in person. Such a report will advance the cause far more than putting it on paper and entrusting it to a long and uncertain journey.

The instructions concerning the status of these Gentiles at the present time are the same that were recommended to your Excellency by your Council and transmitted by the Commandant here. They continue their good cooperation, but their promises of submission are sometimes pretexts for delay, some alleging illnesses and disagreements among them, while others in their perplexity make frivolous proposals and lack the unity to settle in the towns. But it is true that some evidences of particular friendliness continue to indicate favorable response to our efforts.

It cannot be denied that the personally directed management of the Indians by Colonel Don Diego Ortiz Parrilla has protected them and decreased their antagonism. It is even more surprising that in so short a time he has not only secured this advantage, but has also accomplished the difficult and necessary task of founding a Presidio, with the improvement in this essential service manifested in the discipline and efficiency of the troops and the growing number of persons maintained. All this together has been the diligent and painstaking task of this officer. Consequently it seems to us more and more as though this new settlement has been longer established and more improved than others in which we have lived in the Interior Provinces.

These considerations also convince me and my religious colleagues that the said Colonel, as well as ourselves, should accept the responsibility of proposing to your Excellency and to your Captaincy General certain measures which we consider basic and essential, although there would be no need of your Excellency's presence in this region, pending such time as further provisions may be put into effect. The Colonel and his well-trained officers and men carry out the plans and regulations through peaceable procedures compatible with the Catholic powers and aims of his Majesty, to whose royal service we dedicate our proposals and purposes. Of the greatest importance, we solicit the superior authorization of your Excellency for these measures, which will in no way burden the royal treasury. Rather, having duly considered the matter, we are willing ourselves to assume the expense of this long journey as well as the other costs in provisions and the great fatigue.

BISHOP TAMARON'S DESCRIPTION OF NEW MEXICO

[In the year 1760, Bishop Pedro Tamarón y Romeral of Durango made an episcopal tour of his diocese, including New Mexico. He visited every settlement of any consequence where there was a church or a mission. His description of the tour gives a precise and, in some points, detailed picture of affairs in the frontier colony, for he noted not only matters pertaining to the church but to the population, the economy, and the defense system as well.]

El Paso

This town's population is made up of Spaniards, Europeanized mixtures, and Indians. Its patron saints are Our Lady of the Pillar [of Saragossa] and St. Joseph. There is a royal presidio with a captain and fifty soldiers in the pay of the King.

The cure of souls is in charge of the Franciscan friars of the

From "Bishop Tamarón's Visitation of New Mexico, 1760," Eleanor B. Adams, ed., in: *Publications in History*, February 1954, of the Historical Society of New Mexico.

Province of the Holy Gospel of Mexico. Two friars are serving there. One is the Custos, who is prelate of all the New Mexico missionaries. The other, who has the title of guardian, is the parish priest of that large town. Two secular priests also reside there. I found that one of them held the office of vicar and ecclesiastical judge, and for good reasons I decided to give the vicariate to the Father Custos, without prejudice to the rights of the episcopal jurisdiction, even though the one' who was exercising it had given no cause for his removal from this office.

El Paso has 354 families of Spanish and Europeanized citizens, with 2479 persons. There are 72 Indian families with 249 persons.

They gave me a solemn reception here, for not only did the captain of the presidio, Don Manuel de San Juan, who is also the chief magistrate, the Father Custos, and the vicar come out to the Río de Santa María, but when I entered El Paso, everyone came marching out in fine order and display. This cost me a night's sojourn in the country three leagues from El Paso, which I did not like at all, because it is a very dangerous region, even though I had been in the same situation for the six preceding nights from the time I left Janos since there are no settlements en route. But this last night was at their request so that they might make better preparations for my reception, for I was then near enough to have been able to enter El Paso that night. But I arrived on the following day, April 23, 1760.

El Paso is in latitude 32°9', longitude 261°40'.

There is a large irrigation ditch with which they bleed the Río del Norte. It is large enough to receive half its waters. This ditch is subdivided into others which run through broad plains, irrigating them. By this means they maintain a large number of vineyards, from which they make *generoso* wines even better than those from Parras, and also brandy, but not as much. They grow wheat, maize, and other grains of the region, as well as fruit trees, apples, pears, peaches, figs. It is delightful country in summer. . . .

Tomé

This is a new settlement of Spanish citizens which could become the best in the kingdom because of its extensive lands and the ease of running an irrigation ditch from the river, which keeps flowing there. A decent church has already been built. It is thirty-three varas long by eight wide, with a transept and three altars. It is dedicated to the Immaculate Conception. There is a house for the parish priest, who is the one of the villa of Albuquerque. I confirmed 402 persons that afternoon. The population of this settlement is not recorded here because it was included in the census of the town to which it is subordinate [Albuquerque]. The Father Custos was charged to assign a friar to Tomé, separate from Albuquerque, and I believe that he has already done so.

Albuquerque

This villa is composed of Spanish citizens and Europeanized mixtures. Their parish priest and missionary is a Franciscan friar. It is ten leagues north of Tomé. There are 270 families and 1814 persons.

On the following day, May 21, I celebrated the announcement of my visitation. The edict concerning public sins was read, and then the commands of the Roman ritual were executed. The parish books were examined. Various faculties were conferred on the parish priest, and the title of vicar and ecclesiastical judge of this villa was issued to him because of the distance from Santa Fe, for there had never been one there. . . .

Santa Fe

This villa is the capital of New Mexico. It is four leagues east of the house of El Alamo, which I left the afternoon of the same day. And a half a league before we reached Santa Fe, the governor came forth with a numerous and brilliant retinue. He dismounted from his horse and joined me in the coach. This reception was very noteworthy. We proceeded to the villa among a crowd of people, and my entrance to Santa Fe was made with the same solemnity that the Roman ceremonial prescribes for cathedrals. After this function the governor himself lodged me in the very casas reales, and he moved to another house. And he provided food during my sojourn there. I accepted this, and the same from the captain at El Paso, because there was no other way of obtaining it; and they conformed, according to what I heard, to the practice of their predecessors with my predecessors, as likewise with regard to providing mules and horses.

On May 25, which was Whitsunday, the visitation was made with all possible solemnity in the principal church, which serves as the parish church. It is large, with a spacious nave and a transept adorned by altars and altarscreens, all of which, as well as the baptismal font and the other things mentioned in the Roman ritual, were inspected after the edict concerning public sins had been read and a sermon on the aims of the visitation given.

Two Franciscan friars serve continually in this villa, one with the title of Vice-Custos and the other as parish priest, with the status of missionary. To each of these friars, and to all who serve in New Mexico, the King contributes 300 pesos annually; and in addition to this, they receive their obventions in accordance with a fixed schedule. A secular priest also serves in that villa as vicar. He is paid 300 pesos a year from the tithes. This was the only vicar in the kingdom, and for that reason I decided to add the vicarship of Albuquerque and that of the Villa de la Cañada, so that decisions might be handed down with greater ease.

This villa of Santa Fe has 379 families of citizens of Spanish and mixed blood, with 1285 persons. Since I have confirmed 1532 persons in the said villa, I am convinced that the census they gave me is very much on the low side, and I do not doubt that the number of persons must be at least twice that given in the census. . . .

Pecos

A Franciscan missionary parish priest resides in this Indian pueblo. It is eight leagues from Santa Fe to the southeast. There are 168 families, with 344 persons, and 192 persons were confirmed.

Here the failure of the Indians to confess except at the point of death is more noticeable, because they do not know the Spanish language and the missionaries do not know those of the Indians. They have one or two interpreters in each pueblo, with whose aid the missionaries manage to confess them when they are in danger of dying. And although they recite some of the Christian doctrine in Spanish, since they do not understand the language, they might as well not know it.

This point saddened and upset me more in that kingdom than in any other, and I felt scruples about confirming adults. I remonstrated vehemently with the Father Custos and the missionaries, who tried to excuse themselves by claiming that they could not learn those languages. In my writs of visitation I ordered them to learn them, and I repeatedly urged them to apply themselves to this and to formulate catechisms and guides to confession, of which I would pay the printing costs. . . .

I take little satisfaction in these confessions through an interpreter when the latter is an Indian or a negro. I had experience of this when I was a parish priest in Caracas with the negroes brought there under the English contract. Many died soon after they arrived. I made repeated experiments with those of their own nation who had been in the land for some time. Although we granted confession, I never felt reassurance when this means was used. And I attempted to accomplish something in New Mexico by using interpreters, and their version is nothing but confusion on the subject of catechism and confession. In trade and temporal business where profit is involved, the Indians and Spaniards of New Mexico understand one another completely. In such matters they are knowing and avaricious. This does not extend to the spiritual realm, with regard to which they display great tepidity and indifference. . . .

Taos

The titular patron of this Indian pueblo is San Jerónimo. To reach it we traveled through pine forests and mountains until we descended to the spacious and beautiful valley they call the valley of Taos. In this valley we kept finding encampments of peaceful infidel Apache Indians, who have sought the protection of the Spaniards so that they may defend them from the Comanches. Then we came to a river called Trampas, which carries enough water. The midday halt was made at the large house of a wealthy Taos Indian, very civilized and well-to-do. The said house is well walled in, with arms and towers for defense. In the afternoon the journey through that valley continued. Three rivers of similar current and water were crossed. The first one in particular provides abundant ditches for irrigation. They are about a league and a half from one another. And, crossing the last one we entered the pueblo of Taos, where a Franciscan missionary parish priest resides.

It is twelve leagues north of Picuris. It is the last and most distant pueblo of that kingdom. In this direction, it lies at the foot of a very high sierra and in latitude 40°. This pueblo has 159 families of Indians, with 505 persons. There are 36 families of Europeanized citizens, with 160 persons. There is a very decent and capacious church.

I also put forth every effort there to induce those best acquainted with Spanish to perform the act of contrition and confess. I therefore left this group until last, confirming the children first. And in fact some did confess, and, encouraged to contrition, were confirmed. But since they do not know the catechism except in Spanish, I did not feel as pleased and easy in my mind as I should have liked. Therefore I reprimanded the mission father and duly reminded him of his duty, ordering him to continue receiving their confessions.

This pueblo is divided into three many-storied tenements. It would have been better, as I told them, if they had been kept together, for one is on the other side of the river about two hundred varas away. There is a wooden bridge to cross the river. It freezes every year, and they told me that when it is thus covered with ice, the Indian women come with their naked little ones, break the ice with a stone, and bathe them in those waters, dipping them in and out. And they say it is for the purpose of making them tough and strong.

When I was in the pueblo two encampments of Ute Indians, who were friendly but infidels, had just arrived with a captive woman who had fled from the Comanches. They reported that the latter were at the Río de las Animas preparing buffalo meat in order to come to trade. They come every year to the trading, or fairs. The governor comes to those fairs, which they call *rescates* [barter, trade], every year with the majority of his garrison and people from all over the kingdom. They bring captives to sell, pieces of chamois, many buffalo skins, and, out of the plunder they have obtained elsewhere, horses, muskets, shotguns, munitions, knives, meat, and various other things. Money is not current at these fairs, but exchange of one thing for another, and so those people get provisions. I left Taos on June 12, and a few days later seventeen tents of Comanches arrived. They make these of buffalo hide, and they say that they are good and well suited for defense; and a family occupies each one. And at the end of the said month of June seventy of these field tents arrived. This was the great fair.

The character of these Comanches is such that while they are peacefully trading in Taos, others of their nation make warlike attacks on some distant pueblo. And the ones who are at peace, engaged in trade, are accustomed to say to the governor, "Don't be too trusting. Remember, there are rogues among us, just as there are among you. Hang any of them you catch."

In that year, 1760, I left that kingdom at the beginning of July. And on the fourth day of August, according to what they say, nearly three thousand Comanche men waged war with the intention of finishing this pueblo of Taos. They diverted, or provoked, them from a very large house, the greatest in all that valley, belonging to a settler called Villalpando, who, luckily for him, had left that day on business. But when they saw so many Comanches coming, many women and men of that settlement took refuge in this house as the strongest. And, trusting in the fact that it had four towers and in the large supply of muskets, powder, and balls, they say that they fired on the Comanches. The latter were infuriated by this to such a horrible degree that they broke into different parts of the house, killed all the men and some women, who also fought. And the wife of the owner of the house, seeing that they were breaking down the outside door, went to defend it with a lance, and they killed her fighting. Fifty-six women and children were carried off, and a large number of horses which the owner of the house was keeping there. Forty-nine bodies of dead Comanches were counted, and other trickles of blood were seen.

As soon as the governor, Don Francisco Marín del Valle, learned about it, he summoned his men with all possible speed. He set out on their trail with a thousand men and pursued them almost two hundred leagues. By this time the Apache auxiliaries were tired and dispirited. Food supplies were running out. They returned. They spent forty days reconnoitering a large area without accomplishing anything.

It is said, that they told me, that this numerous, strong, warlike tribe of Comanches came and showed themselves on the New Mexico front in the years 1717 or 1718. And they said that it had taken them twelve moons to travel from their lands. The immensity of those unpopulated regions may be deduced from this.

THE PEOPLE OF TEXAS IN 1767

[Pierre Marie François de Pagès was a career officer in the French Navy who inexplicably jumped ship in Santo Domingo on June 30, 1767, and journeyed around the world for the next four years. The first leg of his travels took him to New Orleans, then through Texas to Mexico. It is uncertain whether his tour of Texas was just to satisfy his own curiosity or whether it was to gain information for the French government, which still entertained unspecified designs on the Spanish colony. Pagès's narrative of his wanderings was translated into English under the title *Travels Round the World in the Years 1767–1771* and published in 1791. As such, it was the first description in English of the Texas region and its people. Three portions of Pagès's account are reprinted here: descriptions of Adaes and San Antonio and comments on the American Indian.]

The settlement of Adaés consists of about forty miserable houses, constructed with stakes driven into the ground. It is situated on the declivity of a hill, the top of which, formed into a square, and inclosed with Palisadoes, such as I saw in Nachitoches, served as a kind of fortress to the village. These forts or redoubts, in the language of the country are named *presidio*. The houses are scat-

From "Across Texas in 1767: The Travels of Captain Pagès," Marilyn McAdams Sibley, ed., in: *Southwestern Historical Quarterly*, April 1967.

tered about the west side of the fort; and a little valley lying in the same quarter separates the village from a considerable eminence, on which stands a church and convent of Franciscans. A few straggling trees, and a heath overgrown with briars and thickets, and bounded everywhere by the woods, compose the cheerless prospect of the inhabitants.

The soil is almost entirely destitute of water; which unhappy circumstance, joined to the natural indolence of the people, frequently reduces them to the want of the most common necessaries of life. The chief means of their subsistence is Indian corn, which they boil, mixed with quick-lime, whereby the husk is dissolved to a kind of powder, and the grain considerably softened. Having washed and bruised it on a chocolate-stone, it is formed into a lump of paste, which they knead between their hands. Of this dough they make a sort of cake, which is toasted on a plate of iron laid over the fire. This bread is the native food of the people in New Spain; and indeed, when these thin cakes, or rather wafers, named by the Spaniards *tortillas*, are well baked, they are far from being unpleasant.

The inhabitants of Adaés, consisting in a species of cavalry, live by an appointment of nearly a piastre a day; but whether it be owing to the extraordinary expence they incur by sending for their clothing from Mexico, or rather, perhaps, their idle and sluggish dispositions, which oblige them to import even their daily bread from a distance, the pay of Spain is scarce equal to a bare subsistence. The intervals of public service are employed in play, of which they are particularly fond; in relating their exploits in battle, the perils and hardships they have encountered in wild and inhospitable regions; and on horseback, in visiting, and taming their cattle. Their bodies are strong and muscular, though sadly broken by their severe campaigns against the savages, whom they name, probably in derision, *Mecos*, or by no less ruinous consequences of their youthful debaucheries. They are, in general, obliging, humane, compassionate, and brave; eminently distinguished in the exercise of hospitality, they are known to share, under the immediate pressure of hunger, their last morsel of bread with the first stranger who happens to come under their roof. But, on the other hand, they are extremely proud; and, probably owing in a great measure to necessity, little addicted either to truth or honesty.

That of stealing I have observed is in common to almost all savage nations, and seems to arise from an instinctive movement of nature, upon the first impulse of which a man is prompted to gratify his wants, without waiting for the deliberate interference of his reason. This principle, besides, is much strengthened by that community of goods which every individual is ready to exercise against, as well as in favour of his own interest: but this description of mankind have one great advantage over their more civilized brethren, namely, that it is much more easy to convince them of their ignorance, and reclaim them from their vices.

The half-savage Spaniards of this settlement are dressed in the most fantastic manner: a sort of under-waistcoat and breeches without a seam, but pieced together with buttons of gold and silver, are commonly ornamented with lace, stockings made of skins, and shoes whose upper-leathers are cut into thongs, affording free access to the dirt and dust as well as to the air, compose their ordinary apparel. A large hood and short cloak, adorned round the neck with broad stripes of gold lace, seems to be considered as a full uniform, and is only worn on horseback. But, in spite of all this finery, one often meets the Spaniard without either hat or shirt, while his sumptuous uniform, torn by the briars and thorns of the woods, hangs in a thousand tatters about his person. His heels are usually armed with a pair of enormous spurs about five or six inches in length. His armour consists in a helmet of deer-skin, a carabine, and a long broad sword. Two little leathern boxes placed before the saddle serve to hold provisions for his march. The carabine rests commonly in the stock, but is used as a pillar, during the night, for a kind of tent, which is reared occasionally with the Spanish hood, in order to protect him from rain. His saddle-leathers, neatly dressed, and stamped with various ornamental designs, are garnished round the edges with trinkets of steel, which, like as many little bells, are kept perpetually ringing by the motion of the horse. The rider rests his feet in a couple of stirrups at least fifty pounds of weight, which are composed of four massy bars of iron arranged in the form of a cross. To keep the horseman steady in his seat, and to constrain his limbs to that position which is deemed most graceful among the Spaniards, are the chief purpose of those ponderous stirrups. Riding in them, however, to a novice, is a pretty severe trial of his patience; for, in my short experience of these accoutrements, I caught a swelling in my legs, and an almost entire dislocation of my joints. If the horse is strong enough not to be oppressed with their weight, I am uncertain, after all, whether they may not contribute to his ease, since they form a sort of balance below to the gravity of the rider on his back. The bits of their bridles, which are of an oblong shape, and extremely well adapted to their purpose, have a strong resemblance to those in use among the Arabs, who as every one knows, excel in the art of horsemanship all other nations in the world. In fine, the half-savage Spaniard, with all this singular extravagance, is an excellent rider, and when completely equipped and mounted never failed to revive in my mind all the ideas of ancient chivalry. . . .

I have had frequent opportunities to observe moral dispositions in the men we call savages, that would do much honour to the most civilized European; dispositions whose influence on their conduct is only interrupted under the violence of an unruly passion; but even in such situations, the first sallies of his rage having soon subsided, that equanimity of which the savage affords an eminent example resumes its ascendency over his mind. But will it be said, that reason, depraved by education and the example of others, so often to be met with in civilized nations, or a dark and designing policy, which in obedience to sober judgment contrives, executes, or delays the blackest villainies, ever enter into the character or conduct of the savage? No: in the school of nature he learned to be generous, compassionate, friendly and grateful; and if occasionally he falls into great irregularities, such as thefts, cruelty, or licentiousness, either he has been corrupted in his acquaintance with Europeans, or he is subject to a particular ardency of blood which precipitates him into those excesses. In the province of Louisiana I observed with sincere concern that the French had communicated the impurities of their immoral lives to several families among this simple race of men. At Naquadoch I saw a handsome girl, born and educated in the woods, who having had the misfortune to lose her virtue, abandoned her person, I will not say to any one without distinction, but to such as were inclined to make her a trifling present. Evil communication, and frequent intercourse with foreigners, creating a taste for luxury and convenience, have sown the first seeds of depravity among a people who otherwise might have continued to enjoy the happy innocence of their woods. The rustic simplicity of the savage restraining his desires within a narrow compass, and discouraging his mixing easily in the company of strangers, forms the greatest security to the purity and integrity of his manners. A close attention to what passes among the other animals, which in the original movements of their nature differ little from our own species, has greatly confirmed me in the truth of this observation. Before I dismiss these short strictures on the character of the savage, I must add to the list of his unfashionable virtues a native love of justice and fair dealing; who, as I have often had occasion to remark, pays his little debts with all the punctuality his good or bad fortune in hunting may permit. Chastity, in fine, seems equally natural to simple and undisciplined minds with any other virtue. One day I accidentally stumbled on a couple who had been lately married as they lay under their bearskins, and saw with pleasure the unaffected disconcertion of modesty in the timid Indian beautifully contrasted with the manly confidence and security, untinged with jealousy or shame, on the part of her husband. . . .

Fort San Antonio stands in a valley of an oblong form, one side of which fronts an angle of a small river in its vicinity. The different avenues leading to the settlement are defended by large pallisadoes, while the houses built upon its circumference serve the purpose of walls: but being of very considerable extent, and as many of the houses are in ruins, it is but weakly fortified, and has much occasion for a stronger garrison. It is besides much incumbered from without by several miserable villages, which give encouragement to the incursions of the enemy. The space too inclosed by the angle of the river is crowded by a multitude of huts, which are occupied by a number of emigrants from the Canary Isles. In other respects the settlement is pleasantly situated, on a small peninsula sloping gently towards the river; and commands an agreeable prospect over the opposite grounds. The object of my greatest surprise in this part of the world is the immense swarms of cranes which frequent the borders of the rivers. The houses of the settlement may perhaps amount to two hundred, two-thirds of which, are built of stone. Upon the roof is a kind of earthen terrace, which, on account of the small quantity of rain, and the temperate nature of the climate, are found abundantly lasting; and indeed, since my leaving New Orleans, I did not experience twenty days in all of rainy weather. I am told, however, that the climate of Red River, Nachitoches, and Adaés, are wet, cold, and unwholesome; but the rains of Nachitoches and Adaés never extend so far as this settlement, which stands in the middle of a plain, and is only surrounded by thick woods of the mesquitte. If we except a few clumps of large trees which are found on the banks of the Guadeloupe, the noble forests of massy timber on this route totally disappear in the neighborhood of Red River or Colorado.

This military station is the most important of four, comprehended within the bounds of this province: to wit, Adaés, at seven leagues distance from Nachitoches; Acoquissas [Orcoquisac], a hundred leagues south-west from Adaés; Labadie de Spiritu Sancto [La Bahía del Espiritu Santo], two hundred to the west-south-west; and Fort San Antonio, two hundred and fifty leagues west and west-south-west from the same point of Adaés: west and a quarter north-west from San Antonio, there is also a station of San Saba. On the banks of that river, and at the distance of a hundred leagues from San Antonio, stands the post of Rio Grande [San Juan Bautista del Rio Grande]; and nearly in the same direction, at the distance of two hundred and fifty leagues from the same point, are Passe de Nord [El Paso] and Santa Fé, in the province of New Mexico. It appears from this detail, that geographers lay down New Mexico on the map much further towards the north than it actually is; and though the circuitous path necessarily described by travellers in traversing uninhabited countries must frequently deceive them as to distance, yet I am convinced that the most northerly of the Spanish settlements in those regions lies between the 33rd and 34th degree of latitude. The province of Cuvilla is at least fifty leagues more to the south than it is represented on the map; whilst that of Sonora, which borders on California, lies southwest of Cuvilla. It is true, the Spaniards had formerly possessions further northward; but the turbulent temper and frequent inroads of the savages at length compelled them to give them up; and it was not without great difficulty they were able to maintain their ground at San Saba, Santa Fé, and Passe de Nord; insomuch that the first of these was once ordered by the Spaniards to be evacuated and demolished. The roads leading from Nueva Sonora to the mines of Serro Prietto, being rendered almost impassable by the savages, I saw a very considerable force called out in order to clear them of the molestation of the northern tribes. But how are we to reconcile those facts with the number of Spanish posts we find on the map to the northward of the settlements above mentioned? The fact seems to be, according to the best information I have been able to obtain from sensible Indians, who have travelled over the northern extremities of this kingdom, that they only exist in the imagination of certain geographers. In this opinion I do not commit my credit with the public on my own conjectures, but on the information of men employed to carry the different articles of clothing to the Spaniards in their most northern settlements; as well as on the veracity of several in the suite of the governor, who came from Nouvelle-Sonora, and who had been instructed to take plans of all the posts situated within the boundaries of the northern savages.

In the settlement of San Antonio we find a Spanish colony from the Canary Isles; whilst all their other stations consist merely of soldiers, and a few Indians who have been seduced from the innocence of savage life. Their principal employment is to rear horses, mules, cows, and sheep. Their cattle, commonly allowed to roam at large in the woods, are once in two months driven into fields adjoining to the houses of their owners, where every means is used to render them tame and tractable. After having been subjected to hunger and confinement, they receive their liberty, and are succeeded by others, which experience in their turn a similar course of discipline. Such of the inhabitants as are at pains to prevent their herds from running entirely wild, are found to possess five or six thousand head of cattle.

The inhabitants of San Antonio are excellent horsemen, and particularly fond of hunting or *lacing* [lassoing] their wild animals. Having entered the field, and started an animal they mean to take alive, they give him chase at full speed from wood to valley, till his fatigue enables them to come within a certain distance of him. Here the hunter, holding the running noose of a strong lash or thong coiled around his arm in his right hand, throws it with such dexterity, that he seldom fails to catch him round the neck or horns; and in the same instant, by pulling up his horse, or turning him abruptly from the line of his career, he checks his prey, and obliges him to stand still. A custom very similar to this is described in Anson's Voyages, and represented by the author as peculiar to the coast of Patagonia.

They have likewise the use of tame animals, which, besides being serviceable to them in milk, supply them with fat and dried flesh for their extensive peregrinations. Their horses and mules are no sooner a little broken in, than they are offered to sale; but here the market price is so extremely low, as indeed may be imagined, that I have seen a good horse sold for a pair of shoes. Having only one or two keepers for all the cattle of the settlement, even their domestic animals run day and night in the woods.

The keen eye which the habit of close and minute attention has bestowed on those people is truly surprising. Discovering in the morning that one of their cattle has disappeared in the course of the night, they are at much pains to examine the inclination of the grass over which he must have passed, when they can distinguish by the prints of his feet whether he is a horse or mule, and whether he quitted his pasture grazing or in flight: nor do they despair of finding him before they have gone fifteen perhaps twenty leagues from home. In their wars with the savages this extreme nicety of fight is still of great consequence; but as each party are on their guard against the discernment of the other, and both have the same motives to conceal the direction of their flight, it is usual to set fire to the sward as they retreat, leaving three or four leagues of black desert behind them.

They are often in danger of losing their way in the meadows, but in order to secure themselves against this inconvenience they are accustomed to give much attention to particular trees, and the position of the adjacent woods, which serve to assist their recollection, and answer the purpose of conducting posts in civilized countries. In their excursions through the woods they discover the quarter of the north by observing the side of the tree which, being hidden from the solar rays, acquires a coat of greenish moss, whilst that exposed to the south retains a neat clean skin of a whitish colour. In the neighborhood of this settlement, and situated on the river, at the distance of two or three leagues from one another, are four missions, consisting of a couple of Franciscans each. In the houses of those missionaries savages who have been captivated in war, and on whom the reverend fathers have conferred marriage and baptism, receive their maintenance and education. In this manner each house entertains seven or eight men, with their wives and children, who are employed, under the direction of these monks, in certain articles of industry, the profits of which are applied to the emolument of the mission. The rules of those missions, as to temporal affairs, are nearly the same with those observed by the Jesuits in their settlements in Paraguay; but they are applied by the disciples of St. Ignatius in a manner much more liberal and conciliating to the minds of their savage proselytes, than they are here by the followers of St. Francis.

The savages of Tegas are the last who have taken to the use of the firelock, and maintain any intercourse with the French. Those of Apaches, living about fifty leagues northward from San Antonio, as well as all the maritime tribes between the stations of Acoquissas and Labadie de Spiritu Sancto, still use the bow and arrow. Certain Europeans have represented the latter, named Coumaches, as a race of cannibals; but according to the Spaniards, who are probably better acquainted with their manners, they are merely a cruel dastardly kind of savages, who only escape the yoke of slavery by taking refuge among the rocks, bays, and fastnesses of the sea-coast.

The Spaniards make war upon those miserable tribes, which still retain the bow and arrow, almost in impunity. In case of engagement, the Spaniards, covering their heads with a sort of shield, and their bodies with a great coat, consisting of three or four folds of deer-skin, quilted with cotton, are in condition to set the darts of the enemy at defiance. If the savages happen to be few in number, and the Spanish cavalry think themselves ensured of an easy victory, reserving their fire for situations of greater necessity, they use the thong, and lace them like wild horses. As soon as a savage has been caught in the noose, he is bound hand and foot, and carried to the residence of a missionary, who makes it his business by threats, persuasion, severe fasting, gentleness, and last of all by marriage, to tame and civilize the manners of his prisoner. Having been instructed in the existence of a Supreme Being, providence, and the more peculiar doctrines of Christianity, he is admitted to the privilege of baptism.

The violent prejudices of the Spaniards not only restraining them from all intercourse with the more warlike tribes, but having engaged them in a system of policy most vexatious to those nations, their patience was at last exhausted, and they abandoned a vast tract of uninhabited country to the north of New Spain. Whether this immense territory could have been obtained by open and avowed war is doubtful; at least it must have been purchased by the Spaniards at a very great expence, both of blood and treasure.

THE INTERIOR PROVINCES IN 1772

[The end of the Seven Years' War in 1763 saw the elimination of France as a colonial power in North America and the consequent transfer of Louisiana to Spain. The new situation called for a revamping of Spain's colonial policies, and several other factors pointed in the same direction. First of all, the very existence of the most northern provinces was continually threatened by Indian raids, and the efforts of the missionaries were of no apparent avail in bringing the turbulent tribes around to more peaceful ways. Second, the home treasury was virtually depleted by years of war, and it therefore seemed a good time for retrenchment and consolidation of gains. Two men were sent out from Spain to survey colonial problems and make recommendations: the Marqués de Rubí, who inspected all the presidios from Sonora to Texas, and José de Gálvez, who went to Mexico to reform the administration there. Rubí's report of 1769 spoke of the necessity of making the presidios of the northern provinces a buffer against Indian attacks, and Gálvez's report urged detaching the provinces from the authority of the Viceroy and putting them under a military commander. Based on these reports, the Royal Regulations of 1772 were issued creating the Interior Provinces of Texas, Sonora, New Mexico, California, Nuevo León, Nuevo Santander, Sinaloa, Nueva Vizcaya, Chihuahua, and Coahuila, under one commandant inspector supervised by the Viceroy. The pacification of the Interior Provinces was to be important not only in itself but also as providing a land base from which California could be more easily colonized. Preliminary to the occupation of California, Sonora, one of the nearer provinces, had been fairly well rid of the Indian menace between 1768 and 1771. In 1772, the Viceroy requested from the governors of all the northern provinces reports bearing on a council of war for defending the colonies. The

From "A Description of Sonora in 1772," by Alfred Barnaby Thomas, in: *Arizona Historical Review*, January 1933.

report below was sent in by Governor Mateo Sastre of Sonora and gave a general description of conditions in his colony.]

The settlements exist generally with very little difference in their number as previously, with the exception of the Villas of Culiacan and Sinaloa which have become smaller due to the inundation which they suffered, particularly Sinaloa where destruction occurred when the river carried off the church and most of the houses. Because of this event, many settlers abandoned it. Some have returned and I have seen the building of different houses on other terrains more elevated. Accordingly, I conjecture that it will soon be in its original state. The pueblo of Charay which consisted of more than five hundred Mayo Indians is in a similar condition as that of Sinaloa, almost entirely destroyed, situated, as it is, three-quarters of a league more or less on a height above the Rio del Fuerte (or as others say, the Suaqui), which had risen to this height (over a space of) some five leagues and a half. Because of this the houses and church were carried away. They were in a very decent condition and considerable people were drowned. Besides this misfortune, the said Mayos were at war by reason of their last uprising and some had been executed. As a final misfortune, a pestilential sickness carried off a very large number of them. It has been reduced to some thirty families more or less. But it is true that of some of the missing ones, there are some families established in the hills and heights close to the peublo. That of Saracahe is entirely depopulated as your Excellency is aware. That of Sayopa is likewise depopulated; that of San Antonio which was a pueblo quite large in the time of its mines and placers, is now being depopulated without other reason than that of the great decline in the riches which it had and that its inhabitants have been leaving to seek those which La Cienega is now supplying. The latter is in the same condition as that which your Excellency was pleased to indicate to me in your letter dated April 4 of this year. To avoid a similar misfortune, I shall avail myself of the resources that may appear proper to me and shall give your Excellency a report concerning them.

Regarding the mines, I have written your Excellency from Culiacan, dated May 30th. I suspended the inspection of them by reason of the order from your Excellency of the 27th of April which transferred this responsibility to the Intendant, *ad interim*, Don Pedro Corbalan, because it was an affair attaching to his office and that from his inspection many useful results can come to the royal treasury. He no doubt will give a report to your Excellency of the state of them.

On the point of the presidios, although I have not yet seen more than two, it appears to me their companies are complete and well equipped with arms and horses. Only that which is called the Flying Company, attached to the presidio of Terrenate, I have taken some care with them because of the desertion which it has experienced in the last few days. As I came (into the province) I gathered men from Sinaloa where they were awaiting to present themselves to me. Of this I shall report to your Excellency, separately. Having despatched these to their proper company, it is now complete and ready for service like the rest.

Agriculture is moderately advanced among the nations of the Yaquis, Opatas and Egudebes who sow with some systematic order and reap abundantly wheat, corn, garbanzos, beans, and lentils, but the others such as the Piatos, or Pimas Altos, Mayos, Guaimas, and Pimas Bajas, although they reap their crops of corn, and some maize and very little of the other seeds, they carry on their work without any skill. I am not surprised at this, as they have had no director to teach them but practice itself in time will supply without doubt competent direction.

Concerning the missions, I am stating to your Excellency that they were much better administered and equipped with supplies before the expulsion of the Jesuits than now, as they had an abundance of herds of all kinds and an abundance of grains. Now they are quite poverty stricken. Some have declined since the time of the transfer of the haciendas and the rest of the things to the administrators who were appointed for them. Although they were delivered with an inventory to the new fathers missionaries, they tell me some missions lacked a great many things and, in short, that the delivery was very rapid. It is true that the decline of the herds is due in a great part to the lack of rain which has occurred, a drouth unknown ever to have existed in these provinces. Likewise a large number of the animals have died and been stolen by enemies.

With regard to the Pueblo of Charay, it is now without a regular church and with regard to what can be done for the advance of God among them, may your Excellency be pleased on reflecting upon this circumstance to commend a new one constructed at the expense of the royal treasury. They need it so much that I pray for the very benign and Christian action of your Excellency.

Having understood that the *mariscadas* will be the pearl fisheries, I report to your Excellency that, as I am informed, these have ceased operation since the past year because I am told also, that there are a number of them along the coasts of California and on those of Tepoca, close to the Isla de Tiburon, on the north. Their *placeres* being much more abundant than those of the first stopping place of (Lower) California I do not believe anything would be lost if your Excellency commanded that the larger of the two, Tahuas del Rey, be armed and that the fishery be developed at the expense of his Majesty. This can be done quickly by the Yaqui Indians who are skilled, because of the extensive experience they have had. From that some profit should redound to the royal treasury.

The successes which have been achieved since the Expedition into this province are that they have remained almost entirely peaceful, as they have not suffered any major uprisings. Occasionally individuals of the nations reduced attack travelers, steal or kill any herds which they encounter. Thus as to those, I consider them, as I have already stated to your Excellency, but some vagabonds, petty thieves, whose people no longer recognize them, since the measures I have taken concerning patrols, about which I have reported to your Excellency. Even yet, I am not very certain of the Suaquis or Sibupapas because of the reasons which in a letter I have signified to your Excellency under date of the 28th of July and because of late advance I have made in reducing the Tiburones. The latter also have been increased, up to today, by more than two hundred and fifty families which have settled on a secure footing in La Cieneguilla, without counting either the Yaquis and different Indians of other nations, or many *hombres de razon* who are at work, whose number amounts to more than five thousand souls, compared with the latter, I am persuaded that the former is more numerous.

JUNIPERO SERRA REPORTS ON THE MISSIONS OF CALIFORNIA

[The colonization of California was the logical culmination of Spain's expansion to North America, but it might have been deferred even longer had not Spain become suddenly alarmed over possible Russian incursions on the Pacific seaboard south of Alaska. Spain had been casually aware of upper California for more than two centuries prior to 1769, but only the threat of Russian rivalry nudged it into action. José de Gálvez, visitor-general to Mexico City on behalf of the crown, commissioned the opening up of the new colony in 1769. The two leaders of the settlement party were Captain Gaspar de Portolá, appointed governor of the province, and Fray Junípero Serra, a Franciscan missionary who had been in Mexico since 1749 and in Baja California, during most of 1768. The San Diego mission was founded on July 16, 1769, the first of twenty-one that the Franciscans would build by 1823. Father Serra spent the first years in California opening and supervising missions from San Diego to Monterey. Four years after the founding of San Diego, he was back in Mexico City seeking support for the new missions and helping to plan the overland expedition under Juan Bautista de Anza that would found the city of San Francisco. While at the capital, Father Serra prepared an extensive "Report on the general condition and needs of the missions of Upper California" for the Viceroy, Antonio Maria de Bucareli y Ursua, from which the following paragraphs are reprinted. The report was dated March 13, 1773.]

From Antonine Tibesar, ed., *Writings of Junipero Serra*, Washington, D.C., 1955. Vol. I, pages 295–327.

It is of the utmost importance that the missions be provided with laborers, to till the land, and so raise the crops for their maintenance and progress. We would already have made a start in so doing, were it not for the opposition of the Officer at the presidio—a situation I have described recently in a letter to the Reverend Father Guardian of our College, written about the middle of October, from San Diego. The original of that letter was turned over to the government offices of Your Excellency, where you may see it.

The easiest method seems to me the one we have presented from the beginning. I explained it in the said letter. It is this. Along with the sailors aboard ship, there should be a number of young men from the vicinity of San Blas. I should think that it would not be hard to find among them day laborers, cowboys and mule drivers. These should be divided among the missions—six to each, or four at least. But a rule should be made that the Officer of the presidio has no right to change them for a whole year; and that stipulation will inspire confidence in their minds. Otherwise, not a single one will be found to be willing to stay, especially as matters go now. Also, during the year their pay should be on the same basis as that of the sailors at San Blas; and in the missions they should receive free rations. And if at the end of the first year they wish to stay a second year, the same treatment should be continued. If they prefer to return to San Blas, by boat, they should be granted their request, and others should be provided to take their place.

It is of no less importance that, when the livestock arrives, which Your Excellency, in virtue of your decree, orders to be forwarded from California for the equipment of the Monterey missions, some Indian families from the said California should come, of their own free will, with the expedition, and that they should receive every consideration from the officials. They should be distributed, at least two or three being placed in each mission. By taking such measures two purposes will be accomplished. The first will be that there will be an additional two or three Indians for work. The second, and the one I have most in mind, is that the Indians may realize that, till now, they have been much mistaken when they saw all men, and no women, among us; that there are marriages, also, among Christians. Last year, when one of the San Diego Fathers went to California to get provisions, which had run short in that mission, he brought back with him, along with the rest of his company, two of the said families. At his arrival, there was quite a commotion among the new Christians, and even among the gentiles; they did not know what to make of these families, so great was their delight. Just to see these families was a lesson as useful to them as was their happiness at their arrival. So if families other than Indian come from there, it will serve the same purpose very well—that is, if we can provide for them. . . .

As regards our food supply—to last us a year, and to leave something over to give, at least, to the little Christian boys and girls—I intended to say a great deal, but will limit myself to this: that our sufferings are great; never have we, the religious, been in such dire straits, and never has the said Officer been living in such plenty, as since the time he and we arrived in Monterey. May our poverty be accepted for the love of God, and may his plenty—I do not envy him it—do him good. What I do want and ask for is, that the missions be maintained, that there should be a mouthful over and above to give to our Christians and catechumens, and that Christianity be extended.

Only two Indians from California still remain at my San Carlos Mission. The rest I distributed among the other missions. When the Officer was partitioning out what was brought by pack train, and marked for Monterey, I asked him to make an entry in his accounts for the two said Indians, to which he replied that he would not give anything to any Indian, and that if I wanted to chase them away, I should do so.

To sum up the whole situation, my opnion is that, without a doubt, whatever, in your goodness, Your Excellency, or the King—whom God keep—sends us—and without it at the present time we could not keep going, nor could the missions be kept in existence—should be sent from here marked and addressed separately. I have already mentioned in the letter referred to, that this year the Missions of San Diego and San Gabriel are in poorer condition than last year, even though two boats arrived, while there was only one the year before. The explanation is that last year there was sent from here the full quota of supplies for San Diego, on the supposition that the packet boat *San José* had never reached there. And, in point of fact, it never did arrive. . . .

In view of what I have just told you, I earnestly ask Your Excellency for an additional forge and blacksmith. If it were set up at the Carmel Mission it could also serve the Missions of San Antonio and San Luis. Not only would we get better service, but we would be able to have some of the newly converted youths learn the trade. This the Fathers of said missions, in their last letters, are most insistent upon. They are tired of dealing with the presidio, where the Officer does not absolutely refuse, but where repairs are done very slowly, and, all too frequently, a bad job is made of them. With a blacksmith in San Diego, the missions nearby can be served from there, and the one in Carmel can serve those of San Antonio and San Luis.

I beg of Your Excellency that, for the setting up of the two said forges, you order that there be sent and delivered to the two missions a goodly supply of iron—mostly in bars, partly in sheets—and that it be clearly stated that it be sent for the missions. In that way, so as to get possession of it, we will avoid any further difficulties or counterclaims on the part of the presidio.

We are in as much need of two carpenters as we are of two blacksmiths, one for the missions near Monterey, and the other to be located at Mission San Gabriel de los Temblores, where San Diego and San Buenaventura can make use of him. Both of them should come equipped with the tools of their trade. All of these matters could easily be attended to, if Your Excellency would give whatever orders seem suitable to you to someone in Guadalaxara. There could easily be sent from there the two blacksmiths, the two carpenters, and all of their equipment. But they should be clearly given to understand that the equipment is not their own, but the property of the respective missions. . . .

It seems to me that it would be most helpful if Your Excellency were to give strict orders to the said Commissary at San Blas, that he take greater care than he has till now taken in the packing of provisions forwarded for the maintenance of these missions and presidio. If the corn is put on board when it has already been attacked by grubs, and is full of maggots—and the same goes for the rest of the supplies—what will be its state when it arrvies at its destination, and what condition will it be in when the time comes to eat it? The corn that has been on board fresh and in good condition has arrived there in the same good condition. But sometimes, when we received it with the kernels empty, the Captain of the boat answered that that was the way it was loaded in San Blas. Last year there was no meat; and this year, what did come, besides being small in quantity, was so maggoty and putrid that very reasonably it was said to be the same that was to have come the year before; and not having much room in the boat, our meat supply was neither much, nor little, but nil.

There is nothing in greater abundance in the countryside around San Blas than herds of cows. Counting this year, it will now be two years since our poor men have been promised—ever since we got there—as part of their daily ration, half a pound or six ounces of meat. They have practically not tasted any other meat than what they have obtained from the gentiles or from hunting.

But, this last year the greatest pity of all has been concerning the flour, which is, of all the things that are sent us, or may be sent, the most helpful and most basic for the sustenance of life. It was put in plain sacks of poor material made of burlap or hemp, and consequently ran out at every motion or contact; and so the assignments arrived minus much that should have been there. And it is not hard to picture how much more they would be diminished when, after a lengthy journey, they arrived at their respective missions. How much money is thus thrown to the winds, both for what is lost—of the better quality—and for what is saved! If Your Excellency would kindly order the said article to be sent under the same stipulations that the Most Excellent Marqués de Croix laid down, such great losses would be avoided; and, with the same number of boatloads, there would be food to eat for a much longer time. . . .

I also ask Your Excellency that you allow a bounty for those, be they soldiers or not, who enter into the state of marriage with girls of that faraway country, new Christian converts. On that point, the Most Illustrious Inspector General gave repeated orders to Don Pedro Fages, but I was not able to ascertain the exact terms and conditions. However, whatever the case may be, it seems to me that anyone who marries after this fashion should be allowed to stay permanently attached to his wife's mission, without being removed to another; that he should be allowed an animal, immediately for his own use, if he is without one; and that, after he has worked a year or more on the mission farms, he be given from the royal herd two cows and a mule, or whatever may appear most suitable to Your Excellency. Lastly that, as time goes on, he might be assigned a piece of land for his own personal use provided he has nothing else to fall back upon.

AMONG THE YUMA INDIANS OF ARIZONA

[The chief threat to the survival of the upper California colony during the 1770's was the great distance between it and its source of supplies in Mexico City. Communication by sea was sporadic at best. What was needed was a practicable land route. In 1774, after one unsuccessful attempt, Juan Bautista de Anza led an expedition that made its way through Arizona into southern California to the mission of San Gabriel, in the vicinity of present-day Los Angeles. Anza had no sooner returned to Mexico than he was given the job of taking a colony of settlers to occupy the San Francisco Bay area. The party reached Monterey in January, 1776, and a colony was founded on the site of San Francisco later that year. One of those who accompanied Anza's second expedition was Fray Pedro Font, who kept one of the many diaries of Anza's journeys. The short passage from Font's diary reprinted here recounts the events of Tuesday, November 28, 1775, when the party was being entertained by the Yuma Indian tribe of Arizona.]

From Herbert E. Bolton, ed., *Font's Complete Diary*. Berkeley, 1933. Pages 71–74.

Tuesday, November 28.—I said Mass, which was attended by both captains with great quiet, modesty, and attention. We set out from the pass and banks of the Gila River at a quarter past nine in the morning, and at two in the afternoon halted on the beach of the Colorado River, after crossing the Gila a third time, and having traveled some five leagues to the west by south.—Five leagues.

The Yumas entertained us in an arbor which Captain Palma had ordered erected here as soon as he learned of our coming, and many Indians of both sexes assembled to visit us, very festive and joyful and very much painted in various modes and colors. The Gila River joins the Colorado about a league below this site, which is the one called by the last expedition the Island of La Trinidad, because then this area was made an island by the Gila River and a branch of the Colorado. But now there was no such island, because of the shifting of the land effected by the rivers when in flood. On our arrival the soldiers were ordered to fire a few shots to reciprocate the pleasure manifested by these people at our coming. This pleased the Yumas greatly and they responded to the musket-shots with a great shouting and hullabaloo.

A little after we arrived, Carlos, the new governor of the Opas, came with his alcalde, Francisco, and others, to make the peace treaties. He began his harangue while on horseback, passing in front of the Indians. Captain Palma did not like this, and gave him to understand that if he came with a good heart to ratify the treaties he must dismount and talk to him on foot, as he was, and not go in front of everybody in that way. So he dismounted, and Carlos and Palma, sitting down on the ground with their canes, talked for a while, the rest of the people being all round about. Then Pablo, the preacher captain, took the helm. Getting up on his feet in the midst of them all, he delivered a great harangue, all of which amounted to saying that now they no longer wished war, for thus we had ordered it, pointing to the commander and to me and the other fathers, who were present. Then, pointing to the four winds and in all directions, he said many times in a very loud voice, with movements, gestures, and grimaces, and with much fervor, that now with all the tribes and people they wished to be relatives and friends or "Queyé," which means "fellow citizens." In conclusion, the commander ordered Captains Palma and Carlos to embrace. They did so, and in imitation of them the rest of the people likewise embraced.

This peace began to be established during the former expedition, when the commander told him that the king did not wish them to have wars, and that if any tribe injured another, Spaniards would come to avenge the wrong. Previously Father Garcés had urged them to the same end, and it was from this perhaps that they began to trade with each other; for last year there was scarcely an Indian seen with a blanket, and now we saw some with blankets of cotton which the Opas make, and a few with blankets of black wool of the kind they make in Moqui, and which the Jalchedunes and other friends obtain from the Moquinos. We went to dine, and Captain Palma, with permission obtained beforehand from the commander, took Governor Carlos and all his people to his house to eat, in confirmation of the peace treaties, and the next day he gave him a supply of beans, péchita, and other things such as they have, for his journey when he might wish to return.

At night the Yumas and the Opas remained until late around the fire, stretched out on the ground half buried in the sand, heaped up like pigs, as is their custom, singing in their funereal fashion, and playing on the drum with a corita. I remained with them for a short time. Then I took Captain Palma and an interpreter, and in the arbor I had with him a long conversation as to whether he wished that I and other fathers should come to live there with his people. To this he replied that he would be very much pleased by it, and all his people likewise. I continued by telling him that for this it was necessary that he should learn the doctrine in order that they might be Christians; likewise that they would have also to learn masonry and carpentry, and to till the soil, etc., and that they must live together in a pueblo, which would have to be formed by the people, in order that they might live close together in their houses and not scattered out as now; and that they would have to make a house for the father and a church.

To all this Palma replied that they would do these things with great pleasure, although now his head was pretty hard for learning, and that he greatly wished that we would come now and not "soon." He said also that for building the pueblo there was, on the other side of the river, a hill or mesa which the river does not reach, and which he had already examined with a view to our living there, and that this mesa was the one at the Puerto de la Concepción. I told him that I would have to return to report this opinion of his to the king, adding that now that he and his people wished to be Christians, and be friends with the Spaniards, no doubt next year the king would say that we must return to live with them, and that if I should come I would have to teach them to work and likewise to sing. To all of this Palma listened so pleased that he began to sing the *Alabado* with me. Then he bade me goodbye with many embraces and demonstrations of pleasure, saying in conclusion that now he was a Spaniard and I a Yuma, and Queyé.

REPORT ON THE TEXAS MISSIONS IN 1785

[Fear of French encroachments on Texas ended with the cession of Louisiana to Spain in 1762. From that time on, Spain gradually lost interest in the far eastern outposts of the Texas colony. For the sake of economy, the whole east Texas mission field was abandoned in 1773, and most of the settlers were eventually concentrated in the vicinity of San Antonio and La Bahía (or Goliad). In 1779, former settlers at Los Adaes insisted on returning east, and they founded the settlement of Nacogdoches. During the last two decades of the eighteenth century, Spain's hold on Texas was indeed feeble, confined as it was to these three towns and some scattered missions. The report on the Texas missions reprinted in part here gives some indication of the state of decay into which the province had fallen. The report was issued on August 4, 1785, by Fray José Francisco López who was in charge of the Texas mission field at the time.]

These missions, as stated in the title of this report, are in the Province of Texas, which belongs in its secular aspects of the Command [*Comandancia*] of the Internal Provinces of New Spain, and

From "The Texas Missions in 1785," trans. by J. Autry Dabbs, in: *Mid-America*, January 1940.

in its ecclesiastical affairs to the Bishopric of Neuvo León. The missions consist of towns protected by walls, with houses for inhabitants, each house roofed with timber and mud, and provided with a good floor. Some, according to the facilities of each mission, have façades of carved wood, and iron locks in the houses as well as in the ramparts. In this protective wall there are three or four doors for varying purposes and on different sides. In the center and at the most advantageous place in these missions are the houses for the missionaries, with sufficient room for living quarters and the other needs. Adjoining this house, or not far away from it, is the church and sacristy as described in the individual reports.

These missions were . . . founded, organized, and developed by the Apostolic Missionaries of the Order of Saint Francis, who have kept and tended them, as sons of the College of the Holy Cross of Querétaro and of Our Lady of Guadalupe of Zacatecas, in the seven pueblos as already described. These are San Antonio de Valero, La Purísima Concepción de Acuña, San José de Aguayo, San Juan de Capistrano, Nuestro Padre San Francisco de la Espada (which are in an area of three or four leagues along the banks of the San Antonio River), El Espíritu Santo de la Bahía, and Nuestra Señora del Rosario, which, as already stated, is abandoned and in ruins today as a result of the flight of its Indians to the coast from where they were brought. These missions in the beginning were founded for and organized with Indians of the most diversified nations, . . . nearly all . . . reduced to one language, which is common or uniform in meaning and differs only in the greater or less stress or speed with which some Indians, called Bozales, because they use and understand very little Spanish, are being instructed. In spite of what has been said, Spanish is generally and commonly spoken among both Spaniards and Indians, although, in the case of the latter, with noticeable imperfection or (in the common expressions) with stones in their mouths.

As already stated, these missions were organized and founded by the Apostolic Franciscan Missionaries, some by the sons of the Apostolic College of la Santisima Cruz de Querétaro, and others by those of Nuestra Señora de Guadalupe de Zacatecas. Today the latter have charge of the administration of all the missions. In them there are employed nine missionaries as follows: six resident, one in each mission, one supernumerary who substitutes for the sick or unavoidably absent, and two in the new settlement of Nacogdoches, as mentioned in the discussion of that establishment. . . . The precision and punctuality with which these missionaries discharge the duties of their ministry may be inferred by remembering that they are continually under the supervision of a Father President, who with the authority of a legitimate prelate granted and delegated to him by the Reverend Guardian of his College, resides in the locality of the missions. . . . And from time to time when it is deemed necessary and opportune, the College designates by a unanimous vote of its Senior Council a serious-minded missionary

as an Inspector. . . . He makes a very careful examination of every
phase of life pertinent to the missions and missionaries; but especially he inquires if they comply well with the duties of the ministry
to which they have been assigned and if they manage the property
of the Indians with the greatest personal disinterestedness, legality,
and exactness. Likewise he examines whether the missionaries
properly look after the needs of their indigent constituents. They
remove at once those who have fallen into serious fault, acting in
this matter with more asperity than leniency. Page by page he in-
spects the records of income and expenses, in which very punctilious
note is made of each item. As soon as these missionaries reach
their respective assignment, they make the most diligent attempt to
learn, through use and daily intercourse, the languages of their
charges. This is the only means they have for communication, although usually the missionaries insist that the Indians understand
and use Spanish, as is ordered by the laws of the kingdom. This
order is complied with by speaking often with the adults and by
teaching the children usually or always to read, and, if it is deemed
practical (which is not always the case) to write and figure. The
piety of our Lord the King (May God keep him) has appropriated
for the missionaries the prebend or annual *sínodo* of 450 *pesos*
This amount is paid from His royal treasury and is drawn by the
Apostolic Treasurer, acting as representative of the missionaries,
with certificates from the royal judges of the region and by order
of the Commandant of these Interior Provinces. Neither now nor
ever have the missionaries demanded or received any compensation
or fees, large or small, from either the Indians or the Spaniards.
On the contrary they added the prebend to the products from the
missions, limited themselves to a most meager allowance, and
leaving the balance for the Church expenses and the Divine Cult.
In these churches and towns there are no confraternities or brother-
hoods, for there is barely time for more than the teaching of the
Faith and the administration of baptism. . . .

The wealth of these missions is derived from the cultivation of
corn, beans, chile, or pimentos, and fruits like watermelons, cantaloups, pumpkins, and garden produce, as well as from the breeding
of sheep, goats, and cattle. . . .

Although there are some wild berries that the Indians eat readily,
they are not as abundant or as appetizing as the bananas, guanavas,
cherimolas, otes, chicos, mameys, cocoanuts, Brazilian nuts, and
other fruits that grow on some coasts or along the sea shore. Nevertheless, there is cultivation of vegetables, fruits, etc., which would
give a good, large yield if the weather were not so changeable and
if there were fewer of the locusts, grasshoppers, ants, beetles, plant
lice, etc., that abound here. All the planting done in these missions,
as well as the cultivation and distribution of the crops, is by communal labor. Those, however, who are considered most apt are
assigned plots of land to cultivate with delicacies, such as vegetables, watermelons, cantaloups, and cucumbers. But here, just as

in the case of the corn and beans that are gathered, no scruples are spared to divide them equally among all, even though, to do this, it is necessary to act with thorough forethought and prudence. Although the Indians in every other way are very limited in comprehension and lacking in reasoning ability, in the matter of concealing idleness or laziness by unostentatious excuses and the appearance of pious sanctity, which they do with consummate hypocrisy, they are very skillful. Thus they avail themselves of the assignment to the gardens or private work, only to slip away from the task and very shamelessly, profit from the toil of the others, regardless of whether the latter be their fathers, sons, or brothers. . . .

The present state of these missions, and also that for the last twelve or fifteen years, may well be compared in personnel and property with that of the Kingdom of the Indies [New Spain] during the fifties and sixties—particularly as regards the Interior Provinces. At that time there flourished several rich mines; the farms were all rich estates; and, with the exception of one or two years when they suffered setbacks, they were very fertile and abundant, whereas in these years all is poverty and want. Most of the mines have been depopulated on account of their extreme destitution, and those that persist do so in the face of indescribable hardships and work. Many of the most prosperous ranches have become wildernesses, deserted by man and beast. In short, decay and dissolution continue. . . . For the Indians scarcely have enough to eat and wear, while previously they had enough to adorn their temples and lived in relative comfort.

A POLICY FOR THE COLONIZATION OF CALIFORNIA

[California was a mission colony administered by the Franciscan order. The priests who conducted the missions were accompanied by soldiers, officials, and a small civilian population, but the military presidios and the civil pueblos served as supports for the missions and were not intended to have a life of their own. The missions, from San Diego in the south to San Francisco in the north, were situated about a day's journey on horseback apart, an average of thirty miles. The missions, apart from their religious efforts, tended to become self-contained economic units, with substantial Indian populations treated as wards. The Indians, under the direction of the priests, did the manufacturing work and performed the agricultural labor. By the year 1800, the missions were flourishing, with herds and flocks, orchards, vineyards, fields, and workshops. The province of California was well on its way to becoming self-supporting, as indeed it nearly had to be. The lines of communication with Mexico City were long and uncertain, and, had the missions and the colonists depended on supplies from Mexico, they would not have survived. Distances were too great and administrative red tape was insurmountable. Spain had not intended that its distant province become self-sufficient and prosperous, for California was meant only as a defense outpost on the borders of the empire. The scope of Spain's failure to deal with the Californians' complaints can be discerned in the following letter written on May 14, 1796, by Fray José Señán to the Viceroy, the Marqués de Branciforte. Father Señán had spent the previous eight years at the Mission San Carlos Borromeo (Carmel) in California, and, in 1797, he was assigned to Mission San Buenaventura. He would eventually become president of the California Missions. Señán's letter is at once a criticism of

From Lesley Byrd Simpson, ed., *The Letters of José Señán, O.F.M.*, trans. by Paul D. Nathan. Ventura County (Calif.) Historical Society, 1962. Pages 1-9.

Spain's dealings vis-à-vis California and an unwitting explanation of
why Spanish policy failed, for his suggestions were never followed
up.]

My Lord, the means which would best facilitate the colonization of
New California and foment its material progress are, it seems to
me, as follows:

First: Those who are to establish themselves there and erect
towns must be persons of honest Christian character. If they are
industrious as well, your Excellency in your zeal may confidently
look forward to substantial progress. This is a fundamental principle that should be taken for granted, for no one who is given to
vice and indolence can contribute to the well-being of society.
Nevertheless, I must call it to the high attention of your Excellency
because of the peculiar circumstances prevailing in that region.
The population still consists chiefly of gentiles, who stand in need
of a particularly good example. But the opportunities afforded by
the necessary travels of our people among the natives—and other,
more furtive errands—have led to notorious excesses.

It is equally necessary that new settlers be energetic workers;
otherwise the settlements will be in danger of sharing the sad fate
of the towns of San José de Guadalupe and Nuestra Señora de los
Angeles de Porciúncula. These two towns, your Excellency, were
founded in the days when Señor Don Felipe de Neve was Governor
of the Peninsula. In the regulations he drew up for the Province,
the Governor included certain measures for the stability of the
towns and the contentment of their inhabitants, who were to receive
grants of land for cultivation, cattle for breeding, and certain speci-
fied privileges and exemptions. These regulations won the approval
of our late Monarch, Charles III (may he rejoice in glory!). Despite
all this, however, and despite the continuing efforts of the central
government to encourage the founding of additional communities
(which I believe ought to be done to the greatest extent), the settlements I have mentioned are even today hardly worthy to be called
towns, for they remain formless or embryonic. The main fault, in
my opinion, lies in the indifference of the colonists and their dis-
inclination toward hard work; they prefer to hold in hand a deck
of cards rather than a hoe or plow. What little progress is being
made must be credited to the population of the neighboring gentile
rancherías and not to the settlers. The Indians cultivate the fields,

do the planting, and harvest the crops; in short, they do almost
everything that is done. Yes, your Excellency, such indeed is the
current state of affairs. Still more painful is the effect of all this
upon the natives who, being in contact with the colonists, or *gente
de razón*, should have been the first to receive Holy Baptism. But
because of the bad example set them, and perhaps for their own
private reasons, these natives still abide in the shadows of paganism.
Most of the Indians of the outlying villages, on the other hand,
have entered the fold of the Holy Church.

Second: It is my opinion that the information of settlements and
their prosperity would be greatly enhanced if the inhabitants were
permitted, through certain advantages and privileges, to enjoy the
fruits of their own labor and make some profit therefrom. Thus
the heavy tasks of agriculture would be made less burdensome
and their application to other industries encouraged. Your Excellency, I have good reason to accuse the settlers of laziness, but
there is equally good reason to excuse them in large part. Their
lack of enthusiasm for their work is not surprising, inasmuch as
they regard most of its as fruitless.

How can the colonist be expected to apply himself willingly to his
work, tending his fields to produce grain for sale to the presidios in
order to cover his own nakedness and that of his children, and procure implements for his farm and utensils for his house, when he
knows that he cannot succeed and that his efforts are largely in
vain? In the entire Province there is not a single store or warehouse, other than the Quartermaster's depots, where he can hope to
obtain the above-mentioned articles. Supposing, for example, that a
certain colonist has on hand 100 fanegas of corn and 50 of beans to
be used as rations for the troops. He goes to the Quartermaster,
offering his products and stating his needs for equipment and
supplies. But the answer he usually hears (or rather, one that
pierces his heart) is almost sure to be as follows: "There aren't
any! There aren't any! The troops come first! Maybe we'll have
some later on. We've received very little this year. . . ." and so
on and so on and so on.

I have no desire to blame the Quartermaster unjustly; after all, he
merely distributes what is sent him, and besides, of course, the
goods are intended primarily for the troops. But does this state of
affairs in any way console the colonist? Is it any wonder that he
feels averson toward his toil, from which he derives such scant
reward? Even if he were paid in cash for his grain, the colonist
would still be unable to obtain the things he needs; there is no
place to go to purchase them, and his very real unhappiness remains as keen as ever. Such, your Excellency, is the lot of those
unfortunate settlers, and when they are paid in money, they
squander it or gamble it away because there is no way to spend
it profitably. Their only alternative is to accept from the Quartermaster whatever may be left after the troops and their families
have been supplied. The colonist must be satisfied with taking

home some trifle or other and with the knowledge that he has a small credit balance on the Quartermaster's account books.

Besides all this, the colonist has to sell his produce at absurdly low prices while being charged exorbitantly for whatever goods he can procure, which in my opinion is seeing his work wasted. . . . Supposing, for example, that the Quartermaster requires 200 fanegas of grain and 100 of beans to feed the troops. He approaches a farmer, who fills these requirements. The farmer thus contributes to the subsistence of the military through the sweat of his brow. He does not tell the purchasing agent to go to Mexico City or Guadalajara for his provisions, at much greater cost. Rather, they may be had right there on the spot as a result of the farmer's work. But how differently it turns out for the poor fellow! He asks the Quartermaster, in return, for certain goods, but he does not get them. Although the farmer has sold his grain at a miserable price, he is told to buy the things he needs in Mexico City or Guadalajara. Is it any wonder, your Excellency, that these wretched people feel no love for their work? They might fairly justify themselves by replying, "If that's the way matters stand, I cannot let you have my grain at such a price. You can't supply the goods I need, and it will cost me a great deal more, both in money and effort, to try to get them elsewhere. Both of us must exist in the same country; therefore both should share its hardships in just co-operation instead of one party suffering while the other gains advantage. . . ."

But all this, your Excellency, is impossible, for two reasons: (1) The price of produce purchased for the troops is fixed by government regulation; (2) the seller must submit because he has no choice. The only recourse open to him—and an unhappy one—is to hold off, awaiting the arrival of the supply ship. But what sort of solution is this, your Excellency? Aboard each supply ship are certain private individuals who offer goods for sale. These persons are hungry for money, and besides, the things they usually bring in are not prime necessities. The country could well do without this sort of merchandise, all the more so because badly needed articles are not included. Instead, vanity among our women and intemperance among our men are fostered by this fatal commerce. So it is that the sweat of the wretched settlers is wasted, while they themselves contribute to this result by reason of their own frailties.

In matters concerning grain, similar difficulties affect the missions. They contribute all their surplus (after providing for the needs of their own neophytes) to the maintenance of the presidios. But all they receive in return is a credit entry in the account book. Whenever these entries reach a considerable amount, a draft on Mexico City is issued, but it is impossible to draw on it that same year. Thus, for example, two years must elapse before the missions can realize their profit on grain delivered to the presidios today. Furthermore, if the goods required by the missions are purchased for them by the Father Procurator in this city [Mexico], a large part of the credit balance must be spent for freight charges because of the great distance between Mexico City and the port of San Blas. The missionary fathers consequently find themselves in virtually the same position as the settlers. The grain produced by the toil of the neophytes is turned over to the presidios at very low prices, and even these small proceeds are largely eaten away by high freight charges.

Even so, there are those who claim that the prices paid for grain are too high, although it is hard to understand how or why they can say so. One suspects that such persons underestimate the grievances and tribulations of the sellers and therefore condemn them unjustly. In my opinion the price of grain is not excessive; on the contrary, it ought to be increased so as to establish a proper relationship between the seller and the buyer. Besides all this, your Excellency, the purchasers of grain on the Peninsula [of California] enjoy greater advantages than any others in the world. The price-fixing by a government agency is as invariable as an Article of Faith. In a year of abundance, prices remain the same as in a year of scarcity. . . .

I know very well, your Excellency, that there are a hundred necessary evils, but I do not believe that the one of which I speak may properly be numbered among them. I feel sure that the late Governor of that Province, Don Felipe Neve (a man of insight and prudence), would have concurred in his view. When the missionary fathers complained about the established rates for grain, he replied that it should be paid for in the form of merchandise required to fill the needs of the seller, at prices prevalent in Mexico City. Under these conditions, the prices offered would be regarded as equitable. Such was his judgment, your Excellency, but it was never put into practice.

The third measure to facilitate the founding of settlements and to further their material progress, it seems to me, would be to appoint in each town a person to exercise authority over its residents and to act as their representative. His authority should derive not only from the prestige of his office, but also (as far as possible) from his own distinction and honesty, and his judicious conduct of affairs. He should be an enlightened and understanding person, one who would faithfully execute the instructions of the Governor of the Province. He would also be expected to discourage bad conduct among the colonists and help them overcome laziness, the chief enemy of their peace and happiness. I am not unaware, your Excellency, that the established towns already have their alcaldes and commissioners. But these men are looked upon as intimates or companions of the settlers, with the result that everyone in town does as he pleases. Officials of this sort serve no useful purpose; indeed, they cause nothing but utter confusion.

Finally: Towns cannot exist without people; as the number of inhabitants increases, so do the opportunities for their well-being. I therefore believe that under no circumstances should retired soldiers or others with special credentials who wish to settle in the

Province be permitted to establish themselves separately in remote areas or in villages outside the towns, a practice that I have seen tolerated these past few years. Such persons should rather be required to reside in the towns, as lands and adequate water supplies become available for their maintenance; otherwise we shall never have towns. The consequences to be expected from scattered and isolated colonization are distressing to contemplate. Colonists thus openly exposed are likely to suffer mischief at the hands of the native gentiles, which has already happened more than once, even in less vulnerable areas, with no one to correct or punish them. In short, they live in those remote regions without King to rule or Pope to excommunicate them; but such considerations, your Excellency, do not trouble them. Indeed, for these very reasons, and perhaps because of a certain spirit of independence, quite a few of these persons refuse to take up residence in the towns. They picture themselves, if they did so, as obligated, when called upon, to stand guard or ride patrol. Duties of this kind do not appeal to them, although they are absolutely necessary for the peace of the community, security of the livestock, and protection against surprise attacks and cattle raids. What can the gentiles think, your Excellency, of such indifference on the part of civilized persons? It is no small part of the missionary fathers' task to maintain their neophytes congregated in the missions, as members of society, so as to subdue the savage nature which impels them, like wild beasts, to live in the deserts and forests. When they see our own people taking up the same mode of life they lose faith in us, or conclude that our real purpose is to deprive them of their lands. Outlying settlements of this kind must therefore be prohibited. It is directly contrary to our policy in establishing new towns.

THE STRENGTHS AND WEAKNESSES OF THE CALIFORNIA PROVINCE

[It is not possible to trace all the origins of "manifest destiny," the impulse of the United States to extend its hegemony to the Pacific Coast. But, if this westward movement did not culminate until the 1840's, it was certainly in the minds of some Americans much earlier. It must have occurred to some citizens as early as 1803, the year when the Louisiana Purchase doubled the size of the nation. If thoughts of continental expansion were preoccupying Americans in the opening years of the nineteenth century, the journal of William Shaler's visit to California probably aroused their interest a good deal. Shaler had set out, as captain of the ship *Lelia Byrd* late in 1801, to become involved in the China trade and, on his way from South America, stopped in both lower and upper California. By 1804, he had sailed to China with his cargo of otter skins and returned to California. On his second visit, he made a number of careful observations of the population, government, economy, and defenses of the Spanish province, noting particularly the weakness of Spain's hold on the colony. His *Journal of a Voyage Between China and the North-Western Coast of America* was published in 1808 for all Americans to read and ponder.]

From *The American Register*. Vol. III, 1808.

The Indians that inhabit the shores and islands of the canal of Santa Barbara seem to be a race of people quite distinct from the other aboriginals of the country. They are a handsome people, remarkably sprightly, courteous, and intelligent, and display great ingenuity in all their arts. They make fine canoes of small pine boards, sewed together in a very curious manner; these are generally capable of carrying from six to fourteen people, and are in form not unlike a whale boat; they are managed with paddles, and go with surprizing velocity: they besides make a great variety of curious and useful articles of wicker work, and excellent pots and mortars of stone. The other Indians of this country differ very little among each other in their persons, genius, and manners: they are a dull, stupid people, of the ordinary stature, and far from comely. The fathers informed me, that, notwithstanding their apparent stupidity, they have some rude notions of astronomy; they distinguish the season by the movements of the heavenly bodies, and mark the hours of the night by the positions of the *great bear* and *pleiades*. The canoes used on all this coast, except in the canal, are a very rude kind of machines, made of flags. The Indians of the canal have a tradition of a race of white men being shipwrecked on their coast, at some remote period: this they assign as the cause of the great difference in their favour before mentioned.

The inhabitants of California were formerly very numerous. In the journal of a voyage performed by Sebastian Viscayno, in 1602, to explore the western coast, and by father Gonsag, a jesuit, in 1746, to explore the gulf of California, by order of the court of Spain, it is remarked, that all along, wherever they passed, they found great multitudes of people. I have touched at a great number of the same places in the course of my voyages to this country, which are now solitary and desert; not a soul is to be seen, except now and then a straggler from the neighbouring missions. One of the missionaries informed me, that, fifty years ago, they numbered 7000 souls at the mission of the Purissima, in latitude 26° 30′, and that at present they do not exceed fifty persons. At present, Lower California is nearly depopulated: no mission there numbers above 350 Indians; not more than three exceed 250; and the greater part have less than fifty persons. It is difficult to imagine what can have been the cause of this extraordinary depopulation, in a country where no establishments but missions and garrisons have been made. At present, the miserable remains of these people are almost universally infected with the venereal disease, and numbers perish daily, in the most deplorable manner, with that loathsome disorder: as no pains are taken to stop it, there is reason to suppose, that in a few years it will entirely exterminate them. Upper California is still populous, and the same disorder rages there with the same violence. Captain Vancouver speaks in high terms of the successful practice of medicine and surgery by the Franciscan missionaries in this country: I have had a pretty large acquaintance with those gentlemen, and I have not known any one among them who appeared to have the least tincture of any science. This observation may also be extended to the Dominicans, who are a much politer order of men. They were always soliciting medicines and medical advice of me, and lamented the unfortunate situation of the country in that respect: many of them assured me, that there was not in all California one qualified physician or surgeon. I have also reason to think that captain Vancouver has likewise overrated their abilities in the arts as well as sciences, as they have not as yet erected a single mill in Upper California, though the country abounds in materials and excellent situations, for both wind and water mills. In such circumstances, such a useful, and necessary, and simple piece of mechanism would hardly have been neglected, if they had known how to direct their construction. At present, all their grain is ground by the tedious process of rubbing it by hand between stones, or beating it in mortars.

The Spanish population of the Californias is very inconsiderable; by the best information I could obtain, it hardly exceeds 3000 souls, including the garrisons, among which, even the latter, the officers excepted, there are very few white people: it principally consists of a mixed breed. They are of an indolent, harmless disposition, and fond of spirituous liquors. That they should not be industrious, is not surprising; their government does not encourage industry. For several years past, the American trading ships have frequented this coast in search of furs, for which they have left in the country about 25,000 dollars annually, in specie and merchandize. The government have used all their endeavours to prevent this intercourse, but without effect, and the consequence has been a great increase of wealth and industry among the inhabitants. The missionaries are the principal monopolizers of the fur trade, but this intercourse has enabled the inhabitants to take part in it. At present, a person acquainted with the coast may always procure abundant supplies of provisions. All these circumstances prove, that, under a good government, the Californias would soon rise to ease and affluence.

The government of this country may be considered as altogether military, although civil causes may be carried before the audience of Guadalaxara, in New Spain. The governor rules every thing, and no one undertakes to dispute the legitimacy of his decisions. The missionaries are also under his jurisdiction in civil matters, but he does not interfere with the Indians attached to the missions, except at the request of the fathers, who are their sovereign magistrates.

The political and military arrangements for the government of the Californias are as follows: the whole country is divided into six military districts, called *presidios*, or garrisons; these are, beginning with the northernmost, San Francisco, Monterrey, Santa Barbara, San Diego, San Vicente, and Loreto. In these *presideos* are distributed about four hundred cavalry, which forms the whole military force of California: they are each commanded by a lieutenant, except San Vicente, which is not properly a *presideo*, and is commanded by an ensign. The *presideos* furnish the necessary guards to the missions under their protection; generally from three to five soldiers, with a sergeant or corporal, to each mission. The soldiers also do the duty of couriers; and every occurrence of the least consequence is immediately transmitted by express to the governor. During the last war, small detachments of artillery were quartered in the principal *presideos*, but they were withdrawn at the peace.

The Californias have, until lately, been under one government, of which Monterrey was the capital; but I am informed that they are now separated. The division is at San Diego, and Loreto is the capital of Lower California. I am also informed that considerable reinforcements of troops are ordered to be raised in New Spain for that country.

The plan of civilization in the missions is to instruct the Indians in the catholic religion, the Spanish language, the necessary arts, agriculture, &c.; but the notion of private property is not admitted among them; so that each mission forms an indivisible society, of which the fathers are the kings and pontiffs. The missionaries of the Franciscan order, in Upper California, have salaries of 400 dollars per annum; the Dominicans that are established below have but 350 dollars. The missions of California may be considered as so many valuable estates or plantations belonging to the king of Spain, and capable, in case of a conquest of this country, of furnishing abundant supplies of all kinds of provisions, horses, &c. . . .

The Spaniards have complete possession of the peninsula of California; but that is not the case above: there their domination is bounded by the Sierra Madre, which in no part is far removed from the coast; so that in reality they are masters of the maritime part of the country only. Beyond that range of mountains the country is remarkably fine, well watered, and covered with forests: these they have not as yet been able to penetrate, on account of their being thickly inhabited by warlike tribes of Indians. I am informed that the government have it in contemplation to establish lines of missions and garrisons from San Francisco to New Mexico, and by the country of the Colorado Indians to the same place, and by these means to complete the conquest of the country. But that is a project that does not seem likely to be very soon realized. . . .

The conquest of this country would be absolutely nothing; it would fall without an effort to the most inconsiderable force; and as the greatest efforts that the Spanish government would be capable of making towards its recovery would be from the shores of New Spain, opposite the peninsula, a military post, established at the bay of Angels, and that of San Diego fortified and defended by a competent body of troops, would render such an attempt ineffectual. The Spaniards have few ships or seamen in this part of the world; the arsenal of San Blass would be their only resource on such an occasion, and that might be very easily destroyed. But, admitting that the inactivity of the invaders should permit them to transport troops over to the peninsula, those that come from New Spain could not be very formidable, either in point of numbers or courage, and they would have to penetrate through Lower California, where they would not find even water in their march: all the other resources of that desolate country could be easily removed out of their way. They could not march round the head of the gulf: the natural obstacles to such an expedition would be very numerous; and they must besides force their way through many warlike nations of savages.

An expedition by sea to Upper California would be equally difficult for them: the bad weather they must encounter in winter, and the great length of the passage in summer, on account of the prevailing north-west winds, would render it a very precarious undertaking. In a word, it would be as easy to keep California in spite of the Spaniards, as it would be to wrest it from them in the first instance.

Part Two

THE MEXICAN SOUTHWEST, 1810–48

Strictly speaking, the Mexican era in the Southwest did not begin until 1821, the year the revolution against Spanish rule was won. This chapter is dated from 1810, because it was in that year that Father Miguel Hidalgo y Costillo first raised the cry of revolt. From then on, Mexico was in turmoil until independence was achieved, and indeed for years afterwards.

During the decades covered by this chapter, Mexico was also on the defensive, not always knowingly, against the "presence" of the United States. In 1803, Napoleon had sold the Louisiana Territory to the young nation, bringing the American dominion for the first time into direct contact with Mexico's Interior Provinces in the Southwest. The moment the United States became a trans-Mississippi power, the promptings of Manifest Destiny began to urge the nation on to the Pacific Coast. Such a spirit eventually had to bring a confrontation with Mexico, and it is this meeting of peoples and cultures that is emphasized in the selections dating from these years.

The arrival of the Anglo-Americans in the Southwest after 1800 was slow at first. But gradually the strangers increased in numbers, and, in the case of Texas, there was a substantial immigration. The rate of increase was slow enough, however, so that the authorities in Madrid, and later in Mexico City, did not regard it as a threat. There was apprehension as to the intentions of the United States, but the occasional early visitors to Santa Fe, Texas, and California were considered chiefly as nuisances.

Different visitors came for different reasons. Many of the earlier ones were adventurers or explorers. Zebulon M. Pike is the best-known of these. He arrived in New Mexico in 1806, but for what purpose the officials at Santa Fe never did fathom. That he represented an expansionist policy on the part of his country was not very likely at that early date, but the New Mexicans could not help wondering. The mountain men—fur trappers—came to the Southwest for profit, and they cared little whether the Spaniards or Mexicans wanted them there or not. A giant commercial step was taken in 1822, with the opening of the Santa Fe Trail by William Bicknell. The trade was profitable in spite of the exhorbitant taxes levied by the Mexican officials, and, being profitable, it brought Anglos into Santa Fe to live.

A few Americans ventured beyond the Rockies in search of land. By conforming to the laws of Mexico, they could receive large land grants and lead prosperous lives. By 1840, nearly 400 outsiders had shown up in California, and, by 1846, this number had almost doubled.

It was Texas that became most Americanized after 1820. In the next decade, the population of the province quadrupled, most of the newcomers being Anglos. These new settlers would provide the revolutionary fervor that would rend Texas from Mexico and eventually take the remainder of the Southwest as well. Anglo colonization began in 1821, with a grant given to the family of Moses Austin by the governor of the province, Antonio Martínez. In 1824, the Mexican Congress speeded the colonization movement by a liberal new law. But, by 1830, Mexico had become alarmed, and it passed a decree—the famous Decree of April 6, 1830—prohibiting any future immigration from the United States. From that time on, in spite of attempts to resolve differences, militant attitudes dominated affairs in Texas, as the Anglos grew more determined to secure their rights, safeguard their land titles, and clear the way for further immigration from the East. Their grievances, coupled with the assumption of dictatorial powers by President Santa Anna, paved the way for the Texas Revolution and independence. And the abrasiveness of relations between Mexico and the United States from 1836 to 1846 was mainly caused by the issue of Texas's future.

In the history of La Raza, the period from 1810 to 1848 is significant because of the increasing contact between Anglo and Mexican. This encounter saw the genesis of a cultural-ethnic conflict that endures to this day in the United States. During the years covered by this chapter, the confrontation involved two nations, meeting each other in the same place and getting acquainted. But with the ending of the Mexican War, this equality was removed, and the Mexicans of the Southwest became the Mexican Americans, an ethnic-cultural minority in an Anglo-American world.

THE BEXAR REVOLUTION IN TEXAS

[On September 16, 1810, Father Miguel Hidalgo y Costillo raised "el grito de Dolores," the shout from Dolores, calling upon the masses of Mexicans to revolt and throw off the yoke of Spain. Although Hidalgo himself became a casualty in the rebellion he initiated, the revolution eventually succeeded in 1821, after more than ten years of turbulence. In the capital of Texas, an abortive, but not insignificant, sequel to the Hidalgo revolt took place early the following year. Under one Juan Bautista de Las Casas, a former army captain, a number of men who sympathized with Hidalgo, led a short-lived revolt on January 22, 1811. By early March, a counterrevolution took place guided by Juan Mañuel Sambrano, and Las Casas was executed. But the spirit of revolt and disaffection manifested by the "Béxar revolution" endured in the province for decades, and it was fed by the continual arrival of colonists from the United States. The following selection reprints a statement issued by the loyalist junta under Sambrano of April 3, 1811, to the military commandant of the Interior Provinces, describing the rebellion at San Antonio de Béxar and its successful overthrow by Spanish loyalists.]

From "The Governing Junta of Texas and Its President, Juan Manuel Sambrano to the Commandant General," in: *Yanaguana Society Publications*. Vol. VI, San Antonio, 1941. Pages 112–114.

The morning of January 22, just passed, was when Captain of Militia Juan Bautista Casas, accompanying the auxiliary troops of Nuevo Santander, took the command from our governor, Lt. Col. Manuel de Salcedo, also taking prisoners, the commander of said bodies, Lt. Col. Simon de Herrera; and Captains Gerónimo de Herrera, Martin Echavarría, José Goceascoechea, Miguel de Arcos, Juan Ignacio Arrambide, José Joaquín Ugarte, Lieutenants Juan José Elguezábal, Bernardino Montero and Gregorio Amador, and other Europeans who had their residence in Béxar, generally confiscating all their properties and treating them as prisoners in the most execrable manner, and abrogating the authority of the government of the province, submitting it to the·Captain General of the insurgents in Saltillo, Mariano Ximénez, taking all the arms, munitions, and artillery.

Thus, they prevented the loyalists from taking any action; but with their combinations, they decided on the night of March 1, to address themselves to Subdeacon Juan Manuel Sambrano, Ignacio Pérez, José Antonio Saucedo, Erasmo Seguin, Martin Beramendi, Francisco Ruiz, Lt. Miguel Muzquiz, Luis Galan, José Maria Sambrano, José Angel Navarro, Gabino Delgado, and others, who in greatest secrecy, proceeded to the headquarters of the militia, where all the forces of the troop and artillery were deposited and immediately took possession of them, arresting the principal followers of the insurrection, persuading them with the most lively and efficacious reasons to desert the iniquitous party which they had embraced. Finally, in one way or another, we managed to install a governing junta, as reported under separate cover. As soon as we entered the Capital of Béxar, we let it be known that the president of the governing junta was now the subdeacon Juan Manuel Sambrano; presenting the names of the members of the Junta by seniority, the undersigners, with the exception of two [Capt. Luciano García and Juan José Sambrano, who took oath on March 11 and 22, respectively] who were absent. Their secretary was Antonio Saucedo.

In this way winning the confidence of the majority of voters, who were submerged in the inky darkness of the insurrection, they authorized us to arrest them, unwittingly thinking perhaps that the purpose of the movement was directed to extinguish forever the legitimate authorities. Under this erroneous impression they continued for some time as did some members of the junta.

After each had voted, oath was taken, with greatest formality, to remain faithful to Religion and Patriotism, and to put into effective and immediate effect the measures dictated by the said junta, the president of it, in the presence of the troop, and the same was done from the first member to the secretary, and at day break, at the head of about four hundred armed troops, the inhabitants gathered, and all went to the Government House to take the command from the said Casas, keeping his person under good custody, and sure imprisonment. From that moment on, steps were taken for good government, tranquility and public peace, and for the reestablishing of the old order. Great changes had taken place, a continued movement and agitation, into which we had all been thrown. We were now liberated from the evil influences of those discontented perverts, and enjoyed just government, which was established and lasted [in Béxar] until the 25th of March, the eve of our march from the Villa de Laredo, at the head of 400 [500] men, the Governing Junta taking along with them those under suspicion, to prevent their interrupting good order, which had already been established by our government; and so our country was rid of them and the security of our prisoners assured, as reported under separate cover.

The desires of this Governing Junta never have been and never shall be other than those to render distinguished service to God, the King, and the Country, without overlooking the subjection due their immediate superior Chief the Commandant General of these Provinces, Brig. Nemecio Salcedo, or any other legitimate authority who might succeed him, whose superior orders we hold inviolate, as the sole Chief we recognize, without the misfortune of incurring the infamous charge of neglect. The delay in communicating with you in regard to these decisions is not criminal in view of the fact that all communication was intercepted and the distance that separates our country afforded us no concrete news of the whereabouts of Your Excellency.

May God preserve you many years. Villa de Laredo, April 3, 1811. Juan Manuel Sambrano, President, Antonio Saerri [sic], Ignacio Pérez, Miguel de Músquiz, Luciano Garcia, Santiago Tixerina, Pedro Prieto, absent, Manuel Barrera, Juan José Sambrano, Vizente Gortari, absent, Gavino Delgado, José Antonio Saucedo, Secretary.

THE PEOPLE OF
NEW MEXICO IN 1818

[Most of Spain's northern Interior Provinces were highly vulnerable to attack during the second decade of the nineteenth century. That New Mexico was no different from the rest is evident from this selection, which is taken from a curious document entitled "Notes concerning the Province of New Mexico Collected on My Mission to the West." The unknown author of the piece was certainly not Spanish or Mexican and very likely not an American, since the original work was written in French. The nature of the "Mission to the West" is not known, but it may well have been to survey the military vulnerability of the Southwest for the United States or even some European power. The most likely potential enemy seemed to be the United States, apparently intent on seizing Florida and trying to negotiate a Louisiana-Texas boundary a little too far west for Spain's comfort. In any case, the "Notes" came into the hands of the Viceroy at Mexico City, who ordered immediate steps taken to strengthen the military fortifications of New Mexico.]

Population. I have not been able to procure any accredited list of the population of New Mexico. It is composed of free whites and

From "An Anonymous Description of New Mexico, 1818," Alfred B. Thomas, ed., in: *Southwestern Historical Quarterly*, July 1929.

civilized Indians, a very few European Spaniards, and absolutely no negro slaves. It may be estimated at fifteen or twenty thousand souls . . . .

The people are generally poor, having neither industry nor commerce. The little foreign merchandise which is found in the country comes principally from the province of Sonora, where the English introduced it in contraband by way of the Gulf of California. This business is in some manner tolerated. The smugglers captured are only condemned to pay double duty (alcabala). It comes also from Chihuahua, now the residence of the Governor General of the Provincias Internas, whence the merchants obtain it through the more usual but very costly routes from Vera Cruz, crossing Old Mexico. But this commerce is diminishing every day, not being able to sustain itself concurrently with the illicit commerce of Sonora. They also have some (trade) with the savages who live throughout the mountains on the waters of California, and also with those who live to the east of the mountains on the waters of the Arkansas. But as there can only be procured with a great deal of trouble, the articles of merchandise necessary to the savages, and because they have only a very small market for the furs which they receive in exchange, it follows that this commerce is unimportant. These savages who are envying the fortune of their neighbors on the north and east, who have frequent communication with the English and Americans, are doing everything possible to allure the traders of these two nations to themselves. They could accordingly at the instigation of one or the other of these peoples, or better, by some of their traders become very dangerous enemies for Spain and certainly in case of war with Spain, America will not neglect a means, which in augmenting her commerce, would likewise greatly disturb the Spanish frontiers, and which could, if well directed, ruin a part of those provinces, or assure their conquest. It would, then, be prudent for the Spanish government to search for means of furnishing these nations with the things which have become absolutely necessary to them. For there is no doubt that in the hands of one or the other governments, these savages would become either important means of defense or an important means of attack.

The principal wealth of the inhabitants of this Province is the herds of bulls, cows, horses, and mules, but principally sheep, for which the country and the climate appear very favorable. They manufacture with the wool some very good blankets, a kind of very ordinary cloth, and some stockings.

Aspect of the Country and Mines. The country is generally mountainous, watered by a large number of very pretty rivers, all of which empty into the Rio del Norte. One finds there very fine appearing uplands of excellent soil, and beautiful plains along the rivers, principally along that of the del Norte.

There is absolutely no doubt but that this Province is rich in silver mines. Some of this precious mineral has been found in different parts. However, no mine has ever been worked there except

one of copper, not far from Taos which was exploited some years
ago by a private individual who himself manufactured this metal
into kitchen utensils, but after some years, the demand for these
objects, having diminished, and not finding any other market he
abandoned this mine which has not been worked since. The few
objects of this class, which are still found in the country came from
this mine.

The iron which is used in the country comes from Chihuahua but
I have not been able to learn where that town acquires it. It comes
at a price so exorbitant that if the commerce were open, it could
be procured from St. Louis on the Mississippi more cheaply. . . .

Civilized Indians. The civilized Indians in New Mexico are various
little tribes of Apaches and Yutas (Utes). They are converted to
Christianity and reside in their ancient villages, situated on some
steep rocks, of difficult access. Although force of custom makes
them remain in such places, yet they cultivate the plains at the foot
of the rocks. This requires of them a great deal of time and hardship to harvest them, carrying on their heads, in baskets, the corn
which they cultivate on the plains. They think they live there in
perfect security but they have not yet been able to achieve this idea
of perfect security. Each village has its ancient hereditary chief who
receives from the Spanish government a baton with a silver point
and has the title of Gobernocito. But there resides also in each
village a Spanish Alcalde who tyrannizes over them and often even
beats them. The chief of the village is obliged to furnish to the
troops of the king, when they pass there, water and fire, and nothing
else. But in spite of these very humane ordinances these unfortunate
ones on such occasions are exposed to all sorts of vexations, and
are ordinarily very happy to have their fowls taken from them and
their pigs eaten, and to escape in that way from worse treatment,
and that under the eyes of an Alcalde whom a paternal government
had placed there only to protect them.

These civilized Indians are armed like (the militia) in the center
of the country serving with it often and like it on horseback. They
are of a very amiable character, are the best cultivators of the
country, and show a great deal of ingenuity and skill in the manufacture of many of the little objects they make in their villages,
such as pottery, baskets, shields, etc. If they were treated with less
harshness and after the spirit of the laws made in their behalf by
the king of Spain, which could not be wiser, there is no doubt that
they would become a real acquisition to a country which only needs
people to become important. In the same way there could be civilized many other tribes, but these unhappy ones (the Pueblos)
embittered and discouraged by haughtiness and bad treatment of
those miserable ones established among them to protect them are
of little advantage to the country. They will certainly become for
Spain very dangerous auxiliaries and very valuable for a power,
which, in attacking these provinces, would know how to win their
friendship by promises and presents. Spain by following a policy

different from that which she pursues now, could easily make friends of them, or better said, faithful and devoted objects. For this they would only need to relieve them of the Alcaldes and of the quartering of troops. . . .

Communication between the United States and New Mexico. The communication of St. Louis with New Mexico would be very easy as far as the Huerfano. The country offers nothing, as I have said, but immense high prairies or perfectly joined plains, where no difficulty would be encountered in making a way for carriages or artillery, except at the passages of the rivers, which, being almost always crossed towards their sources, would not present, by leaving St. Louis at a good season, that is to say, about the end of April, any other difficulties than that of cutting down the banks and making a road to descend into their beds. That, at the most, could be done in some hours.

These provinces offer everywhere an excellent pasturage for horses, whatever number one may have, and immense herds of buffalo for the sustenance of men. Consequently there is no need to transport provisions. If a military expedition should be made against New Mexico, it would be necessary to send ahead some men who with some thousands of pesos in merchandise would win over the savages who live to the east of these mountains and with them be able to take possession of the passes.

The governor of the province sends out from time to time parties to come to the east of the mountains to reconnoitre the country and see what is going on there. But these parties, where they go customarily never encounter enemies, (and) are very negligent. Besides, they are almost always commanded by some ignorant under-officers and composed in very large part of a badly armed militia. It would be very easy, accordingly, either to avoid them, take possession of the pass, and cut off their retreat, or to vanquish them and not give them time to stop in the pass to fortify themselves there while waiting for the rest of the army. One can with good horses go from St. Louis to Taos in thirty-five or forty days.

From the Arkansas River, the road, following the course of the river, is also good and the shortest. From the mountains, taking the pass of La Sangre de Cristo, that is to say from the river of La Trinchera, to Taos there are about one hundred miles; from Taos to Santa Fe, about eighty miles.

I consider New Mexico, in its present position, as one of the most vulnerable points of the Provincias Internas, and because of the facility of communication by land with the United States, because of the ease of fortifying and maintaining it, as one of the most advantageous for the Insurgents, if they succeed in taking possession of it.

THE MISSION SYSTEM OF MEXICAN CALIFORNIA SEEN THROUGH BRITISH EYES

[For more than three years, from 1825 to 1828, the British ship *Blossom* participated in a global expedition, part of whose mission was exploration of the Bering Strait. The ship was commanded by Captain Frederick W. Beechey of the Royal Navy. On November 26, 1826, the Blossom arrived in San Francisco Bay, and Captain Beechey spent a good deal of time inspecting the area. His visit was not solely out of casual curiosity, for Britain had great interest in the West Coast of North America. The Oregon issue was only temporarily resolved at the time, and the future of California was still an open question. It was known that Mexico's hold on the province was weak, as had been Spain's before 1821. Foreigners from several nations, notably the United States, were showing interest in the area, and the importance of a West Coast port for the Far East trade was lost on no one. The following passages from Beechey's *Narrative* detail some of the weaknesses of the San Francisco presidio and the operation of the mission system in the decade prior to secularization of the missions.]

From Captain F. W. Beechey, *Narrative of a Voyage to the Pacific and Beering's Strait.* London, 1831. Vol. II, pages 10–23.

The garrison of San Francisco consists of seventy-six cavalry soldiers and a few artillerymen, distributed between the presidios and
the missions, and consequently not more than half a dozen are at
any time in one place.

They appeared to us to be very dissatisfied, owing not only to their
pay being so many years in arrear, but to the duties which had
been imposed both on the importation of foreign articles, and on
those of the Mexican territory, amounting in the first instance to
forty-two and a half per cent.; whereas under the old government,
two ships were annually sent from Acapulco with goods, which were
sold duty free, and at their original cost in that country, and then,
also, their pay being regularly discharged, they were able to purchase what they wanted. A further grievance has arisen by the refusal of the government to continue certain privileges which were
enjoyed under the old system. At that time soldiers entered for a
term of ten years at the expiration of which they were allowed to
retire to the Pueblós—villages erected for this purpose, and attached to the missions, where the men have a portion of ground
allotted to them for the support of their families. This afforded a
competency to many; and while it benefited them, it was of service
to the government, as the country by that means became settled,
and its security increased. But this privilege has latterly been withheld, and the applicants have been allowed only to possess the land
and feed their cattle upon it, until it shall please the government to
turn them off. The reason of this, I believe, was that Mexico was
beginning to turn her attention to California, and was desirous of
having settlers there from the southern districts, to whom it would
be necessary to give lands; and until they could see what would be
required for this purpose and for the government establishments,
and had the limits of the property already allotted defined, they
did not wish to make any new grants. The real cause, however, was
not explained to the soldiers; they merely heard that they would
not have the land ceded to them for life as usual, and they were
consequently much dissatisfied.

The same feeling of discontent that was experienced by the garrison, pervaded the missions, in consequence of some new regulations of the republican government, the first and most grievous of
which was the discontinuance of a salary of 400 dollars per annum,
heretofore allowed to each of the padres: the support the former
government had given to the missions amounted, according to
Langsdorff, to a million piastres a year. Another grievance was, the
requisition of an oath of allegiance to the reigning authorities,
which these holy men considered so egregious a violation of their
former pledge to the king of Spain, that, until he renounced his
sovereignty over the country, they could not conscientiously take
it; and, much as they were attached to the place in which they had
passed a large portion of their lives, and though by quitting it they
would be reduced to the utmost penury—yet, so much did they
regard this pledge, that they were prepared to leave the country,

and to seek an asylum in any other that would afford it them. Indeed, the Prefect, preferring his expulsion to renouncing his allegiance, had already received his dismissal, and was ready at the
seaport of Monterey to embark in any vessel the government might
appoint to receive him. A third grievance, and one which, when
duly considered, was of some importance, not only to the missions
but to the country in general, was an order to liberate all those
converted Indians from the missions who bore good characters,
and had been taught the art of agriculture, or were masters of a
trade, and were capable of supporting themselves, giving them
portions of land to cultivate, so arranged that they should be divided into parishes, with curates to superintend them, subservient
to the clergy of the missions, who were to proceed to the conversion of the Indians as usual, and to train them for the domesti-
cated state of society in contemplation.

This philanthropic system at first sight appeared to be a very
excellent one, and every friend to the rights of man would naturally
join in a wish for its prosperity; but the Mexican government could
not have sufficiently considered the state of California, and the disposition of the Indians, or they would have known it could not
possibly succeed without long previous training, and then it would
require to be introduced by slow degrees.

The Indians whom this law emancipated were essential to the
support of the missions, not only for conducting their agricultural
concerns, but for keeping in subordination by force and example
those whom disobedience and ignorance would exempt from the
privilege; and as a necessary consequence of this indulgence the
missions would be ruined before the system could be brought into
effect, even supposing the Indians capable of conducting their own
affairs. So far from this being the case, however, they were known
to possess neither the will, the steadiness, nor the patience to provide for themselves. Accustomed, many of them from their infancy,
to as much restraint as children, and to execute, mechanically, what
they were desired and no more, without even entertaining a thought
for their future welfare, it was natural that such persons, when
released from this discipline, should abandon themselves entirely
to their favourite amusements, pastimes, and vices. Those also who
had been converted in later life would return to their former habits,
and having once again tasted the blessings of freedom, which confinement and discipline must have rendered doubly desirable, would
forget all restraint, and then being joined by the wild discontented
Indians, they would be more formidable enemies to the missions
than before, inasmuch as they would be more enlightened. But I
will not anticipate the result, which we had an opportunity of seeing
on our return the following year; and from which the reader will
be able to judge how the system worked. . . . .

The object of the missions is to convert as many of the wild
Indians as possible, and to train them up within the walls of the
establishment in the exercise of a good life, and of some trade, so

that they may in time be able to provide for themselves and become useful members of civilized society. As to the various methods employed for the purpose of bringing proselytes to the mission, there are several reports, of which some were not very creditable to the institution: nevertheless, on the whole I am of opinion that the priests are innocent, from a conviction that they are ignorant of the means employed by those who are under them. Whatever may be the system, and whether the Indians be really dragged from their homes and families by armed parties, as some assert, or not, and forced to exchange their life of freedom and wandering for one of confinement and restraint in the missions, the change according to our ideas of happiness would seem advantageous to them, as they lead a far better life in the missions than in their forests, where they are in a state of nudity, and are frequently obliged to depend solely upon wild acorns for their subsistence.

Immediately the Indians are brought to the mission they are placed under the tuition of some of the most enlightened of their countrymen, who teach them to repeat in Spanish the Lord's Prayer and certain passages in the Romish litany; and also to cross themselves properly on entering the church. In a few days a willing Indian becomes a proficient in these mysteries, and suffers himself to be baptized, and duly initiated into the church. If, however, as it not unfrequently happens, any of the captured Indians show a repugnance to conversion, it is the practice to imprison them for a few days, and then to allow them to breathe a little fresh air in a walk round the mission, to observe the happy mode of life of their converted countrymen; after which they are again shut up, and thus continue to be incarcerated until they declare their readiness to renounce the religion of their forefathers.

I do not suppose that this apparently unjustifiable conduct would be pursued for any length of time; and I had never an opportunity of ascertaining the fact, as the Indians are so averse to confinement that they very soon become impressed with the manifestly superior and more comfortable mode of life of those who are at liberty, and in a very few days declare their readiness to have the new religion explained to them. A person acquainted with the language of the parties, of which there are sometimes several dialects in the same mission, is then selected to train them, and having duly prepared them takes his pupils to the padre to be baptized, and to receive the sacrament. Having become Christians they are put to trades, or if they have good voices they are taught music, and form part of the choir of the church. Thus there are in almost every mission weavers, tanners, shoemakers, bricklayers, carpenters, blacksmiths, and other artificers. Others again are taught husbandry, to rear cattle and horses; and some to cook for the mission: while the females card, clean, and spin wool, weave, and sew; and those who are married attend to their domestic concerns.

In requital of these benefits, the services of the Indians, for life, belong to the mission, and if any neophyte should repent of his apostacy from the religion of his ancestors and desert, an armed force is sent in pursuit of him, and drags him back to punishment apportioned to the degree of aggravation attached to his crime. It does not often happen that a voluntary convert succeeds in his attempt to escape, as the wild Indians have a great contempt and dislike for those who have entered the missions, and they will frequently not only refuse to re-admit them to their tribe, but will sometimes even discover their retreat to their pursuers. This animosity between the wild and converted Indians is of great importance to the missions, as it checks desertion, and is at the same time a powerful defense against the wild tribes, who consider their territory invaded, and have other just causes of complaint. The Indians, besides, from political motives, are, I fear, frequently encouraged in a contemptuous feeling towards their unconverted countrymen, by hearing them constantly held up to them in the degrading light of *béstias!* and in hearing the Spaniards distinguished by the appellation of *génte de razón*.

The produce of the land, and of the labour of the Indians, is appropriated to the support of the mission, and the overplus to amass a fund which is entirely at the disposal of the padres. In some of the establishments this must be very large, although the padres will not admit it, and always plead poverty. The government has lately demanded a part of this profit, but the priests who, it is said, think the Indians are more entitled to it than the government, make small donations to them, and thus evade the tax by taking care there shall be no overplus. These donations in some of the missions are greater than in others, according as one establishment is more prosperous than another; and on this, also, in a great measure, depends the comforts of the dwellings, and the neatness, the cleanliness, and the clothing of the people. In some of the missions much misery prevails, while in others there is a degree of cheerfulness and cleanliness which shows that many of the Indians require only care and proper management to make them as happy as their dull senses will admit of under a life of constraint.

The two missions of Sán Francisco and Sán José are examples of the contrast alluded to. The former in 1817 contained a thousand converts, who were housed in small huts around the mission; but at present only two hundred and sixty remain—some have been sent, it is true, to the new mission of Sán Francisco Solano, but sickness and death have dealt with an unsparing hand among the others. The huts of the absentees, at the time of our visit, had all fallen to decay, and presented heaps of filth and rubbish; while the remaining inmates of the mission were in as miserable a condition as it was possible to conceive, and were entirely regardless of their own comfort. Their hovels afforded scarcely any protection against the weather, and were black with smoke: some of the Indians were sleeping on the greasy floor; others were grinding baked acorns to make into cakes, which constitute a large portion of their food. So little attention indeed had been paid even to health, that in one hut there was a quarter of beef suspended opposite a window, in a very offensive and unwholesome state, but its owners were too indolent to throw it out. Sán José, on the other hand, was all neatness, cleanliness, and comfort; the Indians were amusing themselves between the hours of labour at their games; and the children, uniformly dressed in white bodices and scarlet petticoats, were playing at bat and ball. Part of this difference may arise from the habits of the people, who are of different tribes. Langsdorff observes, that the Indians of the mission of Sán José are the handsomest tribe in California, and in every way a finer race of men; and terms the neophytes of Sán Francisco pigmies compared with them. I cannot say that this remark occurred to me, and I think it probable that he may have been deceived by the apparently miserable condition of the people of Sán Francisco.

The children and adults of both sexes, in all the missions, are carefully locked up every night in separate apartments, and the keys are delivered into the possession of the padre; and as, in the daytime, their occupations lead to distinct places, unless they form a matrimonial alliance, they enjoy very little of each other's society. It, however, sometimes happens that they endeavor to evade the vigilance of their keepers, and are locked up with the opposite sex; but severe corporeal punishment, inflicted in the same manner as is practised in our schools, but with a whip instead of a rod, is sure to ensue if they are discovered. Though there may be occasional acts of tyranny, yet the general character of the padres is kind and benevolent, and in some of the missions, the converts are so much attached to them that I have heard them declare they would go with them, if they were obliged to quit the country. It is greatly to be regretted that, with the influence these men have over their pupils, and with the regard those pupils seem to have for their masters, the priests do not interest themselves a little more in the education of their converts, the first step to which would be in making themselves acquainted with the Indian language. Many of the Indians surpass their pastors in this respect, and can speak the Spanish language, while scarcely one of the padres can make themselves understood by the Indians. They have besides, in general, a lamentable contempt for the intellect of these simple people, and think them incapable of improvement beyond a certain point. Notwithstanding this, the Indians are, in general, well clothed and fed; they have houses of their own, and if they are not comfortable, it is, in a great measure, their own fault; their meals are given to them three times a day, and consist of thick gruel made of wheat, Indian corn, and sometimes acorns, to which at noon is generally added meat. Clothing of a better kind than that worn by the Indians is given to the officers of the missions, both as a reward for their services, and to create an emulation in others.

If it should happen that there is a scarcity of provisions, either through failure in the crop, or damage of that which is in store, as they have always two or three years in reserve, the Indians are sent off to the woods to provide for themselves, where, accustomed to hunt and fish, and game being very abundant, they find enough to subsist upon, and return to the mission when they are required to reap the next year's harvest.

Having served ten years in the mission, an Indian may claim his liberty, provided any respectable settler will become surety for his future good conduct. A piece of ground is then allotted for his support, but he is never wholly free from the establishment, as part of his earnings must still be given to them. We heard of very few to whom this reward for servitude and good conduct had been granted; and it is not improbable that the padres are averse to it, as it deprives them of their best scholars. When these establishments were first founded, the Indians flocked to them in great numbers for the clothing with which the neophytes were supplied; but after they became acquainted with the nature of the institution, and felt themselves under restraint, many absconded. Even now, notwithstanding the difficulty of escaping, desertions are of frequent occurrence, owing probably, in some cases, to the fear of punishment—in others to the deserters having been originally inveigled into the mission by the converted Indians or the neophytes, as they are called by the way of distinction to Los Gentíles, or the wild Indians—in other cases again to the fickleness of their own disposition.

MEXICAN POLICY ON IMMIGRATION TO TEXAS

[Probably the most serious blunder committed by Mexico with respect to Texas was encouraging colonization by immigrants from other nations, particularly the United States. The first grant had been made by Spain to Moses Austin in 1821, but Mexico issued a new colonization law in 1824 with provisions so generous that many citizens from the United States and various European countries arrived to found settlements. In all the years of Spanish occupation, Texas had amassed a population of only 4,000 persons; but now, within the single decade of 1820 to 1830, the population more than quadrupled. And most of the newcomers were "Anglos." The fact that each colony was practically free to run its own affairs—apart from a general oath of loyalty to Mexico—did not make for strong ties to the government at Mexico City. And it was natural that the incoming settlers from the United States should shape their social institutions and attitudes according to what they had known "back East" rather than accommodate themselves to the Mexican life style. There was bound to be a clash, both of interests and of ethnic groups, in Texas. Between 1825 and 1830, official Mexican attitudes on the colonization of Texas began to shift, and the government became uneasily aware of the dangers inherent in allowing unlimited numbers of "Anglos" to enter. For one thing, for several years, the U.S. Government had been making repeated offers to purchase Texas. Occasional articles appeared in American newspapers demanding that the Louisiana Territory boundary be extended to the Rio Grande. And Mexico was forewarned of future possibilities by the

From: 1. "A Trip to Texas in 1828," by José María Sánchez, trans. by Carlos E. Castanada in *Southwestern Historical Quarterly*, April 1926.
2. and 3. "Causes and Origin of the Decree of April 6, 1830," by Alleine Howren, in: *Southwestern Historical Quarterly*, April 1913.

unsuccessful "Fredonian Rebellion" late in 1826, led by an American, Hayden Edwards, whose colonization contract had been summarily canceled by the governor because of a misunderstanding. Although the short-lived rebellion was easily put down by January 1827, Mexico could see in it the danger of divided loyalties among the Anglo colonists. The government began to think of putting limits on the number and source of immigrants, as information arriving at the capital from Texas suggested that time was fast running out on the effort to keep Texas within the Mexican federation of states. Spain's solution to the problem was the decree of April 6, 1830, which, among other things, specifically forbade the immigration of additional colonists from the United States. The decree only added fuel to an already smoldering fire. This selection consists of three readings that throw light on events in Texas in the 1820's and 1830's. In 1827, the Mexican Government appointed a commission headed by General Manuel Mier y Terán to tour Texas, ostensibly to survey the boundary between the province and Louisiana. The recommendations of the commission, particularly of Mier y Terán himself, were influential on the eventual promulgation of the 1830 decree. The first reading below is taken from a journal kept by the draftsman of the boundary commission, José María Sánchez. His insights into the dangers lurking in the Austin colony were prophetic. The second reading comprises most of a letter written by General Mier y Terán from Nacogdoches on June 30, 1828, to President Guadalupe Victoria of Mexico. The last reading is the Decree of April 6, 1830.]

1. THE SPARK THAT WILL START THE CONFLAGRATION

By a conservative estimate it may be said that the Mission of San Antonio de Bejar, on the banks of the beautiful river that bears the same name and whose head waters are about two leagues to the northwest, was founded between 1690 and 1693. Both the temple and the fortifications built as a defense against wild Indians are still preserved. The small settlement within the inclosure is composed of one company of frontier troops known as the Alamo Company, the name given to the place. In 1730, the missions of Concepción, San José, and San Francisco were moved from the frontier of Texas and rebuilt in the vicinity of the Mission of San Antonio. In the same year the *Villa de San Fernando* was founded on the opposite bank of the river and was joined to the settlement of the *presidio* or Mission of the Alamo by a bridge of trees that was built, the two making one place, as one might say, through the middle of which runs the aforementioned river. The streets are not exactly straight, for they curve at various points, and the buildings, though many are of stone, show no beauty, nor do they have any conveniences. There are two squares, almost joined together, being divided merely by the space occupied by the parochial church, but neither one is worthy of notice. The commerce, which is carried on by foreigners and two or three Mexicans, is very insignificant, but the monopoly of it is very evident. I could cite many instances to prove by assertion, but I do not wish to be accused of ulterior motives. Although the soil is very rich, the inhabitants do not cultivate it because of the danger incurred from Indian attacks as soon as they get any distance from the houses, as the Indians often lurk in the surrounding country, coming in the silence of the night without fear from the troops, for by the time the latter notice the damage done it is already too late. No measures can be taken for the maintenance of a continuous watch on account of the sad condition of the troops, especially since they lack all resources. For months, and even years at times, these troops have gone without salary or supplies, constantly in active service against the Indians, dependent for their subsistence on buffalo meat, deer, and other game they may be able to secure with great difficulty. The government, nevertheless, has not helped their condition in spite of repeated and frequent remonstrances. If any money arrives, it disappears instantly, for infamous hands are not lacking to take it and give the poor soldiers goods at double their normal value in exchange for what they have earned, suffering the inclemencies of the weather while these inhuman tyrants slept peacefully in their beds. I am not exaggerating; on the contrary, I keep silent about many worse things I could say. The character of the people is carefree, they are enthusiastic dancers, very fond of luxury, and the worst punishment that can be inflicted upon them is work. Doubtless, there are some individuals, out of the 1,425 that make up the total population, who are free from these failings, but they are very few. The temples and old mission buildings that constituted the missions of Concepción, San José, San Juan, and La Espada, are within a league of the city. These, with the exception of that of San José, founded in 1720 by Fray Antonio Margil, were first established on the frontier of Texas and were moved to the San Antonio River in 1730, when San Fernando de Bejar was founded. The missionaries undertook the reduction of the gentiles with their accustomed zeal, but in our day the glamor of learning has come upon us so suddenly that it has blinded some of the very few persons of judgment [in Bejar], property owners in the main, who clamored loudly: "Out with the friars, out with the good-for-nothings." Thus they abolished the missions and divided among themselves the lands they have not known how to cultivate and which they have left in a sad state of neglect. . . .

The Americans from the north have taken possession of practically all the eastern part of Texas, in most cases without the permission of the authorities. They immigrate constantly, finding no one to prevent them, and take possession of the *sitio* [location] that best suits them without either asking leave or going through any formality other than that of building their homes. Thus the majority of inhabitants in the Department are North Americans, the Mexican population being reduced to only Bejar, Nacogdoches, and La Bahía del Espíritu Santo, wretched settlements that between them do not number three thousand inhabitants, and the new village of Guadalupe Victoria that has scarcely more than seventy settlers. The government of the state, with its seat at Saltillo, that should watch over the preservation of its most precious and interesting department, taking measures to prevent its being stolen by foreign hands, is the one that knows the least not only about actual conditions, but even about its territory. This fact is corroborated by the report given to the boundary commission by the government itself with regard to the lands granted in Texas to *empresarios* which when compared by us with the map showed that grants of the same lands had been made over and over again. Another amusing instance is that of the deputy from the Department who in 1828 wrote to a friend in Nacogdoches begging him to tell him about the region from the Guadalupe on, and about all that was noteworthy, in order that he might be able to speak about them in the legislature when the occasion arose. Admirable fathers of their country! Alas, wretched republic! Repeated and urgent appeals have been made to the Supreme Government of the Federation regarding the imminent danger in which this interesting Department is of becoming the prize of the ambitious North Americans, but never has it taken any measures that may be called conclusive, either because it has always been involved in those fatal convulsions that have destroyed the republic, or because secret agents, deceiving the officials, have made them believe that all is but the exaggeration of weak and cowardly spirits. Thus the vigilance of the highest authorities has been dulled while our enemies from the North do not lose a single opportunity of advancing though it be but a step towards their treacherous design which is well known. . . . But let us turn to something else. . . .

Villa de Austin [San Felipe de Austin], April 27.—We continued along hills without trees, the ground being wet and muddy, until we arrived at a distance of four or five leagues from the settlement of San Felipe de Austin, where we were met by Mr. Samuel Williams, secretary of the empresario, Mr. Stephen Austin; and we were given lodging in a house that had been prepared for the purpose.

This village has been settled by Mr. Stephen Austin, a native of the United States of the North. It consists, at present, of forty or fifty wooden houses on the western bank of the large river known as *Rio de los Brazos de Dios*, but the houses are not arranged systematically so as to form streets; but on the contrary, lie in an irregular and desultory manner. Its population is nearly two hundred persons, of which only ten are Mexicans, for the balance are all Americans from the North with an occasional European. Two wretched little stores supply the inhabitants of the colony: one sells only whiskey, rum, sugar, and coffee; the other, rice, flour, lard, and cheap cloth. It may seem that these items are too few for the needs of the inhabitants, but they are not because the Americans from the North, at least the great part of those I have seen, eat only salted meat, bread made by themselves out of corn meal, coffee, and home-made cheese. To these the greater part of those who live in the village add strong liquor, for they are in general, in my opinion, lazy people of vicious character. Some of them cultivate their small farms by planting corn; but this task they usually entrust to their negro slaves, whom they treat with considerable harshness. Beyond the village in an immense stretch of land formed by rolling hills are scattered the families brought by Stephen Austin, which today number more than two thousand persons. The diplomatic policy of this empresario, evident in all his actions, has, as one may say, lulled the authorities into a sense of security, while he works diligently for his own ends. In my judgment, the spark that will start the conflagration that will deprive us of Texas, will start from this colony. All because the government does not take vigorous measures to prevent it. Perhaps it does not realize the value of what it is about to lose.

2. ENMITY BETWEEN MEXICANS AND FOREIGNERS

. . . As one covers the distance from Béjar to this town, he will note that Mexican influence is proportionately diminished until on arriving in this place he will see that it is almost nothing. And indeed, whence could such influence come? Hardly from superior numbers in population, since the ratio of Mexicans to foreigners is one to ten; certainly not from the superior character of the Mexican population, for exactly the opposite is true, the Mexicans of this town comprising what in all countries is called the lowest class— the very poor and very ignorant. The naturalized North Americans in the town maintain an English school, and send their children north for further education; the poor Mexicans not only do not have sufficient means to establish schools, but they are not of the type that take any thought for the improvement of its public institutions or the betterment of its degraded condition. Neither are there civil authorities or magistrates; one insignificant little man—not to say more—who is called an *alcalde,* and an *ayuntamiento* that does not convene once in a lifetime is the most that we have here at this important point on our frontier; yet, wherever I have looked, in the short time that I have been here, I have witnessed grave occurrences, both political and judicial. It would cause you the same chagrin that it has caused me to see the opinion that is held of our nation by these foreign colonists, since, with the exception of some few who have journeyed to our capital, they know no other Mexicans than the inhabitants about here, and excepting the authorities necessary to any form of society, the said inhabitants are the most ignorant of negroes and Indians, among whom I pass for a man of culture. Thus, I tell myself that it could not be otherwise than that from such a state of affairs should arise an antagonism between the Mexicans and foreigners, which is not the least of the smoldering fires which I have discovered. Therefore, I am warning you to take timely measures. Texas could throw the whole nation into revolution.

The colonists murmur against the political disorganization of the frontier, and the Mexicans complain of the superiority and better education of the colonists; the colonists find it unendurable that they must go three hundred leagues to lodge a complaint against the petty pickpocketing that they suffer from a venal and ignorant *alcalde*, and the Mexicans with no knowledge of the laws of their own country, nor those regulating colonization, set themselves against the foreigners, deliberately setting nets to deprive them of the right of franchise and to exclude them from the *ayuntamiento*. Meanwhile, the incoming stream of new settlers is unceasing; the first news of these comes by discovering them on land already under cultivation, where they have been located for many months; the old inhabitants set up a claim to the property, basing their titles of doubtful priority, and for which there are no records, on a law of the Spanish government; and thus arises a lawsuit in which the *alcalde* has a chance to come out with some money. In this state of affairs, the town where there are no magistrates is the one in which lawsuits abound, and it is at once evident that in Nacogdoches and its vicinity, being most distant from the seat of the general government, the primitive order of things should take its course, which is to say that this section is being settled up without the consent of anybody.

The majority of the North Americans established here under the Spanish government—and these are few—are of two classes. First, those who are fugitives from our neighbor republic and bear the unmistakable earmarks of thieves and criminals; these are located between Nacogdoches and the Sabine; ready to cross and recross this river as they see the necessity of separating themselves from the country in which they have just committed some crime; however, some of these have reformed and settled down to an industrious life in the new country. The other class of early settlers are poor laborers who lack the four or five thousand dollars necessary to buy a *sitio* of land in the north, but having the ambition to become landholders—one of the strong virtues of our neighbors—have come to Texas. Of such as this latter class is Austin's colony composed. They are for the most part industrious and honest, and appreciate this country. Most of them own at least one or two slaves. Unfortunately the emigration of such is made under difficulties, because they lack the means of transportation, and to accomplish this emigration it has become necessary to do what was not necessary until lately: there are empresarios of wealth who advance them the means for their transportation and establishment.

The wealthy Americans of Louisiana and other western states are anxious to secure land in Texas for speculation, but they are restrained by the laws prohibiting slavery. If these laws should be repealed—which God forbid—in a few years Texas would be a powerful state which could compete in productions and wealth with Louisiana. The repeal of these laws is a point toward which the colonists are directing their efforts. They have already succeeded in getting from the Congress of Coahuila a law very favorable to their prosperity: the state government has declared that it will recognize contracts made with servants before coming to this country; and the colonists are thus assured of the employment of ample labor, which can be secured at a very low price in the United States. This law, according to the explanation made to me by several, is going to be interpreted as equivalent to permission to introduce slaves.

In spite of the enmity that usually exists between the Mexicans and the foreigners, there is a most evident uniformity of opinion on one point, namely the separation of Texas from Coahuila and its organization into a territory of the federal government. This idea, which was conceived by some of the colonists who are above the average, has become general among the people and does not fail to cause considerable discussion. In explaining the reasons assigned by them for this demand, I shall do no more than relate what I have heard with no addition of my own conclusions, and I frankly state that I have been commissioned by some of the colonists to explain to you their motives, notwithstanding the fact that I should have done so anyway in the fulfillment of my duty.

They claim that Texas in its present condition of a colony is an expense, since it is not a sufficiently prosperous section to contribute to the revenues of the state administration; and since it is such a charge it ought not to be imposed upon a state as poor as Coahuila, which has not the means of defraying the expenses of the corps of political and judicial officers necessary for the maintenance of peace and order. Furthermore, it is impracticable that recourse in all matters should be had to a state capital so distant and separated from this section by deserts infected by hostile savages. Again, their interests are very different from those of the other sections, and because of this they should be governed by a separate territorial government, having learned by experience that the mixing of their affairs with those of Coahuila brings about friction. The native inhabitants of Texas add to the above other reasons which indicate an aversion for the inhabitants of Coahuila; also the authority of the *comandante* and the collection of taxes is disputed.

That which most impressed me in view of all these conditions is the necessity of effective government in Nacogdoches at least, since it is the frontier with which the Republic is most in contact. Every officer of the federal government has immense districts under his jurisdiction, and to distribute these effectively it is necessary to give attention to economy as well as to government and security. The whole population here is a mixture of strange and incoherent parts without parallel in our federation: numerous tribes of Indians, now at peace, but armed and at any moment ready for war, whose steps toward civilization should be taken under close supervision of a strong and intelligent government; colonists of another people, more progressive and better informed than the Mexican inhabitants, but also more shrewd and unruly; among these foreigners are fugitives from justice, honest laborers, vagabonds and criminals, but honorable and dishonorable alike travel with their political constitution in their pockets, demanding the privileges, authority and officers which such a constitution guarantees. The most of them have slaves, and these slaves are beginning to learn the favorable intent of the Mexican law toward their unfortunate condition and are becoming restless under their yoke, and the masters, in the effort to retain them, are making that yoke even heavier; they extract their teeth, set on the dogs to tear them in pieces, the most lenient being he who but flogs his slaves until they are flayed.

In short, the growing population, its unusual class, the prosperity and safety of the nation, all seem to me to demand the placing at this point of a *jefe politico* subordinate to the one at Béjar, and also a court of appeals. This done, I do not believe so radical a step as the separation of Texas from Coahuila, now desired by the inhabitants, would be necessary.

I must ask your forbearance for this long letter, but I desire to forward to you at once my observations of this country and not withhold them until the day when I make full report to the government, for fear the time for remedy will be past.

3. THE DECREE OF APRIL 6, 1830

Article 1. Cotton goods excluded in the Law of May 22, 1829, may be introduced through the ports of the Republic until January 1, 1831, and through the ports of the South Sea until June 30, 1831.

Article 2. The duties received on the above mentioned goods shall be used to maintain the integrity of Mexican territory, to form a reserve fund against the event of Spanish invasion, and to promote the development of national industries in the branch of cotton manufacturers.

Article 3. The government is authorized to name one or more commissioners who shall visit the colonies of the frontier states and contract with the legislatures of said states for the purchase, in behalf of the federal government, of lands deemed suitable for the establishment of colonies of Mexican and other nationalities; and the said commissioners shall make with the existing colonies whatever arrangements seem expedient for the security of the Republic. The said commissioners shall supervise the introduction of new colonists and the fulfilling of their contracts for settlement, and shall ascertain to what extent the existing contracts have been completed.

Article 4. The chief executive is authorized to take such lands as are deemed suitable for fortifications or arsenals and for the new colonies, indemnifying the states for same, in proportion to their assessments due the federal government.

Article 5. The government is authorized to transport the convict-soldiers destined for Vera Cruz and other points to the colonies, there to establish them as is deemed fit; the government will furnish free transportation to the families of the soldiers, should they desire to go.

Article 6. The convict-soldiers shall be employed in constructing the fortifications, public works and roads which the commissioners may deem necessary, and when the time of their imprisonment is terminated, if they should desire to remain as colonists, they shall be given lands and agricultural implements, and their provisions shall be continued through the first year of their colonization.

Article 7. Mexican families who voluntarily express a desire to become colonists will be furnished transportation, maintained for one year, and assigned the best of agricultural lands.

Article 8. All the individuals above mentioned shall be subject to both the federal and state colonization laws.

Article 9. The introduction of foreigners across the northern frontier is prohibited under any pretext whatever, unless the said foreigners are provided with a passport issued by the agents of this Republic at the point whence the said foreigners set out.

Article 10. No change shall be made with respect to the slaves now in the states, but the federal government and the government of each state shall most strictly enforce the colonization laws and prevent the further introduction of slaves.

Article 11. In accordance with the right reserved by the general congress in the seventh article of the Law of August 18, 1824, it is prohibited that emigrants from nations bordering on this Republic shall settle in the states or territory adjacent to their own nation. Consequently, all contracts not already completed and not in harmony with this law are suspended.

Article 12. Coastwise trade shall be free to all foreigners for the term of four years, with the object of turning colonial trade to the ports of Matamoras, Tampico, and Vera Cruz.

Article 13. Frame houses and all classes of foreign food products may be introduced through the ports of Galveston and Matagorda, free of duty, for a period of two years.

Article 14. The government is authorized to expend five hundred thousand dollars (*pesos*) in the construction of fortifications and settlements on the frontier, in the transportation of the convict-soldiers and Mexican families to same and their maintenance for one year, on agricultural implements, on expenses of the commissioners, on the transportation of troops, on premiums to such farmers among the colonists as may distinguish themselves in agriculture, and on all the other expedients conducive to progress and security as set forth in the foregoing articles.

Article 15. To obtain at once one-half of the above sum, the government is authorized to negotiate a loan on the customs proceeds which will be derived from the ordinary classes of cotton goods, said loan to pay a premium of three per cent monthly, payable at the expiration of the periods fixed in the tariff schedule.

Article 16. One-twentieth of the said customs receipts shall be used in the promotion of cotton manufactures, such as in the purchase of machines and looms, small sums being set aside for the installing of the machinery, and any other purpose that the government shall deem necessary; the government shall apportion these funds to the states having this form of industry. The said funds shall be under the control of the Minister of Relations for the purpose of promoting industries of such importance.

Article 17. Also three hundred thousand dollars (*pesos*) of the above mentioned customs receipts shall be set aside as a reserve fund on deposit in the treasury, under the strict responsibility of the government, which shall have power to use the same only in case of Spanish invasion.

Article 18. The government shall regulate the establishment of the new colonies, and shall present to Congress within a year a record of the emigrants and immigrants established under the law, with an estimate of the increase of population on the frontier.

ANTONIO BARREIRO'S GLIMPSE OF NEW MEXICO IN 1832

[In 1831 Antonio Barreiro was sent from Mexico City to be a legal adviser to the provincial officials in New Mexico. While engaged in his duties at Santa Fe, Barreiro prepared a lengthy descriptive sketch of New Mexico and its problems. As part of his report, he made an analysis (not reprinted here) of the military preparedness of the province, should an invasion, presumably from the United States, occur. He found the defenses inexcusably weak and suggested remedies for the situation: Bring in more troops, move the main garrison from Santa Fe to the center of the province at Valverde, open a military academy for the training of soldiers, and raise and train a civil militia. Barreiro's advice was not heeded, however, and the weakness of New Mexico's defenses made possible a bloodless conquest by General Stephen Kearny's troops in 1846. The reprinted portions of Barreiro's report deal with the commercial, political, and religious life of the province.]

The commerce of New Mexico must be considered under three aspects, namely: the foreign trade carried on with North America,

From "Barreiro's *Ojeada Sobre Nuevo-Mexico*," by Lansing B. Bloom, in: *New Mexico Historical Review*, Vol. III, 1928.

that carried on with the neighboring states, and the trade which it
has internally.

The commerce with the United States of North America is carried on by means of regular caravans which arrive in Santa Fe
usually in July. These caravans are composed of ninety or a hundred wagons well loaded with goods and escorted by their respective owners. They elect officers from among themselves to whom
they yield obedience on the road. At all times they try to proceed
with the greatest care so as not to be surprised by the countless
barbarous and warlike Indians who inhabit the dreadful deserts
which intervene between New Mexico and Missouri for a distance
of more than two hundred and fifty leagues. When a caravan has
stopped in the afternoon, they make a circle with the wagons,
within which the people and the stock sleep, while a sufficient number of sentinels are on watch all night, in order, when occasion
arises, to fire upon the enemy and by all means to save their property.

Generally by July, as I have said, these caravans arrive at Santa
Fe, and that is the time when this capital presents a very festive
appearance. Then on all sides clothing stores are opened and a
considerable number are seen who come to this kind of fair from
the pass of the north, from Sonora, and from all parts of the Territory. That is the time when all the Anglo-American merchants are
returning who, during the year, have gone to the neighboring states
to transact business, and then in short is when one beholds a traffic
which is truly pleasing. Goods become extremely cheap, for many
merchants "burn their profits" so as to return to the United States
in August, and purchases are made with the greatest ease. Upon
the invoices from Philadelphia or Saint Louis goods are sold wholesale at an advance of scarcely 80, or 90, or 100%, and indeed they
are often sold at an advance of only 50%. These crazy bargains have
ruined many merchants, for the losses of the company which came
the past year are estimated to have been at least 30 to 40,000 *pesos*.

In August the caravans start back, only those merchants remaining who are interested in the trapping of beaver, of which a considerable exportation is made.

As the exportation of beaver has no duty imposed, the American
merchants try upon their return journey to carry beaver instead of
money, because thus they secure two advantages: first, that of paying no duties upon the exportation of coin, and second, that of
carrying to their own country an effect which is there of great
value to them and which here is duty-free.

These caravans originated in 1821 when some adventurers began to enter; but subsequently more formal companies of men were
organized, until of late years merchants of means have been coming with ventures on a large scale and under conditions very different from those existing at first. . . .

*The Commerce which New Mexico has with the neighboring
States.*—This also is worthy of attention, as Sonora and Chihuahua

are supplied to a large extent by the foreign goods which are imported from here, with the resulting benefit that the Americans who carry on this commerce bring in a considerable amount of money which circulates in this country, both through the payment of duties made upon their return, as well as through the sums which they spend necessarily upon their living.

The New Mexicans also carry on a fairly active commerce with the neighboring States, for yearly they export flocks of sheep, skins, pine-lumber, coarse woolen goods, tobacco and other goods which they sell at good prices. There are persons who have contracts in Durango by which they are to deliver annually 15,000 or more head of sheep which, marketed there, bring nine *reales* or more. A few persons have the trade in sheep monopolized, so that it cannot be considered as beneficial as the trade in skins, coarse woolens, etc., since the latter trade is well distributed among all classes in New Mexico, especially among the lower and middle classes. The general eagerness found among New Mexicans for commerce with the neighboring States is certainly astonishing. In October especially a multitude of people are seen to set out with this in view and to scatter in all directions. Some head for Chihuahua, others for Pitic or Guaymas; some go even to the fairs of Aguascalientes or San Juan; others to Durango, and others finally as far as the Californias.

The internal commerce of the country.—This is ordinary, and the usual manner of conducting it is by barter. Sheep are held in high esteem, almost more even than money, for the purchase of whatever may be desired. Let me add that such traffic as a regular thing is effected by credit from one year to another, and even for a longer time. I have already spoken of the cheapness of foreign goods; those of the country on the other hand, such as chocolate, rice, sugar, olive oil, almonds, and others of this character, are exceedingly dear and at times are very scarce, and furthermore those which are brought here are always of inferior quality.

The commerce which is carried on with the Gentiles.—This also demands our attention. With vermillion, knives, biscuits, ovened bread, powder, awls and other trifles are bought exquisite skins which are resold at a profit and from which [trade] great advantage might be drawn, were the enlightenment of the country different from what it is. Were there revenue and export duties on such rich and abundant peltries, enough could be produced at very little cost to load whole pack-trains. What an immense field in Mexico lies open to industry! What seeds of prosperity are under our hands on every side! Even those most remote places which are now occupied by the barbarians allure us with things of value but with which we are not yet acquainted; those rivers which in their lands teem with valuable beaver; those virgin, untouched fields where fair Nature displays herself in all her beauty; those affable climes which offer to agriculture and to stock-raising their powerful influence; those timber-clad mountains and beautiful marbles which seem to be sketching the plans of magnificient cities, [all these] surely are powerful incentives to make us think seriously upon developing the elements of true happiness which we possess. Revolutionary aspirants! Infernal spirits of discord! Cast one single GLANCE OVER YOUR COUNTRY, and hasten to bury yourselves forever in the abysses by reason of the furious remorse which will torment ye when ye shall perceive how this soil, blessed by the adorable hand of Providence, invites the Mexican people with riches and products of every sort, and which they do not enjoy nor even know as yet because of your criminality and perverse designs! . . .

Whoever figures to himself the enormous distance of more than eight hundred leagues at which this Territory lies from its *audiencia;* he who knows the lack of resources with which these unhappy people generally find themselves, for undertaking a ruinous journey even to the capital of Mexico in order there to defend their rights; whoever has a slight conception of the ignorance which reigns in this country, will not require other colors in order to paint vividly the deplorable and doleful state in which the administration of justice finds itself. Should I attempt to unfold any one of the very grave faults from which this most interesting branch suffers, I believe that I should fill many sheets without having done, and so I shall simply indicate some points in passing.

Impunity of crimes.—Never are crimes punished because there is absolutely no one who knows how to draw up a verbal process, to conclude a defense, nor to fill the office of attorney general. It is going on two years that I have been here and in this time I have advised the continuance of numberless cases with the greatest clearness and minuteness, but to date I do not know the result of my advice. I have tried to put to rights the course of other civil proceedings, but I have obtained the same outcome. The vicar general, Don Juan Rafael Rascon, has assured me that in the nearly four years that he has held the vicarate he has been unable to arrange the matters and proceedings of his [ecclesiastical] court. In effect, the appointment of an attorney general is advised, and the judge raises the objection that there is no one who would be able to discharge such an office; so after this fashion one indicates the course of the law, but all are blind for following it. In fine, one cannot recount the obstacles which ignorance presents in New Mexico to the correct administration of justice.

Jails.—There are no other than certain filthy rooms with this appellation in the capital. The prisoners are rewarded instead of punished when they are incarcerated in them, because they pass the time much diverted in merry frolics and chatter; and they take their imprisonment with the greatest ease, for at night they escape to the bailes and by day to other diversions. How reprehensible is such laxness on the part of the judges!

The only measures which right now I view as timely are the reestablishment of a learned tribunal for New Mexico, and the enactment of the other measures which the most excellent minister of justice, Don. José Ignacio Espinosa, has introduced in the august chambers.

The spiritual administration finds itself in a truly dismal condition. Nothing is more common than to see numberless sick folk die without confession and extreme unction, and nothing is rarer than to see the eucharist administered to them. Corpses remain unburied many days, and infants are baptized at the cost of a thousand sacrifices. There are unfortunate ones in considerable number who pass most Sundays of the year without hearing mass. The churches are almost destroyed, and most of them are surely unworthy of being called temples of God.

The missions and curacies which do not have pastors are in charge of missionaries and temporary curates and most of these parishioners are visited only a few days in the year. How shall not the poor people who suffer this neglect feel great resentment at seeing that from their crops and herds they have to pay for the maintenance of a priest who does not live with them and who perhaps does not aid them with the consolations of religion in that last hour when they most need them?

There is an absolute deficiency of ministers, for almost all the curacies and missions of the Territory are vacant. The causes which have brought it about that said missions and curacies should have been, and should be, for so extended a time in such great abandonment are very clear; for many ecclesiastics aspire only to hold fat curacies from which to make a fortune, or to maintain a luxury which is surely opposed to the spirit of the Gospel. On the other hand, the curates and missionaries of this Territory have to subsist on a scanty competence; they find themselves separated from cultured intercourse with other people, isolated in these corners of the Republic where only disagreeable objects and oftentimes dangers are near them; they are deprived of the pleasures with which civilized places allure them; they come to live on some miserable ranch and to endure privations which weigh not a little on the spirits of men who are used to a different order of things. And if to those considerations are added the gloomy idea that they have to pass the best of their life in solitude and privation, seeing themselves in the last days of their career without any succor from their poor parishes which from the weariness of years they will now be unable to serve, and therefore reduced to subsist at the expense of charity or off the miserable revenue of some chaplaincy—on these terms, I say, what ecclesiastics will be willing to seek such unhappy lots, unless they be animated by a spirit truly apostolic? It is true that in them they could acquire merits which are very laudable and befitting the obligations of their ministry and of Christian charity, but certain it is that all flee from them.

In order partly to remedy this evil, it would be very fitting that ecclesiastics, when they have served ten years in the cure of souls in these towns with the approbation of the supreme government, should be given preferment for obtaining prebends in the cathedrals of the Republic, for only in this manner would it be possible to induce ecclesiastics of virtue and dignity to come and give their labors on behalf of these unhappy people.

With a saving of revenue and advantages worth considering the missions of this Territory might be secularized, being made into competent curacies which would be sufficient to maintain their rectors in decorum and decency.

It is more than seventy years since a bishop has stepped in New Mexico, and it might be figured that scarcely any age could have an episcopal visit in a country so remote as this, distant more than four hundred leagues from its Metropolis.

The radical way in which to make the spiritual administration is to erect a sacred mitre and a collegiate seminary, as was decreed by the Cortes of Spain on January 26, 1818. With the tithes of New Mexico, now bid off annually at ten or twelve thousand pesos which is scarcely a third of what they produce, there will be sufficient to meet the expenses of the bishop and college. Now the tithes serve only to enrich three or four private parties without profit either to the spiritual welfare of New Mexico or to the temporal good of the Republic.

I will conclude [my notes] upon the ecclesiastical branch, and in summary will say that Christian piety is indignant at seeing the abuses which are committed in New Mexico in the nurture and cure of souls, and charity requires a veil to be thrown over many things the relation of which would occasion scandal . . . As sole remedy for so many ills, the Territory clamors for the shepherd of her church. *The harvest is plentiful but laborers are lacking. Let us pray the Lord that reapers may enter upon it.*

SECULARIZATION OF THE CALIFORNIA MISSIONS

[When Spain came to the New World, members of the several monastic orders of the Church, notably the Franciscans and the Dominicans, came along to found missions among the Indians. As part of its colonial policy, Spain decreed that these missions, once well established, would be secularized: that is, the care of them would be turned over to the secular priests. This policy was not always routinely followed, however, for a variety of reasons. In some cases, there was a scarcity of secular priests, but frequently it happened that the missions founded by the orders developed into powerful economic and religious interests, which the orders were not willing to give up. This situation prevailed in Mexican California, which had, after all, been founded entirely as a mission colony under the aegis of the Franciscans. By the time of the Mexican Revolution, the missions had obtained possession of nearly all the best land in California and had thousands of Indians under their control. They had made the province prosperous and virtually self-sufficient. Secularization was eventually accomplished there in 1834, but, only after a protracted struggle lasting many years, during which there was no lack of intrigue, scheming, wrangling, and name-calling by partisans of both sides of the question. The issue was complicated by the mixed motives of all concerned. Government officials pressed for secularization ostensibly to free the Indians for land ownership and the exercise of the rights of citizenship. But there was also much pressure upon these officials from colonists who wanted some of the mission lands confiscated. Then, too, the loyalty of the Franciscans was called into question, for they had not always bothered to hide

From Zephyrin Engelhardt, *The Missions and Missionaries of California.* San Francisco, 1913. Vol. III, pages 488–495.

their antipathy toward the government at Mexico City and their
devotion to the Spanish monarchy. The Franciscans had their own
good reasons for wanting to hold the missions. They eventually became reconciled to turning them over to secular clergy, but were
understandably hesitant, fearing that Indian rights would be violated and the land confiscated. A law of 1813, passed under Spanish
rule, had set the conditions for secularization, but it had never been
put into effect in California. But the accession in 1832 of a liberal
Mexican regime bent on reform finally gave the needed impetus.
Governor José Figueroa of California at first tried the gradualist
measure of "emancipating" Indians, but met with little success. In
August, 1832, Figueroa asked the advice of the two leading officials,
Fathers Garcia Diego and Narciso Durán. Father Durán replied in
a letter of October 3, reprinted below, spelling out his reasons for
being reluctant to go along with immediate secularization. But the
policy did go into effect the following year, and, in general, the
Franciscans' fears concerning the rights of the Indians and the
confiscation of the land were realized.]

I shall divide this reply in the following manner:—1. The missions
which can be secularized in conformity with the law of September
13th, 1813.—2. The obstacles, difficulties, and dangers which will be
encountered.—3. The ways and means which seem to me more adequate to accomplish a general secularization happily.

With regard to the first point it may forthwith be set down as a
matter of fact that all the missions of Upper California exceed the
ten years of existence demanded by the law, some by twenty, thirty,
and forty years, so that, if ten years is to be the rule, all may be
secularized. However, Your Honor must be convinced of the defect
in this rule. It is clear that, owing to the distance of the place where
the law was framed, no consideration was taken of even the topo-
graphical and geographical peculiarities of this country. It appears
to me that another principle of maturity ought to be adopted, one
that is less exposed to irreparable and sad mistakes, and which
would not involve the loss of what has been achieved in half a century. This principle, according to which we should judge a mission
ripe for secularization, should be gathered from the neophytes. It
should regard the shorter or longer period since which the last
pagans were received into the mission, and the greater or less aptitude noticed in them for living by themselves in a civilized manner;
for it is evident that the less connection these Christian missions
have with the pagan, the more must they be considered to have

abandoned the vicious habits of the latter, and to have advanced in civilization; and from the greater or less inclination observed in them for work, the greater or less must their fitness to live by themselves be judged.

Following this principle, I am of the opinion that a trial secularization could be made at the missions of San Juan Capistrano, San Buenaventura, Santa Barbara, Purisima, San Antonio, San Carlos, Santa Cruz, and San Francisco; for in all these missions it is many years since a pagan Indian was admitted. On the other hand one sees in these neophytes some interest to cultivate their little gardens, which they care for moderately well and raise some produce when conditions are favorable, as when they are given the aid of implements, animals, and other conveniences, though not without the pain of seeing them lose those articles through the vice of drink, which has spread among them horribly. These might be secularized along with the missions if a certain amount of property which they might enjoy as their own were allotted to them. The rest of the property could be reserved in order that there might always be a fund or capital belonging to the community, and administered by themselves through mayordomos of their own choice and race, for expenses of Divine Worship, spiritual administration and others that might occur. In the beginning it would be well that the missionary have some kind of authority over said fund, but without any coercion of the mayordomos and alcaldes, because these are to bear all the responsibility before the government for the losses that may result for not appreciating the fatherly advice of the missionary. All this should be carried out with the warning to the neophytes that they will be put back to the old conditions under the missionaries, whenever it should be discovered that through sloth, preference for wild fruits, or an inclination to vagrancy or other vices, they neglect their property and frustrate the advance of civilization and agriculture which the government expects of them. At the same time, the government should see that similar results are observed in the white people, so that the natives may receive practical lessons through the eyes, which is the shortest road to progress. With these precautions the difficulties and drawbacks following the secularization of the missions may partly be overcome.

However, as soon as the experimental secularization of the said eight missions has been decreed, two difficulties will present themselves to the government. The one is the indifferent and slothful disposition of the neophytes, the other is the necessity of supporting a hundred burdens which circumstances have rendered inevitable, namely, the maintenance of the troops who for twenty-three years have been subsisting upon the toil of the unfortunate Indians to the not little hardship and worry of the missionaries; for the latter are compelled to regard themselves as executioners, as it were, of these poor neophytes, inasmuch as they are forced to increase the amount of work to satisfy the demands of the soldiery, and also owing to the lack of consideration on the part of the military storekeepers (habilitados) in their demands and sometimes in the manner in which they make their requests. The indolent and slothful disposition of the neophytes is surely notorious and evident, since any one can observe with what little eagerness they do all that pertains to the community, notwithstanding that they know they are working for themselves. Nor is their activity much more lively and steady when working at some private task, or when they cultivate a piece of land allotted to themselves, inasmuch as for the sake of a diversion or some festivity in a neighboring mission they will abandon everything to damage from animals, and in one day with indifference allow the hopes of a whole year to be destroyed. It was only by means of the hard work and care of the missionaries that, under God, the great miracle of supporting these communities has been accomplished. It is true that their indifference and indolence is not quite so remarkable in keeping their own fields and gardens; but when they shall have to supply their own implements and tools, as will have to be the case when they become emancipated proprietors, it is much to be feared that they will not plant nor achieve much. If they evince some interest in having a garden, it is because some exemptions from community work are allowed them, and some liberty to roam about, which they would not have if they did no private planting.

As yet the missionaries have not the pleasure of seeing their neophytes devote themselves to agriculture for love of work; for this is against their naturally wild disposition and habits, which they inherited from their pagan state, so that it costs them much to lay aside the freedom natural to wild beasts, in which condition rude nature in a manner provided the necessaries without personal labor. This is the liberty they still crave. They are barely able to appreciate that which is proper to human beings, except for the faint hope, founded or unfounded, of being able to enjoy in some degree their former liberty of roving about. The truth is, that the labor of the missionaries to make men of them is the most laborious in the world, because what has been said about the character of these California Indians is so common to all that there is scarcely known a single exception. For this I appeal to the testimony of all, Your Honor's included, as well as to that of all those who have come into close contact with them. Inasmuch, however, as it would not be strange that any one should think that I or the missionaries have an interest in undervaluing the Indians, and emphasizing their inaptitude and immaturity for emancipation for the reason that we find ourselves well fixed in the management of their affairs, in my name as well as in the name of all the missionaries of San Fernando College I protest against such a supposition. I moreover sincerely and urgently beseech the Supreme Government and Your Honor to grant us the favor of relieving us from the burden and to place other persons in charge. We shall be satisfied to zealously attend to spiritual matters for only the necessary subsistence until other missionaries arrive to take our places. I assure you, and I protest to Your Honor, that though the bando of José Maria de Echeandía of the 6th of January, 1831, provided it had been feasible and issued in good faith, was for us incomparably more advantageous than the system proposed, we nevertheless would have reason to deplore it.

The other obstacle to secularization is the necessity for these communities to support the troops whom the government does not pay in such a manner that with their pay they can procure subsistence wherever they find it. It is now twenty-three years that these poor soldiers know nothing about their salaries. Had it not been for the communities of Indians under the management of the missionaries, there would not have been any soldiers for the internal peace and the external defense, because they would have perished from hunger. Consequently, after the missions have been secularized, we can no more rely on them for anything; for, if the Indians notice that they must pay taxes on their private property, they will soon manage to have nothing, will abandon everything, and go off to the wilderness and tulares in order to live on the products of nature, and there will be no possibility of forcing them from their haunts. In their opinion they will thus gain, inasmuch as they will find themselves free from necessities whose absence in their savage state they never felt. It is the place of the governor to know his resources, and whether they can support the troops independently of these communities.

The third and last point which I have proposed to answer is to treat of the means for carrying out a universal secularization of the missions without destroying what has been planted and reared with so much labor. To arrive at this goal I find two royal roads which both lead to it. The one is simple and insures quick and happy results, but it is expensive to the government, because for some years it requires aid from the treasury. The other is a little more complicated, and its results cannot be so quick, but it involves no expense. It needs no more than to open a gate which has no bolts nor locks, and it is in the power of the governor to open it with facility.

The first way consists in founding a new chain of missions and presidios to the east of the old missions, and leaving it to the neophytes to join the new establishments or to organize civilized pueblos on the sites of the old missions. The natives near the new missions, as is likely, will attach themselves to them, and those neophytes who remain at the old missions will form civilized pueblos. In this manner the opportunity of scattering in the wilderness and the tulares is shut off, and they would lose the hope of returning to their nomadic life, as they would either have to join the new missions or lead a rational life in the pueblos, so that insensibly, as it were, they would be bound to lead a life of virtue. This seems to me the surest way of securing happy results from a general secularization. Unless these exits are shut off, some think a dispersion is much to be feared without any hope of ever recovering the runaways. There would then be imminent danger for the safety of the country, especially if, some day when allied to the savages of the frontier, they should acquire firearms from foreigners in return for skins. In this there is real danger for Upper California; but as neither the treasury nor the missionaries are in condition to take this road, I desist from enlarging on the proposition, and am satisfied to have pointed it out, until God grants us more favorable times.

The other less rapid road to the end, though safe and inexpensive for the government, is to found a bishopric in Upper California alone and leaving the tithes absolutely to the administration of the bishop. With this help alone he would establish a seminary for the ecclesiastical education of the sufficiently numerous sons of decent and honorable families, who have no goal or suitable career in this limited society. There is hope that many of these might have a vocation for the sacred ministry. These alone would furnish a native and select clergy to serve the Church with honor. From this same nursery in a short time would emerge a surplus of priests for the founding of a second missionary college, of either the secular or regular clergy, and in this way alone provisions could be made for new missions and old pueblos. One man can effect this, a bishop, as long as he does not come to rest, but to work, and by means of the tithes alone, provided they are controlled by the Church alone. Ecclesiastical property allowed to operate freely works wonders for the benefit of all. This is a fact which is evident, of daily experience, and proved by all nations. The Church in her organization is economical, and her hands seem to be those that multiplied the bread in the deserts. Let the governor but protect her, when it may be taken for certain that in a few years she will have her seminary for ecclesiastical education, the college for missionaries, a cathedral, the rest of the ministry in running order, and the old pueblos supplied with select laborers. Then a general secularization of all the missions can be effected without the risk of scattering the newly-made Christians; then with giant strides will the natives advance in civilization; and among the white people will also be banished vagrancy which is the real pest of California society.

These ideas which I have the honor of explaining to Your Honor in obedience to your orders have come to me during the twenty-seven years which I have spent in the service of these missions, and they are almost as old as my office of missionary. I express myself thus in proof of my impartiality, and I protest that I only aim to help as well as I can, in order that the government may be enlightened to choose with understanding among so many projects and plans which are offered to benefit California those that seem more suitable to this end, and in order that in a moment may not be destroyed what has been reared during more than half a century at the cost of so much expense and toil.

A MEXICAN ACCOUNT OF THE ALAMO

[The battle of the Alamo, in 1836, was the beginning of the end of Mexico's rule over Texas and was viewed by Texans as a heroic effort in the struggle for independence. Understandably, President Antonio López de Santa Anna of Mexico took a markedly different view: He considered the Texans to be traitors, with only those rights due to such as initiate revolution. The Texas Revolution of 1835–36 was the outgrowth of a number of grievances against Mexico, but its foremost cause was the subversion by Santa Anna of the 1824 constitution and his assumption of dictatorial powers. The first battle went to the Texans at San Antonio, with the defeat of General Martín Perfecto de Cos on December 10, 1835—an insult that Santa Anna immediately set out to avenge. The Mexican forces, numbering more than 6,000, appeared at San Antonio on February 23, 1836, and laid siege to the Alamo, a fortress near the town. A force of 187 Texans led by William Barrett Travis, and including Davy Crockett and Jim Bowie, defended the post. On March 6, the Mexicans made an overwhelming assault, captured the Alamo, and killed all of its defenders. Texas had meanwhile, on March 1, declared its independence of Mexico; the declaration became a reality in April, when the Texas forces under General Sam Houston defeated Santa Anna's army. The following short narrative is a reminiscence written in 1849 by Vicente Filisola, who had been present among the Mexican attackers on March 6, 1836. His account gives little credit to Santa Anna's judgment at the time.]

From "A Critical Study of the Siege of the Alamo and of the Personnel of Its Defenders," by Amelia Williams, in: *Southwestern Historical Quarterly*, July 1933.

On this same evening, a little before nightfall, it is said that Barrett Travis, commander of the enemy, had offered to the general-in-chief, by a woman messenger, to surrender his arms and the fort with all the materials upon the sole condition that his own life and the lives of his men be spared. But the answer was that they must surrender at discretion, without any guarantee, even of life, which traitors did not deserve. It is evident, that after such an answer, they all prepared to sell their lives as dearly as possible. Consequently, they exercised the greatest vigilance day and night to avoid surprise.

On the morning of March 6, the Mexican troops were stationed at 4 o'clock, A.M., in accord with Santa Anna's instructions. The artillery, as appears from these same instructions, was to remain inactive, as it received no order; and furthermore, darkness and the disposition made of the troops which were to attack the four fronts at the same time, prevented its firing without mowing down our own ranks. Thus the enemy was not to suffer from our artillery during the attack. Their own artillery was in readiness. At the sound of the bugle they could no longer doubt that the time had come for them to conquer or to die. Had they still doubted, the imprudent shouts for Santa Anna given by our columns of attack must have opened their eyes. As soon as our troops were in sight, a shower of grape and musket balls was poured upon them from the fort, the garrision of which at the sound of the bugle, had rushed to arms and to their posts. The three columns that attacked the west, the north, and the east fronts, fell back, or rather, wavered at the first discharge from the enemy, but the example and the efforts of the officers soon caused them to return to the attack. The columns of the western and eastern attacks, meeting with some difficulties in reaching the tops of the small houses which formed the walls of the fort, did, by a simultaneous movement to the right and to left, swing northward till the three columns formed one dense mass, which under the guidance of their officers, endeavored to climb the parapet on that side.

This obstacle was at length overcome, the gallant General Juan V. Amador being among the foremost. Meantime the column attacking the southern front under Colonels José Vicente Miñon and José Morales, availing themselves of a shelter, formed by some stone houses near the western salient of that front, boldly took the guns defending it, and penetrated through the embrasures into the square formed by the barracks. There they assisted General Amador, who having captured the enemy's pieces turned them against the doors of the interior houses where the rebels had sought shelter, and from which they fired upon our men in the act of jumping down onto the square or court of the fort. At last they were all destroyed by grape, musket shot and the bayonet.

Our loss was very heavy. Colonel Francisco Duque was mortally wounded at the very beginning, as he lay dying on the ground where he was being trampled by his own men, he still ordered them on to the slaughter. This attack was extremely injudicious and in opposition to military rules, for our own men were exposed not only to the fire of the enemy but also to that of our own columns attacking the other fronts; and our soldiers being formed in close columns, all shots that were aimed too low, struck the backs of our foremost men. The greatest number of our casualties took place in that manner; it may even be affirmed that not one-fourth of our wounded were struck by the enemy's fire, because their cannon, owing to their elevated position, could not be sufficiently lowered to injure our troops after they had reached the foot of the walls. Nor could the defenders use their muskets with accuracy, because the wall having no inner banquette, they had, in order to deliver their fire, to stand on top where they could not live one second.

The official list of casualties, made by General Juan de Andrade, shows: officers 8 killed, 18 wounded; enlisted men 52 killed, 233 wounded. Total 311 killed and wounded. A great many of the wounded died for want of medical attention, beds, shelter, and surgical instruments.

The whole garrison were killed except an old woman and a negro slave for whom the soldiers felt compassion, knowing that they had remained from compulsion alone. There were 150 volunteers, 32 citizens of Gonzales who had introduced themselves into the fort the night previous to the storming, and about 20 citizens or merchants of Bexar.

Considering the disposition made for attack, our loss should have been still greater if all the cannon in the fort could have been placed on the walls, but the houses inside prevented it, and from their situation they could only fire in front. Furthermore, they had not a sufficient number of gunners. Indeed, artillery cannot be improvised as readily as rebellions. Also our movement from the right and the left upon the north front, and the movement executed by Miñón and Morales with their column on the western salient, changing the direction from the southern front as instructed, rendered unavailable the pieces of artillery which the enemy had established on the three other fronts.

Finally, the place remained in the power of the Mexicans, and all the defenders were killed. It is a source of deep regret, that after the excitement of the combat, many acts of atrocity were allowed which are unworthy of the gallantry and resolution with which this operation had been executed, and stamp it with an indelible stain in the annals of history. These acts were reproved at the time by those who had the sorrow to witness them, and subsequently by the whole army, who certainly were not habitually animated by such feelings, and who heard with disgust and horror, as becomes brave and generous Mexicans who feel none but noble and lofty sentiments, of certain facts which I forebear to mention, and wish for the honor of the Mexican Republic had never taken place.

In our opinion the blood of our soldiers as well as that of the enemy was shed in vain, for the mere gratification of the inconsiderate, purile, and guilty vanity of reconquering Bexar by force of arms, and through a bloody contest. As we have said, the defenders of the Alamo, were disposed to surrender, upon the sole condition that their lives should be spared. Let us even grant that they were not so disposed—what could the wretches do, being surrounded by 5,000 men, without proper means of resistance, no possibility of retreating, nor any hope of receiving proper and sufficient reinforcements to compel the Mexicans to raise the siege? Had they been supplied with all the resources needed, that weak enclosure could not have withstood for one hour the fire of our twenty pieces of artillery which if properly directed would have crushed it to atoms and leveled down the inner buildings. . . . The massacres of the Alamo, of Goliad, of Refugio, convinced the rebels that no peacable settlement could be expected, and that they must conquer, or die, or abandon the fruits of ten years of sweat and labor, together with their fondest hopes for the future.

A PROCLAMATION ON PUBLIC EDUCATION FOR NEW MEXICO

[Under normal circumstances, Albino Pérez would probably have been a very satisfactory governor for New Mexico. But the times were far from normal in 1835, when he was appointed to the position. First, Pérez was not a native of New Mexico, a fact resented by most of the residents who had become accustomed to having one of their own chosen for governor. Second, he represented the new centralizing policies of Santa Anna's administration in Mexico City. Part of this centralization program was the direct collection of taxes from the lucrative Santa Fe trade—from which New Mexico officials had been used to pocketing large amounts for themselves. Together with a general decree for taxing the citizens of New Mexico, this direct tariff on the trade route combined with several other grievances to bring about the successful revolt of 1837, in which Governor Pérez and his associates lost their lives and, after a short interim, Manuel Armijo became governor. During 1836, while still in office, Governor Pérez issued a proclamation on the establishment of a public education system, the first such ever issued by a governor of New Mexico. It was a forward-looking document that spoke to a definite need within the province, a need that was not to be supplied adequately for several decades.]

From Ralph Emerson Twitchell, *The Leading Facts of New Mexican History*, Cedar Rapids, Iowa, 1912. Vol. II, pages 57–59.

Ignorance, and idleness, have always been the cause of infinite evil among men in society, and to diminish them, the only remedy and the most efficacious adopted in all countries of the world, is the education of Youth. In this valuable and interesting province securing the good of the people being the principal object, the true lovers of the public weal should attend to this, and it is also the most sacred obligation of the local authorities. This important branch is in a sad state throughout the territory, and more especially in this capital, which by its very nature and elements, does not think profoundly on the means to overcome these false difficulties, which seem by their continuation, to justify the neglect. Running the streets are children who ought to be receiving the education so necessary at the fitting and proper age; youths of evil disposition, abandoned to laziness and licentiousness, practicing vices; useless aims which only serve to corrupt, like the plague, the city that tolerates and feeds them; and above all, what are the results? Robbery, immorality, poverty, desertion, and the most humiliating shame of the city, which if it were cared for by its municipal authorities, should be the enviable example of others composing a most interesting part of the Mexican Nation.

Moved by such salutary reflections, and the love I bear to the inhabitants of this soil, and by the obligation imposed upon me by my position, I issue for the relief of the Royal Municipality the following Plan of Regulation of Public Instruction.

Art. 1. There shall be in this city two schools, particularly of primary instruction, in charge of Masters who may present themselves to conduct them, and who have the proper capacity in the judgment of a commission named by the corporation, which shall examine them in reading, writing, and counting.

2. The schools of the same nature now existing, gone through by heads of families, shall be destroyed, provided always that the Masters who conduct them have not the capacity and the approval required by the preceding article, to which end they may present themselves for examination, in opposition.

3. The Masters shall enjoy such salary or recompense as may be agreed upon with the heads of families, and shall receive pay from those known to be poor, in products of the soil, teaching gratis, orphan children, or those of the absolutely miserable, who have no livelihood or power to pay.

4. All Fathers or Guardians who have children in their care from the age of five to twelve years, are obliged to send them to one of the schools whichever best suits them, and the youths of twelve years or more [must be] in houses of artisans in the different branches of industry, that they may earn a living by honest occupation.

5. Those who fail to comply with the first part of the preceding article, by omission or neglect, shall be required by law, to pay a fine of from, one to five p. according to their means, in the first, double in the second, and triple in the third, and those who are still recalcitrant, and those who cannot pay the fine, shall be punished by law with three days arrest, doubling this punishment in the same way as the pecuniary one.

6. The Youths spoken of in the second part of the fourth article who do not consent to learn a trade, or who have no honest occupation, shall be treated as vagrant or vicious, and be tried and sentenced by the established Court and the laws governing such cases.

7. The Justices of the Wards, the wardens or deputies of the police, may arrest youths of twelve years or over, whom they find in the streets and public places engaged in betting games, at the end of eight days giving notice to one of the magistrates for the recognizance; and the children of twelve or under whom they find behaving ill, they shall take to the school that they may there suffer the same penalty of detention, advising the Master to punish them without fail.

8. Every one or two wards shall form two blocks proportionately, and designated by known names and fixed numbers.

9. To facilitate the better carrying out of this proclamation there shall be in each block a commissioner of Public Instruction, named by three justices unanimously whose duties shall be;

First. To make exact lists of the inhabitants of their blocks, with a statement of ages and occupations by which they live.

Second. To make another list of the children who shall attend the school, and go to each of the two, in order to learn if they are there; an account of the youths who ought to apply themselves to a trade, in what shop and with what Masters, and of the day laborers and where, they work, so that they can certify to the correctness of all this.

Third. To announce, courteously, one, two, or three times, to the fathers of families or guardians of children, what is set forth in the clauses of the preceding articles.

Fourth. To give notice in writing, to the magistrate of the precinct of those who, having been admonished, still do not comply, so that through him, or by advising the judge, the law may inflict the penalty, to which they have made themselves liable.

Fifth. To give notice, in the same manner, of all those living in idleness, who, having been admonished, do not find occupation, declaring all they can testify as to the proper or objectionable habits of the individuals.

Sixth. To give notice also, of any suspicious persons that may be in their blocks, who are spending money without knowing whether they come by it honestly, with the grounds for the suspicion.

Seventh. To visit every month, the schools to which the children go, to learn from the Masters whether they attend, and to get the information for their guidance. Similar visits shall be made to the workshops for the same purpose.

Eighth. They shall make note, in their lists, of the inhabitants who leave their blocks, to what others they go, and of those who come to live in their own.

Ninth. They shall be charged with the cleanliness of the streets and public places in their blocks, giving to the magistrate of the precinct of any neglect they notice.

Art. 10. Any person interfering with the commissioner in the discharge of his duty, shall be punished by a fine of from five to twenty-five p. without prejudice that if the fault be serious, he may be punished according to the laws relating to ordinary transgressions.

11. The duty of a commissioner of Public Instruction shall be a compulsory one, and no one can be excused from discharging it; it is obligatory for six months, without being required to continue, this term completed, until the end of the year, and the magistrates can remove him, for sufficient cause as neglect or bad management, if proven.

12. For any offense committed by the commissioner in the discharge of his duties, he shall be punished by a fine of from ten to thirty p. and deprivation of duty; and if the offence be the concealment of mischievous persons, or the toleration of them without giving notice to the Judges there shall be exacted fifty p. or two months forced labor.

13. This ordinance may be amended in whole or in part when the R. Ayuntamiento may deem proper, being convinced of its advantages or invalidity.

RICHARD HENRY DANA'S CALIFORNIA

[Richard Henry Dana came of an aristocratic Boston family and was intended for the law. But, after two years at Harvard, an attack of measles weakened his eyesight and his doctor recommended a sea voyage. Dana did not take a genteel trip to Europe but instead shipped as an ordinary seaman aboard the brig *Pilgrim*. The vessel left Boston for its long and perilous journey around Cape Horn and to California on August 14, 1834; Dana had just turned twenty. He kept detailed notes of his life as a sailor and of the places he visited, and, in 1840, he published the now classic *Two Years Before the Mast*. Interspersed with this chronicle of a seaman's life are descriptive passages on California, a place more and more Americans were thinking of in the 1840's and for which thousands of them would be heading by 1849. The portions of Dana's book printed here provide a general look at California institutions with special attention to the social life of the province's first families, the Californios. Dana, of course, sees with the eyes of a sophisticated New Englander, but an "Anglo" nonetheless.]

The government of the country is an arbitrary democracy; having no common law, and no judiciary. Their only laws are made and

From R. H. Dana, *Two Years Before the Mast*. New York, n.d. Pages 176–179, 244–252.

unmade at the caprice of the legislature, and are as variable as the legislature itself. They pass through the form of sending representatives to the congress at Mexico, but as it takes several months to go and return, and there is very little communication between the capital and this distant province, a member usually stays there, as permanent member, knowing very well that there will be revolutions at home before he can write and receive an answer; and if another member should be sent, he has only to challenge him, and decide the contested election in that way.

Revolutions are matters of constant occurrence in California. They are got up by men who are at the foot of the ladder and in desperate circumstances, just as a new political party is started by such men in our own country. The only object, of course, is the loaves and fishes; and instead of caucusing, paragraphing, libeling, feasting, promising, and lying, as with us, they take muskets and bayonets, and seizing upon the presidio and customhouse, divide the spoils, and declare a new dynasty. As for justice, they know no law but will and fear.

A Yankee, who had been naturalized, and became a Catholic, and had married in the country, was sitting in his house at the Pueblo de los Angelos, with his wife and children, when a Spaniard, with whom he had had a difficulty, entered the house, and stabbed him to the heart before them all. The murderer was seized by some Yankees who had settled there, and kept in confinement until a statement of the whole affair could be sent to the governor-general. He refused to do anything about it, and the countrymen of the murdered man seeing no prospect of justice being administered made known, that if nothing was done, they should try the man themselves.

It chanced, that, at this time, there was a company of forty trappers, and hunters from Kentucky, with their rifles, who had made their headquarters at the Pueblo; and these, together with the Americans and Englishmen, in the place, who were between twenty and thirty in number, took possession of the town, and waiting a reasonable time, proceeded to try the man according to the forms in their own country. A judge and jury were appointed, and he was tried, convicted, sentenced to be shot, and carried out before the town with his eyes blindfolded. The names of all the men were then put into a hat, and each one pledging himself to perform his duty, twelve names were drawn out, and the men took their stations with their rifles, and firing at the word, laid him dead. He was decently buried, and the place was restored quietly to the proper authorities.

A general, with titles enough for an *hidalgo*, was at San Gabriel, and issued a proclamation as long as the foretop bowline, threatening destruction to the rebels, but never stirred from his fort, for forty Kentucky hunters, with their rifles, were a match for a whole regiment of hungry, drawling, lazy half-breeds. This affair happened while we were at San Pedro (the port of the Pueblo), and we had all the particulars directly from those who were on the spot.

A few months afterwards, another man, whom we had often seen in San Diego, murdered a man and his wife on the highroad between the Pueblo and San Luis Rey, and the foreigners not feeling themselves called upon to act in this case, the parties being all natives, nothing was done about it; and I frequently afterwards saw the murderer in San Diego, where he was living with his wife and family.

When a crime has been committed by Indians, justice, or rather vengeance, is not so tardy. One Sunday afternoon, while I was at San Diego, an Indian was sitting on his horse, when another, with whom he had had some difficulty, came up to him, drew a long knife, and plunged it directly into the horse's heart. The Indian sprung from his falling horse, drew out the knife, and plunged it into the other Indian's breast, over his shoulder, and laid him dead. The poor fellow was seized at once, clapped into the *calabozo*, and kept there until an answer could be received from Monterey.

A few weeks afterwards, I saw the poor wretch, sitting on the bare ground, in front of the *calabozo*, with his feet chained to a stake, and handcuffs about his wrists. I knew there was very little hope for him. Although the deed was done in hot blood, the horse on which he was sitting being his own, and a great favorite, yet he was an Indian, and that was enough. In about a week after I saw him, I heard that he had been shot. These few instances well serve to give one a notion of the distribution of justice in California.

In their domestic relations, these people are no better than in their public. The men are thriftless, proud, and extravagant, and very much given to gaming; and the women have but little education, and a good deal of beauty, and their morality, of course, is none of the best; yet the instances of infidelity are much less frequent than one would at first suppose. In fact, one vice is set over against another; and thus, something like a balance is obtained. The women have but little virtue, but then the jealousy of their husbands is extreme, and their revenge deadly and almost certain. A few inches of cold steel has been the punishment of many an unwary man, who has been guilty, perhaps, of nothing more than indiscretion of manner. The difficulties of the attempt are numerous, and the consequences of discovery fatal.

With the unmarried women too, great watchfulness is used. The main object of the parents is to marry their daughters well, and to this, the slightest slip would be fatal. The sharp eyes of a *duenna*, and the cold steel of a father or brother, are a protection which the characters of most of them—men and women—render by no means useless; for the very men who would lay down their lives to avenge the dishonor of their own family, would risk the same lives to complete the dishonor of another.

Of the poor Indians, very little care is taken. The priests, indeed, at the missions, are said to keep them very strictly, and some rules are usually made by the *alcaldes* to punish their misconduct; but it all amounts to but little. Indeed, to show the entire want of any sense of morality or domestic duty among them, I have frequently known an Indian to bring his wife to whom he was lawfully married in the church, down to the beach, and carry her back again, dividing with her the money which she had got from the sailors.

If any of the girls were discovered by the *alcalde* to be open evil livers, they were whipped, and kept at work sweeping the square of the presidio, and carrying mud and bricks for the buildings; yet a few *reales* would generally buy them off. Intemperance, too, is a common vice among the Indians. The Spaniards, on the contrary, are very abstemious, and I do not remember ever having seen a Spaniard intoxicated.

Such are the people who inhabit a country embracing four or five hundred miles of seacoast, with several good harbors; with fine forests in the north; the waters filled with fish, and the plains covered with thousands of herds of cattle; blessed with a climate, than which there can be no better in the world; free from all manner of diseases, whether epidemic, or endemic; and with a soil in which corn yields from seventy to eighty fold.

In the hands of an enterprising people, what a country this might be, we are ready to say. Yet how long would a people remain so, in such a country? The Americans (as those from the United States are called) and Englishmen, who are fast filling up the principal towns, and getting the trade into their hands, are indeed more industrious and effective than the Spaniards; yet their children are brought up Spaniards, in every respect, and if the "California fever" (laziness) spares the first generation, it always attacks the second. . . .

Wednesday, Jan. 6th. Set sail from Monterey, with a number of Spaniards as passengers, and shaped our course for Santa Barbara. The "Diana" went out of the bay in company with us, but parted from us off Point Pinos, being bound to the Sandwich Islands. We had a smacking breeze for several hours, and went along at a great rate, until night, when it died away, as usual, and the land breeze set in, which brought us upon a taut bowline.

Among our passengers was a young man who was the best representation of a decayed gentleman I had ever seen. He reminded me much of some of the characters in "Gil Blas." He was of the aristocracy of the country, his family being of pure Spanish blood, and once of great importance in Mexico. His father had been governor of the province, and having amassed a large property, settled at San Diego, where he built a large house with a courtyard in front, kept a great retinue of Indians, and set up for the grandee of that part of the country. His son was sent to Mexico, where he received the best education and went into the first society of the capital.

Misfortune, extravagance, and the want of funds, or any manner

of getting interest on money, soon ate the estate up, and Don Juan
Bandini returned from Mexico accomplished, poor, and proud, and
without any office or occupation, to lead the life of most young
men of the better families—dissolute and extravagant when the
means are at hand; ambitious at heart, and impotent in act; often
pinched for bread; keeping up an appearance of style, when their
poverty is known to each half-naked Indian boy in the street, and
they stand in dread of every small trader and shopkeeper in the
place.

He had a slight and elegant figure, moved gracefully, danced
and waltzed beautifully, spoke the best Castilian, with a pleasant
and refined voice and accent, and had, throughout, the bearing of
a man of high birth and figure. Yet here he was, with his passage
given him (as I afterward learned), for he had not the means of
paying for it, and living upon the charity of our agent.

He was polite to everyone, spoke to the sailors, and gave four
reales—I dare say the last he had in his pocket—to the steward
who waited upon him. I could not but feel a pity for him, especially
when I saw him by the side of his fellow passenger and townsman,
a fat, coarse, vulgar, pretending fellow of a Yankee trader, who had
made money in San Diego, and who was eating out the very vitals
of the Bandinis, fattening upon their extravagance, grinding them
in their poverty; having mortgages on their lands, forestalling their
cattle, and already making an inroad upon their jewels, which were
their last hope.

Don Juan had with him a retainer, who was as much like many
of the characters in "Gil Blas" as his master. He called himself a
private secretary, though there was no writing for him to do, and
he lived in the steerage with the carpenter and sailmaker. He was
certainly a character; could read and write extremely well; spoke
good Spanish: had been all over Spanish America, and lived in every
possible situation, and served in every conceivable capacity, though
generally in that of confidential servant to some man of figure.

I cultivated this man's acquaintance, and during the five weeks
that he was with us—for he remained on board until we arrived at
San Diego—I gained a greater knowledge of the state of political
parties in Mexico, and the habits and affairs of the different classes
of society, than I could have learned from almost anyone else.

He took great pains in correcting my Spanish, and supplying me
with colloquial phrases, and common terms and exclamations in
speaking. He lent me a file of late newspapers from the City of
Mexico, which were full of the triumphal reception of Santa Ana,
who had just returned from Tampico after a victory, and with the
preparations for his expedition against the Texans. *"Viva Santa
Ana!"* was the byword everywhere, and it had even reached California, though there were still many here, among whom was Don
Juan Bandini, who were opposed to his government, and intriguing
to bring in Bustamente. Santa Ana, they said, was for breaking
down the missions; or, as they termed it—"Santa Ana *no quiere*

religion." Yet I had no doubt that the office of administrator of San Diego would reconcile Don Juan to any dynasty, and any state of the church. In these papers, too, I found scraps of American and English news; but which were so unconnected, and I was so ignorant of everything preceding them for eighteen months past, that they could not satisfy. One article spoke of Taney as *Justicia Mayor de los Estados Unidos* (what had become of Marshall? was he dead, or banished?), and another made known, by news received from Vera Cruz, that *"El Vizconde* Melbourne" had returned to the office of *"primer ministro,"* in place of Sir Roberto Peel. (Sir Robert Peel had been minister, then? and where were Earl Grey and the Duke of Wellington?) Here were the outlines of a grand parliamentary overturn, the filling up which I could imagine at my leisure. . . .

Sunday, January 10th. Arrived at Santa Barbara, and on the following Wednesday slipped our cable and went to sea, on account of a southeaster. Returned to our anchorage the next day. We were the only vessel in the port. The "Pilgrim" had passed through the Canal and hove to off the town, nearly six weeks before, on her passage down from Monterey, and was now at the leeward. She heard here of our safe arrival at San Francisco.

Great preparations were making on shore for the marriage of our agent, who was to marry Doña Anneta De G____ De N____y C____, youngest daughter of Don Antonio N____, the grandee of the place, and the head of the first family in California. Our steward was ashore three days, making pastry and cake, and some of our stores were sent off with him.

On the day appointed for the wedding, we took the captain ashore in the gig, and had orders to come for him at night, with leave to go up to the house and see the *fandango.* Returning on board we found preparations making for a salute. Our guns were loaded and run out, men appointed to each, cartridges served out, matches lighted, and all the flags ready to be run up. I took my place at the starboard after-gun, and we all waited for the signal from on shore.

At ten o'clock the bride went up with her sister to the confessional, dressed in deep black. Nearly an hour intervened, when the great doors of the mission church opened, the bells rang out a long discordant peal, the private signal for us was run up by the captain ashore, the bride, dressed in complete white, came out of the church with the bridegroom, followed by a long procession.

Just as she stepped from the church door, a small white cloud issued from the bows of our ship, which was full in sight, the loud report echoed among the surrounding hills and over the bay, and instantly the ship was dressed in flags and pennants from stem to stern. Twenty-three guns followed in regular succession, with an interval of fifteen seconds between each, when the cloud cleared away, and the ship lay dressed in her colors, all day.

At sundown, another salute of the same number of guns was fired, and all the flags run down. This we thought was pretty well—

a gun every fifteen seconds—for a merchantman with only four guns and a dozen or twenty men.

After supper, the gig's crew was called, and we rowed ashore, dressed in our uniform, beached the boat, and went up to the *fandango*. The bride's father's house was the principal one in the place, with a large court in front upon which a tent was built, capable of containing several hundred people.

As we drew near, we heard the accustomed sound of violins and guitars, and saw a great motion of the people within. Going in, we found nearly all the people of the town—men, women, and children —collected and crowded together, leaving barely room for the dancers for on these occasions no invitations are given, but everyone is expected to come, though there is always a private entertainment within the house for particular friends.

The old women sat down in rows, clapping their hands to the music, and applauding the young ones. The music was lively, and among the tunes, we recognized several of our popular airs, which we, without doubt, have taken from the Spanish.

In the dancing, I was much disappointed. The women stood upright, with their hands down by their sides, their eyes fixed upon the ground before them, and slided about without any perceptible means of motion; for their feet were invisible, the hem of their dresses forming a perfect circle about them, reaching to the ground. They looked as grave as though they were going through some religious ceremony, their faces as little excited as their limbs; and on the whole, instead of the spirited, fascinating Spanish dances which I had expected, I found the Californian *fandango*, on the part of the women at least, a lifeless affair.

The men did better. They danced with grace and spirit, moving in circles round their nearly stationary partners, and showing their figures to great advantage.

A great deal was said about our friend Don Juan Bandini, and when he did appear, which was toward the close of the evening, he certainly gave us the most graceful dancing that I had ever seen. He was dressed in white pantaloons, neatly made, a short jacket of dark silk, gayly white stockings and thin morocco slippers upon his very small feet.

His slight and graceful figure was well calculated for dancing, and he moved about with the grace and daintiness of a young fawn. An occasional touch of the toe to the ground, seemed all that was necessary to give him a long interval of motion in the air. At the same time he was not fantastic or flourishing, but appeared to be rather repressing a strong tendency to motion. He was loudly applauded, and danced frequently toward the close of the evening.

After the supper the waltzing began, which was confined to a very few of the *gente de razón*, and was considered a high accomplishment, and a mark of aristocracy.

Here, too, Don Juan figured greatly, waltzing with the sister of

the bride (Doña Angustia, a handsome woman and a general favorite) in a variety of beautiful, but to me, offensive figures, which
lasted as much as half an hour, no one else taking the floor. They
were repeatedly and loudly applauded, the old men and women
jumping out of their seats in admiration, and the young people
waving their hats and handkerchiefs. Indeed, among people of the
character of those Mexicans, the waltz seemed to me to have found
its right place.

The great amusement of the evening—which I suppose was owing
to its being carnival—was the breaking of eggs filled with cologne,
or other essences, upon the heads of the company. One end of the
egg is broken and the inside taken out, then it is partly filled with
cologne, and the whole sealed up.

The women bring a great number of these secretly about them,
and the amusement is to break one upon the head of a gentleman
when his back is turned. He is bound in gallantry to find out the
lady and return the compliment, though it must not be done if the
person sees you.

A tall, stately Don, with immense gray whiskers, and a look of
great importance, was standing before me, when I felt a light hand
on my shoulder, and turning around, saw Doña Angustia (whom
all knew, as she had been up to Monterey, and down again, in the
"Alert,") with her finger upon her lip, motioning me gently aside. I
stepped back a little, when she went up behind the Don, and with
one hand knocked off his huge *sombrero*, and at the same instant
with the other broke the egg upon his head, and springing behind
me, was out of sight in a moment.

The Don turned slowly round, the cologne running down his face,
and over his clothes, and a loud laugh breaking out from every
quarter. He looked around in vain for some time, until the direction
of so many laughing eyes showed him the fair offender. She was his
niece, and a great favorite with him, so old Don Domingo had to
join in the laugh.

A great many such tricks were played, and many a war of sharp
maneuvering was carried on between couples of the younger people,
and at every successful exploit a general laugh was raised.

Another singular custom I was for some time at a loss about.
A pretty young girl was dancing, named, after what would appear
to us the sacrilegious custom of the country—Espíritu Santo, when
a young man went behind her and placed his hat directly upon her
head, letting it fall down over her eyes, and sprung back among the
crowd. She danced for some time with the hat on, when she threw
it off, which called forth a general shout; and the young man was
obliged to go out upon the floor and pick it up.

Some of the ladies, upon whose heads hats had been placed,
threw them off at once, and a few kept them on throughout the
dance, and took them off at the end, and held them out in their
hands, when the owner stepped out, bowed, and took it from them.

I soon began to suspect the the meaning of the thing, and was afterward told that it was a compliment, and an offer to become the lady's gallant for the rest of the evening, and to wait upon her home. If the hat was thrown off, the offer was refused, and the gentleman was obliged to pick up his hat amid a general laugh.

Much amusement was caused sometimes by gentlemen putting hats on the ladies' heads, without permitting them to see whom it was done by. This obliged them to throw them off, or keep them on at a venture, and when they came to discover the owner the laugh was often turned upon them.

The captain sent for us about ten o'clock, and we went aboard in high spirits, having enjoyed the new scene much, and were of great importance among the crew, from having so much to tell, and from the prospect of going every night until it was over; for these *fandangos* generally last three days.

The next day, two of us were sent up to the town, and took care to come back by way of Captain Noriego's, and take a look into the booth. The musicians were still there, upon their platform, scraping and twanging away, and a few people, apparently of the lower classes, were dancing. The dancing is kept up at intervals, throughout the day, but the crowd, the spirit, and the *élite*, come in at night.

The next night, which was the last, we went ashore in the same manner, until we got almost tired of the monotonous twang of the instruments, the drawling sounds which the women kept up, as an accompaniment, and the slapping of the hands in time with the music, in place of castanets.

We found ourselves as great objects of attention as any persons or anything at the place. Our sailor dresses—and we took great pains to have them neat and shipshape—were much admired, and we were invited, from every quarter, to give them an American sailor's dance; but after the ridiculous figure some of our country-men cut, in dancing after the Spaniards, we thought it best to leave it to their imaginations.

Our agent, with a tight, black, swallow-tailed coat, just imported from Boston, a high stiff cravat, looking as if he had been pinned and skewered, with only his feet and hands left free, took the floor just after Bandini; and we thought they had had enough of Yankee grace.

The last night they kept it up in great style, and were getting into a high go when the captain called us off to go aboard, for, it being southeaster season, he was afraid to remain on shore long; and it was well he did not, for that very night, we slipped our cables, as a crowner to our fun ashore, and stood off before a southeaster, which lasted twelve hours, and returned to our anchorage the next day.

A SANTA FE TRADER LOOKS AT NEW MEXICO

[The Santa Fe trade began about 1822, along a route from Independence, Missouri, through Council Grove, Arkansas, to Cimarron Spring and Las Vegas and on into the capital of New Mexico. Because of this commercial contact with the United States, New Mexico went through a small economic revolution. For the first time, the province was able to receive an adequate supply of goods from the outside world at a cheaper rate than they could be brought from Mexico, and the trade was also an outlet for the region's own products. Apart from the commercial aspects, the trade also meant the arrival of numerous Americans, many of whom settled in Santa Fe. Thus, New Mexico, like Texas and California, gained a population whose loyalties were not to Mexico and whose social and religious institutions were at variance with those of the older inhabitants. One of the American Santa Fe traders was James Josiah Webb, who first arrived in New Mexico in October, 1844, two years before the Mexican War. In an autobiographical work describing his three years in the trade, he wrote the following account of people and institutions in Santa Fe.]

From James Josiah Webb, *Adventures in the Santa Fe Trade, 1844–1847*, Ralph P. Bieber, ed. Glendale, California, 1931. Pages 91–104.

My first arrival in Santa Fé was in October after a journey of seventy days, which at that time was not considered a specially long trip. My first impressions I can but imperfectly describe after the lapse of so long a time—forty years—but I well remember that there was nothing to induce me to entertain a desire to become a resident or to continue in the trade except as an adventurer and the possible advantages the trade might afford of bettering my fortune. The people were nearly all in extreme poverty, and there were absolutely none who could be classed as wealthy except by comparison. The Pinos and Ortizes were considered the *ricos*, and those most respected as leaders in society and political influence; but idleness, gambling, and the Indians had made such inroads upon their means and influence that there was but little left except the reputation of honorable descent from a wealthy and distinguished ancestry. The houses were nearly all old and dilapidated, the streets narrow and filthy, and the people, when in best attire, not half dressed. And even those who could occasionally afford a new and expensive dress, would make it up in such a way that it would appear extravagantly ridiculous.

There were but a very few houses north of the Palace on the street now called Palace avenue. Don Agustín Durán, Don Félix García, Don Antonio Sena y Baca, and James Conklin and one or two others lived not far from where the Presbyterian church now stands and had quite grand houses for the time; and some of them [had] two or three acres cultivated in corn, beans, and red peppers, and a few apricot trees, the only fruit then raised in the town. There were three residences on Palace avenue, extending from the corner of Washington street towards the *ciénaga*, in one of which we quartered for a few days when we first arrived, and where I afterwards lived a year with my family, owned by Don Juan Sena. The northeast corner of the plaza was the government storehouse, or *lóndiga*, devoted in ancient times to the storage of corn by [the] government to sell to the poor and improvident in time of necessity, but this year used as a government warehouse to store our goods while being examined by the customhouse officers. . . .

The west side of the plaza was nearly all residences. Near the center was the post-office, where a mail sometimes arrived from the south, and also the *estanquillo*, where the government sold a limited amount of cigars and tobacco. There were but a few houses on the *loma* south of the river. The principal one was owned and occupied by "Old Taosenian"; and he used to give a *fandango* once or more a week, according to the number of strangers visiting the city and the demand for amusement.

A Mexican *fandango* in those days was a curiosity. The *sala*, or dancing hall, [was] from twenty to thirty feet long, and fifteen to eighteen feet wide, with sometimes benches on the sides (but frequently without seats of any kind) and packed full, only leaving sufficient space through the center for the couples to waltz through, up and down. When the dance began, the men would place themselves in line on one side, and when the line was complete, the women would begin to rise and take their positions opposite the men, almost always in regular order without manifesting any choice of partners; and when the numbers were equal, the music would strike up and the dance proceed.

I have witnessed some most ludicrous scenes at these *fandangos*. It was not anything uncommon or surprising to see the most elaborately dressed and aristocratic woman at the ball dancing with a peon dressed only in his shirt and trousers open from the hip down, with very wide and full drawers underneath, and frequently barefoot, but usually with moccasins. And such disparity of ages! On one occasion I saw at a ball given by Governor Armijo an old man of eighty or over dancing with a child not over eight or ten. I could not help the reflection that it was a dance of the cradle and the grave. They do literally dance from the cradle to the grave. And I have never seen anything lascivious or [any] want of decorum and self-respect in any woman in a *fandango*, whatever might be her reputation for virtue outside. I have known of disorders and serious brawls in *fandangos*, but it was almost invariably where Americans and whiskey were found in profusion. . . .

I forgot to say, while speaking of the Pinos and the Ortizes, that Don [Pedro Bautista] Pino, the father of Don Miguel and Don Facundo Pino, was much beloved and honored by the early traders, having proved a true and trusted friend to them in all their business and social relations, and one on whom they could rely for counsel and assistance in all dealings with the authorities. Mr. Vaughn often spoke of him with the highest respect and admiration, and to illustrate the esteem in which he was held by the Americans, delighted in relating a dream of an old trader who was quite a wag and related by him the day after the funeral of his old friend. It was the habit to close the stores from twelve till two every day for dinner and siesta, and the Americans would meet at one of their places of business to talk over various matters and have a social chat. This wag came in one day, and Mr. Pino's death coming up as the subject of conversation, he said he had a very peculiar dream the night before, and it had made such an impression on his mind [that] he must be excused for relating it.

"I dreamed," said he, "that I died, and was transported directly to the gates of Paradise. On arriving, I knocked at the door and was admitted by St. Peter in person, and invited into the anteroom for examination. There were many ahead of me, and among them Mr. Pino. When his turn came, St. Peter asked his name and where he was from. He replied

" 'My name is [Pedro Bautista] Pino, from New Mexico.'

" 'How dare you attempt such a trick upon me?' said St. Peter. 'You are a fraud and an imposter. There is no such a place on earth as New Mexico. Go to your place, where you will find plenty of company of your kind.'

CLa relacion que oio Aluar nu=
ñez cabeça de vaca oe lo acaefcido enlas Jndias
enla armada oonde yua po2 gouernado2 ɲ̃
philo oe narbac3 oefde el año oe veynt
y fiete hafta el año o treynta y feys
que boluio a Seuilla con tres
oe fu compañia.:.

Title Page of Cabeza de Vaca's Report

Álvar Núñez Cabeza de Vaca was one of the few survivors of the ill-fated expedition led by Pánifilo de Narváez that reached Florida in 1528. The amazing stories he told of his captivity and travels among the Indians in the areas north of Mexico inspired Spanish authorities to send out expeditions to explore much of what now constitutes the American Southwest. Above is the title page of the report delivered to the King of Spain in 1542.

Spanish Monastery in California in 1769

Spain's earliest settlement in the Southwest was in New Mexico. Juan de Oñate founded the first colony there in 1598. But it was not until the early eighteenth century that serious attempts were made to establish a colony in Texas, which never really prospered and was almost totally neglected once the French threat to Spanish territories was removed by the Louisiana Purchase. On the other hand, the California province, founded as a mission colony in 1769, flourished, largely because of the Franciscans' concern for temporal as well as spiritual matters.

N. Y. Public Library Picture Collection

Old Engraving of the Mission of Monterey in 1792

One of the earliest sites of Spanish presence in California was Monterey. Juan Rodríguez de Cabrillo visited the area in 1542, and, in 1602, Sebastian Vizcaíno named it in honor of the count of Monte Rey, governor of New Spain. In 1770, Father Junípero Serra, who arrived with the expedition of Gaspar de Portolá, established the mission of San Carlos Borromeo and later made Monterey the headquarters for his missionary activities throughout upper California.

New York Public Library
Picture Collection

Father Junípero Serra

The Bettmann Archive

Don Pío Pico, Last Mexican Governor of California

American settlers began arriving in California in 1840. At first, they were respected and well received. But, before long, they were in almost complete control of some areas in the inner valley and were in positions of great influence in many cities on the coast. Mexicans began to speak of a Yankee threat. In 1846, just before the outbreak of the Mexican-American War, Don Pío Pico, the last Mexican governor of California, wrote, "We find ourselves suddenly threatened by hordes of Yankee emigrants . . . whose progress we cannot arrest."

VOLUNTEERS!

Men of the Granite State!
Men of Old Rockingham!! the
strawberry-bed of patriotism, renowned for bravery and devotion to Country, rally at this call. Santa Anna, reeking with the generous confidence and magnanimity of your countrymen, is in arms, eager to plunge his traitor-dagger in their bosoms. To arms, then, and rush to the standard of the fearless and gallant CUSHING---put to the blush the dastardly meanness and rank toryism of Massachusetts. Let the half civilized Mexicans hear the crack of the unerring New Hampshire rifleman, and illustrate on the plains of San Luis Potosi, the fierce, determined, and undaunted bravery that has always characterized her sons.

Col. THEODORE F. ROWE, at No. 31 Daniel-street, is authorized and will enlist men this week for the Massachusetts Regiment of Volunteers. The compensation is $10 per month---$30 in advance. Congress will grant a handsome bounty in money and ONE HUNDRED AND SIXTY ACRES OF LAND.

Portsmouth, Feb. 2. 1847.

Mexican War Recruiting Poster

From the beginning of Anglo-American settlement in Texas, there had been strong sentiment in favor of union with the United States. During the nearly ten years that Texas was an independent republic, this sentiment continued to grow and created friction between the United States and Mexico, which had never accepted the loss of Texas as final. On March 2, 1845, Texas was formally annexed, and, a year later, the U.S. Congress issued a declaration of war with Mexico. The doctrine of Manifest Destiny, which had been invoked to support annexation of Texas, was soon used to advocate acquisition of not only New Mexico and California, which the United States had tried unsuccessfully to purchase, but all of Mexico.

The Bettmann Archive

A Mexican Lancer, *ca.* 1847

The treaty of Guadalupe Hidalgo, which ended the Mexican War in 1848, ceded to the United States vast blocks of territory that now include New Mexico, Colorado, Utah, Nevada, Arizona, and California. It brought about a change among a people who had preserved many Spanish traditions and adopted many customs of the Indians. And proud figures such as this lancer found themselves second-class citizens in a foreign land.

"Mr. Pino gently reminded him that there was such a place, that he had just arrived from there, and [that] if he had a map handy, he would show it to him—in the mountains truly, and far distant from any other christian population. St. Peter took him to a map, where he showed him New Mexico plainly laid down and the location of many christian churches. St. Peter looked astonished and confounded that there should be such a place and he not know it, but finally excused himself by saying that on reflection his mistake was not so singular after all, as he was the first person that ever came from there, and this was the first occasion he had ever had to refer to it on the map—then very blandly opened the door and allowed him to pass in without further questioning."

A look at the resources of the country was not encouraging. The only products, beyond the immediate needs of the people, were wool (which would not pay transportation), a few furs, a very few deerskins, and the products of the gold mines, which did not amount to more than $200,000 a year when in bonanza, and very seldom to anything near that amount. Another resource of the country was from the proceeds of sheep driven to the low country in large flocks (amounting to from 50,000 to 100,000 a year), the proceeds from which would be in the hands of a very few of the *ricos.* And the only chance I could see of getting any portion of it was from the little that might be in the hands of a very few who might want to start a little store and had not yet got in the way of going to "the States" for goods, or [who] might indulge in the national propensity of gambling and thus put some portion of it into general circulation.

The system of peonage, or voluntary servitude, was a fixed institution. The wages of the laborers was only from three to six dollars a month, and a ration to the laborer only. From this he would have to support his family and pay the dues to the priest for marrying, baptizing, and burial of seven dollars and upwards, according to the ability and ambition of the individual desiring the services. An inflexible rule with the priests was: no money, no marrying; no money, [no] baptizing; no money, no burying. Or as they put it: *no haya dinero, no hay casamiento; no haya dinero, no hay bautismo; no haya dinero, no hay entierro.* As a consequence the poor were extremely so, and without hope of bettering their condition. The priesthood [was] corrupt, vicious, and improvident. Is it strange, then, that with such a heartless, demoralized, and utterly impious, yet very religious, priesthood, the people in such abject poverty could see no merit in virtue or honesty?

In a conversation with Dr. Connolly some years after the establishment of the Territorial government, and after his marriage to the widow Chávez, he was boasting of the improved condition of his servants under his liberal management. He had raised the wages of his shepherds from two and three, to four and six, dollars a month, and the peons on the hacienda to six and eight, and teamsters with his wagon train to ten; and some of the best and most industrious laborers he had allowed to work a portion of the land on shares. And he flattered himself that he was treating them with great generosity and kindness, and was doing more to improve the condition of his servants than any of his neighbors.

"Well, doctor," [I said], "how many servants have you on your hacienda?"

"Big and little, 108."

"Well, I suppose you furnish them all [with] work through the winter?"

"Oh no. The crops are all gathered and stored, and I have no further work for them until time to plant the [?]."

"Of course they have a good store of corn and other provisions laid up for the winter?"

"Not an ear—not a thing."

"But how are they to live with nothing in store, and nothing to do to earn a living?"

He saw the point, and laughingly replied, *Steal from Otero.*"

"And how are Otero's servants to live, who you said were not as well cared for as yours?"

"Oh, they will steal from me—if they have the chance. It is considered dishonorable to steal from the master, but neighborly stealing is no disgrace."

This was the condition of the laboring classes of old New Mexico, and in view of the example set by the religious fathers, and their entire dependence upon their masters, is it strange [that] they were, as John Randolph very truly but uncharitably called them, "a blanketed nation of prostitutes and thieves?" Let us withhold our denunciations until we in imagination have put ourselves in their places, and ask ourselves what we would do. We can and ought to thank God that in mercy He placed us [in] a christian land under a free and liberal government, and under pious and moral teachings, where honest labor is liberally rewarded and there is no necessity of resorting to immoral or dishonest practices to live in comfort and decency. Let us watch and pray lest we be led astray by false doctrines of religious and political teachers, and fall into a like condition or entail it upon posterity.

THE TREATY OF GUADALUPE HIDALGO

[Reading the Treaty of Guadalupe Hidalgo, which ended the Mexican War in the light of the events of the past century and a quarter provides illuminating insights into the sorry performance of the United States in adhering to the treaty provisions. To say that the treaty had been honored *only* in the breach is an exaggeration, because the religious rights of the Mexican Americans have been fairly consistently protected. But in no other area have their rights been paid much heed. As the only minority, apart from the Indians, ever acquired by conquest, the Mexican Americans have been subjected to economic, social, and political discrimination, as well as a great deal of violence at the hands of their Anglo conquerors. During the period from 1865 to 1920, there were more lynchings of Mexican Americans in the Southwest than of black Americans in the Southeast. But the worst violence has been the unrelenting discrimination against the cultural heritage—the language and customs—of the Mexican Americans, coupled with the economic exploitation of the entire group. Property rights were guaranteed, but not protected, by either the federal or state governments. Equal protection under law has consistently been a mockery in the Mexican-American communities. Economically, the Mexican Americans have been relegated, both legally and by informal arrangement, to the bottom of the labor ladder. Yet, for all of the inequities perpetrated upon the Mexican Americans, the Treaty of Guadalupe remains the key document for the understanding of the place of this minority within American society. The fact that most of its provisions remain to be fulfilled is both the complaint and the hope of Mexican Americans, as the movement

From Hunter Miller, ed., *Treaties and Other International Acts of the United States of America.* Washington, D.C., 1937. Vol. V, pages 207–236.

toward social justice slowly gains ground in the United States among those for whom the rewards of American life have been all too meager.

The treaty was concluded on February 2, 1848, between Nicholas Trist, for the United States, and representatives of the Mexican government. By it, Mexico gave up all claims to Texas and sold the rest of the Southwest, including Arizona, California, New Mexico, Utah, Nevada, and part of Colorado, for $15,000,000 to the United States.]

In the name of Almighty God:

The United States of America, and the United Mexican States, animated by a sincere desire to put an end to the calamities of the war which unhappily exists between the two Republics, and to establish upon a solid basis relations of peace and friendship, which shall confer reciprocal benefits upon the citizens of both, and assure the concord, harmony and mutual confidence, wherein the two peoples should live, as good neighbours, have for that purpose appointed their respective Plenipotentiaries: that is to say, the President of the United States has appointed Nicholas P. Trist, a citizen of the United States, and the President of the Mexican Republic has appointed Don Luis Gonzaga Cuevas, Don Bernardo Couto, and Don Miguel Atristain, citizens of the said Republic; who, after a reciprocal communication of their respective full powers, have, under the protection of Almighty God, the author of Peace, arranged, agreed upon, and signed the following

Treaty of Peace, Friendship, Limits and Settlement between the United States of America and the Mexican Republic.

Article I.

There shall be firm and universal peace between the United States of America and the Mexican Republic, and between their respective countries, territories, cities, towns and people, without exception of places or persons.

Article II.

Immediately upon the signature of this Treaty, a convention shall be entered into between a Commissioner or Commissioners appointed by the General in Chief of the forces of the United States, and such as may be appointed by the Mexican Government, to the end that a provisional suspension of hostilities shall take place, and that, in the places occupied by the said forces, constitutional order may be reestablished, as regards the political, administrative, and judicial branches, so far as this shall be permitted by the circumstances of military occupation. . . .

Article V.

The Boundary line between the two Republics shall commence in the Gulf of Mexico, three leagues from land, opposite the mouth of the Rio Grande, otherwise called Rio Bravo del Norte, or opposite the mouth of it's deepest branch, if it should have more than one branch emptying directly into the sea; from thence, up the middle of that river, following the deepest channel, where it has more than one, to the point where it strikes the southern boundary of New Mexico; thence, westwardly, along the whole southern boundary of New Mexico (which runs north of the town called *Paso*) to it's western termination; thence, northward, along the western line of New Mexico, until it intersects the first branch of the river Gila; (or if it should not intersect any branch of that river, then, to the point on the said line nearest to such branch, and thence in a direct line to the same;) thence down the middle of the said branch and of the said river, until it empties into the Rio Colorado; thence, across the Rio Colorado, following the division line between Upper and Lower California, to the Pacific Ocean.

The southern and western limits of New Mexico, mentioned in this Article, are those laid down in the Map, entitled *"Map of the United Mexican States, as organized and defined by various acts of the Congress of said Republic, and constructed according to the best Authorities. Revised Edition. Published at New York in 1847 by J. Disturnell:"* of which Map a Copy is added to this treaty, bearing the signatures and seals of the Undersigned Plenipotentiaries. And, in order to preclude all difficulty in tracing upon the ground the limit separating Upper from Lower California, it is agreed that the said limit shall consist of a straight line, drawn from the middle of the Rio Gila, where it unites with the Colorado, to a point on the coast of the Pacific Ocean, distant one marine league due south of the southernmost point of the Port of San Diego, according to the plan of said port, made in the year 1782 by Don Juan Pantoja, second sailing master of the Spanish fleet, and published at Madrid in the year 1802, in the Atlas to the voyage of the schooners *Sutil* and *Mexicana:* of which plan a copy is hereunto added, signed and sealed by the respective plenipotentiaries.

In order to designate the Boundary line with due precision, upon authoritative maps, and to establish upon the ground landmarks which shall allow the limits of both Republics, as described in the present Article, the two Governments shall each appoint a Commissioner and a Surveyor, who, before the expiration of one year from the date of the exchange of ratifications of this treaty, shall meet at the Port of San Diego, and proceed to run and mark the said boundary in it's whole course, to the Mouth of the Rio Bravo del Norte. They shall keep journals and make out plans of their operations; and the result, agreed upon by them, shall be deemed a part of this Treaty, and shall have the same force as if it were inserted therein. The two Governments will amicably agree regarding what may be necessary to these persons, and also as to their respective escorts, should such be necessary.

The Boundary line established by this Article shall be religiously respected by each of the two Republics, and no change shall ever be made therein, except by the express and free consent of both nations, lawfully given by the General Government of each, in conformity with it's own constitution.

Article VI.

The Vessels and citizens of the United States shall, in all time, have a free and uninterrupted passage by the Gulf of California, and by the River Colorado below it's confluence with the Gila, to and from their possessions situated north of the Boundary line defined in the preceding Article: it being understood, that this passage is to be by navigating the Gulf of California and the River Colorado, and not by land, without the express consent of the Mexican Government.

If, by the examinations which may be made, it should be ascertained to be practicable and advantageous to construct a road, canal or railway, which should, in whole or in part, run upon the river Gila, or upon it's right or it's left bank, within the space of one marine league from either margin of the river, the Governments of both Republics will form an agreement regarding it's construction, in order that it may serve equally for the use and advantage of both countries.

Article VII.

The river Gila, and the part of the Rio Bravo del Norte lying below the southern boundary of New Mexico, being, agreeably to the fifth Article, divided in the middle between the two Republics, the navigation of the Gila and of the Bravo below said boundary shall be free and common to the vessels and citizens of both countries; and neither shall, without the consent of the other, construct any work that may impede or interrupt, in whole or in part, the exercise of this right: not even for the purpose of favouring new methods of navigation. Nor shall any tax or contribution, under any denomination or title, be levied upon vessels or persons navigating the same, or upon merchandise or effects transported thereon, except in the case of landing upon one of their shores. If, for the purpose of making the said rivers navigable, or for maintaining them in such state, it should be necessary or advantageous to establish any tax or contribution, this shall not be done without the consent of both Governments.

The stipulations contained in the present Article shall not impair the territorial rights of either Republic, within it's established limits.

Article VIII.

Mexicans now established in territories previously belonging to Mexico, and which remain for the future within the limits of the United States, as defined by the present treaty, shall be free to continue where they now reside, or to remove at any time to the Mexican Republic, retaining the property which they possess in the said territories, or disposing thereof, and removing the proceeds wherever they please; without their being subjected, on this account, to any contribution, tax or charge whatever.

Those who shall prefer to remain in the said territories, may either retain the title and rights of Mexican citizens, or acquire those of citizens of the United States. But they shall be under the obligation to make their election within one year from the date of the exchange of ratifications of this treaty: and those who shall remain in the said territories, after the expiration of that year, without having declared their intention to retain the character of Mexicans, shall be considered to have elected to become citizens of the United States.

In the said territories, property of every kind, now belonging to Mexicans, not established there, shall be inviolably respected. The present owners, the heirs of these, and all Mexicans who may hereafter acquire said property by contract, shall enjoy with respect to it, guaranties equally ample as if the same belonged to citizens of the United States.

Article IX.

The Mexicans who, in the territories aforesaid, shall not preserve the character of citizens of the Mexican Republic, conformably with what is stipulated in the preceding article, shall be incorporated into the Union of the United States and be admitted, at the proper time (to be judged of by the Congress of the United States) to the enjoyment of all the rights of citizens of the United States according to the principles of the Constitution; and in the mean time shall be maintained and protected in the free enjoyment of their liberty and property, and secured in the free exercise of their religion without restriction.

[One of the amendments of the Senate struck out Article 10.]

Article XI.

Considering that a great part of the territories which, by the present Treaty, are to be comprehended for the future within the limits of the United States, is now occupied by savage tribes, who will hereafter be under the exclusive controul of the Government of the United States, and whose incursions within the territory of Mexico would be prejudicial in the extreme; it is solemnly agreed that all such incursions shall be forcibly restrained by the Government of the United States, whensoever this may be necessary; and that when they cannot be prevented, they shall be punished by the said Government, and satisfaction for the same shall be exacted: all in the same way, and with equal diligence and energy, as if the same incursions were meditated or committed within it's own territory against it's own citizens.

It shall not be lawful, under any pretext whatever, for any inhabitant of the United States, to purchase or acquire any Mexican or any foreigner residing in Mexico, who may have been captured by Indians inhabiting the territory of either of the two Republics, nor to purchase or acquire horses, mules, cattle or property of any kind, stolen within Mexican territory by such Indians.

And, in the event of any person or persons, captured within Mexican Territory by Indians, being carried into the territory of the United States, the Government of the latter engages and binds itself in the most solemn manner, so soon as it shall know of such captives being within it's territory, and shall be able so to do, through the faithful exercise of it's influence and power, to rescue them and return them to their country, or deliver them to the agent or representative of the Mexican Government. The Mexican Authorities will, as far as practicable, give to the Government of the United States notice of such captures; and it's agent shall pay the expenses incurred in the maintenance and transmission of the rescued captives; who, in the mean time, shall be treated with the utmost hospitality by the American authorities at the place where they may be. But if the Government of the United States, before receiving such notice from Mexico, should obtain intelligence through any other channel, of the existence of Mexican captives within it's territory, it will proceed forthwith to effect their release and delivery to the Mexican agent, as above stipulated.

For the purpose of giving to these stipulations the fullest possible efficacy, thereby affording the security and redress demanded by their true spirit and intent, the Government of the United States will now and hereafter pass, without unnecessary delay, and always vigilantly enforce, such laws as the nature of the subject may require. And finally, the sacredness of this obligation shall never be lost sight of by the said Government, when providing for the removal of the Indians from any portion of the said territories, or for it's being settled by citizens of the United States; but on the contrary special care shall then be taken not to place it's Indian occupants under the necessity of seeking new homes, by committing those invasions which the United States have solemnly obliged themselves to restrain.

Article XII.

In consideration of the extension acquired by the boundaries of the United States, as defined in the fifth Article of the present Treaty, the Government of the United States engages to pay to that of the Mexican Republic the sum of fifteen Millions of Dollars.

Part Three

THE ANGLO-AMERICAN CONQUEST, 1849–1910

La Raza has a lost
history. It is the period from 1849 to 1910, from the end of the
Mexican War to the beginning of the substantial immigration from
Mexico. The scene was the same—the Southwest—but the protag-
onists for the most part were the thousands of Americans who came
West to seek fortune, land, or fame. The Mexican Americans were
there, but, in most cases, they were losing more than they gained.
They were a generally passive community around which the events
of the day moved rapidly.

It was a time of change in a land and among a people that had
changed very little over the generations. They had preserved the
ways of Old Spain and many of the ways of the Indians. But they
had not improved. Their culture was rooted in the past, in traditions, usages, and social attitudes that had become stultified. Of
manufacturing they had none; Spain had made sure of that with
her mercantilist policies. The closest thing to industry was the
craftsmanship of the local wood- and metal-workers, but they did
not devise new techniques, only new styles. Agriculture, the main-
stay of the region, was also tied to the practices of past centuries.

Little wonder that the Mexican Americans were overwhelmed by
the newcomers. Almost at once, they became outsiders in their
own homeland, as the Anglos poured in by the thousands with new
ideas and ways, and an apparently boundless energy and desire to
make everything work. The first great lure was the promise of quick
riches in the newly found gold fields of California. Within two

decades, mining possibilities were being explored and exploited all over the Southwest. But, for most fortune hunters, mining was a transitory undertaking in which many more failed than succeeded. And even most of those who did strike it rich did not stay in mining. Sooner or later, the time came to settle down, and, for most Americans of the nineteenth century, settling down meant getting hold of a piece of land and farming it.

When the Anglos turned their covetous eyes on the lands of the Southwest, it was the undoing of Mexican-American society. The forty years after the Mexican War witnessed the greatest land grab in American history, at least since the Indian tribes were first dispossessed. In retrospect, the whole episode appears to have been inevitable. When the Anglos arrived, particularly in New Mexico and California, they found most of the land assigned to the holders of a few thousand old Spanish or Mexican land grants. The best land was not available for the taking. This was a new and disquieting experience for Americans, with their tradition of open, accessible land on the frontier. The situation was obviously intolerable—to find millions of acres of soil unused and begging to be tilled, only to be told that it was tied up in some old grant handed down in Madrid or Mexico City. And, when the extent of many of the land grants was realized—some as large as 50,000 acres—such holdings seemed positively immoral to men who were accustomed to thinking of farms in terms of a section (640 acres) or fractions thereof.

The Treaty of Guadalupe Hidalgo protected the Mexican Americans in all their property rights. But this treaty, like all of the treaties and agreements with the Indians, became mere paper when the matter at issue was land ownership. Not all transfers of land came about through chicanery, fraud, theft, or violence. There was at least an aura of legality to the whole business, and many of the final settlements were made in court, even the U.S. Supreme Court. But it has to be realized that, with the conquest of the Southwest, two systems of land ownership and law met head on, and the conqueror won. When the generalities of the old land grants became subject to the legal technicalities of the Anglos, and their holders to precise proof of ownership, the Mexican Americans were bound to get the worst of it. Their land, even if valid title could be proved, was often sold to pay taxes, legal fees, or their debts. In the long run, whatever the details, the lands of the Southwest passed largely into the control of Anglo owners.

However, it was not the small, family farm-owner who was the winner. For time has proved that the theory behind the old Spanish grants was valid, even if the grants themselves were frequently excessive. In the arid lands, only large holdings make economic sense, and their supposed immorality has long been forgotten.

During the second half of the nineteenth century, then, the Mexican Americans were transformed from masters in their own domain to minority status in a nation whose language and cultural orientation were different. One is forced to say that they became second-class citizens in what was to them a foreign land. This is not too strong an assertion when one considers the discrimination and violence to which La Raza was subjected from the opening of the Mexican War until well into the twentieth century. The number of killings of Mexican Americans in the Southwest from 1850 to 1930 exceeds the number of lynchings of blacks for the same period. For the Texas Rangers, it was always open season on Mexicans on either side of the border.

But La Raza did not spend all of its time between 1848 and 1910 being oppressed or losing its land. For one thing, most Mexican Americans had little land to lose. It was mostly the *ricos*, the rich ones, who were victimized by land titles, debts, legal fees, and court cases. The bulk of the Mexican-American population simply noted the exchange of one oppressive regime for another and went on working and living as they had before. In their religion and social customs, they were relatively unaffected by the change of governments. The coming of the Anglo-Americans did bring the public school system to the Southwest. Prior to 1848, what education there was, and that was precious little, occurred under the auspices of the church, or in the home, or abroad, if one were wealthy.

With the Anglos there also came money: capital to develop the economy of the whole region. Between the Civil War and 1890, the railroads also arrived. This meant more goods brought in from the East and a means to ship produce out. The railroads served as an impetus to the development of the cattle and sheep industries and of farming. Most of the productive mines ended up in the hands of large companies. In all of these fields, except railroading, the Mexican Americans became the core of the labor force, for they had the know-how that accrued from generations of experience. When they did not turn to wage labor—always low-paying at best—they remained on the land, either as subsistence farmers or sheep ranchers. Many ended up as tenants working the land for others, but hopeful that someday they would have acreage or a flock of their own.

HOSPITALITY IN NEW MEXICO

[From 1853 to 1856, William Watts Hart Davis was U.S. Attorney for the Territory of New Mexico. During those years, he kept a diary of his observations and experiences, from which he wrote the book *El Gringo, or, New Mexico and Her People*. This volume is probably the fullest and most trustworthy account of life in New Mexico during its early years as an American territory. The following narrative of a visit with one of the wealthier families of Santa Fe is from one of Davis's chapters on the "manners and customs of the people."]

We next call upon a Mexican family, in order to obtain some knowledge of the manners and customs of the people in their social intercourse. A few steps bring us to the house of a friend, and we stand before the large door that leads into the *patio*, knocking for admittance. While the old *portero* is coming to inquire who is there and to let us in, I will say a few words more about the houses and their mode of construction. It will be borne in mind that the material is simple earth in its raw state, and that all, whether in town or country, are built in the form of a square, with a court-

From William W. H. Davis, *El Gringo, or, New Mexico and Her People*. New York, 1857. Chapter 7.

yard in the centre. The style of building was borrowed from the East, and is as ancient as the time of Moses, and was essential here in early time because of the hostility of the Indians. The roof is called *azotea la puerta del zaguan*. An *adobe* is about six times the size of an ordinary brick, and they cost, delivered, from eight to ten dollars the thousand. Neither skill nor practice are required in order to make them. A piece of ground is selected for the purpose, upon which water can be turned from an acequia, and the earth is dug up and mixed until about the consistency of mortar. Each adobe maker has a frame the proper size, which he fills with the soft mud, strikes off the top evenly, when he empties it out upon the ground to dry in the sun. The adobes are very seldom laid in lime and sand, but with the same kind of mud they are made of. In time the walls become quite solid, and houses are in use, built in this manner, which have stood for nearly two hundred years; but they would not last long in the States, amid the great storms that prevail there.

By this time the porter has made his appearance at the door, where we have been standing some two or three minutes. There is great dread of robbers among the people, and they will not always admit you before you are known. The porter, therefore, as a matter of precaution, salutes us in the first place with *Quien es?* (Who is it?) to which we respond, *Amigos* (friends), when he opens the door sufficiently wide to see who we are, and permits us to enter. Being now assured that we are not robbers, he conducts us across the patio, and ushers us into the *sala*, or reception-hall, where we remain seated until the family come in to welcome us. While they are making their appearance—which may be some minutes, if the hour is afternoon, and they have not arisen from their *siesta* (afternoon nap)—we will, in imagination, make an excursion around the house to notice the *locus in quo*, as a lawyer would say, or, to speak more familiarly, to observe the manner in which it is furnished and the style thereof. The internal arrangement of a Mexican house is as different from that of an American as the building itself. The style is essentially Spanish, blended with which are observed many traces of the Moors, their early ancestors. As has been remarked before, all the rooms open into the patio, except some which communicate directly with the sala and with each other. It is a very rare thing to see a board floor in a Mexican house, the substitute being earth, cheaper in the first place, and more easily repaired. A coating of soft mud is carefully spread over the earth, which, when dry, makes a firm and comfortable floor. The common covering for the floors, when they are covered at all, is a coarse article of domestic woolen manufacture, called *gerga*, which answers the purpose of a carpet. The inside walls are whitened with calcined *yezo* or gypsum, which is used instead of lime, but it does not adhere to the walls with the same tenacity, and comes off upon every article that touches it. To prevent this, the rooms are lined with calico to the height of four feet, generally of bright colors. The coating of mud and yezo on the inside of the house is generally put on by females, who make use of their hands and a piece of sheep-skin with the wool on for that purpose, instead of brushes and plasterers' tools.

The ceiling is never plastered, but in those of the wealthier classes the beams that support the roof are planed and painted in various colors, and sometimes an artificial ceiling is made by tacking bleached muslin to them. In some sections of the country, small round sticks are laid from beam to beam in herring-bone style, and painted red, blue, or green; but it is only a choice room that is ornamented in this manner. The fire-place is built in one corner of the room, and occupies a small space. The mouth is somewhat in the shape of a horseshoe, not generally more than eighteen inches or two feet in height, and the same in width at the bottom. The back is slightly concave instead of being a plane surface, and the little circular hearth in front is raised a few inches above the level of the floor. The use of andirons is unknown, the wood being placed on end against the back of the fire-place. These small fire-places appear to give out more heat than the larger ones in use in American houses, and, being in a corner of the apartment, they occupy less space. I do not remember to have ever seen shovels or tongs in a Mexican house. When the house becomes dingy, if outside, they besmear it with a new coating of soft mud; or if inside, the walls are again daubed with yezo, followed by a coat of fresh mud on the floor. This renovation suffices instead of the semi-annual house-cleaning which causes American housewives so much annoyance.

The furniture, as well as the manner of arranging the same, differs materially from the style in the States. Few chairs or wooden seats of any kind are used, but in their stead mattresses are folded up and placed around the room, next to the wall, which, being covered with blankets, make a pleasant seat and serve the place of sofas. This is an Eastern custom, and was undoubtedly borrowed from the Moors. At night they are unrolled and spread out for beds; and it is customary for the whole family to sleep in the same room at night that they sit in during the day. Bedsteads are almost unknown, and if the mattress is raised at all above the floor, it is placed on a low wooden frame. Bureaus and other furniture of that description, in such common use in American houses to contain the clothing of the family, are seldom seen among the Mexicans, their place being supplied by an increased number of trunks and antiquated chests. In the houses of the wealthier classes a few chairs and cumbrous settees are found, generally made of pine, but among the peasantry such articles of luxury are unknown. This economy in articles of furniture was an absolute necessity in early times, caused by the almost entire absence of mechanics in the country; and such as they possessed were handed down from generation to generation as heir-looms in the family. At the present day, although there are American mechanics, but few of the people have adopted our style of furniture, but cling to that of olden times. Every article of this description sells at a price enormously high, and ordinary pine furniture costs more than that made of mahogany in the Atlantic States. The females in particular, prefer the easy *colchon*—folded mattress—to the straight and stiff-backed chairs and settees; and frequently they spread a single blanket in the middle of the floor, upon which they sit at work and receive visitors.

The kitchen utensils are equally meagre in their appointment. They cook almost universally in earthen vessels, which bear the general name of *tinaja*, and it is a rare thing to see any other description of culinary articles. I have never seen a stove in a Mexican house. The *sala* is the largest room about the establishment, and in the colder parts of the country it is only used during warm weather, when, for the time being, the family literally live there, lounge among the *colchons* during the day, receive their visitors, sleep at night, and hold the *baile*. The family room is adorned with a number of rude engravings of saints, among which the Virgin of Guadalupe is always conspicuous.

It has been stated elsewhere that the *tortilla*, a thin cake made of corn, is one of the principal articles of food among all classes of the people. The duty of making them has devolved upon the women from the earliest times, and they pride themselves upon the skill and rapidity with which they can prepare them. While we are in the kitchen, should we extend our adventures in that direction, we will see the manner in which the tortilla is made. The corn is boiled in water with a little lime, to soften the skin so that it can be peeled off, when they grind it into a paste upon an oblong hollowed stone, called a *metate*. The operator kneels down behind it, and takes in both hands another long round stone like an ordinary rolling-pin, between which and the *metate* she mashes the corn. To bake, the *tortilla* is spread upon thin sheets of tin or copper, and in a few minutes they are ready for use. They are quite palatable when warm, but when cold are almost as tasteless as so much shoe-leather. This, with the bean called *frijole*, makes the staff of life of all classes of the population. In Southern Mexico it is the custom for women, with small portable furnaces on their backs or strapped to a burro, to travel the streets of the large towns making and vending *tortillas* and *frijoles* to the passers-by.

By this time the siesta of *La Senora* has come to an end, and she makes her entrance into the sala where we have awaited her coming. The people of all classes receive their friends with much genuine affection, and it is customary to embrace each other when they meet. Our hostess upon this occasion, if perchance I am on intimate terms with herself and family, will encircle me with her fair arms, or, in common parlance, salute me with what is vulgarly called a *hug*, while you, who are a stranger, must be content with a shake of the hand. To make this distinction between a person and his friends is certainly aggravating to him who falls in the vocative, but a short acquaintance will place the outsiders upon an equally pleasant footing. If all the family should make their appearance, each one in turn will embrace you, which is by no means an unpleasant performance when the pretty daughters are a party to the operation, but it is much less agreeable to be hugged in the brawny arms of the father and brothers. This custom is universal among all classes, and even the filthy beggars in the streets meet and embrace each other with an affection truly laughable.

The Mexicans are distinguished for their politeness and suavity, and the *lepero*, covered with abominations, often exhibits a refinement of manners and address that would well become a prince, and which they as well practice toward each other as toward strangers. In their houses they are particularly courteous, and in appearance even outdo the most refined code of politeness. It is customary for them to assure you that you are in your own house the moment you cross their threshold, or to place themselves entirely at your disposal. If you admire an article, the owner immediately says to you, *"Tomele Vmd., Señor, es suyo"* (Take it, sir, it is yours). But in these flattering expressions the stranger must bear in mind that the owner has not the most remote idea that he will take him at his word—that he will either command his household, lay his personal services under contribution, or carry off whatever pleases his fancy.

We have already gone through with the hugging and kissing, and are now seated in the presence of our fair hostess. One of the first acts of courtesy of the mistress of the house is to invite you to smoke. She carries about her person a small silver tobacco-box, in which she keeps the noxious weed, and also has at hand a little package of corn-husks, one of which she fills with the fine-cut tobacco, rolls it up into a *cigarrito*, lights it, and hands it to you to smoke. The American cigar is rarely used by the men, and never by the females, both substituting the article here named. The *cigarrito* is made by each person as he requires them, who always has on hand for that purpose his box of tobacco and package of husks. Gregg, in his "Commerce of the Prairies," says upon this subject, "The mounted vaquero will take out his *guagito* (his little tobacco-flask), his packet of *hojas* (or prepared husks), and his flint, steel, etc., make his cigarrito, strike his fire, and commence smoking in a minute's time, all the while at full speed; and the next minute will perhaps lazo the wildest bull without interrupting his smoke." Smoking is habitual with all classes, not excepting the most lovely and refined females in the country. The habit is bad enough in men, but intolerable in women. The *cigarrito* seems to be an abiding presence, being handed round at the dinner-table as a refreshment, and served up in the ballroom; and it is common to see ladies smoking while they are engaged in waltzing and dancing, and some even indulge the luxury while they lie in bed. In Southern Mexico the ladies use a pair of golden tongs to hold the *cigarrito* while they light it, and the coal of fire is brought by a servant on a small silver salver.

In the more southern cities of Mexico, next to providing the guest with the means of smoking, chocolate and sweet bread are served up, the former being a delicious article of domestic manufacture, and the latter a superior quality of sponge-cake. During our stay, the mistress of the establishment and her daughters will endeavor to make the time pass as agreeably as possible. They are great talkers, and we will have enough to do to maintain the negative side of the question, now and then throwing in a word, in order to draw out the colloquial powers of our fair companions. When we come to take leave, the same ceremony is used as at the arrival, and you are passed around the family circle to receive an embrace from each member. This custom is as much a matter of course as that of shaking hands among the Americans, touching noses among the Chinese, or grunting among the North American Indians; and the most modest lady in the land has no scruples about giving and re-ceiving such salutation. The whole family accompany us to the door, and wait there until we have fairly made our exit, instead of turning us over to an impudent lackey, as has become the *fashion* in the States.

MEXICAN LAND CLAIMS IN CALIFORNIA

[The issue of land ownership in California after the Mexican War was dominated by two factors: the enormous amount of acreage claimed under Spanish and Mexican grants, and the insatiable hunger for land on the part of thousands of "Anglos" arriving every year from the East. Something had to give, and, in the end, it was the land grants of the older California residents, the Treaty of Guadalupe Hidalgo notwithstanding. During 1849 and 1850, two entirely contradictory reports on the validity of the old land grants were made for the federal government. One, under the auspices of the Department of the Interior, generally confirmed the grants, but the other, made by Captain Henry W. Halleck for the territory of California, called virtually all of them into question. To resolve the land problem, Congress created a Land Commission in 1851 to pass upon the validity of all titles. The commission was heavily weighted in favor of American land seekers, but it must be said in fairness that some of the grants were enormous and of a thoroughly unmanageable size. The following article by John S. Hittell, rather favorable to the original claimants, sums up the work of the Land Commission.]

From *Hutchings' California Magazine*, July 1857.

The establishment of the American dominion in California, made it necessary that the titles to land, owned in the State, under grants from Mexico, should be recognised and protected in accordance with the principles of American law. Protection was due to the land owners under the general principles of equity and the laws of nations, and had been expressly provided in the treaty of Guadalupe Hidalgo. It was necessary that the protection should be in accordance with the principles of American law, because the vast majority of the population soon came to be composed of Americans, who naturally introduced their own system of law,—the only system suited to their method of conducting business.

But there was a question of much difficulty as to how this protection should be furnished. The Mexican titles were lacking in many of the conditions necessary to a perfect title under the American laws. The land systems of the two countries were constructed on entirely different principles and with different objects. The Mexican system was a good one for the purposes to be attained by it; it was suited to the wants of the natives of California. They were stock-growers;—their only occupation, and wealth and staple food was furnished by their herds. They owned immense numbers of horses and horned cattle, and to furnish them with pasture, each ranchero required a large tract of land, which might be used by his own stock, exclusively. The public land in California was very extensive; it was worth nothing; there was little demand for it; no evils had been experienced, none were feared from the accumulation of great tracts, in the hands of a few owners; every grant was supposed to be a benefit to the State, by furnishing a home to a new citizen; and so, large grants were made without stint, on nearly every application. If the applicant could show that the land was public property, and unoccupied, he could obtain from 10,000 to 50,000 acres without expense, on condition that he would make the ranch his home, build a house on it, and place several hundred head of horned cattle upon it. These grants were usually made without any accurate description of the land; there never had been any government survey of any portion of the territory; there were no surveyors in the country to locate the boundaries; neither would the applicants have been willing in most cases to pay for surveys; nor was there any apparent need for them, land being very cheap and quarrels about boundaries very rare. Sometimes the land granted was described with certain fixed natural boundaries. In other cases, the grant might be described as lying in a narrow valley, between two ranges of mountains, and extending from a tree, rock, or clump of willows, up or down the valley far enough to include three, six, or ten square leagues. The most common form of grant was for a certain number of square leagues, lying in a much larger district, bounded by well known land-marks. Thus the famous Mariposa grant of Fremont is for ten square leagues—44,386 acres, equivalent to a tract about nine miles square—in the district bounded by the San Joaquin river on the west, the Sierra Nevada mountains on the east, the Merced river on the north, and the Chowchillas on the south; which district includes nearly 100 square leagues. Under such a grant, the Mexican law allowed the grantee to select any place within the larger limits, and make it his home.

The grants made were not carefully registered. The law prescribed that the petitions for land should all be preserved, and a record of them kept, and that a registry should be made of all the lands granted; but the affairs of the Governor's office were loosely conducted; and in many cases where the claimants have been in possession for twenty years, and have an undoubted title, there is nothing in the archives or records of the former government to show for it. In many respects the California governor had been very careless about granting lands. Some times they would grant the same lands to several persons; and there was one instance wherein Gov. Micheltorena ordered that every person in the Northern District of California, who had petitioned for land before a certain date, and whose petition had not been acted upon, should be the owner of the land asked for; provided the nearest Alcalde should certify that it belonged to the public domain. In these cases no title to the grantees was ever made by the Governor.

I have thus briefly mentioned the main peculiarities of the Mexican system of disposing of the public land in California, as distinguished from the American system. The Mexican government made no survey of the land; granted it away in immense tracts, without any fixed boundaries, leaving the grantee a wide discretion in regard to location, and keeping no careful registry of the grants.

When the great immigration of '49 filled the land with Americans, it became necessary to provide for the recognition and protection of the good Mexican titles by the American Courts. But how was this to be done? By the ordinary State Courts? The judges would not be sufficiently able, and would be ignorant of the laws under which the grants had been made; and the juries would be composed of Americans whose interests would lead them to do injustice to the large land-owners. Besides, the lawmakers and judges elected by a deeply interested populace could not be depended upon to do justice under such circumstances.

Or should the protection be rendered by the appointment of a commission, instructed to make a summary examination of all claims, declare all those valid which had been in possession previous to the conquest, and of which some record might be found in the archives; leaving the other claims to be tried in the U. S. Courts? This was the policy which should have been pursued.

But that plan was not to prevail. Mr. Gwin's bill "to ascertain and settle the private land claims in the State of California," became a law, on the 30th of March, 1851. This act provides for the appointment of a special Judicial Committee, (to be composed of three judges) before which all claimants to land, in the State, under Mexican titles, should bring suit against the Federal Government, within two years after the date of the act, under penalty of forfeiting their land. It provided further, that a law agent should be appointed, who should "superintend the interests of the United States in every case." It provided further, that appeals might be taken in these land cases, from the judgments of the Commission to the U. S. District Court, and from the latter, to the Supreme Court of the United States. It provided further, that in the trial of these cases, the Commission and the courts should "be governed by the treaty of Guadalupe Hidalgo, the law of nations, the laws, usages and customs of the country from which the claim is derived, the principles of equity, and the decisions of the Supreme Court of the United States."

This act provided that the owners of land should sue the Government or lose their land. But why be subjected to so severe a condition? The land owners had committed no offence, that they should be threatened with spoliation. It was not their fault that the Mexican land system differed from the American. The introduction of a new system by the Government did not justify the invalidation of titles, which had been good before, and the subjection of the owners to tedious and expensive litigation. When the American Government took California, it was in honor bound to leave the titles to property as secure as they were at the time of the transfer, and express provision to this effect was made in the treaty. Let us imagine that California were to be again transferred to some other power, whose land system is far more complex and strict than our own, and that all our present titles should be declared incomplete and insecure, and that every land owner should be taxed to one-fourth of the value of his land to pay for defending his title before a foreign and hostile Court, and, if successful, should not get his title until six or eight years after the commencement of the litigation;—would we not exclaim against it as extremely unjust? But what is the difference between that supposed case and the actual one under consideration? There is no difference between the principles involved in the two cases; each supposes a great wrong—such a wrong as has been committed by the Federal Government of the United States upon holders of land in California under Mexican grants.

The Land Commission was opened in this city, January 1st, 1852, and in the ensuing fourteen months, 812 suits were brought, and these were all decided previous to the 3d of March, 1855, at which time the Commission dissolved.

It was severe hardship for owners of land under grants from Mexico, that they should be required to sue the government of the United States, (which ought to have protected—not persecuted them,) or lose their land; but this hardship was rendered much more severe by the peculiar circumstances under which the suits had to be tried. The trials were to be had in San Francisco at a time when the expenses of traveling and of living in San Francisco were very great, and the fees of lawyers enormous. The prosecution of the suits required a study of the laws of Mexico, in regard to the disposition of the public lands, and this study had, of course, to be paid for by the clients. In many cases the claimants had to come to San Francisco from remote parts of the State; having three hundred miles to travel, bringing their witnesses with them at their own expense. The witnesses were nearly all native Californians, and it was necessary to employ interpreters at high prices.

Meanwhile the claimant could not dispose of his land, on account of the cloud there was on his title: neither could he have it surveyed by the U. S. Surveyor so as to give notice to the public where his land really lay. As he could not give a secure title, nor, in most cases, tell where his boundaries were, the Americans were not disposed to buy the land. Many squatters were, no doubt, glad of a pretext under which they might take other people's land and use without paying rent; but the circumstances were often such that they were justified in refusing to buy. The number of settlers or squatters became large; they formed a decided majority of the voters in several of the counties; their political influence was great; politicians bowed down before them; all political parties courted them; and most of the U. S. Land Agents, and District Attorneys, appointed under the influence of the California Congressmen, became the representatives of the settler interest, and failed to represent the true interest of the United States. Every device known to the law was resorted to to defeat the claimant, or delay the confirmation of his grant, as though it were the interest of the Federal Government to defeat every claimant, or to postpone his success as long as possible.

Eight hundred and twelve important suits, to be tried according to the principles of strange laws, and on evidence given in a strange tongue, and where the testimony, in many of the cases, covered hundreds of pages of manuscript, were not to be disposed of in any brief period. In fact, the Commission did not clear its docket until more than three years after its organization. This delay, which would have been disastrous in any country, was doubly so in California. During the greater portion of this time, the titles to most of the good farming land in the settled districts of the State, were declared to be unsettled. The delay was an encouragement to dishonest, and often a justification of honest squatters. They wanted to cultivate the ground; they could not learn whether the land they wished to occupy, was public or private property; they knew the question would not be decided soon, and therefore they might know, if dishonest, that they might make a profit by seizing land which they were morally certain would be, and should be, confirmed to the claimant; and if honest, they could not be expected to pay for property, to which, in many cases, the title was one in which they could place no confidence. The consequence of the system was, that a large portion of the most valuable farming land in the State was occupied by squatters. This occupation contributed greatly to injure the value of the property. The land owner could not sell his land, nor use it, and yet he was compelled to pay taxes. His ranch brought serious evils upon him. It was the seat of a multitude of squatters, who—as a necessary consequence of antagonistic pecuniary interest,—were his bitter enemies. Cases we know, where they fenced in his best land; laid their claims between his house and his garden; threatened to shoot him if he should trespass on their inclosure; killed his cattle if they broke through the sham fences; cut down his valuable shade and fruit trees, and sold them for fire-wood; made no permanent improvements, and acted generally as tho' they were determined to make all the immediate profit possible, out of the ranch. Such things were not rare: they are familiar to every person who knows the general course of events during the last five years in Sonoma, Napa, Solano, Contra Costa, Santa Clara, Santa Cruz and Monterey Counties. Blood was not unfrequently spilled in consequence of the feuds between the land holders and the squatters; the victims in nearly every case, belonging to the former class.

After the Federal Government had committed the error of compelling every Californian land owner to bring suit for his own land, which he had held in indisputable ownership under the Mexican dominion, and even before the independence of Mexico and Spain,—and after the Government stubbornly contested every case before a tribunal whose learning, ability, and honesty, was and is, universally admitted,—after all this, it is strange that those persons, whose claims were confirmed, and who had been in possession of their land before the American conquest, and in cases where there was no suspicion of fraud, were not allowed to take their own property once for all. But no; Uncle Sam told all the Californians who had gained their suits, that they should not take their land till they had sued him again; he would appeal every case; the claimant must make another fight for his property, or be despoiled.

Here, then, was the whole work to be gone over again in the Federal District Courts, of which there are two in the State; and in each district there are about four hundred claims, to be tried by a judge, much of whose time is occupied with the trial of admiralty cases. The land suits must all be defended, or attended to, by the United States District Attorney, much of whose time is occupied with criminal cases, and civil business in which the Federal Government is interested. The result is delay upon delay. . . .

Only two pleas have been made to extenuate or justify the stubborn opposition made by the agents of the Government to the recognition of the Californian land holders. These pleas are, *first*, that many of the claims are fraudulent; and, *secondly*, that the Californians claim too much land.

It is not true that *many* of the claims are fraudulent. The Land Commission did not reject one claim, and the District Courts have rejected only two, on the ground of fraud. There may be twenty-five fraudulent claims in all; I believe not more. There may be many claims which would not have been valid under the Mexican law; but these are not fraudulent, and have been, or will be rejected. But even if there were a hundred, that would be no reason why the

Government should attempt to rob the holders of land under titles undoubtedly good in equity and under the Mexican law. A distinction might be made between the two classes, of the suspicious and the undoubtedly good claims. But the Federal Government made no distinction. The Peralta grant, which was made in the last century, and has been in constant possession ever since, under a perfect title according to the Mexican law, was subjected to the same litigation and vexatious delay, and was given over to the tender mercies of the squatters in the same manner with the most questionable title in all the land.

The other plea is still worse. It may be that the welfare of the people requires the land to be equally divided among them; but shall that justify the Government in robbing—directly by violence, or indirectly by litigation—the owners of large tracts? If it be wrong for me to rob my neighbor of his dollars, is it right for Uncle Sam to rob Peralta, or any other Californian, of his land? And let it be remembered that temporary dispossession is morally as wrong as entire and final spoliation. I admit that it were far better for the country that the Mexican grant-holders should not own so much land; I admit that it were better, looking at the question abstractly, that the settlers should own all the land they claim; I admit that the settlers are more active and industrious, and contribute vastly more, in proportion to their means, to the development and wealth of the State, than do the native holders of the large grants; but all this has nothing to do with the main question. . . .

Not only has the system adopted by the Federal Government, in regard to Mexican grants, been most injurious and unjust to the claimants, but it has also been very injurious to the country at large. It has deprived the people in the most populous agricultural districts, of permanent titles; has prevented the erection of fine houses, valuable improvements, permanent homes; has contributed to make the population unsettled; to keep families from coming to the country; and, in fine, has been one of the chief causes of the present unsound condition of the social and business relations of California.

THE "ROBIN HOOD"
OF SOUTH TEXAS

[Juan Nepomuceno Cortina became a folk hero for the Mexicans along the Rio Grande border during the difficult years when Texas was first part of the United States. Texas, like most of the Southwest, was the scene of a clash of cultures—between the "Anglo" and Mexican residents—and the latter usually got the worst of it. Adding fuel to the already present hostility were frequent Indian depredations, after which the raiders would cross the border into Mexico, apparently with impunity. Cortina first leaped into prominence when he occupied the city of Brownsville, Texas, on September 28, 1859. The "Cortina War," with raiding by Cortina and his followers, on the one hand, and expeditions by Texas Rangers and U.S. Army units to find Cortina, on the other hand, lasted into the first half of 1860, when excursions by American military units into Mexico put a stop to the raids. Cortina himself was never captured and, in fact, went on to an illustrious career as a Mexican patriot, with occasional relapses into banditry. This selection reprints a proclamation to the Mexican Americans of South Texas, issued by Cortina on November 23, 1859, from his stronghold at the Rancho del Carmen in Cameron County. It is a remarkably literate composition for a man who could neither read nor write. Needless to say, the grievances of the Mexican Americans were not resolved by the punitive raids engaged in by Cortina and his band.]

From 36 Congress, 1 Session, House Executive Document No. 52: "Difficulties on Southwestern Frontier." Pages 79–82.

The Mexicans who inhabit this wide region, some because they were born therein, others because since the treaty Guadalupe Hidalgo, they have been attracted to its soil by the soft influence of wise laws and the advantages of a free government, paying little attention to the reasoning of politics, are honorably and exclusively dedicated to the exercise of industry, guided by that instinct which leads the good man to comprehend, as uncontradictory truth, that only in the reign of peace can he enjoy, without inquietude, the fruit of his labor. These, under an unjust imputation of selfishness and churlishness, which do not exist, are not devoid of those sincere and expressive evidences of such friendliness and tenderness as should gain for them that confidence with which they have inspired those who have met them in social intercourse. This genial affability seems as the foundation of that proverbial prudence which, as an oracle, is consulted in all their actions and undertakings. Their humility, simplicity, and docility, directed with dignity, it may be that with excess of goodness, can, if it be desired, lead them beyond the common class of men, but causes them to excel in an irresistible inclination towards ideas of equality, a proof of their simple manners, so well adapted to that which is styled the classic land of liberty. A man, a family, and a people, possessed of qualities so eminent, with their heart in their hand and purity on their lips, encounter every day renewed reasons to know that they are surrounded by malicious and crafty monsters, who rob them in the tranquil interior of home, or with open hatred and pursuit; it necessarily follows, however great may be their pain, if not abased by humiliation and ignominy, their groans suffocated and hushed by a pain which renders them insensible, they become resigned to suffering before an abyss of misfortunes.

Mexicans! When the State of Texas began to receive the new organization which its sovereignty required as an integrant part of the Union, flocks of vampires, in the guise of men, came and scattered themselves in the settlements, without any capital, except the corrupt heart and the most perverse intentions. Some, brimful of laws, pledged to us their protection against the attacks of the rest; others assembled in shadowy councils, attempted and excited the robbery and burning of the houses of our relatives on the other side of the river Bravo; while others, to the abusing of our unlimited confidence, when we intrusted them with our titles, which secured the future of our families, refused to return them under false and frivolous pretexts; all, in short, with a smile on their faces, giving the lie to that which their black entrails were meditating. Many of you have been robbed of your property, incarcerated, chased, murdered, and hunted like wild beasts, because your labor was fruitful, and because your industry excited the vile avarice which led them. A voice infernal said, from the bottom of their soul, "kill them; the greater will be our gain!" Ah! this does not finish the sketch of your situation. It would appear that justice had fled from this world, leaving you to the caprice of your oppressors, who become each day more furious towards you; that, through witnesses and false charges, although the grounds may be insufficient, you may be interred in the penitentiaries, if you are not previously deprived of life by some keeper who covers himself from responsibility by the pretence of your flight. There are to be found criminals covered with frightful crimes, but they appear to have impunity until opportunity furnish them a victim; to these monsters indulgence is shown, because they are not of our race, which is unworthy, as they say, to belong to the human species. But this race, which the Anglo-American, so ostentatious of its own qualities, tries so much to blacken, depreciate, and load with insults, in a spirit of blindness, which goes to the full extent of such things so common on this frontier, does not fear, placed even in the midst of its very faults, those subtle inquisitions which are so frequently made as to its manners, habits, and sentiments; nor that its deeds should be put to the test of examination in the land of reason, of justice, and of honor. This race has never humbled itself before the conqueror, though the reverse has happened, and can be established; for he is not humbled who uses among his fellow-men those courtesies which humanity prescribes; charity being the root whence springs the rule of his actions. But this race, which you see filled with gentleness and inward sweetness, gives now the cry of alarm throughout the entire extent of the land which it occupies, against all the artifice interposed by those who have become chargeable with their division and discord. This race, adorned with the most lovely disposition towards all that is good and useful in the line of progress, omits no act of diligence which might correct its many imperfections, and lift its grand edifice among the ruins of the past, respecting the ancient traditions and the maxims bequeathed by their ancestors, without being dazzled by brilliant and false appearances, nor crawling to that exaggeration of institution which, like a sublime statue, is offered for their worship and adoration.

Mexicans! Is there no remedy for you? Inviolable laws, yet useless, serve, it is true, certain judges and hypocritical authorities, cemented in evil and injustice, to do whatever suits them, and to satisfy their vile avarice at the cost of your patience and suffering; rising in their frenzy, even to the taking of life, through the treacherous hands of their bailiffs. The wicked way in which many of you have been oftentimes involved in persecution, accompanied by circumstances making it the more bitter, is now well known; these crimes being hid from society under the shadow of a horrid night, those implacable people, with the haughty spirit which suggests impunity for a life of criminality, have pronounced, doubt ye not, your sentence, which is, with accustomed insensibility, as you have seen, on the point of execution.

Mexicans! My part is taken; the voice of revelation whispers to me that to me is entrusted the work of breaking the chains of your slavery, and that the Lord will enable me, with powerful arm, to fight against our enemies, in compliance with the requirements of that Sovereign Majesty, who, from this day forward, will hold us under His protection. On my part, I am ready to offer myself as a sacrifice for your happiness; and counting upon the means necessary for the discharge of my ministry, you may count upon my coöperation, should no cowardly attempt put an end to my days. This undertaking will be sustained on the following bases:

First. A society is organized in the State of Texas, which devotes itself sleeplessly until the work is crowned with success, to the improvement of the unhappy condition of those Mexicans resident therein; exterminating their tyrants, to which end those which compose it are ready to shed their blood and suffer the death of martyrs.

Second. As this society contains within itself the elements necessary to accomplish the great end of its labors, the veil of impenetrable secrecy covers "The Great Book" in which the articles of its constitution are written; while so delicate are the difficulties which must be overcome that no honorable man can have cause for alarm, if imperious exigencies require them to act without reserve.

Third. The Mexicans of Texas repose their lot under the good sentiments of the governor elect of the State, General Houston, and trust that upon his elevation to power he will begin with care to give us legal protection within the limits of his powers.

Mexicans! Peace be with you! Good inhabitants of the State of Texas, look on them as brothers, and keep in mind that which the Holy Spirit saith: "Thou shalt not be the friend of the passionate man; nor join thyself to the madman, lest thou learn his mode of work and scandalize thy soul."

THE QUICKSILVER MINES OF NEW ALMADEN, CALIFORNIA

[Mexican-American miners had centuries of experience behind them as a result of the working of copper, silver, and other deposits by Spain and Mexico in the Southwest. The craftsmanship they could lay claim to was to prove most useful to the Anglo-Americans, generally late arrivals on the mining scene, who came pouring into the region after 1849. Unfortunately, the Mexican Americans were rarely adequately rewarded for their expertise, and frequently, as in California, they were driven from the mine fields, under the "Foreign Miners Law" of 1851. But, in the larger company-owned mines, the Mexican American continued to be an indispensable, if underpaid, laborer. This selection comprises portions of an article on the quicksilver, or mercury, mines near San Jose, California. Quicksilver was necessary in the refining of gold, silver, tin, lead, zinc, and other metals. The discovery of the "cinnabar," or quicksilver, mines in northern California opened up one of the world's largest supplies of the metal.]

From *Harper's New Monthly Magazine*, June 1863.

From San José to the quicksilver mine of New Almaden is twelve miles. The road winds for that distance through the most fertile part of the valley of Santa Clara, which gradually widens into a verdant plain, richly carpeted with wild flowers, and every foot of it "claimed," fenced, and settled upon by those who have come to California not to "make a pile" and return, but to build up and improve a home. . . .

The ascent to the range of mountains, on the slope of which the mine is situated, is very gradual—scarcely perceptible. The first indication of one's proximity to it is a small village, or collection of tasteful cottages, neatly painted and inclosed by paling fences, with here and there the evidences of woman's industrious hand in the cultivation of flower-gardens and the fancy trellis-work for wood-bine and honey-suckle vines which clamber luxuriantly over some of the dwellings. The families of the superintendents of the works reside here, and live in the enjoyment of rural life, while the constant arrivals of visitors from San Francisco at this romantic spot keeps them "posted" in relation to city affairs and the minutiæ of more fashionable life.

Beyond appear the brick buildings of the "works." These consist of the business offices of the directors, the residences of the workmen, storehouses for flasks and general material for repairs and additions, and houses for the reception of ore and bricks. Together they form a collection of solid and substantial houses, apparently built for a century's use. Here also are the furnaces in which the ore is smelted.

The process of extracting the quicksilver is an interesting study; and as our conductor promised an explanation of its mysteries on our return, we accepted his offer to visit the mine with us. The discovery and subsequent history of the New Almaden is briefly told. Some years before the gold discovery an opening was observed in the hill-side, into which the main shaft has been since run. It had been repeatedly traced by the native Californians for fifty or a hundred feet, but nobody seems to have considered it any thing but a natural cave—one of the many crevices or caverns which have been formed in all parts of California by freaks of nature. It was at last ascertained to be an artificial excavation, and one of great antiquity. The vaqueros and taciturn old dons of the neighborhood, when questioned concerning it, replied, with the usual shrug, and *"Quien sabe?" "Son cosas muy antiquos,"* until the débris was cleared away from the lower part of the shaft; in doing which a number of skeletons, a quantity of rounded stones from the brook, and other interesting relics were disclosed. These, it was evident, were the remains of aborigines, who had resorted here to obtain the cinnabar from which to manufacture vermilion for ornamental purposes, according to their savage customs. This was the only place where this primitive paint could be obtained on the coast; and it is now ascertained that savages visited it even from the confines of Oregon, a distance of several hundred miles. Ignorant of the art of propping up their drifts as they each year worked farther into the earth, they had been suddenly overtaken by a natural catastrophe, and were buried alive in a grave of their own digging, after which the tribes appear to have abandoned it.

Conjecture was for a long time at a loss to know the object of the Indians in thus penetrating the mountain. On the discovery of the gold mines some experiments with rockers and pans are said to have been made in search of the precious metals, but of course without success, as the auriferous soil of California does not extend into the coast range. But soon after a gentleman, at present one of the principal proprietors in the quicksilver mine, in prosecuting the search for gold, first attempted to retort some of the ore, or what then appeared to be a species of red earth or ochre, when, standing over the crucible, he inhaled some of the mercurial vapor, and shortly afterward began to experience symptoms of salivation. The result of this dangerous but fortunate experiment he communicated to his brother, one of a wealthy commercial firm in Mexico; and other tests yielding similar proofs of the richness of the ore, the land for a league or two was purchased at a very reasonable rate from its proprietor, who then held it under an original Spanish grant. . . .

The main entrance to the mine is a tunnel, commenced in 1850, in the side of the mountain, in a line with the patio, and which has already been carried to the distance of 1800 feet, by 10 wide and 10 feet in height to the crown of the arch, which is strongly roofed with heavy timber throughout its entire length. Through this an iron rail track passes, the cars receiving the ore as it is brought upon the backs of carriers (tanateros) from the excavations. These cars are calculated to carry about a ton each, and are pushed rapidly in and out by hand.

We enter the car and in a few moments are rumbling along this under-ground railroad, with no sound to break the silence besides the heavy breathing of our human propellers, who, with swarthy visage lighted up by the dim rays of the candles, seem almost ghastly as they bend to their work. These laborers are all Mexicans, and have generally served a sort of apprenticeship in the silver mines of Spanish America. Soon we reach the terminus of the rail-road, and step out upon a damp soil beaten hard by the incessant tramp of the ore-carriers. Here the sensation of chilling dampness usually possessing the novice on entering a subterranean cavern seizes one, and makes him for a moment doubt the prudence of the adventure; but this gradually wears away, and a feeling of curiosity succeeds.

With a stout Mexican to act the part of torch-bearer, we pass along a damp passage-way, through the arched roof of which the water trickles, and in the rainy months hangs in drops, glittering like gems in the light of the candles. We next pass down a perpendicular piece of accommodation, known among the miners as an *escalera,* or ladder, which consists of a notched stick of timber some twelve feet in length, answering to the common "samson-post" in a ship's lower hatchway. This leads to a small landing-place, from which we gaze down into a black pit, the darkness made visible by the uncertain flicker of the candles. It is dainty treading along the little shelf, where a misstep would send you headlong into some unknown chasm, whose depth is indicated by the noises of the laborers far below, which ever and anon come faintly up. A short interval of groping, with the peculiar uncertain feeling of not knowing whether the next step is likely to be upon solid ground or into emptiness, and we commence the descent of a flight of steps cut into the wall of rock, which leads into a still deeper cave. Here, feeling our way cautiously among loose stones and along craggy sides of the cave, we follow the glimmering candles, now down a slippery inclined plane, and again struggling up the precipitous base of some vein of cinnabar, which in its erratic course seems to have shot through the solid heart of the mountain, in much the zigzag course that a drop of quicksilver would describe in rolling about the surface of a plate. It is not until the lowest and inner excavations are reached that we realize the labyrinthine intricacies we have traversed. We are more than 200 feet below the patio and 600 below the summit of the mountain.

For many months after the working of the mine was commenced the proprietors labored under every difficulty; or, rather, a parsimonious spirit and ignorance of the true method to be pursued prevented its development. The system adopted was so in accordance with the desultory style used in the gold mines of the interior, that at one time the under-ground workings, as shown by a map exhibiting the subterranean topography, had assumed the appearance of a gigantic rabbit warren, extending in innumerable holes and crooked windings, like the streets of a city without system or economical order. A German overseer, however, gradually put matters to rights. About 300 persons are employed in the mine. The work was formerly given out to them by *empresarios* or "bosses," who took the job to deliver at the mouth of the mine a certain number of tons of ore, and, of course, hired their workmen at the lowest possible wages. The laborers in the mine *(barateros)* are a distinct fraternity from the ore-carriers *(tanateros)*. Each have their respective calling, and are not willing nor are they ever expected to assume each other's places. The tanateros are most muscular and the best proportioned of all those engaged in the mine. Long practice has inured them to the labor, and a first-rate man will pack 200 pounds up the escalaras without stopping to rest. This method of raising the ore is preferred to any machinery that has been suggested, as the men supply all that the works can distill, and the cost to the company is only in proportion to the amount furnished. A large sack or pannier of hide, open at the top, is slung to the back, and supported by a strap passing over the shoulders and around the forehead. The whole weight is thus supported by the muscles of the neck, a method in which Spanish Americans seem to have great faith.

Two hundred pounds being the average load, it becomes a matter of pride to preserve the physical reputation. It is impossible to witness the straining nerves and quivering muscles of the carriers, as they pass slowly up from the depths below, without feeling that the heavy breathing and painful expression of face is produced by such labor as human beings can not long endure. Yet they seem cheerful, and as they deposit their burdens into the cars, light their cigarros, and join in the laugh produced by the jokes of some Joe Miller of the gang. Their dress is confined to a pair of pantaloons with the legs cut off above the knees, and a calico shirt, which is generally stowed away in some crevice until the day's work is over. A pair of leathern sandals fastened at the ankle is sometimes added to the costume. Flight after flight up perpendicular steps these muscular fellows will ascend, winding through deep caverns, or threading passages of Egyptian darkness, or, as the openings often lead up in following the tortuous windings of the veins, they may be seen cautiously descending the notched logs toward the main entrance; yet it is affirmed that no accident has ever happened. Their course is dimly lighted by the candles placed in the niches of the walls. A single misstep would dash the man and his load into the dismal abyss below; but by constant practice they attain to a wonderful degree of precision, and ascend and descend with all the certainty of mules scaling the rocky fastnesses of the South American sierras. An efficient tanatero will make from twenty to thirty trips a day. Groping about the mine, and following the glimmering light which barely illumines the way, we happen upon little groups of the barateros hard at work with crow-bars and picks breaking down the sterile rock. These fellows are, if possible, more scantily clad than their ore-carrying brethren. Some may be seen following the serpentine lead of a vein of cinnabar which has just been found to dip from the horizontal toward the base of the mountain. They have dug themselves out of sight, and their half-smothered grunts and exclamations come curiously up from the cave whose length they are slowly extending. A feeble light glimmers out of the excavation—a cave within a cave. A little farther, and we find a plank stretched across a narrow chasm upon which two or three swarthy broadchested miners are standing, drilling their way into the solid rock above them, where a rich lead has just been found. . . .

At the patio the principal part of the mechanical labor of the works is performed. Here may be seen actively employed blacksmiths, carpenters, bricklayers, weighers, sifters. The mechanics, who are mostly Americans, receive full city wages—from five to seven and the laborers from two to three dollars a day. These last are fair specimens of the reckless, improvident Spanish-American race. With them the only use for money is to get rid of it as quickly as possible. It is of little consequence how much or little they receive. Monte and the other games of cards generally swallow up the week's earnings. . . .

At an elevation of a few hundred feet above the patio, on the mountain side, is situated a village inhabited exclusively by the miners. Here may be seen a genuine Mexican *aldea* in full perfection. The houses, or rather huts, are thatched with straw; placid-looking donkeys stand musing at the doors; chocolate-colored brats with huge paunches and shocks of frouzy hair sprawl about in the sunshine screaming and quarreling in infantile Spanish; mangy dogs, pigs, goats, and fleas wander in and out at random *à la* Mexico; bedraggled señoritas pass by with the peculiar careless saunter of the *aguadora*, balancing her burden on her head; and here, as in every other collection of Spanish Americans, no matter how far removed from home, one may notice the adherence to the national customs, to which the Mexican in particular is as religiously bound as the Turk to his turban and petticoats, or the Indian to his moccasin.

Sometimes on *dias de fiesta*, and on Sundays, they send to San José for a *guitarrista* and a violin or two, and get up a spirited dance, in which the whole population assist. Here repair the *vaqueros* and mantilla'd *muchachas* of the neighborhood; and after a day of general breakdown and jollification, in which cigars, bad brandy, horse-racing, fandango, and monte are the component parts, the assemblage breaks up with a general stampede on horseback, and the little village subsides into its usual quiet.

Nor do they neglect the forms of religion. Like devout Catholics they attend mass at stated periods at Santa Clara, and now and then have the Padre come over to help along their labors with a benediction or two. Besides this, they have in one of the recesses a shrine appropriated and dedicated to the holy protectress of the mine. This is a niche hewn with more than ordinary care out of the solid rock, in which is placed a small figure of the tutelary saint before whom propitiatory candles are constantly kept burning. Her ladyship is clad in a handsome white gown with red morocco slippers, bead eyes, and any quantity of head-dress and ornaments. This is "Nuestra Señora de Guadelupe," before whom the miners regularly prostrate themselves to supplicate her protection from fire-damps, cavings, and sudden outbursts of water. Of the first, as has already been remarked, there is no danger; of the second, no instance has occurred, as the galleries are well stanchioned; and though of the latter all live in constant anxiety, the mine has remained so dry up to this time as to need no artificial drainage.

THE WORK OF
ARCHBISHOP LAMY
IN NEW MEXICO

[Prior to New Mexico's incorporation into the United States, its churches had been part of the huge archdiocese of Durango, but, once territorial status was attained, a new diocese was organized, with headquarters at Santa Fe. A young cleric, thirty-seven-year-old, French-born Jean Baptiste Lamy, was selected by Rome to head the new organization. He left his mission parish in Kentucky and traveled to New Mexico, arriving there in 1851, accompanied by a fellow clergyman and friend, Joseph P. Macheboeuf. Lamy's large diocese included New Mexico, Arizona, and parts of Utah, Colorado, and Nevada. Besides building up the diocese in terms of schools and hospitals, there was much work to be done reforming many parishes. Over the years of Spanish and Mexican domination, many lax practices had crept into the churches, and several priests were found to be thoroughly unfit to lead congregations. The work of reform was frequently an uphill battle for Lamy and his associates, because the Spanish-speaking priests were well-entrenched in their parishes and had loyal followers. The selection below consists of two readings illustrating the work of Lamy at Santa Fe. The first is a statement by Father Macheboeuf detailing his experiences at Albuquerque, where he was given the task of ousting the parish pastor, José Manuel Gallegos. The second reading is the report by Archbishop Lamy for 1866 to the Central Council for the Propagation of the Faith at Rome.]

From: 1. Ralph Emerson Twitchell, ed., *The Leading Facts of New Mexican History.* Cedar Rapids, Iowa, 1912. Vol. II, pages 832–834.
2. Louis H. Warner, *Archbishop Lamy: An Epoch Maker*, Santa Fe, 1936. Chapter 14.

1. REFORMING THE PARISH AT ALBURQUERQUE

My position was sufficiently delicate and difficult, for he was very popular in his set. I took advantage of his temporary absence in Old Mexico to take possession of the church and to announce from the pulpit the sentence of the Bishop, suspending him from the exercise of any priestly function. Some time later, when I was visiting some Indian parishes in the mountains, about seventy-five miles from Alburquerque, I heard that the Padre had returned and was going to dispute the possession of the church with me the next Sunday. This did not alarm me, but I thought it best to be prepared, so I sent a messenger in haste to the Bishop to get a confirmation in writing of the sentence pronounced upon the Padre, and my authorization in clear terms to administer the affairs of the parish. I returned to Alburquerque on Saturday night, and on Sunday morning I went to the church an hour earlier than usual in order to be on the ground and ready for anything that might happen. What was my astonishment upon arriving here to find the Padre in the pulpit and the church filled with people whom I knew to be his particular friends. These he had quietly gathered together, and now he was inciting them to revolt, or at least to resistance. I tried to enter the church through the sacristy, but this communicated with the presbytery, which he still occupied, and I found the doors locked. Going then to the main door of the church I entered, and assuming an air of boldness I commanded the crowd to stand aside and make room for me to pass. Then, as one having authority, I forced my way through the crowd and passed up by the pulpit just as the Padre pronounced the Bishop's name and mine in connection with the most atrocious accusations and insulting reflections. I went on until I reached the highest step of the sanctuary, and then turning I stood listening quietly till he had finished. Then all the people turned to me as if expecting an answer. I replied, and in the clearest manner refuted all his accusations, and I showed, moreover, that he was guilty of the scandals which had brought on his punishment. I then took from my pocket the letter which my courier had brought me from the bishop, and I read it in a loud voice. To finish, I called upon him to justify himself, or at least to answer, if he had any reply to make. But, not a word; he went out as crestfallen as a trapped fox and left me in peaceful possession of the church. I sang the high mass as usual, and preached on the Gospel of the day without making the least allusion to the scene which had just taken place. A few days later, to repair his humiliating defeat, he went to the neighboring villages and used every means to arouse the people, and he succeeded in getting together twenty-five or thirty of the most influential and the richest, with some of his intimate friends from Santa Fé. These, profiting by the absence of the Prefect, who was an intimate friend of mine, came to me in a body, and, with an air of insolence and bravado, ordered me to leave the parish, adding that they did not want any of my administration, and if I did not go they would have recourse to other measures. At that moment the good God must have given me patience and strength that were more than natural, for I answered them with firmness that I had come to take possession of the parish by order of the highest ecclesiastical authority, and that I would receive no orders except from that same authority. I told them that they might take such measures as they saw fit, but, like the sentinel on guard, I would not quit my post, and as the shepherd of the flock I was ready to die for my sheep rather than abandon them.

This short and forcible answer disconcerted them; they did not have a word to say in reply, but returned to the Padre to apprise him of the little success of their mission. They did not know that I was an Auvergnat. *Latsin pas.* Never give up!

Hardly had they left me when the Prefect, whom some one had notified of the affair, came up in a fury. He had already given orders for their arrest and appearance in court, but I reasoned with him and finally persuaded him to drop the matter, for I was sure that such a course would be the best in the end. This, in effect, was the case, for a re-action took place in my favor and several deputations waited upon me to offer their services and protect me if necessary. I thanked all of them for their good will, but I declined any protection, as I did not fear any trouble. This scene took place on Saturday, and on Sunday morning I went to the church unattended by anyone except by the sacristan, and the only change I noticed was that everyone I met saluted me with apparently greater respect than ever. There were only three men from Alburquerque who took part in the rebellion; all the rest were from the Ranchos, or villages on the lands of the rich proprietors.

From that moment the Padre lost all hope of driving me away, and, abandoning the Church, he went into politics. There was no doubt about his talents, and he used them to good effect in his new field, for through them he worked every kind of scheme until he succeeded in getting himself elected to the Congress of the United States as Delegate from the Territory of New Mexico. . . .

2. ARCHBISHOP LAMY'S REPORT FOR 1866

When I arrived in Santa Fe, sixteen years ago, my first care was to get missionaries and open schools. Divine Providence has blessed in a most visible manner our efforts, despite all kinds of difficulties that had to be conquered.

We have already been able to repair the majority of the old churches, and build 85 new ones, all of adobe. They are of moderate dimensions with no architectural character, and as poor in the interior as the exterior. But, thanks to God, they are well frequented. The majority of our Catholics approach the Sacraments, and First Communions are established in every place where there is a priest. The total number of Churches and Chapels is 135.

We have three schools directed by the Christian Brothers in full prosperity; those of the Episcopal City never have less than 200 pupils, many times 300. They are taught English, Spanish, reading, writing, geography, history and arithmetic. Almost all our missionaries have at least one school under their direction, some have more, according to the places they have to visit.

The Sisters of Loreto have five houses in the Diocese; the first novitiate is numerous, and many novices belong to the first families.

On the 1st of January, 1866, four Sisters of St. Vincent de Paul have opened an Orphanage and Hospital in Santa Fe; for this work I have donated the house inhabited by me.

The foremost difficulties in our missions are first, the traversing of the immense plains which isolate us from the rest of the United States. After crossing the ocean, after traveling six hundred leagues by rail, the most difficult and most costly part of our trip has yet to be made.

Up to this time, we have had at our service the comforts of the civilized countries, now we have to travel 300 leagues without finding on our way a hut or even a bridge over the rivers, and, are always exposed to the arrows of the Indians. Rarely do these savages fail to attack caravans, at times very large ones. In the fall of 1855, six of our Christian Doctrine Brothers, traversed the plains while coming to Santa Fe. As a precaution they joined a caravan of 500 open carts, loaded with provisions and merchandise for New Mexico. It took them two and one-half months to make the trip; they were attacked several times by the Indians, who, defying the 1200 men of the caravan, killed and wounded numerous people.

The expense of equipping a caravan is enormous. It is necessary to buy both animals and wagons, to carry the baggage of the Missionaries and the effects of the churches and schools; to take also provisions for two months, and camping outfits. After the Civil War, the cost of transportation, is from Frs. 1.50 to Frs. 2.00 per kilogram. In New Mexico we have only the most rigorously necessary things for our existence, as bread and meat. There are no factories of any kind here. The majority of the inhabitants raise sheep and cattle and horses, but they get very little profit out of them. It may be for lack of a market or on account of the savage Indians who steal the flocks, kill the shepherds or take them prisoner. In these beautiful and vast prairies Providence has placed innumerable droves of buffalos, the meat of which serves as food, and the hides as clothing for half a million of savages.

Since these savages are at war with the government, the crossing of the plains is more dangerous than ever before. It was only by an especial protection from God that in 1865, the 10 young missionaries that one of my Priests brought from Lyons could traverse these 300 leagues. They were twice attacked by savages and exposed to death by hunger and cold. New Mexico is the most populated of the three territories that to this day comprise the Diocese of Santa Fe; we have 110,000 Mexicans and 15,000 Catholic Indians. Colorado has 10,000 Catholics in a settlement of 40,000 souls. Arizona has 8,000 Catholics. The present number of our Priests in missions is 41, five in charge of Colorado, three in Arizona, the rest in New Mexico. I have made three pastoral visits into Colorado, and only one into Arizona, but this took me six months, from the 1st of November 1863 to the 1st of May 1864. I traveled over a thousand leagues on horseback. In some places we had to sleep under the moon and to travel spaces from 20 to 25 leagues without a drop of water, walking to rest my horse. But we find ourselves rewarded for all this hardship, at finding such faithful souls. Not having seen a priest for many years, they take advantage of the visits of the missionary to receive the Sacraments with fervor and gratitude.

On Christmas day we were able to celebrate the Holy Sacrifice, to which 20 or 25 persons assisted, kneeling on the ground still covered with the snow which had fallen the day before. We were on the slope of a mountain, surrounded by forests of oak and pinon, silver leaf and cedar trees. The altar placed in the shadow of green, had been improvised with the material on hand, consisting of trunks of trees. Some old boards which had done service, were used as seats and tables. At that time there were only two miserable huts. Today you find in this place the capital of Arizona. The working of the mines can make it a very important city. Upon the great Colorado river, we found a little settlement that had existed only a year, it counted 800 souls almost all Catholics. Here we had to perform a number of baptisms, weddings and many of the faithful approached the Sacraments. Following the road eastward we arrived, after traveling a hundred and fifty leagues, in various places inhabited by the Pimas and Maricopa Indians. These Indians, numbering from nine to ten thousand, are half civilized, industrious and of very simple habits, but have not yet heard a word of the Gospel. The old Mission of San Francisco Xavier is three days journey from the Pimas. Its inhabtiants were converted by the Jesuit at the beginning of the last century. Four thousand Catholics are counted here.

Two Rev. Jesuit Fathers remained here eight months in 1864, and were gratified and consoled in baptizing many adults. The Church in this mission is constructed of large bricks and well preserved, it has two capulas which are to be seen at a great distance, the interior is frescoed and has very nice statues. About a year ago, we placed here two Priests, who administer, not only to the Mission of St. Francis Xavier, but also Tucson, with a settlement of 1,200 inhabitants, mostly Catholics. The Missionaries just finished building a church there. In Arizona are found ruins of monuments constructed by the Aztecs, whose dominion extended over all the Pueblos in Mexico, from an early date to the Spanish conquest. Other more recent ruins testify to the passing of the Spaniards, driven out at the time, by the Apache Indians. The flora of this territory presents one of the most curious of the gigantic cacti. They grow here in such abundance that according to what many of the travelers relate, from them has the country obtained the name of Arizona, which is said to signify in the Indian language: "land of the cactus". The etymology sounds truthful enough. What ever it may be, these gigantic cacti, by their beauty, form and great height, are the most interesting of their species. We have seen many as high as eleven or twelve meters. At a certain height, three, four and even five branches sprout from the main trunk, giving it the form of a real candelabra. The circumference of the trunk is about a meter. This plant yields an exquisite fruit, which the Indians gather by means of a long pole to which is attached a sickle. When we went from the great Colorado river, west of the mission of St. Francis Xavier, we traversed, each day, immense forests of these cacti, which at a distance, appeared like a troop of giants armed for a battle. Arizona has a very healthy climate. Its resources are gold mines, pastures and agricultural lands.

Colorado is much colder, but the great rivers irrigating it make its meadows cooler and the land much better for cultivation. Thousands of farmers have already taken possession of the most beautiful valleys. The main resources of Colorado are gold mines, pastures and valleys, where most of the cereals are raised. The mountains are covered with silver leaf trees and cedars.

New Mexico has the advantage over the other two territories in being populated by inhabitants born in this country, who have their families, their property and their flocks here. The climate is more temperate. Like Arizona, this Territory is rich in minerals, in flocks, cereals and fruits. The southern part produces excellent grapes. As to religion, the New Mexicans are very well disposed. There are very few places where they have not constructed a chapel, and contributed to the support of the Missionary. At a certain place, both church and rectory have been built at the expense of a single family. Their example has been followed by many. Protestants also aid frequently. The Military Commandant in New Mexico has given us $1,000 for the inauguration of the Orphanage in Santa Fe. As a general thing, our Mexicans have large families, and they state with pleasure that the more children they have the richer they are. It is not unusual to meet families of ten, twelve or more children. In the sixteen years we have been here, we have seen fifty to two hundred families emigrating to the more fertile valleys in the West, their first care being the selection of a suitable site for a Church. The Missionary draws the plan and when the good weather comes each family sends workers. At the end of one or two years the church is concluded. This is of a poor style, nevertheless it is the best monu-

ment of the place. The ardent faith of our Mexicans, their respect
for religion, above all, for the Holy Eucharist, their devotion to the
Blessed Virgin, is truly admirable. They realize that the priest is the
representative of our Lord Jesus Christ and they render him the
greatest veneration. Almost the same can be said of the Catholic
Indians. In the Pueblos, not having a missionary, they gather regularly to say their prayers. They are very fond of their priests. Here is
an example, given in the month of July 1865, by the Indians of the
Pueblo of Isleta. I had thought of confiiding to Fr. Jouvet a more
important mission. As soon as the probable change of missionary
was made known to the Indians, they gathered in a mass, the chiefs,
their eyes full of tears, presented themselves before the priest, the
oldest speaking. "Is it true that you are leaving us?" he asked.
"With your permission I will get together all our people, large and
small, counting more than 2,000, and if there is a single one who has
any complaint to make against you, we will let you go. But, if you
will remain with us now that we know you and we have placed all
our confidence in you, we will present ourselves to the Bishop in
Santa Fe; on our knees we will request that he let you remain with
us, and we will not rise until he grants us this grace." Fr. Jouvet
could not resist joining in the request of his parishioners, and remained with them, until the hour, which no one dreamt was so
near, that God called him to Himself. On the 4th of the following
November, the young Missionary died of cerebral fever. Fr. Felix
Jouvet was only a sub-deacon when he arrived in Santa Fe.

Even the most savage tribes respect our priests. One of our
missionaries, Fr. Martin, just recuperating from a serious illness,
started with a caravan to visit a priest in the neighborhood. On
the 4th of March, an extremely cold day, he was again attacked by
the fever. To arrive at his destination the quicker, he separated
himself from the caravan. While on his way, unconscious of any
danger, an arrow shot by an Indian struck him on his breast. When
he dropped dead the savages came out of their hiding places, with
the intention of robbing him of his clothes and dividing them. But
the moment they realized he was a priest, they were struck with
fear, and contrary to their custom they covered the body without
touching it. They took only his horse with them. After a while
we heard that the chief of this band has condemned the guilty one
to death, because the killing of the priest had irritated the Great
Spirit. According to the belief of these savages, a victim of expia-
tion was necessary.

In all this diocese the number of uncivilized Indians exceeds
80,000, comprising the Comanches, the Tejas and their allies, who
spend most of their time in our Territory.

It appears that the government in Washington is contemplating a
plan, which if carried out with prudence and humanity will help us
in their conversion, particularly of their children. It consists of
designating for their use a fixed tract of land, and obliging them to
live on it. This trial towards civilization has been attempted with

the Navajos, and has had a good effect. At the end of the year 1864 I sent Fr. Flourant and two minor clerics among these Indians, with orders to start a Mission and a school. After a few months the missionary had gained the respect, esteem and affection of this tribe, though at the moment that he might have gathered the fruit of his zeal, death, on the 25th of October 1865, snatched him from his dear savages. Miguel Flourant left France, when only a minor cleric, on the 17th of April 1861. I intend to grant him a successor as soon as possible.

Until now, communication between New Mexico and the rest of the United States is difficult and transportation very costly. But railroads are building in the west in California; and from the east in Missouri and Texas. As soon as these are established, the working of the mines, the raising of the flocks, the cultivation of vineyards, will change entirely the condition of things. We will be able to employ laborers at more reasonable wages, construct houses and churches as in the east. We may probably see factories established in this country, where wool is to be obtained in great abundance. In this general increase of resources, this mission will without doubt find extension and a way of sustaining the great, heavy loads, which are always found in new undertakings. Providence will never abandon us, and the Order of the Propagation of the Faith, will, as we hope, continue to help us as heretofore, since the beginning of this See in Santa Fe, of which despite our personal unworthiness we have the honor to be the first Bishop.

WALT WHITMAN'S VEIW OF THE SPANISH ELEMENT IN THE AMERICAN NATIONALITY

[In 1883, Walt Whitman was invited to compose a poem for an anniversary celebration of the settlement of Santa Fe and to come to the New Mexican capital to read it. He declined the invitation, but wrote the city fathers the following letter, remarkable for its appreciation of the Indo-Hispanic heritage of the Southwest.]

Dear Sirs:—Your kind invitation to visit you and deliver a poem for the 333d Anniversary of founding Santa Fé has reach'd me so late that I have to decline, with sincere regret. But I will say a few words off hand.

We Americans have yet to really learn our own antecedents, and sort them, to unify them. They will be found ampler than has been supposed, and in widely different sources. Thus far, impress'd by New England writers and schoolmasters, we tacitly abandon ourselves to the notion that our United States have been fashion'd from the British Islands only, and essentially form a second England only—which is a very great mistake. Many leading traits for our future national personality, and some of the best ones, will certainly prove to have originated from other than British stock.

From *The Complete Prose Works of Walt Whitman.* New York, 1902. Vol. III, pages 116–119.

As it is, the British and German, valuable as they are in the concrete, already threaten excess. Or rather, I should say, they have certainly reach'd that excess. To-day, something outside of them, and to counterbalance them, is seriously needed.

The seething materialistic and business vortices of the United States, in their present devouring relations, controlling and belittling everything else, are, in my opinion, but a vast and indispensable stage in the new world's development, and are certainly to be follow'd by something entirely different—at least by immense modifications. Character, literature, a society worthy the name, are yet to be establish'd, through a nationality of noblest spiritual, heroic and democratic attributes—not one of which at present definitely exists—entirely different from the past, though unerringly founded on it, and to justify it.

To that composite American identity of the future, Spanish character will supply some of the most needed parts. No stock shows a grander historic retrospect—grander in religiousness and loyalty, or for patriotism, courage, decorum, gravity and honor. (It is time to dismiss utterly the illusion-compound, half raw-head-and-bloody-bones and half Mysteries-of-Udolpho, inherited from the English writers of the past two hundred years. It is time to realize—for it is certainly true—that there will not be found any more cruelty, tyranny, superstition, &c., in the *résumé* of past Spanish history than in the corresponding *résumé* of Anglo-Norman history. Nay, I think there will not be found so much.)

Then another point, relating to American ethnology, past and to come, I will here touch upon at a venture. As to our aboriginal or Indian population—the Aztec in the South, and many a tribe in the North and West—I know it seems to be agreed that they must gradually dwindle as time rolls on, and in a few generations more leave only a reminiscence, a blank. But I am not at all clear about that. As America, from its many far-back sources and current supplies, develops, adapts, entwines, faithfully identifies its own—are we to see it cheerfully accepting and using all the contributions of foreign lands from the whole outside globe—and then rejecting the only ones distinctively its own—the autochthonic ones?

As to the Spanish stock of our Southwest, it is certain to me that we do not begin to appreciate the splendor and sterling value of its race element. Who knows but that element, like the course of some subterranean river, dipping invisibly for a hundred or two years, is now to emerge in broadest flow and permanent action?

If I might assume to do so, I would like to send you the most cordial, heartfelt congratulations of your American fellow-countrymen here. You have more friends in the Northern and Atlantic regions than you suppose, and they are deeply interested in the development of the great Southwestern interior, and in what your festival would arouse to public attention.

Very respectfully, &c.,

WALT WHITMAN.

TEXAS TYPES
AND CONTRASTS

[Southeast Texas is
Mexican Texas; even the land has a greater similarity to the region
south of the Rio Grande than to the rest of the state. Texas, along
with California, has been one of the immigration magnets drawing
Mexicans north from their homeland to economic opportunity and
political stability. Even prior to the vast twentieth-century immigration of Mexicans, there were thousands of Mexican Americans
living in south Texas and giving it the color and atmosphere of Old
Mexico. The following article by journalist-historian Lee C. Harby
is a vivid portrayal of this picturesque area, where two civilizations
have met.]

In the many quaint and artistic phases of life which Texas presents
there are none more alluring than those in which the Spanish race
play the principal part.

Wherever found, these Texo-Mexicans are picturesque, and their
admixture with the population renders the State fertile in vivid
contrast and rich local coloring. Even in the large cities, where they
are in such small proportion, these people of the Latin race are
distinctly noticeable from the comparisons they afford. Always
quiet and well-behaved, these city Mexicans—a few foreign waifs on

From *Harper's New Monthly Magazine*, July 1890.

the great sea of American humanity—are thrifty and industrious, living on a mere pittance, being well-content as long as they have their cigarettes and coffee. You meet them everywhere about the streets, grave, dignified, and taciturn. They pass you by with their baskets of *tamales* slung upon their backs, or with great covered cans of *chile con carne*—two modes of preparing meats which are appetizing in the extreme, but fiery to the palate from the amount of pepper used. At the corners you find them with their trays of *nueces dulces;* and following one of the vendors to his home, you come upon a scene which gives attractive variety to the city life which surrounds it. It is a low-roofed, dark shanty, the home of a family of candy-makers. A young man, slim, lithe, and dark-browed, sits on a raised threshold, cracking and shelling pecans. Behind him another stands at a stove, stirring a great kettle of boiling, seething syrup, the while a smooth-faced lad draws an inspiriting dance tune from the strings of his banjo, and a good-looking Mexican woman rocks slowly to and fro in her wide, low chair, and sings softly in unison. Out on the sidewalk three girls dance gracefully and joyously to the spirited measure, while a circle of negro children, with whom mingle two or three ragged whites, stands admiring the gay movements of the dancers. Two flaring gasoline lamps light up the scene, which is within the shadow of one of the handsomest hotels in the State. No place but Texas could afford such a picture, and many subjects for the painter's art could be found in the homes of these people.

The old Dutch masters would have loved to perpetuate the interior of a Mexican restaurant, its patrons showing the cosmopolitan nature of the population of the State. A long, low-roofed room, with bare floor, an uncovered pine table, and hard bench, on which sit three noted politicians taking an evening lunch, and concocting plans for the dear people's benefit. One is fair-skinned and ruddy-haired, as befits his Irish blood; one a typical American; the third a French Canadian. Each has a steaming platter of *chile con carne* before him, and a plate of *tamales* in their hot, moist wrappings of shuck. Behind them stands the Mexican host, tall, dark, dignified, and grave, yet watchful. They are four sharply contrasting types. Over them flicker the dim rays cast by an oil lamp, deepening the shadows, throwing half-lights into the obscurity of the corners. A tiny hairless Mexican dog sits motionless on the door-step, while the sign—written in both English and Spanish—swings creakingly above his head. Outside, the darkness is pierced by long shafts of colored light, which stream from the windows of a Jewish temple, and by the pale glimmer of a lamp in the street car waiting at a switch.

Only in the cities of Texas can be found that peculiar fusion of American civilization with Mexican life which gives rise to such tableaux as were ably depicted by Grenet in his picture "El Jarabe," exhibited at the American Art Exhibition in New York some years ago; still can the tourist be delighted with such scenes, where the grace of the dancer lends a fascination to the surroundings, and even the natural gravity of the race is dispelled by interest and admiration. . . .

Out toward the west—the great Southwest—with its illimitable prairies, its millions of cattle, its cow-boys, and its ever-interesting, distinctive, and primitive Spanish life. On to the very borders, to the Rio Grande country, with its strange formation of hills rising abruptly from the flat face of the prairie, resembling long lines of giant fortifications. The prairies themselves are sandy, loose soil, covered with grass and cactus, but with no undulation, no gradual swell and increase of altitude to lead up to the great hills which tower over their level stretches—hills composed of limestone and rock, and in many places showing the action of water, as if the waves of some great ocean had swept them up from its lowest depths. They present a natural phenomenon which is not found elsewhere in the State. . . .

It is the land of romance and of poetry, of legend, of warrior, and of priest, for from here stretching back to the Nueces lies the home of the Spanish element of the population. Here, in a clearing of the thick chaparral which borders the white winding road, stands an adobe house—earthen-floored and straw-roofed—cool, dark, and secret-looking. The shadows of the night fall thick about it, and soon from within its master comes, leaving its door wide open as he mounts his mustang and rides away to the nearest village, a mile or more distant. The warm red light of the mesquite fire fills up the open portal, and presently into this radiance passes a woman— young, slim, and handsome, with the languor and passion of the South within the depths of her dark Spanish eyes. A moment she stands and peers out, as if to pierce through the night, her form outlined against the glowing background; then drawing her rebozo about her half-bare bosom, she turns, and taking a guitar, sings in sweet high tones a little Spanish song, striking lightly upon her instrument a rippling accompaniment; and thus it would have been in English:

> "As an eagle, brave and free,
>   Is my love.
> Yet he's ever unto me
>   As the dove,
>   Cooing,
>   Wooing,
> But, eagle-like, pursuing
>   If I rove.
>
> "Like the lion, strong and bold,
>   Is my choice;
> But as lamb within the fold
>   At my voice.
>   Heeding,

Speeding,
Come, haste thou at my pleading,
And rejoice!"

The song is evidently a signal; scarcely have its notes died away
before a tall, lithe young Mexican creeps out from the thickest part
of the chaparral and makes his way to the house. He knows his
danger, or fears treachery perhaps, for as their lips meet and the
door closes behind them, the light flashes and plays upon the long,
keen blade of a knife he holds unsheathed in his hand.

The scene is like a little piece of a novel, but one meets with
much of romance—and of tragedy—in the Spanish part of the
State.

El Paso de l'Aguila, to give Eagle Pass its old Spanish name, is
such a mixture of Mexican and American that one can hardly
credit that it was settled as recently as 1849. Yet it was in that year
that General W. S. Harney established Fort Duncan at this point,
and kept his twelve hundred men in health and happiness on the
high bluffs which overlook the Rio Grande. . . .

Around Fort Duncan, then, sprang up the town—a town of jacals
and adobe houses, of dirt floors and grass roofs. Gradually American traders came there from San Antonio and Goliad, and many
who were struck by the gold fever of that year and started for California, choosing the route through Mexico, were harassed by Indians and Mexican banditti, and so turned back and settled here
under the protecting folds of the United States flag. Thus it grew,
and now it presents a wonderful mixture of poverty, ignorance, and
dirt with wealth, culture, and refinement. It is a jumble of all
classes, but Spanish if anything. Every store is a *tienda barata*
(cheap store), and all have names, as *Tienda del Gallo* (store of the
cock), *Tienda de los Mexicanos*, and so forth. They are one-storied
and flat-roofed, the most modern ones built of brick, the others of
adobe, which last forever; they have earthen floors, or cemented
ones, perhaps. Here and there can now be found a wooden building, but, though more pretentious-looking, they do not have the
solid comfort and immunity from fire which the more primitive
structures enjoy.

The town looks as though the skies rained buildings, and they
fell wheresoever they pleased. Everywhere are the jacals, and the
houses of the Americans are but a little more regularly placed. The
jacals of Eagle Pass are vastly superior to those of any other part
of Texas. Here the straw roofs are laid in regular overlapping tiers,
impervious to the elements, and lasting in good repair for thirty
years. Nor is there danger of fire, for this peculiar grass is hard to
ignite, and even when once caught does not blaze, but smoulders
sullenly, and may be extinguished with the bare hand. It is well
that it is so, for many of these dwellings have no chimneys, the fire
of mesquite is built on the earthen floor, and the smoke goes out
of a little hole left in the roof above, or an opening just in the

corner where walls and roof meet. The jacal itself is made by driving four mesquite posts in the ground; then poles are nailed across inside and outside of these uprights, and slender branches are wattled between these poles at certain distances. All the spaces are then filled with the limestone and rock indigenous to the place, and a clay cement is made with which it is plastered in and out. If a chimney is added, it is constructed in the same way. It is all fireproof, it lasts a lifetime, takes but a few days to build, costs nothing for material, and keeps out both heat and cold. All of these jacals have dirt floors, and only one or two openings for windows. Here live the Mexican and his wife and their innumerable children, who seem to swarm around every door. Here also are found the dog and all the chickens, as well as goats without number, which are the milch cows of these primitive folks. In and out of the open door stray the poultry and animals, while the family sit contentedly on the floor, smoking and talking. Most of these houses are innocent of furniture; in some a bed is found, or a chair or two; but dry-goods boxes seem to answer their every purpose, and skins are spread on the hard earthen floor, and there, wrapped in their blankets, they sleep. Above them from the roof hang strings of chile (red pepper) and jerked goat's meat, and outside against the house are fastened bird-cages of their own make, with different kinds of feathered denizens, for they are great bird trappers, and the bird sellers are a feature of the place. The jacals are all clean swept, and the yardways as well; indeed, their cleanliness seems to show itself in this particular manner, for a broom is constantly in the hands of every Mexican woman.

Every yard almost has an oven, built out of earth and rock, half under and half over the ground; here they bake their meats and some kind of cakes, but their own bread is tortillas. These are made by an interesting and peculiar process. The Indian-corn is boiled whole in water, into which a little unslacked lime is thrown, until the grain is tender. It is then taken out, washed, put into clear cold water, and allowed to soak all night. In the morning it is drained dry and crushed into flour between two stones—the bottom one like a three-cornered tray on legs of uneven height, so that it slopes downward; the upper, like a rolling pin. They place the tray upon the floor, and kneeling, they mash and roll the grain until it becomes a beautiful, white, starchy flour. That is then mixed with water into a paste, next kneaded and flattened out between the hands into broad, very thin cakes. In the mean time the mesquite fire in the corner of the jacal has burned into a grand bed of coals; on this is thrown a flat sheet of iron, which is soon hot. Here the cakes are placed, and brown instantaneously; they are turned, and in a minute are ready to be eaten. They are good, too, but need salt, for the Mexican mixes none in this bread. The Mexican of the lower class uses neither fork nor spoon, but rolls a tortilla into a scoop, and so eats his *chile con carne, frijoles,* etc. When too much softened by the gravy to take up the food, he eats his improvised spoon, takes another tortilla, and proceeds as before. They sit on the floor to eat, putting the dish of food in the middle of the circle, and not in one house out of six of the lower order is there a table. They are hospitable in the extreme, welcoming a perfect stranger to their homes, and offering him of their best.

The Mexican cooking, though Americans have a prejudice against it, is exceedingly appetizing, but for most palates too highly peppered, chile entering largely into the composition of every dish. Yet it is a rare good feast one can have by ordering the following bill of fare:

Sopa de Fideo.

Gallina con Chile.   Tamales.

Frijoles Mejicana.   Enchiladas.

Chile con Carne.   Tortillas.

Salza de Chile.

Pastel de Limon. Granadas de China.

Café.

Out in the street, on the sidewalk at night, one finds here and there about the town blazing fires, and over them set great three-cornered pieces of iron sheeting, supported on legs. These sheets have round places cut out of them, and over these holes are tin cans, their contents boiling merrily. Tamales are cooking here, and the Mexican woman who is tending them looks like one of the witches in *Macbeth*, as she moves about in her short red skirt with her black shawl about her wrinkled brown face, while the fire-light falls upon her in fitful gleams, now throwing her figure into broad relief, then leaving it in shadow. Behind her the open door of the jacal shows a blazing fire within, and on the floor, playing gravely in the quivering, dancing light, many children of different hues; for, be it known, this people is not a moral one, and a family of Mexican children may vary in all the shades between black and white. This is, *bien entendu*, of the lower orders.

Crossing the town toward the convent comes the baker, a supple, dark-skinned Mexican, with a large osier basket under his arm, filled with fine loaves baked in those same underground clay ovens; over them is tucked a flaming crimson cloth, so fond are they of color. He is baker and baker's cart too, and now he stops to chat with a butcher—not one of animals in general, but of goats in particular. Here and there are the goat-meat shops, all marked by a flag: little bits of wooden shanties—a packing-box set on end would do almost as well—but here the goats are slaughtered, dressed, and sold, and all Mexicans love the meat. Goat's milk is the only kind they use, and even the American hotels in the place have it upon the table.

Contrasting with all of this rude, primitive life is the fact that this place offers really fine society, and that at the meetings of their literary club, held weekly, much talent is evinced. Fine dances are given too, and the club-house has witnessed many dramatic efforts.

The people generally, high and low, rich and poor, have a lordly disregard for money. As the French have it, they spend with both hands. They do no haggling over prices; if they like a thing, and have the amount, they buy it, no matter what the cost. The poorest Mexican will enter a store and make his purchases with the air of a grand seigneur. Their manners have a grave decorum about them that is worthy of imitation, and they are wonderfully law-abiding, as far as riots and quarrels are concerned; but make no Mexican your enemy, or else avoid the darkness of night and of shadows, should he be within reach. He will smile in your face as you pass, then wheel and sheathe his long, sharp knife in your back. Their warfare is not open, and hence has none of the frank, lusty, rollicking bravado of the cow-boy, who gives a man a chance always in his quarrels, and would as soon be shot at as shoot. . . .

The town of Laredo presents one of the glaring contrasts so common in Texas. To all intents and purposes it is Spanish, showing in its jacals, adobe houses, low-walled, flat-roofed stone buildings, and the barred and grated windows to its dwellings, all the characteristics of old Spain. Its beggars complete the picture, and its water-carriers, with their barrels drawn by sturdy little donkeys called *burros*, add to the illusion. In contradistinction to this, electric lights swing in the narrow, stone-paved streets, and the low-roofed dwellings, with their stone walls of three and four feet thickness, are illuminated with incandescent globes. An ice factory helps to cool the water carted along the streets, and overlooking the straw-thatched and wattled jacals, a magnificent seminary rears its stately proportions.

Along the streets everything is Spanish—the signs, the language, the people—even the dogs, for the hairless Mexican canine called *pelon* is in full force. Americans are there, of course—many of them—but they are lost in the general foreign air which pervades the place. The señoras and señoritas wear no hats, but over their heads the dearly loved shawl, or *tapalo*, which is often used to coquettishly conceal the lower part of the face, leaving only the great dark eyes exposed, thus adding to their effectiveness. The use of this shawl is general, from the great-grandmother, bowed, wrinkled, and leather-colored, to the wee tot just walking alone; they all wear it, and wear it at all times, performing a thousand duties while enveloped in its embarrassing folds as easily as does the domestic who pushes her sleeves out of the way before commencing work.

The men and boys all affect the high-crowned, broad-brimmed Mexican hat of felt, with its twisted silver snakes around the crown and the arms of Mexico embroidered on the side, or else there is a silver filigree lace wound about it, and the whole hat is heavy with ornamentation done in fine threads of the precious metal. These hats cost wonderful sums, and a Mexican ranchero will spend three times as much for his head-gear as he will for all the other wants of his family combined.

Laredo has many lovely Spanish women, handsome enough to be an eternal temptation to the grave but warm-hearted *caballeros*, and so the windows of these houses, which are built immediately on the street, are guarded by iron bars, forming a grating through which one may glance and smile and whisper, perhaps, when the nights are dark and no one is very near, but the lovers' kiss and hand-clasp are things that may not be. Many of these Mexican maidens are beautifully fair, the white of the skin making their eyes darker and larger by contrast, while the lace *rebozo*, which they drape so gracefully about them, lends an almost irresistible piquancy to their charms.

In using the generic title "Mexican" when alluding to the inhabitants of a large part of western Texas, it is for the want of a better term. They are Texans by birth, and their fathers before them, but they are of the Mexican race, and have kept their blood, language, and manners distinct from the Americans. Yet when you question their leaders on which side they would fight in case of war with Mexico, they draw themselves up proudly and say, "We are Texans and Americans; we would fight for the United States." Still, they do not speak the language of this country, and they are accused of not desiring to even understand it.

PIONEER SPANISH FAMILIES IN CALIFORNIA

[The Californios, or Spanish-speaking Californians of the Mexican era, are California's "First Families." They were a small group—the Picos, Vallejos, Carrillos, Alvarados, and others—who formed a sort of early aristocracy by virtue of wealth and land ownership. The Anglo conquest largely dispossessed them of their vast land holdings, so that, by the end of the nineteenth century, their fame and position would have been only a fading memory, had it not been for the development of a nostalgia for the "Spanish heritage" on the part of California residents. This article recapitulates the place of the Californios in the state's history. Its author, Charles Howard Shinn, worked in forestry and agriculture at the University of California for several years.]

The great families of the Spanish pioneer period have mostly representatives at the present day; some of them have retained wealth and influence, especially in the southern counties. Don Romualdo Pacheco, whose mother was Ramona Carrilo, became State senator,

From *Century Magazine*, January 1891.

lieutenant-governor, and one of the leaders of the Republican party. The grandson of Captain Antonio del Valle, who came from Mexico to California in 1819, is now one of the most prominent politicians in the State. Don Juan B. Castro has held many offices of trust and profit in Monterey County. Don Ignacio Sepulveda, a thoroughly educated lawyer, married an American wife, and was long a superior judge in Los Angeles. A number of similar cases might be mentioned in which individuals of the conquered race have found their opportunity in the material development of the Pacific coast. Still, these were but exceptions; most of the old families sank into obscurity, and it is now difficult to trace their connections. Only about thirty Spanish families of California have retained any wealth or influence.

Among the families of the first rank as regards wealth, influence, dignity, and pride of birth were the Castros, Picos, Arguellos, Bandinis, Carrillos, Alvarados, Vallejos, Avilas, Ortegas, Noriegas, Peraltas, Sepulvedas, Pachecos, Yorbas, and their numerous connections. The Estradas, for instance, were relatives of the Alvarados, and Don José Abrego, of Monterey, treasurer of the province from 1839 to 1846, married an Estrada. This made the Abregos allies of the Alvarados. Don José's son married a daughter of Jacob P. Leese, the American, son-in-law of General Vallejo; his daughter married Judge Webb of Salinas: the Alvarado-Vallejo connection had drawn the Abregos towards the Americans. The founder of the Alvarado family was Juan B., a settler of 1769, whose son José was sergeant at Monterey, and whose grandson was the governor. The mother of the governor was Maria Josefa Vallejo; his wife was Martina Castro. The founder of the Arguello family was Don José Dario, who arrived in 1781; his wife was a daughter of the Moragas, and their children intermarried with the best families of the province. One daughter was the famous Maria de la Concepcion Marcela, born in 1790, and remembered because of her romance, of which Bret Harte has told the story. There is little to add to the outlines of the poem, except that the tale of the lady Concepcion Arguello is familiar to all the Spanish families, and one often hears it used to illustrate the "simple faith of the ancient days." One of the ladies of the Vallejo family retired to a convent. The lady Apolinaria Lorenzana, of Santa Barbara and San Diego, whose lover died, devoted her life to teaching and to charity, and was known for half a century as "*La Beata*," to whom all doors were open and all sorrows brought. She planted the famous grapevine of Montecito, long known as the largest in the world, and bearing six thousand clusters in a single season. There were other women as worthy of saintship, of whom the elders still speak.

The well-known family of Pico was founded in 1782, by Don José Maria, the father of the governor. The northern branch of this family sprang from Don José Dolores, who arrived in 1790. The first of the Sotos was Don Ignacio, a pioneer of 1776; and the Moraga family date from the same year, their founder being Comandante José Joaquin, of San Francisco Presidio and San José Pueblo. A large and

prominent Los Angeles family, that of the Avilas, was founded by
Cornelio Avila in 1783. Alcalde Avila was killed in the revolution of
1836. Several daughters married Americans. The Lugos are often
spoken of in histories. They descend from a Mexican soldier, Francisco Lugo, who arrived in 1769, the date which ranks among Spanish Californians as 1849 does among American pioneers. His four
daughters married into the four prominent families of Ruiz, Cota,
Vallejo, and Carrillo. The town of Martinez, near Monte Diablo,
takes its name from the Martinez family, whose founder was an
early alcalde of San Francisco, and three of whose daughters married Americans. A far later arrival was the Jimeno family, one of
whom was Governor Alvarado's Secretary of State, whose widow
became the wife of Dr. Ord, and whose two sons were taken to the
Atlantic States by Lieutenant Sherman in 1850 to be educated. An
intimate friend of this famous secretary was Don José M. Romero,
the most widely known teacher and author of the province, who
wrote and printed the "Catecismo de Ortologia" at Monterey in
1836, and established an advanced school, the best in California until
the days of Enrique Cambuston and José Maria Campina, whom
Governor Alvarado brought from Mexico.

The Bandinis descended from an Andalusian family of high rank,
and were in California by 1771. Old Captain José Bandini was the
first to raise the Mexican flag, which he did on the ship *Reina*, at
San Blas, in 1821. His son Juan married Dolores Estudillo, and, after
her death, Refugio Arguello, and was very prominent in the province
from 1825 to 1845. The extensive Carrillo family and also the great
Ortega family date their Californian record from 1769. The Ortegas
founded Santa Barbara. The Carrillos in the second generation married into the Vallejos, Castros, Pachecos, and many other proud
families. At the time of the conquest they had connections in every
part of the province. The late Judge Covarrubias, of Santa Barbara,
one of the most prominent jurists of Southern California, was connected by marriage with the Carrillos. Captain Noriega, of Santa
Barbara, also married a Carrillo, and when he died, in 1858, he left
more than a hundred descendants. There were large families in
those days of simple, healthy outdoor life; one often reads in the old
documents of from twelve to twenty sons and daughters of the same
parents. Don Cristobal Dominguez, who owned the Las Virgenes
ranch, left fourteen living children, and one hundred and ten living
descendants.

The founders of the early families came from all parts of the
Spanish dominions. The Castros were from Sinaloa, and so were
the Lugos. Old Don Aguirre, a wealthy ship-owner and merchant
who first came in his vessel the *Guipuscuana*, was a Basque, and his
family is still represented in San Diego and Santa Barbara. Another
Basque pioneer was Don José Amesti, a rough, honest fellow, alcalde
of Monterey, and afterwards the governor's secretary, who married
Prudencia Vallejo. General Castro once told me that Don José
"would even say 'carajo' before his children," a thing which "as-

tonished all his friends," for it was not seemly; no other Californian did so. The officer who founded Branciforte, Colonel Pedro Albertia, was a Catalan. The first of the Alvisos, the Valencias, and the Peraltas were from Sonora. José Mariano Bonilla, from the city of Mexico, was one of the first lawyers in the province. The Vacas, descendants of the famous *conquistadore* Captain Vaca, who was under Cortez, came from New Mexico. Don Manuel Requena of Los Angeles came to California from Yucatan. The Suñols, who owned one of the most beautiful of valleys, were from Spain, and the sons were sent to Paris to be educated. Lieutenant Valdez, who was in the Malaspina expedition of 1791, returned to Europe and was killed at Trafalgar. This noted expedition, under Alejandro Malaspina, consisted of two royal corvettes of Spain, which left Cadiz in 1789, reached California in 1791, and went around the world. In ways like these, and from a thousand channels of commerce and adventure, every province of Spain and Mexico became represented among the pioneer families of California.

The Vallejo family traces its descent from soldiers and nobles of the heroic days of Spain, and is as well known in the mother country as in California. A copy of the genealogical record of the family, which has been kept with great precision, was filed in 1806 in the Spanish archives of Alta California. It states that Don Alonzo Vallejo commanded the Spanish troops on board the vessel which brought the royal commissioner Bobadilla to America with orders to carry Columbus a prisoner to Spain. Another famous Vallejo was a captain under Cortez, followed that illustrious cutthroat to the complete conquest of Mexico, and became governor of the province of Panuco, lord of great silver mines, and master of peons innumerable.

Bilbao, the ancient capital of Burgos, Spain, was the place from which the branch of the Vallejos that is known in California started for the New World. Of this branch came Don Ignacio Vicente Vallejo, born in 1748, in the city of Guadalaxara, Mexico, and designed, as were many of the family before him, for holy orders and the service of the Church. The young man rebelled, volunteered under Captain Rivera y Moncada in Padre Junipero Serra's famous expedition, landing at San Diego in 1769, and thus became a pioneer among the Spanish pioneers themselves. He soon became prominent in the colony, and was not only made military commander of various towns, but was long the only civil engineer in the province, laying out most of the greater irrigation works of the Missions and pueblos, and becoming the owner of extensive and valuable estates. . . .

The link between the old and the new, between the quiet and happy pastoral age of the beginning of the century and the age of American growth and change that followed fast on the conquest, was that remarkable man, General Mariano Guadalupe Vallejo, whose children, as he once told me, "were born under three administrations—Spanish, Mexican, and American." One of his daughters said, "Two of us, when we were small, were called by our brothers and sisters 'the little Yankees.'" General Vallejo, the eighth of the thirteen children of Don Ignacio, was born in 1808, in the old seaport town of Monterey, long the capital of the province, and died January 18, 1890, in Sonoma, once the northern fortress of the province and guarded by the . . . general's soldiers. . . .

One has to go back to the days of the famous Spanish "marches," or frontier towns built and defended in Spain's heroic age by her proudest knights, to find a fit parallel in history to the position held by General Vallejo during the closing years of the Mexican rule in California. He had absolute sway for a hundred miles or more, and he "kept the border." His men rode on horseback to Monterey and to Captain Sutter's fort on the Sacramento, bringing him news and carrying his letters. Spanish families colonized the fertile valleys under his protection, and Indians came and built in the shadows of the Sonoma Mission. He owned, as he believed by unassailable title, the largest and finest ranch in the province, and he dispensed a hospitality so generous and universal that it was admired and extolled even among the old Spanish families. J. Quinn Thornton, who visited the coast in 1848 and published his experiences, says: "Governor-General Vallejo owns 1000 horses that are broken to the saddle and bridle, and 9000 that are not broken. Broken horses readily bring one hundred dollars apiece, but the unbroken ones can be purchased for a trivial sum." More and more in the closing years of the epoch and the days of the conquest General Vallejo became the representative man of his people, and so he has received, among many of the old families, the reproachful name of a traitor to California and to his nation. The quiet intensity of this bitterness, even to-day, is a startling thing. I have seen men of pure blood, famous in provincial history, leave the room at the name of Vallejo. . . .

In his younger days General Vallejo not only knew almost every one of the five thousand Spanish Californians in the province, the greater part of the Mission Indians, and the chiefs of the wild tribes, but he gathered up, even in his youth, the traditions of the pioneers, and tested their accuracy by every possible documentary and other evidence. His journals are full of variety, and form a complete picture of the entire Spanish period. . . .

Everywhere, in the most picturesque portions of California, are the old adobes that once were social centers of the stately life of nearly a century ago. Most of them are merely ruins, but many are still the homes of the descendants of the first families of the province. The years that brought such change and wreck to the old days have now carried them so far back into the mists of tradition that they seem centuries away. Vallejo's fortress on the frontier is now a town, as dull and unromantic as Yonkers. About the ancient pueblo of Los Angeles has sprung up an intensely modern city. A railroad extends through the very graveyard of San Miguel Mission. Much needs to be done by Californians to preserve the memorials of the past that was so fair and so fruitful a beginning of the story of the commonwealth. The agency through which this is to be accomplished is likely to be the association known as the Native Sons of the Golden West, under whose public-spirited direction was conducted the recent successful celebration of the admission of California.

THE LAND OF POCO TIEMPO

[Charles Fletcher Lummis was a journalist, historian, explorer, and folklorist, to name a few of his many vocations and interests. Most of his exploring was in the Southwest and in Central and South America. On the basis of several years of living in New Mexico, he wrote a highly readable description of the state and its people called *The Land of Poco Tiempo*. Prior to publication of the book, he published an article by the same title, reprinted in part below, in a leading journal of his time.]

Sun, silence, and adobe—that is New Mexico in three words. If a fourth were to be added, it need be only to clinch the three. It is the Great American Mystery—the National Rip Van Winkle—the United States which is *not* United States. Here is the land of *poco tiempo*—the home of "Pretty Soon." Why hurry with the hurrying world? The "pretty soon" of New Spain is better than the "Now! Now!" of the haggard States. The opiate sun soothes to rest, the adobe is made to lean against, the hush of day-long noon would not be broken. Let us not hasten—*mañana* will do. Better still, *pasado mañana*.

From *Scribner's Magazine*, December 1891.

New Mexico is the anomaly of the Republic. It is a century older to European civilization than the rest, and several centuries older still in a happier semi-civilization of its own. It had its little walled cities of stone before Columbus had grandparents-to-be; and it has them yet. The most incredible pioneering the world has ever seen overran it with the zeal of a prairie-fire three hundred and fifty years ago; and the embers of that unparalleled blaze of exploration are not quite dead to-day. The most superhuman marches, the most awful privations, the most devoted heroism, the most unsleeping vigilance wrested this bare, brown land to the world; and having wrested it, went to sleep. The winning was the wakefullest in history—the after-nap eternal. It never has wakened—one does not know that it ever can. Nature herself does little but sleep, here. A few semi-bustling American towns wart the Territorial map. It is pockmarked with cattle-ranches and mines, where Experience has wielded his costly birch over millionaire pupils from the East and the Continent. But the virus never reached the blood—the pits are only skin-deep. The Saxon excrescences are already asleep too. The cowboy is a broken idol. He no longer "shoots up the town," or riddles heels reluctant for the dance. His day is done; and so is that of the argonaut. They both are with us, but their lids are heavy. And around them is New Spain again, dreamy as ever after their rude but short-lived nudging. The sheep—which feed New Mexico—doze again on the mesas, no longer routed by their long-horned foes; and where sheep are, is rest. The brown or gray adobe hamlets of the descendants of those fiery souls who wreaked here a commonwealth before the Saxon fairly knew there was a New World; the strange terraced towns of the aboriginal pioneers who out-Spaniarded the Spaniards by unknown centuries; the scant leaven of incongruous American brick—all are under the spell. And the abrupt mountains, the echoing, rock-walled cañons, the sunburnt mesas, the streams bankrupt by their own shylock sands, the gaunt, brown, treeless plains, the ardent sky, all harmonize with unearthly unanimity.

"Picturesque" is a tame word for it. It is a picture, a romance, a dream, all in one. It is our one corner that is the sun's very own. Here he has had his way, and no discrepancy mars his work. It is a land of quaint, swart faces, of oriental dress and unspelled speech; a land where distance is lost, and the eye is a liar; a land of ineffable lights and sudden shadows; of polytheism and superstition, where the rattlesnake is a demigod, and the cigarette a means of grace, and where Christians mangle and crucify themselves—the heart of Africa beating against the ribs of the Rockies.

There are three typical races in New Mexico now—for it would be wrong to include the ten per cent. "American" interpolation as a type. With them I have here nothing to do. They are potential, but not picturesque. Besides them and around them are the real autocthones, a quaint ethnologic trio. First, the nine thousand Pueblo Indians—peaceful, fixed, house-dwelling and home-loving, tillers of the soil; good Catholics in the churches they have builded with a patience infinite as that of the Pyramids; good pagans everywhere else. Then the ten thousand Navajo Indians—whose other ten thousand is in Arizona—sullen, nomad, horse-loving, horse-stealing, horse-living vagrants of the saddle; pagans first, last, and all the time, and inventors of the mother-in-law joke gray centuries before the civilized world awoke to it. Last of all, the Mexicans; in-bred and isolation-shrunken descendants of the Castilian world-finders; living almost as much against the house as in it; ignorant as slaves, and more courteous than kings; poor as Lazarus, and more hospitable than Croesus; Catholics from A to Izzard, except when they take occasion to be Penitentes—and even then fighting to bring their matted scourges and bloody crosses into the church which bars its door to them. The Navajos have neither houses nor towns; the Pueblos have nineteen compact little cities; and the Mexicans several hundred villages, a part of which are shared by the invader. The few towns of undiluted gringo hardly count in summing up the Territory of three hundred by four hundred miles. . . .

The most unique pictures in New Mexico are to be found among its unique pueblos. Their quaint terraced architecture is the most remarkable on the continent; and there is none more picturesque in the world. It remains intact only in the remoter pueblos—those along the Rio Grande have been largely Mexicanized into one-storied tameness. Laguna, on the Atlantic & Pacific Railroad, has some three-story terraced houses still. Acoma, on its dizzy island-cliff, twenty miles southwest, is all three-storied; and Taos, in its lovely, lonely valley far to the north, is two great pyramid-tenements of six stories.

And the Pueblos—they are picturesque anywhere and always, but particularly in their dances, races, and other ceremonials. These are Indians who are neither poor nor naked; Indians who feed themselves, and ask no favors of Washington; Indians who have been at peace for two centuries, and fixed residents for perhaps a millennium; Indians who were farmers and irrigators and six-story-house builders before a New World had been beaten through the thick skull of the Old; Indians who do not make pack-beasts of their squaws—and who have not "squaws," save in the vocabulary of less-bred barbarians. They had nearly a hundred republics in America, centuries before *the* American Republic was conceived; and they have maintained their ancient democracy through all the ages, unshamed by the corruption of a voter, the blot of a defalcation or malfeasance in office. They are entitled, under the solemn pledge of our government in the treaty of Guadalupe Hidalgo, to every privilege of citizenship, but have received few, if any. Their numerous sacred dances are by far the most picturesque sights in America, and the least viewed by Americans, who never found anything more striking abroad. The mythology of Greece and Rome is less than theirs in complicated comprehensiveness, and they are a more interesting ethnologic study than the tribes of inner Africa, and less known by their white countrymen.

The flat Mexican towns themselves are picturesque—for the ardent sun of the Southwest makes even an adobe beautiful when it can pick it out in violent antitheses of light and shade. Their people—ragged courtiers, unlettered diplomats—are fast losing their pictorial possibilities. The queue and the knee-breeches, the home-woven poncho with a hole in the centre whereby the owner may thrust his head through the roof of his combined umbrella and overcoat, are past or passing away; and in their place have come the atrocities of the Hebrew clo'man. But the faces—they are New Spain still. . . .

Life is the least vital feature of New Mexico. The present is a husk—the past was a romance and a glory. The Saxon invasion which came with the railroad has reacted almost to syncope. It is in little hope of revivification until the settlement of land titles shall be effected, and a national shame of forty years effaced. The native, stirred to unwonted perspiration by the one-time advent of the prodigal *peso*, has dropped back to ease with dignity—dignity in rags, mayhap, but always dignity. To the old ways he has not wholly returned—just to the old joy of living, the broad content of sitting and remembering that one has lungs for this ozone and eyes for this day-dream. I would not be understood that it is idleness. There is work; but such unfatal work! The *paisano* has learned to live even while he works—wherein he is more wise than we, who slave away youth (which is life) in chasing that which we are past enjoyment of when we overtake it. He tills his fields and tends his herds; but there is no unseemly haste, no self-tripping race for wealth. *Lo que puede*—that which can be—is enough. It needs not to plough deep, nor to dun the land with fertilizers. The land has taken it easy, too, and after three centuries of uncrowded fruition appears not exhausted, but restful and conservative. Why urge it? There will be enough! The river's wily pulse circulates in ten thousand *acequias*, and gives drink to the thirsty fields, cupped with their little irrigating-beds. Its sediment is fertilizer sufficient. So shall the brown bean, the quenchless chile, the corn and the wheat, fill the storeroom—and what need of more? . . .

Society is little bitten with the unrest of civilization. The old ways are still the best ways; and the increasing reprobates who would improve upon their fathers are eyed askance. The social system is patriarchal, and in many degrees beautiful. Mexican and Pueblo children are, as a class, the best-mannered, the most obedient, the least quarrelsome in America. Respect for age is the corner-stone of society. A son, untouched by our refining influence, would as soon put his hand in the fire as smoke before his parents—even though he have already given them grand-children. A stranger, be he poor or princely, is master of the house to which he shall come. It may be the veriest hut of a *jacal* amid the farther ranges; it may contain but a single crust of bread and a sheepskin upon the clay floor; but house and crust and couch are his, though his hosts sleep supperless upon the bare adobe—and all with a high, gentle courtesy that palaces might study. The Anglo-Saxon is not born to intrinsic hospitality, and can understand its real meaning as little as anything else one has to *learn*. He promulgates the Brotherhood of Man; but to him man *means* his brothers, and not his fifty-ninth cousins. It is partly because of this that he disavows, and is infested with, the tramp. Hospitality is as Latin in fact as in name. It is in the blood; and outside that blood it is not. In the old days, one might zigzag the whole incomparable area of Spanish America, without money or letters, with no introduction beyond his patent of humanity, and be assured everywhere of a "welcome to your own house, Señor." It is very much so to-day, and the traveller in the outer darkness will meet a hospitality as utter as he shall find the lack of it in the few "civilized" communities along his way. There are some Mexicans and some Pueblos who have learned in bitterness to shut their doors upon the hospitality-robber of late years; but they are very few. Almost every Spanish home in New Mexico is a home too for the wayfarer; and in the pueblos it is the sacred office of the Cacique to see that no stranger is uncared for. There are poor people among both races—fewer in the Indian ranks—but no Mexican and no Pueblo since time began ever went hungry, unless lost in the wilderness; and none ever suffered for the necessaries of life, and none was ever outcast of his kind. One or two Pueblos in a generation, and several Mexicans in a week, go behind the bars; but if the Southwest were peppered with poorhouses, no soul of either race would ever be found therein. To Saxons who are associable, both peoples are the kindliest, the most thoughtful, and the least meddlesome of neighbors. . . .

As the burro is the spiritual type of the Southwest, so is the sheep the material symbol. He rendered the Territory possible for three centuries, in the face of incomparably the most savage and interminable Indian wars that any age or any country ever knew. He fed and clothed New Spain, and made its customs, if not its laws. He reorganized society, led the fashions, caused the only machinery that was in New Mexico in three hundred years, made of a race of nomad savages the foremost of blanket-weavers, and invented a slavery which is unto this day in despite of the Emancipation Proclamation. The first sheep that touched what is now United States came to New Mexico with Coronado in 1540; but they did not last. Half a century later, Oñate brought the merino flocks whose descendants remain. The modest wool-bearer soon came to the front. He was the one available utilization of New Mexico. Society gradually fell apart into two classes—sheep-owners and sheep-tenders. One man at the beginning of this century had two million head of sheep, and kept a thousand peons always in the field with them, besides the thousands more who were directly dependent. That was the Spanish governor Baca. "El Quero" Chaves, the first governor of

New Mexico under the Mexican Republic, had a million sheep. The last of the great sheep-kings, Don José Leandro Perea, of Bernalillo, died a few years ago leaving two hundred thousand. Since his time, the largest flocks range from eighty thousand to one hundred and ten thousand; and there are more than a dozen individual holdings of over fifty thousand head.

The social effects of such a system, wherein four-fifths of the Caucasian male population were servants at five to eight dollars a month to a handful of mighty *amos,* are not far to trace. The most conscientious of these frontier czars had perforce a power beside which the government was a nonentity; and the unscrupulous swelled their authority to an unparalleled extent. It was easy to get a few hundred poor shepherds into one's debt; and once in, the *amo,* with the aid of complaisant laws, took good care that they should never get out. He was thenceforth entitled to the labor of their bodies—even to the labor of their children. They were his *peons*—slaves without the expense of purchase. And peonage in disguise is still effective in New Mexico. . . .

Cumulative penitence is a deep-rooted custom of both races. With the Indians, the tribal vicars mortify the flesh in behalf of their people, but almost solely by excessive fasts. Among the Mexicans still survives that astounding perversion of the once-godly Franciscan Third Order, the Penitentes, but now confined to a few remote hamlets. These fanatics do penance for themselves only, and in Lent achieve their sin-washing for the year. They flay their bare backs with plaited scourges, wallow naked in beds of cactus, bear crushing crosses, and on Good Friday actually crucify one of their order, chosen to that supreme honor by lot. This is not all of the past. The Penitente crucifixions had not missed a year up to 1891. Hundreds of Americans have witnessed this ghastly passion-reality; and I have had the privilege of photographing it.

With the superstitions dwells the simple folk-lore. That of the Mexicans is scant; but that of the Indians infinite and remarkably poetic. And both races have great store of folk-songs—composed by Those of Old, or by lonely shepherds.

These are but fugitive glimpses of the Land of Pretty Soon. A picture of sharp outline and definite detail would better diagraph some of the contents of New Mexico, but it would not be a true picture of the country. Landscape and life are impressionist, and will submit neither to photography nor to figures. Years of study and travel do not itemize the picture—there still remain in the memory but a soft, sweet haze of shifting light and shade, a wilderness of happy silence, an ether of contentful ease, wherein we live and die and are glad.

GOVERNOR MIGUEL A. OTERO'S PLEA FOR NEW MEXICAN STATEHOOD

[New Mexico became a U.S. territory at the end of the Mexican War in 1848, but it was not until 1912 that statehood was granted. Between the two dates lay a long struggle fraught with numerous setbacks and a great deal of political dealing. Responsibility for the long delay can be about evenly divided between the federal government and the people of New Mexico. When there was willingness on one side, it was absent on the other. While Miguel Antonio Otero, a Mexican American, was governor of New Mexico (1897–1906), he actively promoted statehood. In 1901, he and Governor N. O. Murphy of Arizona arranged for both of their territories to hold separate statehood conventions, at which both governors would speak. The first convention was held at Albuquerque on October 15. Governor Otero's short speech to the convention is reprinted below. His efforts, regrettably, did not result in statehood, for the idea of joint statehood for Arizona and New Mexico was put forward, and Otero found himself working against statehood as long as New Mexico could not come into the Union under its own flag.]

From Miguel A. Otero, *My Nine Years as Governor of the Territory of New Mexico.* Albuquerque, 1940. Appendix, pages 389–391.

Fellow citizens: It is with pride and pleasure that I greet you on this occasion when for the 21st year the metropolis of New Mexico celebrates her territorial fair.

This occasion is one of unusual significance and importance to you and the whole territory, as upon your action today will largely depend the action of Congress in regard to that question of supreme importance to our future, our admission as a state of the Union.

My own views upon this subject are too well known to need repetition here; in each message to the legislature, and in every report to the secretary of the interior, I have urged the passage of an enabling act and set out in full the reasons and arguments for it. I have issued the proclamation calling this meeting of the people that they might express themselves directly instead of through their legislature or governors.

For more than half a century we have been of, yet not one of, the United States; during all that period we have been true and loyal to the laws and flag of that glorious Union of which we hope to become a part, and have freely given of our blood and treasure to maintain its supremacy and glory. During that time we have seen fifteen states admitted, one of them taken largely from within our borders, and a territory created out of one of our counties; each of these states save one, when admitted had less population and taxable property than we now possess, and none was in any respect better equipped for self government than we.

As early as June, 1850, a constitution was adopted by our people for the formation of a state which prohibited slavery in New Mexico, showing at that early day that our people were fully alive to the dangers that threatened the republic, and the only course it could pursue to carry out the great future which these United States have wrought in proclaiming liberty throughout the world and to the peoples thereof. Under this constitution, two United States senators and a member of Congress were elected, who were not recognized by Congress. But it did in September of that year create us into a territory by the organic act which is still our fundamental law.

Nothing further was done of a public nature towards our admission until 1874, when a bill for that purpose was introduced by Honorable S. B. Elkins, our delegate. This was defeated but the effort was renewed at the next and each succeeding Congress. With every renewed effort and additional reasons for our admission the

opposition has grown the stronger, until the conclusion is irresistible that some strong personal and financial interests are arrayed
against us for selfish aggrandisement. One evidence of this is the
Elephant Butte dam; and another the segregation of large areas of
public domain for so-called forest reserves, and the effort being
made for a government lease law. As a territory, we cannot combat
these schemes; we have no voice in the disposition of that land that
we have struggled so long to maintain as a part of our territory,
while, as a state, we would be able to assert and retain our rights.

In 1889, as distinguished a body of men assembled for the purpose
of framing a constitution for the new state of New Mexico as had
ever gathered for a similar purpose, and after deliberating for
nearly a month, formulated a constitution which is the peer of any
similar document in the Union. It is so fair, so liberal, and so com-
prehensive that I caused it to be published in my last report as the
strongest showing that could be made upon our capacity for self
government. Owing to an unfortunate combination of circumstances,
this most admirable constitution was rejected by the people at the
election held in 1890, but it will stand as a monument to the wisdom
and statesmanship of its framers.

I believe that the time is now ripe for the fruition of our hopes;
that Congress knows the merit of our claims and will not longer
deny us the privilege we have sought so long, and that the action of
this assemblage of representative citizens of the territory will prove
a potent help toward that end.

I do not, on an occasion like this, wish to speak of disagreeable
facts, but it is well that we should realize and face them and then
apply the remedy.

Our ridiculously low assessment for taxation is constantly spoken
of and reflected upon. The present assessed value of the territory is
less than forty millions, while it is a notorious fact recognized by all
who know anything about the subject that it ought to at least be
three times that amount. The figures show that we have dropped
from fory-five millions, in 1890, to less than thirty-eight million, in
1901, and the reduction still goes on, until, as a means of self preservation, in order to protect our credit and pay the actual expense of
the government, the territory board of equalization last month
made a raise on the returned value of all the property it could
reach. This, my fellow citizens, is a lamentable state of affairs and
one that must be remedied by you. You must see to it that proper
men are elected to assess the property and equalize its value, so
that we may appear to the world that we are in fact, as to our
wealth and ability, able to pay our obligations.

This I believe to be the principal objection to our immediate admission, and if at this meeting you will adopt suitable resolutions
upon this most important and vital subject and determine to see
them carried out, you will have taken a long step toward the object
for which we are here assembled.

I understand that some timorous people are afraid of the expense and responsibility attached to our becoming a state, but such fears are unworthy of American manhood; if they were to prevail in the ordinary affairs of life no one would exercise his rights of citizenship, or incur the duties and responsibilities of family life. The history of every newly admitted state is one of growth, advance, and prosperity, and we would be no exception to this rule, but, on the contrary, by our location midway of the oceans which bound the nation, with our natural wealth of mineral, timber, and lands, and the railroad connections we already have, New Mexico will at once assume a commanding position in the sisterhood of states, and the present motto, "Cresit Eundo" on our seal will assume added meaning and significance from the date of our admission.

Part Four

MEXICAN AMERICANS: NATIVE AND ALIEN, 1911–39

La Raza was reinforced substantially after 1890 by immigration from Mexico. The statistics are unreliable, but it is known there were thousands of illegal entrants. The immigration, however, was a highly transient one. Although many Mexicans did eventually settle in this country, it is probable that they had not originally intended to. Work and wages provided the attraction, but Mexico was still home, and money was sent there to help support the family. And it was to Mexico that the immigrants returned when work slackened off north of the Rio Grande.

This immigration from Mexico, eventually numbering hundreds of thousands, cannot be seen as an isolated affair, although it had its own interesting characteristics. The decades from 1890 to 1930 witnessed an enormous immigration of people from nearly all parts of the globe. During those years, more than 22 million persons came to the United States, seeking the opportunities available in the world's most industrialized nation. The Mexicans were but a small portion of this great movement. But, when the gates of immigration were virtually closed by the Reed-Johnson Act of 1924, the Mexicans continued to enter, because the nations of the Western Hemisphere were not included in the ban.

Between 1910 and 1920, the Mexicans had their own urgent reasons for emigrating, for once again their country was in the throes of revolution, as the regime of long-time President Porfirio Díaz was overthrown and various factions fought for supremacy. During Díaz's rule, 90 per cent of the population of Mexico had found itself landless by virtue of a "reform" program that put most of the land into the hands of the wealthy. This was perhaps the original incentive for the emigration that occurred as early as the 1890's. But, in fact, the desperately poor masses of Mexicans needed little additional incentive to look elsewhere for a livelihood.

Up to the end of the nineteenth century, the career of La Raza had been pretty well confined to the Southwest, but, under the pressure of the immigration from Mexico, Mexican Americans and Mexican nationals began to appear in almost every part of the country. Predominantly, of course, it was the Southwest—mainly Texas and California—that drew the most immigration. But, as the immigration continued, job opportunities were heard of in the Northwest and throughout the upper Midwest. Most of the work was agricultural, but the major Northern cities also attracted Mexican workers to their mills, factories, and railroads. The immigration from Mexico also acted as an economic pressure on Mexican Americans of the Southwest. The immigrants were willing to accept jobs for lower wages than native American workers, and, in much of the Southwest, this meant they were competing directly with native-born members of La Raza. The Mexican Americans therefore frequently inaugurated a migration of their own, moving north, where jobs were more plentiful and wages higher and where they could exploit their advantage of being able to speak English.

The immigrants from Mexico provided a source of unskilled labor for American industry and agriculture. Since the demand for agricultural laborers is seasonal, a great part of this labor force usually returned to Mexico at the end of the season. Others followed the crops, working their way from one part of the country to another, and often trying to find temporary work after the harvests were over. This immigrant, transient work force was highly favored by the agricultural interests of the Southwest. These laborers were available when needed, were tractable would work for lower wages, and were not subject to unionization; and a minimum of responsibility needed to be shown for them.

A great portion, perhaps most, of the immigration from Mexico consisted of "wetbacks," those who crossed the border illegally, often by swimming across the Rio Grande. Many of these came over as individuals, but not a few were contracted for by American employers and smuggled in in groups. This illegal crossing was not an issue for many Mexicans, because they felt that they were only entering another part of what was really their country, a land founded and settled by their ancestors centuries ago and where many of their people lived and worked. To enter illegally was also a less humiliating experience than to have to deal with American immigration officials. Deportation of the illegal entrants has never been successful. There were just too many of them, and it was too easy to get back into the United States again even if one was deported. The agricultural interests benefited from the number of Mexicans illegally in the country, for they could hire them until the work was done, then report them to the immigration agents before the seasonal wages had to be paid.

The immigration from Mexico, whether legal or not, has contributed greatly to the economic development of the Southwest. Owing to the labor vacuum created by the Chinese Exclusion Act of 1882 and the "Gentlemen's Agreement" with Japan in 1907, virtually shutting off Oriental immigration, the West needed another source of workers. Mexican nationals and Mexican Americans constituted 80 per cent of the work force in agriculture, 90 per cent of the workers on the Western railroads, and 60 per cent of the labor force in the mines. This is in addition to the sizable numbers who gravitated to the industrial centers of the North or who followed the agricultural seasons in other parts of the nation.

The immigration from Mexico proceeded unhindered until the Great Depression. With the collapse of the economy, many Mexican nationals returned to their homeland, and many others went back in the forced repatriation that was put into effect in parts of the Southwest as a way of getting rid of a labor surplus and of cutting down the relief rolls. Unfortunately, the repatriation was indiscriminately carried out, and, of the approximately 500,000 persons who returned to Mexico, more than half were U.S. citizens. This made for hard feelings between La Raza and the Anglo majority in a region never known to be generous in its attitude toward Mexican Americans.

The effects of the immigration from Mexico on that portion of La Raza native to the United States were not uniform. To some extent, the immigrants represented a cultural and ethnic reinforcement, as had been true among immigrant groups from Europe and the Far East. As the decades passed, these accessions of population became more solidly a part of La Raza in this country. But they were not welcomed with open arms when they first arrived. For one thing, they were direct economic competition. For another, their low educational level and desperate poverty put them at a disadvantage, especially in the eyes of the Hispanos, who considered themselves descendants of the Spanish conquerors with no admixture of Indian blood. And the low educational and economic level, as well as cultural differences, caused many Mexican Americans to fear they would be lumped together with the newcomers by an Anglo population not always discriminating in its ethnic views.

The lot of the Mexican Americans, except as they were affected by the immigration, changed little during this period prior to 1940. In a real sense, they were forgotten Americans; there was little assimilation to the majority society. They remained a Spanish-speaking, largely rural, and generally poor minority. The decline of the small farmer and sheepherder forced many off the land altogether. But even as wage-earners, they received no proper return in comparison to their contribution to the building of the economy of the Southwest.

MEXICAN IMMIGRANTS ON THE LABOR MARKET

[Immigration from Mexico began in earnest about 1900. The impetus toward it was two-fold. Within Mexico, the terrible poverty of the masses under the regime of Porfirio Díaz prompted thousands to move northward for a living. In the mid-1890's, to make matters worse, Díaz instituted agricultural policies that resulted in most of the land coming into large private holdings, while 95 per cent of the ten million poor were left landless. Beginning in 1910, of course, a further decade of revolution and political instability would prompt many Mexicans to emigrate. But, if Mexico itself offered sufficient reason to leave, the United States also provided the great lure of jobs. The labor market, particularly in the Southwest, required a large supply of cheap, unskilled labor for large-scale agriculture, the railroads, and the mines. There were also incentives for many to go further north to the Midwest, so that many areas of the United States that had never known Mexicans became acquainted with them for the first time. Immigration statistics are thoroughly unreliable as indicators of how many Mexicans have come into the country during any given decade. There is a large two-way traffic of illegal entrants, as well as many who enter legally but only stay temporarily. This article by Samuel Bryan, published in 1912, gives a brief account of social and economic aspects of the immigration at the end of its first decade.]

From *The Survey*, September 7, 1912: "Mexican Immigrants in the United States," by Samuel Bryan.

Previous to 1900 the influx of Mexicans was comparatively unimportant. It was confined almost exclusively to those portions of Texas, New Mexico, Arizona, and California which are near the boundary line between Mexico and the United States. Since these states were formerly Mexican territory and have always possessed a considerable Mexican population, a limited migration back and forth across the border was a perfectly natural result of the existing blood relationship. During the period from 1880 to 1900 the Mexican-born population of these border states increased from 66,312 to 99,969—a gain of 33,657 in twenty years. This increase was not sufficient to keep pace with the growth of the total population of the states. Since 1900, however, there has been a rapid increase in the volume of Mexican immigration, and also some change in its geographical distribution, with the result that distinct social and economic problems have arisen.

Until 1908 the officials of the Bureau of Immigration who were stationed upon the Mexican border concerned themselves chiefly with the examination of Japanese and Syrians who sought to enter this country by the way of Mexico. Since that time some effort has been made to secure data with regard to immigrants of Mexican birth, but the results obtained are so obviously incomplete as to be of little value. In 1908 it was estimated that from 60,000 to 100,000 Mexicans entered the United States each year. This estimate, however, should be modified by the well known fact that each year a considerable number of Mexicans return to Mexico. Approximately 50 per cent of those Mexicans who find employment as section hands upon the railroads claim the free transportation back to El Paso which is furnished by the railroad companies to those who have been in their employ six months or a year. Making allowance for this fact, it would be conservative to place the yearly accretion of population by Mexican immigration at from 35,000 to 70,000. It is probable, therefore, that the Mexican-born population of the United States has trebled since the census of 1900 was taken.

This rapid increase within the last decade has resulted from the expansion of industry both in Mexico and in the United States. In this country the industrial development of the Southwest has opened up wider fields of employment for unskilled laborers in transportation, agriculture, mining, and smelting. A similar expansion in northern Mexico has drawn many Mexican laborers from the farms of other sections of the country farther removed from the border, and it is an easy matter to go from the mines and section gangs of northern Mexico to the more remunerative employment to be had in similar industries of the southwestern United States. Thus the movement from the more remote districts of Mexico to the newly developed industries of the North has become largely a stage in a more general movement to the United States. Entrance into this country is not difficult, for employment agencies in normal times have stood ready to advance board, lodging, and transportation to a place where work was to be had, and the immigration officials have usually deemed no Mexican likely to become a public charge so long as this was the case. This was especially true before 1908. Thus many penniless Mexicans who would be rejected at an eastern port have been admitted without question on the Mexican border. . . .

Most of the Mexican immigrants have at one time been employed as railroad laborers. At present they are used chiefly as section hands and as members of construction gangs, but a number are also to be found working as common laborers about the shops and powerhouses. Although a considerable number are employed as helpers, few have risen above unskilled labor in any branch of the railroad service. As section hands on the two more important systems they were paid a uniform wage of $1 per day from their first employment in 1902 until 1909, except for a period of about one year previous to the financial stringency of 1907, when they were paid $1.25 per day. In 1909 the wages of all Mexican section hands employed upon the Santa Fe lines were again raised to $1.25 per day. The significant feature is, however, that as a general rule they have earned less than the members of any other race similarly employed. For example, of 2,455 Mexican section hands from whom data were secured by the Immigration Commission in 1908 and 1909, 2,111, or 85.9 per cent, were earning less than $1.25 per day, while the majority of the Greeks, Italians, and Japanese earned more than $1.25 and a considerable number more than $1.50 per day.

In the arid regions of the border states where they have always been employed and where the majority of them still live, the Mexicans come into little direct competition with other races, and no problems of importance result from their presence. But within the last decade their area of employment has expanded greatly. They are now used as section hands as far east as Chicago and as far north as Wyoming. Moreover, they are now employed to a considerable extent in the coal mines of Colorado and New Mexico, in the ore mines of Colorado and Arizona, in the smelters of Arizona, in the cement factories of Colorado and California, in the beet-sugar industry of the last mentioned states, and in fruit growing and canning in California. In these localities they have at many points come into direct competition with other races, and their low standards have acted as a check upon the progress of the more assertive of these.

Where they are employed in other industries, the same wage discrimination against them as was noted in the case of railroad employes is generally apparent where the work is done on an hour basis, but no discrimination exists in the matter of rates for piece-work. As piece-workers in the fruit canneries and in the sugar-beet industry the proverbial sluggishness of the Mexicans prevents them from earning as much as the members of other races. In the citrus fruit industry their treatment varies with the locality. In some instances they are paid the same as the "whites"—in others the same as the Japanese, according to the class with which they share the field of employment. The data gathered by the Immigration Commission show that although the earnings of Mexicans employed in the other industries are somewhat higher than those of the Mexican section hands, they are with few exceptions noticeably lower than the earnings of Japanese, Italians, and members of the various Slavic races who are similarly employed. This is true in the case of smelting, ore mining, coal mining, and sugar refining. Specific instances of the use of Mexicans to curb the demands of other races are found in the sugar-beet industry of central California, where they were introduced for the purpose of showing the Japanese laborers that they were not indispensable, and in the same industry in Colorado, where they were used in a similar way against the German-Russians. Moreover, Mexicans have been employed as strike-breakers in the coal mines of Colorado and New Mexico, and in one instance in the shops of one important railroad system.

Socially and politically the presence of large numbers of Mexicans in this country gives rise to serious problems. The reports of the Immigration Commission show that they lack ambition, are to a very large extent illiterate in their native language, are slow to learn English, and in most cases show no political interest. In some instances, however, they have been organized to serve the purposes of political bosses, as for example in Phoenix, Arizona. Although more of them are married and have their families with them than is the case among the south European immigrants, they are unsettled as a class, move readily from place to place, and do not acquire or lease land to any extent. But their most unfavorable characteristic is their inclination to form colonies and live in a clannish manner. Wherever a considerable group of Mexicans are employed, they live together, if possible, and associate very little with members of other races. In the mining towns and other small industrial communities they live ordinarily in rude adobe huts outside of the town limits. As section hands they of course live as the members of the other races have done, in freight cars fitted with windows and bunks, or in rough shacks along the line of the railroad. In the cities their colonization has become a menace. The unwholesome conditions of the Mexican quarter in El Paso, Tex., have been described with photographic illustrations in previous articles in THE SURVEY. In Los Angeles the housing problem centers largely in the cleaning up or demolition of the Mexican "house courts," which have become the breeding ground of disease and crime, and which have now attracted a considerable population of immigrants of other races. It is estimated that approximately 2,000 Mexicans are living in these "house courts." Some 15,000 persons of this race are residents of Los Angeles and vicinity. Conditions of life among the immigrants of the city, which are moulded to a certain extent by Mexican standards, have been materially improved by the work of the Los Angeles Housing Commission, upon which Johanna Von Wagner has served as an expert social worker. However, the Mexican quarter continues to offer a serious social problem to the community.

As is to be expected under the circumstances, the proportion of criminals and paupers among the Mexicans is noticeably greater than among the other foreign-born or among the natives. In Los Angeles county, California, the Mexicans comprised 11.4 per cent of the total number of persons bound over for felonies in 1907. In 1908 and 1909 the percentages were 12.6 and 13.4 respectively. During the year ending July 1, 1908, the chief of police of Los Angeles estimates that approximately 20,000 police cases were handled, in 2,357 or 11.8 per cent of which Mexicans were the defendants. In Arizona, where the proportion of Mexicans to the total population is greater than in Los Angeles, a correspondingly large proportion of the inmates of the various penal institutions are of this race. In 1908, 24.2 per cent of the prisoners in the jail at Tucson, Ariz., were Mexicans, while in the Pima county jail they comprised 62 per cent of the inmates. The territorial prison reported in the same year that 61 per cent of those incarcerated were Mexicans. In both Arizona and California the offenses for which they were committed were in the large majority of cases traceable to gambling or excessive drinking. Most of the serious trouble with Mexicans, however, arises from quarrels among themselves which interfere very little with the white population.

In the matter of poor relief, Mexican families were concerned in 11.7 per cent of the cases dealt with by the Associated Charities of Los Angeles in 1908. The proportion has increased since that time, and in 1910 it was estimated that Mexicans comprised fully one-third of those given relief from this source. The county authorities had charge of approximately 3,000 individuals in 1908, of whom about one-third were Mexicans. The proportion of Mexicans among those dependent upon the County Board of Charities has continued about the same, for in the month of November, 1910, which was said to be typical of that year, 30.1 per cent of the applications for aid were made by members of that race.

In conclusion it should be recognized that although the Mexicans have proved to be efficient laborers in certain industries, and have afforded a cheap and elastic labor supply for the southwestern United States, the evils to the community at large which their presence in large numbers almost invariably brings may more than overbalance their desirable qualities. Their low standards of living and of morals, their illiteracy, their utter lack of proper political interest, the retarding effect of their employment upon the wage scale of the more progressive races, and finally their tendency to colonize in urban centers, with evil results, combine to stamp them as a rather undesirable class of residents.

MEXICO IN SAN ANTONIO

[The first two decades of Mexican immigration to the United States coincided with the great wave of "new" immigrants from Eastern Europe as well as with the resurgence of American nativism and its concommitant demands for immigration restriction. In the social atmosphere then prevailing in the United States, any incoming group whose appearance, language, customs, and abilities were ostensibly at variance with the Anglo majority was easily faulted for its very difference. This was the fate of the Mexican immigrants in the two decades after 1900, when the pressures for assimilation were so strong and when American relations with Mexico were touchy because of the revolutionary situation in that country. The immigrants were desired for the places they could fill in the job market, but their presence nevertheless aroused resentment from native Americans who viewed them as a social problem. But it stood to reason that, like other immigrants, the Mexicans for the most part would remain and make new lives for themselves. With this in mind, journalist Alvin S. Johnson, later president of the New School for Social Research, took the following sympathetic look at the Mexican immigrants in Texas, the state to which they went in greatest numbers.]

From *New Republic*, June 24, 1916.

If you wish to form a just estimate of the potentialities of any race, you naturally seek for your laboratory an environment in which the race has had at least a fair chance for development. The Italian and Russian races would be most outrageously misjudged if they were studied exclusively through some of the more wretched peasant communities; China and Japan have been grievously slandered through the occidental assumption that the characteristics of coolies are characteristics of the race. We in America, with our vast experience in the transformation of miscellaneous foreign types into standardized Americans, ought to be safe against the fallacies resulting from a confusion of nature with nurture.

We are not safe, however, and every time we are confronted by a race which presents an appearance of degradation we cry, "Here at last is a race of which no good can ever come." Just now the race whose apparent defects press themselves upon our notice is the Mexican. The Mexican problem is not merely one of foreign policy, although the Mexican in Mexico is perplexing enough. It is also an immigration and labor problem, and a problem of local politics besides. Mexican laborers are steadily crossing the border and dispersing through the country in search of work. They are everywhere in the Southwest, and are appearing in increasing numbers in the northern states of the Pacific slope and of the Rocky Mountains. Some, too, are appearing in the Middle West. Mexican laborers have found work as far away from the border as Milwaukee. There is no legal bar upon Mexican immigration. No head tax is exacted, no records are kept. Is this laissez-faire policy wise? All depends on what kind of man the Mexican really is, not as he appears after he has grown up in oppression, ignorance, superstition, but as he would be if he had a fair chance in life. Where shall we find Mexicans in this condition? Perhaps nowhere, but it is approximated in San Antonio.

Mexicans who are pure Spanish, Mexicans who are pure Indian, and all intermediate grades, as well as Mexicans who are part Scotch, Irish, German, Italian, are to be found in San Antonio. There are Mexicans in plenty whose stocks were settled in Texas before the days of the Texas Republic, and Mexicans driven out by each of the successive waves of revolution in the last six years. Most of the Mexicans are poor, but many of them are rich. As Mexicans, they appear to be excluded from nothing. They play the game on fairly equal terms in business, the professions, politics. They are admitted to social clubs and there is no ban upon mixed marriages. Is there a race prejudice against the Mexicans? A little, of course; toleration comes hard with the Anglo-Saxon. But ask an old San Antonio resident whether he dislikes the Mexicans. "No, I couldn't do that. I've been with them all my life."

If there is anyone who ought to know the Mexicans, it is Mr. W. G. Knox of San Antonio. Mr. Knox is a devoted educator, an excellent representative of the American schoolman, our best national contribution to civilization. Since boyhood he has known the Mexicans and liked them, and for the last sixteen years he has taught them in the Navarro public school, of which he is head. Mexicans are not segregated in the public schools of San Antonio, but the Navarro school is in the Mexican quarter, and of its twelve hundred pupils, more or less, ninety per cent are Mexican. All manner of Mexican children are represented here, blond and black, wee brown sprites born in San Antonio and big fellows of fourteen just over from Mexico. Mr. Knox has watched their steady advance from grade to grade and has followed their progress in the commercial or high schools, or—the usual case—at work. Here, then, is a man who ought to be overflowing with generalizations on race differences. But he isn't. Mr. Knox knows of no characteristic intellectual differences between Mexican and American children. Such differences as he notes are mere matters of degree, and minor degree at that. "At least," you prompt, "the brighter ones are the purest Spanish." "No," says Mr. Knox, "many of my best students are of the darkest types."

The Mexican child, according to Mr. Knox, enters the American public school under a severe handicap. As a rule he knows only Spanish, and his parents are most likely to be illiterate. He is too poor to equip himself fully with books, and he has not learned the virtues of regularity. As an offset, he is more eager to learn than the American child. He comes from a hovel and the school is a wonderland for him. Besides, his parents are vastly interested in his progress. When he can read, it is occasion for celebration among all his kin, and abundant is the little soul's opportunity for showing off. Of course he gets somewhat spoiled. Mexicans spoil their children anyway, loving them beyond the measure known to Anglo-Saxons. Their theories of discipline are drastic. "Do what you will with him, only save me the bones," such are the disciplinary instructions left to the teacher. But at home the little Mexican, especially if he is winning glory through his scholastic achievements, does about what he pleases.

But ambition, with the children, balances the spoiling and the Spanish, and if we omit from consideration the new arrivals of advanced age in every degree of retardation, the Mexican children make as rapid progress through the grades as American. In writing, drawing and music they are better than the American; in mathematics, as good, in English they are inferior. They are good at baseball, inferior at football—a matter of physique. In the early grades they are mainly Spanish-speaking, in the later, English-speaking. The finished product of Mr. Knox's school is abundantly in evidence in San Antonio. In an hour's stroll about town Mr. Knox will introduce you to enough of them to shake out all your preconceptions of white-race superiority. Wherein would you change these straight, frank-eyed, easy-mannered young men? How handsome some of them are, how fair and square they all seem to be in their mental attitude. In El Paso they say a Mexican is unreliable. Ask these San Antonio young men how long they have been with their present employers. Three, six, ten years—the impression you get is one of decided steadiness. Mr. Knox admits that his boys are not noted for saving their money. But what boys, so handsome as some of these, born to bask in the bright sun of San Antonio, would be thrifty?

They are not rhetorical. They argue as pointedly as any young Americans for or against intervention in Mexico, and have a more or less disdainful attitude toward the fiery language of old Mexico, as we of the North have toward the belated representatives of pre-bellum American oratory. All that high-sounding Latin—it's a bit disappointing to discover that it is not temperament but tradition. . . .

Go among the Mexicans that have been long subject to the benignant influence of San Antonio, and you form a conception of the Mexican problem quite different from the conceptions you form on the border or far inland. Here is a people well endowed intellectually, eager to learn, capable of artistic expression, with an emotional life intense, but wholesome, with extremely vital family institutions, and apparently with enough coöperative instinct to manage the practical affairs of life without the capacity for individual accumulation necessary for survival in a race like our own, unsocial, unkind. This people has fallen on evil days; progressive exploitation, followed by general disintegration, has torn apart millions of these intimate family bonds, thrown despair into hundreds of thousands of breasts, made for happiness, demanding so very little for happiness. And we on our side know only to use the thick fingers of diplomacy or the brutal fingers of imperialistic exploitation. Mexico may work out her own salvation, but she will owe few thanks to us. Or she may sink into barbarism, independently or under us, to our immense cost. For if there is one thing needed to enrich our life, it is a contiguous civilized state with something other than the real estate, railroad, banking trust-organizing interests to live for. Such a contiguous civilization we might have in Mexico in one generation if Uncle Sam could be to Mexico what Mr. Knox is to the little brown boys and girls in the Navarro school. This is impossible, you say. Why?

A PLEA FOR MUTUAL UNDERSTANDING BETWEEN MEXICAN IMMIGRANTS AND NATIVE AMERICANS

[The following short paper was presented to the 1920 annual session of the National Conference of Social Work by Ernestine M. Alvarado, of the Young Women's Christian Association of New York City.]

Those who from the immigration offices behold the masses of men, brown-colored, circumspect, silently awaiting their turn with that air of indifference which reminds us of the oriental peoples, have little idea of the enormous forces of individuality represented in that apparently passive throng, and imagine that they must be treated as human cattle, always generalizing, because no one can dream of detaching the individual from the mass which appears to

From "Mexican Immigration to the United States," by Ernestine Alvarado, in: *Proceedings of the National Conference of Social Work*, Chicago, 1920.

the observer so uniform. But, when it comes to distributing them for the various kinds of work, then it is found that each one constitutes a separate problem almost without connection with the others. He who knows how to treat them, takes special care in studying them, giving personal attention to each and every one; and only by this method good results can be obtained.

The Mexicans who come to the United States are of three types, namely, the aristocracy or leisure class, who come for political, educational, or business reasons; the middle class, who come for political reasons, but more often for study, business opportunities, and professional advancement; and the peon or laboring class who come for economic betterment. I shall confine my paper to the Mexicans of this third class.

The Mexicans of the lower class who constitute the greater part of the immigration element to this country, respond generously when rightly treated. They are intelligent and indefatigable workers when they are put in the right place. They are reliable, serious, of quick comprehension, and at the same time calm and reflective. In our country, and owing to causes against which the revolution is still fighting, those men have received almost no education; many of them do not know how to read and write. It is imperative that they be educated by you. You can make of them a very useful element in your social life and in the prosperity of the nation.

They come from Mexico in search of new horizons. They have been told about the prosperity of this country, of the liberty that they may enjoy here, of the big salaries they may obtain, of the practicability and value of your methods, of the low cost of living, and thousands of other things which are growing obsolete. They come seeking that wonderful country wherein they hope to find greater liberty than in their own. The "enganchaores," men who come down to Mexico in order to bring labor, make golden promises, so beautiful and bright that they are the more deceived; and although the Mexican government does its utmost to enlighten them, warning them against false offers, they have inherited wandering habits from Aztecs and Castillians, and they go out in search of the golden treasure like mythological argonauts. This bold spirit, this adventurous impulse toward the unknown, implies a greatness of soul, an aspiration toward betterment, a character, which must be taken into account, and it is "up to you," citizens of the United States, to take care of these bold dreamers in order that they may find in your country, if anywhere, at least something of what they have dreamed.

Up to the present the majority of these men have returned to Mexico taking with them disappointment instead of fortune. They have complained of being treated like cattle; that no one knew how to understand their personality, their individuality; that they have fallen into hands that intended only to exploit their physical resistance, frugality, and unselfishness. They have rarely found anyone who has wisely opened to them the path of education, a course which would have been a thousand times more profitable and more human.

The Mexican has a sentiment of patriotism set in his innermost soul. Its roots are deeply embedded in tradition. Unfortunately, our country is misrepresented and abused nearly everywhere in the United States, in theaters, moving pictures, newspapers, books, and private conversations. Perhaps (I would prefer to believe it so), it is done without ill intention, probably thoughtlessly, but it *is* done. Mexicans find an antagonistic atmosphere for everything that is Mexican, and this fact necessarily tends to make difficult their uniting with you. You could hardly become friends with one who begins by insulting your mother; and for us Mexicans love for our country is not less than love for our mothers.

The best way to attract Mexican immigrants is by educational advantages, not only the education of the immigrants themselves, but also the education of those who are going to be in contact with them. I mean the American people, especially the American workmen. Both American and Mexican workers have a lot to learn from each other. When the time comes that you *understand* our country, as great as it is unfortunate, you will respect and love those good Mexicans who come to you full of hopes, and then you will know how to treat them in order that those hopes may not be in vain.

To found really friendly relations between our two countries, closer contact between American and Mexican labor must be established. But, unfortunately, the Mexican worker finds very often that it is impossible for him to join your workers' organizations. Mexicans go back to Mexico and carry with them the recollection of the animosity they found here. If ever the American worker has found any animosity in Mexico it has been because of the sentiment brought there by Mexicans returning from the United States. All this also will have to disappear when education has taught your laborers that the Mexican laborer does not belong to an inferior race, and should by no means be discriminated against. Fraternity is an international obligation, a duty of humanity. In order that the United States may make effective the high ideals of democracy and liberty, it is necessary for the American laboring man to learn to treat his less fortunate Mexican brother with sympathy and justice.

THE SPANISH HERITAGE IN AMERICA

[Hispanic society in the Southwest is more than three and a half centuries old, and, antedating that, are nearly 100 years of Spain's rule in Mexico itself. This encounter of the Spanish and Indian cultures produced traditional ways of life that have come to characterize much of the Southwest. Not strictly Spanish, nor solely Indian, this heritage represents a synthesis that perhaps sounds more Spanish than it really is. The language, religion, laws, and usages came from Spain. But they were all modified in their new surroundings, so that the emphasis in the following selection by William R. Shepherd on things Castilian is somewhat one-sided.]

The history of the United States is not the history of the Thirteen British Colonies alone and of what grew out of them. Too often has the moment of the arrival of English-speaking folk on the scene provided an excuse for ignoring the achievement of other European peoples who happen not to be of their kin. The part played by Spain and Spanish America in determining the origin and development

From *The Modern Language Journal*, November 1925.

of our country had a much more important share in the process than has grudgingly been accorded them. . . .

To Spain, obviously, the United States owes its very inception, as an area in which the civilization of Europe was to be implanted. Under the banner of Castile sailed the mariner who made known the New World, in the heart of which lay our native land of the future. From Spain came also the mighty men of valor who were the first to discover, explore and settle its vast stretches of primeval wilderness. They supplied the foundations upon which others from overseas were to build. . . .

From the realms of Spain in North America came eventually about two-thirds of our entire continental territory south of the forty-ninth parallel, and out of her possessions in the Caribbean and the Pacific most of our insular dependencies as well. Throughout its wide expanse to the southward and westward linger the memories of her age-long control. From Montana to Texas, from Florida to California, from St. Augustine to Sacramento, from the Strait of Juan de Fuca to the Rio Grande, from the Sierra Nevada to the "Llanos Estacados," they survive in the names of our States, our cities, our rivers, our mountains and our plains. They are embodied in many an edifice; they are cherished in many a custom, and the soft mellifluous tongue of Castile yet moves thousands in our midst to laughter or to tears as it did in the brave old days of long ago.

For her vast empire in the New World Spain devised in the "Laws of the Indies," a magnificent monument of legislation, without parallel in the enactments provided by a governing people for the governed. No code of the sort compiled by any other nation before or since has surpassed or even equalled it: not because of the marvellous machinery of administration alone which it contained, but because of the sheer spirit of humanity with which it was pervaded, converting into legal formulas the second commandment of the New Dispensation: "Thou shalt love thy neighbor as thyself!"

From this great body of colonial enactments, which hark back to the famous "Siete Partidas" of Alfonso the Wise of Castile, passed through the crucible of Mexican law-making, and modified by that of certain of our western states, have been derived highly important features of the law in those commonwealths and of our national legislation. Among them is the introduction of the ganancial system, or the community of interest in the property of husband and wife, whereby the disposition of the common fund cannot be varied by the parties even through mutual agreement, and its devolution can be changed only by the order of a court. This arrangement, so just to the wife and so befitting the young democracy of the Far West, stands out in sharp contrast to the principle of the old common law of England, obtaining for a long period in the eastern states, which made the husband virtually the controller, if not also the owner, of the wife's property. Another legal conception proceeding ultimately from Spain is the right to use the waters of a running stream for purposes of irrigation or the production of power, without heed necessarily to the private ownership of the land through which they flow, and thus to thwart anew the common law that enabled the proprietors of either bank to forbid such use of the waters even if, dog-in-the-manger-like, they did not themselves make use of them. A third benefit to us of the Spanish legal system is the present practice of our Government to grant a lease of the privilege of exploiting the natural resources of an area, whether of mines or minerals or some other public utility, instead of giving away outright, as it had done, the land on which they are situated or selling it at merely a nominal price. The original laws of the State of Louisiana, furthermore, concerned with promises, obligations, sale, purchase and exchange were founded upon the "Siete Partidas."

That Spanish art, architecture and literature have been fruitful sources of beauty and inspiration upon which Americans have been privileged to draw for the enrichment of their life and thought, there is no need to descant at length, for the proofs of it are all too obvious. Because of its historical antecedents, this country may be said to possess a natural receptivity for Spanish culture. Hence the art of Spain has found in our æsthetic development a field for fertile amplification. In multiple blends with our own art, it reflects the filiation with the Iberian land and the essential unity of Spanish civilization. The works of Velasquez, El Greco, Goya, Zuloaga and Sorolla are no less a part of our æsthetic consciousness than of all the world to which those masters of the brush have borne their marvels.

Spanish colonial architecture and the furnishings of the quaint old missions of our Southwest are treasured among us in manifold reproduction. Whatever the form of application, their grace, charm and comfort unite to produce an effect at once curiously exotic and yet susceptible of easy adaptation to environment. The contents of our homes, summer and winter, testify to the service of Spanish craftsmen in interior decoration. Antique designs elaborated by their practiced hand adorn the walls and gladden the eye with a pleasure quick to recall the land whence they came. . . .

Nor can we forget how richly stored our native tongue is with Spanish words and their vivid imagery of expression. From this source the number of terms is legion. They range over a great variety of phenomena; they recall many an episode in history, and they suggest many an idea, institution or article given currency through the Spaniards, and yet so familiar to us that the Spanish origin becomes for the moment lost. They include nautical terms, such as "cargo," "commodore," "embargo," "flotilla," and "armada," and military, like "grenade" and "guerrilla." Since the Spaniards were the first among Europeans to become acquainted with the aborigines of America, their speech and customs, with the products found here or brought hither, and with the earlier operation of European influences, they gave names to many things, and passed on directly or in modified form the Indian expressions for them. They bestowed upon us so bizarre an assortment of things good and bad as "alfalfa," "alligator," "barricade," "bravado," "buffalo," "canary," "cigar," "desperado," "duenna," "Eldorado," "fandango," "gala," "grandee," "indigo," "maroon," "merino," "mosquito," "mulatto," "mustang," "negro," "palaver," "paragon," "parasol," "sarsaparilla," "sierra," "siesta," "sherry," "soda," "sombrero," "stampede," "tornado," and "vanilla." To us they transmitted also "alpaca," "barbecue," "cannibal," "cacao," "canoe," "chocolate," "cocoa," "hurricane," "maize," "potato," "quinine," "savanna," "tobacco," and "tomato"!

These evidences of service afforded by discovery, exploration, settlement, and retention of territory for a longer period than any European state that ever has had dominion over what is now our country; these workings of the spirit, communicated through the ideas and institutions of civilization, might support a claim that the United States be regarded historically and culturally as one of the "Three Spains": the motherland in Europe and the "Two Americas." The three form a species of triangle, of which this land of ours and the Spanish-speaking nations to the southward constitute the base. From it the two great sides of history and civilization stretch forth like giant arms across the seas and meet at the apex in the heart of old Spain!

INTERVIEWS WITH TWO MEXICAN IMMIGRANTS

[During 1926 and 1927, Manuel Gamio and his staff interviewed many Mexican immigrants in both the United States and Mexico in order to gather information for a study published in 1930 under the auspices of the Social Science Research Council. These interviews touched on all important aspects of the immigrants' existence: jobs, education, assimilation, religious attitudes, repatriation, political participation, and home and family life. Two interviews dealing with the problem of assimilation are reprinted here.]

Sra. Ruhe López

This woman is native of Mazatlan, Sinaloa, Mexico. Her father was an Austrian, and her mother a daughter of a Spaniard and a Mexican woman. This lady is white, her hair is rather blonde, and she has adapted herself in almost every way to the American customs, but she says that she is, was, and will be Mexican by heart and by "race" in spite of the fact that she has married an American.

From Manuel Gamio, *The Mexican Immigrant: His Life-Story.* Chicago, 1931. Pages 229–232, 278–285.

"In Mazatlan my father was the owner of one of the best hotels of the place. Europeans, Americans and prominent persons in Mexico were almost the only ones who went to stay at that hotel as they went through Mazatlan. At seventeen years of age I married an American mining engineer with whom I became acquainted at that hotel; he had been introduced to me by my father. My sister married a partner of my husband. Until I was sixteen I attended a private school of Mazatlan where I studied a lot of English, for my father had the idea of sending me to the United States to study. Once married, I traveled with my husband almost all over the Mexican Republic. We went to the Southern and the Central States and to all those where there are mines. He was very good to me in every way. He gave me everything that I wished and which was within his reach. We were married five years and it was almost one continuous honeymoon. But my husband died of fever and I was left a widow and without money. As I had practiced English a lot with him, and besides had made a trip to this country before he died, I decided when I found myself left alone to go and live in Nogales, Arizona. There, as I was still young (in 1917 I was twenty-two years old), I went around a lot with young Americans and Mexicans from Nogales, Arizona, and Nogales, Sonora. I got a job selling stamps in the American post-office of Nogales and got pretty good pay.

". . . . I established a store in Nogales and there I fell in love with a young American who is now my husband. He is a mechanic, much younger than I. He speaks Spanish perfectly for he was brought up on the border. We decided to come and settle in Los Angeles and we have now been here several years. My husband earns six dollars a day and as that isn't enough for I like to dress well, etc., I rent two rooms of our house with which I help to pay the rent. I also work in a real estate office where I earn $15.00 a week for being there in the morning and also two per cent on the houses or land which I am able to sell. Besides, since I have an automobile and know the city well, I hire it with myself as chauffeur to honorable persons, and especially to Mexicans. I do every kind of business that I can, the thing is to earn something to help my husband. Once I even worked as an extra in a moving picture studio where I earned five dollars a day.

"I get up in the morning at seven and make breakfast for my husband and myself. This consists of mush, eggs, milk and coffee. I also prepare his lunch and take him to his work in the automobile which we have bought and then I go to mine. At noon when I come home I make ham and eggs or anything for lunch or take my lunch in a restaurant. I come early in the afternoon if I don't have anything to do, and after I have fixed and swept the house, I get supper ready. That is our big meal, as it is with the Americans. I make Mexican stews, vegetables and American side dishes, chocolate, milk and coffee, *frijoles*, etc. I buy pies and sweets and we have a good supper. Then we go out to a movie or some dance hall or riding in the automobile. We are almost always on our way back by ten at night and then go to bed.

"We always buy the daily, the *Los Angeles Examiner* and we read the principal items. I don't read the Mexican newspapers, because I am hardly at all interested in Mexico anymore, for my family is almost all here. I am thinking of going back but I don't know when, that depends on when the country gets in peace. When it is in peace my husband and I will go and we will establish a modern garage for the sale of oil and gasoline and the repair of automobiles, for I think good money can be made in that business.

"I am Catholic and my husband is also but we hardly ever go to church. I pray at night on going to bed and in the morning when I get up but we don't make confession.

"I think that the American women have good taste in dressing, perhaps better taste than the Mexican women of the capital, and as I like to dress well I always buy stylish dresses.

"I have never had any trouble with the Americans; they have always treated me well. Once when I was introduced to an American family they asked me if I was Spanish and when I said I wasn't, that I was Mexican, they then said that the Mexicans weren't as clean nor as white as I; but I told them that in Mexico there are people as white and blonde, as intelligent and clean as in any other country of the world.

"I have never believed in witches nor do I know of any here. There are probably some among the Mexicans who live on the East Side. Although I like my people very much I don't want to live with them, especially on the East Side, because they are very dirty there; there are many robberies and one can't live comfortably.

"I think of myself as a very modern woman, following the American style but I am not extreme like the American women. For example I never bathe myself in the beaches or other public places because there all the people can see one's body and I wouldn't like that.

"All the furniture of my home is American. I have my gas stove and gas heater also. I have my piano so that I can play it when I want. I also have a radio to listen to the concerts and news. I have always liked to buy everything for cash but I have purchased a few things on installments."

Juan Salorio

Juan Salorio is white, a native of El Paso, Texas.

"My parents were Mexicans, born, I don't know where, in Chihuahua but they were educated in various parts of Texas. In those times there weren't many differences between the Americans and the Mexicans. All those along the border were the same, and there were no difficulties in crossing from one side to the other, nor immigration, nor anything which now creates differences between the Americans and the Mexicans and the Mexicans who were born on one side or the other of the border. My grandmother brought me up. I was her pet; she did everything for me that I wanted. I have other brothers and sisters. There were about seven of us. Some of them had blue eyes and light colored hair but we had a sister who was very dark. When my grandmother died I was taken to live with my brothers. Once, when my older brother, who is now about fifty-eight (I am forty-five) was bathing he asked me to give him his shoes and I threw them from where I was. When he had finished dressing he took hold of me and gave me a good thrashing. As I wasn't used to having anyone touch me I felt that a great deal and I ran away from home but I was brought back again and sent to a Seminary at Las Cruces, New Mexico. I was at this Seminary for a long time and learned many things. I went to Sunday School and had about 10 little kids under my care. I used to ask them questions about the doctrine and taught them other things. But I got tired of being there and then, little as I was, I escaped from the Seminary. In order to get out I deceived the 'head-priest' or rather the director. I told him that I was going to see a sister of charity who liked me a great deal and who was sick. I then ran away and kept going towards Louisiana until I came to the home of a French family where I was taken in as an orphan. I worked there. This family taught me how to speak French. I afterwards was in other parts of the United States, working as a servant, shining shoes, and a lot of other things. Eight years went by without anyone at home knowing anything about me nor me of them until finally I went to San Antonio, Texas. I stayed there a long time and my family after a while came there and we were happily reunited. I learned to be a cook there. I knew how to cook American style very well, rather, I still know how. I got tired of being in San Antonio and I became a sailor. I went to travel all over the world. I have even been in Palestine, in Asia and in Europe. I spent years in the North and South of Europe. I have taken care of goats in the snowy mountains of Europe and I know what it is to suffer there. Sometimes I would arrive at a port and stay there. Then later I would go on with another ship and in that way I went from one place to another. Finally I came back to San Antonio to work, happy to be with my family. I was there when the war came and I volunteered in the Second Division and went to Europe to fight there. I was at the front and was later sent to Paris. I was there about fourteen months. I went to a cafe in Paris where all the English speaking soldiers came together, the Australians, the Americans, the Canadians, the English, etc., for the owners of the cafe were Americans. Once when we were speaking of all the nations the old barmaid began to say that in Mexico there wasn't anything but Indians and that they didn't even know the Spaniards there. I told her that I was an 'American-Mexican' and that my country was Mexico, which was on the border of the United States, and that Spanish was spoken there and that I could prove it. I told them to call a Spaniard who had never been in Latin America and they would see how we could talk. About this time a Spaniard who was a street cleaner passed by and they called him in and we began to talk first in French and then in Spanish. I told him that I was Mexican but he told me that I was wearing an American uniform. I then told him that I was an American citizen because I had been born in the United States but that all of us recognized Spain as our mother country and that there were more than a hundred million inhabitants in Latin America who spoke Spanish. He then invited me to take a drink but I wouldn't let him pay for it. I saw that he was very poor and I paid. He invited me to eat on Sunday at his house and he prepared a delicious Spanish meal and took me to the Spanish club and presented me to many pretty Spanish girls. Another time I was at the largest opera in Paris with an Italian friend of mine. When the Italian told me that they were speaking Spanish nearby in the hall I took notice and saw that it was a gentleman, a lady and a young woman who seemed to be French. All of them were very well dressed. I also was well dressed, for I had a special uniform made for dress purposes. I was then a sergeant. I drew near and, begging their pardon, told them that I had heard them speaking Spanish and that I had wanted to speak to them in our language. They told me that they were Mexicans from Chihuahua and that the young lady was studying in Belgium but they had come for her to take her back to Mexico. They invited me drink some very good wine but I started to leave, saying that I couldn't leave my friend alone. They then told me to invite my friend. All of this happened during an intermission. When the program was going to begin again they gave me their address and I later visited them, becoming a very close friend of the young lady. They went to Mexico by way of Brest and New York but the young lady kept on writing to me. She sent me Mexican sweets, pictures, a thimble and thread and a lot of other things and I also sent her things. She still wrote to me when I returned to the United States but then I began to go around with other girls and we stopped writing to each other. Later a Porto-Rican friend introduced me to some young ladies, through correspondence. They lived in Los Angeles and I in San Antonio. Without seeing her picture I chose one that I liked called Ines, just because of her name, and I wrote to her proposing to her. She told me that she always read her letters to her mother but that she hadn't been able to read the last letter to her. She said that we should become acquainted first. She thought and hoped that as my letters were nice and well written I would be that way also and said that I should come to Los Angeles so that we could become acquainted. I asked her in the next letter if she liked to dance, go to the theatre and other things and she answered that they had been educated in a convent and that they liked music, dancing and the theatre very much but that they hardly ever went out and since then, I don't know why, I stopped writing to them. I then went away again and sailed all along Central and South America. I know Argentina, Chile, Brazil, Colombia and almost all of the countries. We are all brothers—the Latin-Americans—for we are of the same blood. Only the Brazilians don't speak Spanish and are more aristocratic. I was in Porto Rico, in Santo Domingo, Haiti—the latter are countries of mulattoes and negroes but the people of Santo Domingo are very cultured. What is bad is that in a family where all are white and good looking girls suddenly one turns out a negress. That is because the mixture shows its origin again. I have also been in Cuba and in the British Islands. I afterwards returned to San Antonio and took a rest there. Much of my traveling has been done with an American friend who was my pal. We came together to Tucson about a year ago. We arrived quite broke. We hardly had some three dollars between us. I then had the idea that we should make tamales. Although I know about cooking I had never made tamales but I finally made them and then he went out with a can to sell them on the streets. He sold them very quickly and came back very happy for another can, but he later came back very sad and told me that many of the tamales had been returned because they were raw, for I didn't know how to cook them well. We kept on little by little building up our business until I learned how to make tamales well. Then we established this restaurant, to which the best American and Mexican people come. Some don't believe that I am Mexican. They say that I am Greek, or Italian or Spanish but I tell them that I am nothing but Mexican and tell them that I am Yaqui. Sometimes some come and ask me what Spanish dishes I have in my restaurant and I tell them that we don't have any Spanish dishes nor do we know them. What we have is pure Mexican, frijoles, chile con carne, enchiladas, rice, eggs Mexican style and everything. As they see that I am very clean and that everything is served well here so many people come that at times I don't have enough for all of them. I can say that I am the first here to make enchiladas and tamales in true Mexican style. I learned that in San Antonio by remembering how they were made at home. All the clubs and societies here order tamales from me and banquets of all sorts and in spite of the fact that I came here 'broke' I couldn't be bought out for less than $2,000 now.

"The city that I like the best is San Antonio. I have most of my family there and many Mexican acquaintances. Although I was born in El Paso I don't like that city very well. It is like Tucson to me. All those who know me here like me because they say that I am modest and honest.

"I am a citizen of this country because I was born here and if there was a war of course I would have to defend this country because it is my home land and I am a citizen in order to defend it. I know very well, however, that I would be going to fight against my own people. But I don't believe that there will be war between the United States and Mexico unless there was another world war. There may be difficulties, like those which have already come up, as when Veracruz was occupied, for example. I was then in New York City and I kept informed about the affair through the Amer-

ican newspapers. I think that Veracruz was a heroic city like Chapultepec was when General Scott took it and the child heroes died.
I remember that there was in New York then a paper called *Las
Novedades* which I think a South American published (he was a
Spaniard) and it published a picture in which there was a strong
man, who was saying that all the countries of Latin America should
unite against the threatening Eagle of the North. That was very
good and I liked the idea very much, that the Latin Americans
should unite. I see, for example, since I know all of the history of
the civil wars in Mexico, that those men [he is referring to the
Americans] have respected her a good deal and haven't got mixed
up in anything, while on the other hand in small countries like
Santo Domingo, 15 days after a revolution begins they establish
their military rule. The same thing has happened in Cuba, in Nica-
ragua and in other small countries. I would go with the American
army against Mexico, because the United States is my country and
one has to be loyal to one's home-land. The same thing was true in
the world war in which whole regiments of Germans from Pennsylvania went to fight against their mother country because they were
American citizens.

"I know the history of Mexico very well from the time of the Conquest. I know who have been the great Americans and Mexicans because I have always been interested in reading a great deal of literature and history. Although I know almost no part of Mexico, for I
have only been to Chihuahua, I know a great deal about Mexico
from what I have read in the newspapers, in books and from the
pictures which I have seen. I believe that Mexico is my mother country and that all the South Americans, even if they are mulattoes or
negroes, are more or less of the same people.

"I can speak English, French and Spanish. I can write in the three
languages very well and was even thinking of entering the Academy
of Languages of Paris, but I hardly needed to do that for I even
know a little Latin.

"Although I was born a Catholic like all Latin Americans I don't
any longer know what religion to choose. I have read all of the
Bibles and I find some good in all of them and some things which
I don't like. I had a Klu Klux Klan friend who wanted to put a hood
on me and give me a flaming cross and a spear. I told him that he
was a poor fool because George Washington when he made the
Constitution of the United States said that the European peoples
would bring progress and capital here and it has been that way. The
Klu Klux Klan wants all Americans to be one hundred per cent but
even they aren't. I would say to that friend 'All of your ancestors
were immigrants and so are those of all the Americans, for the only
pure Americans are the Indians and the Klu Klux Klan doesn't admit any Indian because they say that he isn't white. So you are
violating the Constitution in everything. You don't know if I am
Catholic or not. I go with a girl who is an Episcopalian and I go
with her to sing hymns some nights and she goes with me to the

Catholic Cathedral on Sunday morning to Mass. If you are my friend it doesn't make any difference to what church you belong. I am your friend wherever you are and as I have read all of the Bibles, Episcopal, Baptist, Methodist and others I don't know which to choose.' I think that I will turn out a free thinker for I only believe in the true God who cares for all the beings that there are on the earth.

"The good man is he who lives from his work and doesn't do harm to others. That is all that I care about. It doesn't make any difference what religion he belongs to. The thing is that he be always and everywhere honorable.

"I say that he who is Mexican here is Mexican anywhere, just as the Chinaman is Chinese everywhere and always gets together with the Chinese. It is true that we Mexico-Americans are different and have other customs but in general we are all like the Mexicans of Mexico and we ought to be brothers, for we are brothers racially.

"I also know almost all of Europe, because when the war was over I stayed as a guard of honor to the Inter-Allied Commission, the Allied Commission in which were all the high officials of Italy, France, England, Portugal and Italy, and all of the allies, and we went to almost all of the European capitals. I had a very good time there."

THE LEAGUE
OF UNITED
LATIN-AMERICAN
CITIZENS

[The emergence of a middle class among Mexican Americans in various parts of the Southwest has given rise to volunteer associations for the purpose of studying and dealing with the problems of Mexican-American communities. Of primary concern are racial bias, equality before the law, equal educational and employment opportunity, and fair political representation. One of the earliest agencies set up by the Mexican Americans was the League of United Latin-American Citizens, founded in Corpus Christi, Texas, in February, 1929. A subsequent convention in May, 1929, drew up a constitution for the League, Article 2 of which is reprinted below.]

From "The League of United Latin-American Citizens: A Texas-Mexican Civic Organization," by O. Douglas Weeks, in: *Southwestern Political and Social Science Quarterly*, December 1929.

The Aims and Purposes of This Organization Shall Be:

1. To develop within the members of our race the best, purest and most perfect type of a true and loyal citizen of the United States of America.

2. To eradicate from our body politic all intents and tendencies to establish discriminations among our fellow citizens on account of race, religion, or social position as being contrary to the true spirit of Democracy, our Constitution and Laws.

3. To use all the legal means at our command to the end that all citizens in our country may enjoy equal rights, the equal protection of the laws of the land and equal opportunities and privileges.

4. The acquisition of the English language, which is the official language of our country, being necessary for the enjoyment of our rights and privileges, we declare it to be the official language of this organization, and we pledge ourselves to learn and speak and teach same to our children.

5. To define with absolute and unmistakable clearness our unquestionable loyalty to the ideals, principles, and citizenship of the United States of America.

6. To assume complete responsibility for the education of our children as to their rights and duties and the language and customs of this country; the latter, in so far as they may be good customs.

7. We solemnly declare once for all to maintain a sincere and respectful reverence for our racial origin of which we are proud.

8. Secretly and openly, by all lawful means at our command, we shall assist in the education and guidance of Latin-Americans and we shall protect and defend their lives and interest whenever necessary.

9. We shall destroy any attempt to create racial prejudices against our people, and any infamous stigma which may be cast upon them, and we shall demand for them the respect and prerogatives which the Constitution grants to us all.

10. Each of us considers himself with equal responsibilities in our organization, to which we voluntarily swear subordination and obedience.

11. We shall create a fund for our mutual protection, for the defense of those of us who may be unjustly persecuted and for the education and culture of our people.

12. This organization is not a political club, but as citizens we shall participate in all local, state, and national political contests. However, in doing so we shall ever bear in mind the general welfare of our people, and we disregard and abjure once for all any personal obligation which is not in harmony with these principles.

13. With our vote and influence we shall endeavor to place in public office men who show by their deeds, respect and consideration for our people.

14. We shall select as our leaders those among us who demonstrate, by their integrity and culture, that they are capable of guiding and directing us properly.

15. We shall maintain publicity means for the diffusion of these principles and for the expansion and consolidation of this organization.

16. We shall pay our poll tax as well as that of members of our families in order that we may enjoy our rights fully.

17. We shall diffuse our ideals by means of the press, lectures, and pamphlets.

18. We shall oppose any radical and violent demonstration which may tend to create conflicts and disturb the peace and tranquility of our country.

19. We shall have mutual respect for our religious views and we shall never refer to them in our institutions.

20. We shall encourage the creation of educational institutions for Latin-Americans and we shall lend our support to those already in existence.

21. We shall endeavor to secure equal representation for our people on juries and in the administration of governmental affairs.

22. We shall denounce every act of peonage and mistreatment as well as the employment of our minor children of scholastic age.

23. We shall resist and attack energetically all machinations tending to prevent our social and political unification.

24. We shall oppose any tendency to separate our children in the schools of this country.

25. We shall maintain statistics which will guide our people with respect to working and living conditions and agricultural and commercial activities in the various parts of our country.

THE SPELL OF NEW MEXICO

[The following affectionate portrayal of New Mexico's Spanish-speaking residents was written by Adelina Otero Warren, a daughter of Manuel B. Otero and, thus, a member of one of most illustrious families in the state's history. When she wrote the article, Mrs. Warren was county superintendent of schools at Santa Fe.]

The spell of my country? Perhaps it is the beauty of it all. To some it is the sunset of a fall afternoon, bathing a little community in its afterglow; turning the vivid yellow of the aspen trees to gold; the red-brown of the scrub oak to bronze; and dark, in the midst of these, the piñon trees. As the sun disappears behind the mountain in the west, its crimson glow is reflected on the snow-covered range in the east. My people watch this with reverence. *"Sangre de Cristo!"* (Blood of Christ) they call these mountains, so named by the early Franciscan missionaries.

Many persons believe New Mexico is a region of plains. But it is in the northern part, into the fertile valleys of the Rio Grande, back into the mountains and their canyons, that my work, as county

From *Survey Graphic*, May 1, 1931. "My People," by Adelina Otero.

superintendent of schools, takes me. Into Cundiyo, situated eight
thousand feet high in the Sangre de Cristo range, reached by a
difficult road down *arroyos* and up over mountains until it seems
that we are to climb Baldy, ten thousand feet above us. Here is a
typical mountain community, entirely occupied by Spanish-Americans, a gentle, industrious, and intelligent people, brown-eyed and
suntanned. The houses are flat-roofed, and are plastered with adobe
of a warm, brown color which conforms to the earth around.
Wherever possible, space has been cleared for gardens and little
farms fed by a stream of crystal water. In the background are the
high pines. It is the fall of the year. The crops have been gathered
from the mountain canyons. The men and women work together.
Corn is husked and separated; the blue for *tortillas* and *atole*, the
white for flour. Both will be taken to the water mill at Nambe to be
ground. The yellow pumpkins are placed on the roofs; the *chili*, red-
der than any sunset, is hung in strings from the *vigas* to dry, and
later will be ground into *chili molido*. Apples are sliced and placed
on boards in the sun.

Since the road was bad, the school nurse and I left my car at
Nambe, the Indian village, and hired an Indian boy to drive us in
his wagon to Cundiyo. There are so many wood roads, it is easy to
lose the way, as we were to learn when we started back. Darkness
comes upon us suddenly in the high mountains, like a curtain lowered to cover our eyes from too much grandeur! But we were fortunate. A moon rose over the range, shedding its white light upon
the countryside. A breeze stirred the pine trees that they might
give forth a fragrance and refresh their guests in the canyons,—
El refresco de la noche! Suddenly I heard a man singing. I looked
back and noticed that he was following us on horseback. It was
Teofilo, one of the school directors.

I asked him,

"Teofilo, where are you going at this hour?"

"*Para* Santa Fe, Señora."

"To Santa Fe! It is thirty miles. You will not arrive there till late.
Can I attend to your business for you?"

"No, Señora. No tenga pena." (Do not be worried.)

We drove on. Our Indian boy never saying a word; Teofilo just
keeping us in sight. The moon, as it rose, gave us more and more
light. At first the tall pines seemed like sentinels one is afraid to
approach, but gradually they became more friendly and Teofilo began to sing:

> *Alli, en un bosque donde yo me hallo, solo se oye mi triste
> peñar.* (In a forest where I find myself alone, I hear my
> sad thoughts.)

The melody of it, the pathos, "*Solo se oye me triste peñar!*" The
little Spanish community; the mountains; the moon; Teofilo's voice
breaking the great silence. *La Hermosura de la noche!* We finally

reached Nambe, and as I thanked and paid the Indian boy and got into my car, I noticed Teofilo was still following. He drew up to the car and addressed me.

"Are you all right, Doña Adelina?"

"*Si, gracias.*"

"You will not have trouble with your car?"

"I think not."

"Well, then, *buenos noches, y Dio la cuide.* I shall return to Cundiyo. But, first would you be so kind as to mail this letter for me in Santa Fe?"

"But you are not going there yourself, then?"

Teofilo smiled, bowed, donned his hat, and rode off into the night. He had followed us for ten miles to see that we were not lost in the canyon! Yes, these are my people, my friends.

In the little community we had left—the teacher had called the school directors to meet with me that day, and the children proceeded to recite their lessons. As I listened I was thinking how to encourage them to preserve the arts, the customs, and the traditions of this New Spain in an effort to save its charm, which is its very life. This is an American school, giving those little children the same reading, writing and arithmetic which is taught in the Far West, the Middle West, and the East. One of the fundamentals of our American education is to train children for life. My people's children have been working at the side of the father and the mother since they were old enough to work—the boy at the plow, herding the sheep, or in the tin shop; the girl a practical exponent of home economics, helping to keep the home and caring for the younger children. A practical effort, theirs, to keep the child in his surroundings. The idea is that the son will inherit the little farm, the sheep, or the tin shop. The girl will become a home maker—the desire and custom of the Spanish-speaking women. I have been lenient about school attendance in the fall of the year since they must bring their children into the work in order to save their crops. It is difficult to get farm hands, even if they could afford it (which they cannot), and as their neighbors are busy with their own farms, there is no alternative. I mention this in an effort to get across a vital point. While I recognize the wonderfully organized educational system of the United States, might it not be beneficial to modify requirements and curricula in other ways?

If we could, for example, in New Mexico include in our rural school curriculum the old arts such as dyeing, blanket-weaving, tin work, needle work, and wood-carving, employing experts in these lines from the community, and give credits in the schools for this work as we do for reading, writing and arithmetic, we might then perpetuate something of lasting educational value for the people. Do you ask why we can not do this now? Because a teacher who has been given her teacher's certificate is not usually expert in these lines, and without such a certificate our laws say that no one may be paid for teaching. Further, if no credits are allowed for these subjects, we will not be able to accredit the students for promotion or for graduation, according to the educational standards of the state. I might add, in passing, that we can not permit the children to speak Spanish in the classroom, and the teachers are instructed to keep the children from conversing in it on the playground, thereby conforming to the national system of education!

But let me go back to the classroom where my twenty-six children from six to sixteen years were gathered. Having recited their lessons, I asked them what they would like to do next. They wanted to sing. It was their way of expressing pleasure at my being with them. (How often since then have I longed to express my joy in a similar way!) "We want to sing to you My Country 'Tis of Thee"—this to show me that they knew our national songs. Then a little chap, with eager brown eyes, asked: "May we sing *one* Spanish song?" And their voices rang out with real feeling in the rhythmical music of La Golondrina, which, according to a legend of our people, was sung by the king of Spain as he looked down on the Moorish siege of Granada:

> *Tambien yo estoy en la region perdido,*
> *O, Cielo santo, y sin poder volar.*
> (I also am in this region lost,
> O, blessed heaven, and unable to fly.)

Into this song went all the love of our natives for their ancestral land—a heritage from their Conquistador forebears. As Gabriela Mistral so beautifully expresses it: *"Una cancion es una respuesta que damos a la hermosura del mundo."* (A song is a response which we give for the beauty of the world.)

The Spaniards made their first stand against the Indian early in the 16th century, and from that time until the territorial division, we had practically reigned supreme over New Spain. With annexation to the American republic, we became a part of *e pluribus unum!* With a people whose traditions and customs had been established for some four hundred years, whose temperament is to live and let live, it has been somewhat difficult to acquiese in the new order, expressed in this instance in the present educational system. The appeal which I make to my people is this: that since the American Occupation in 1846, we have been American citizens, members of *another* great nation, and it is to our best interests that we become educated according to the standards of that nation. It has, for us, its distinct advantages, its definite protection.

Education, in its first sense, is the "leading out" of knowledge and capacities. It requires great skill and a gift to do this without aggressive or hasty imposition of new and unfamiliar ideas. This is especially true in the case of those to whom the "old order changeth." In spite of the tremendous acreage of unsettled and uncultivated land, of sparse population, New Mexico is advancing educationally. Our children are getting their diplomas in reading, writing and arithmetic. Yet we are overlooking their expression of beauty in the native arts and crafts which would be, were these incorporated into the curriculum, a definite contribution to the cultural background of this country.

My visit to Chupadero takes me to Tesuque, a small village about six miles north of Santa Fe. Here I leave my car, and climb into Macario Jimenez' wagon. He has placed a chair in the back for me and over the road we go. We climb one hill after another, into one canyon, and up over a mountain to Chupadero. The schoolhouse comes in sight. The American flag is flying from a pine tree which has been brought down from the mountains. The bark and branches have been carefully cut off, and as carefully our great flag, on a regulation pulley, has been raised to the very top of this one-time sentinel of the hills.

Macario drives me over another mountain pass to Rio en Medio. On the top of this mountain, which is between the two communities, are more *descansos*, silhouetted against the blue sky. These are resting places where the people stop as they carry their dead to the grave. As we begin the ascent, I notice a procession going over the winding road. A wagon grinds its way ahead of a group of men. There are no women. The men are chanting. Macario tells me a young girl from Chupadero has died, and they are taking her to be buried in the church yard at Rio en Medio. The bell tolls in accompaniment to the chanting of the procession. *"Ese doble de campana, no es por el que se murio, sino para recordarme a mi que me he de morir mañana"* ("That tolling of the bell is not for the dead, but to remind me that I may die tomorrow"), says Macario softly as he watches them, with hat in hand. The coffin was a home-made one, covered with pink calico, a white strip making a cross on its lid. A man is driving the team sitting on the box seat, while a young man kneels at the coffin's head, holding a cross. The rest of the men, about a dozen in all, walk bareheaded behind the wagon. At the top of the mountain they halt and a *descanso* cross is erected. The procession winds on, taking the high road. The chanting dies out among the trees as they disappear into the mountains.

After examining the school at Rio en Medio, I visited Macario's home. His wife embraced me, as is the custom among my people, and then invited me to have dinner which had been especially prepared in my honor. It was a delicious repast: *Carne en arroz, frijoles con chile, tortillas, manzanas, secas hervidas, y café*. All of which on an American menu would have appeared as, meat cooked with rice, beans with chile, *tortillas* (which resemble American flapjacks but are used as bread), and stewed dried apples. They have a small adobe house of five rooms, with rag rugs on the floor, a spotless home. One room was set aside as a *sanctuario*, or little chapel,

where candles were burning that day in front of images of the saints
and of Our Lord. The family meet together every evening, light the
candles, and say evening prayers. A devout, religious people whose
religion permeates each thought and action. As these people watch
the snow on the Sangre de Cristo range, they feel that it is a sign
from *Dios* that there will be water in the streams for their crops.
"Why are we Catholics? Because we are Spanish," some of our
people say.

On the long winter evenings I may see this same family sitting
in front of an open fire-place; the father playing the guitar, the
children the flute or the mouth harp, and the rest joining in with
the sheer joy of singing:

> *Ay! ay, ay, ay, canta y no llores,*
> *Porque cantado se alegran, Cielito Lindo, los corazones.*
> (Sing and do not weep, pretty creatures,
> For singing makes the heart glad.)

I have schools in some of the old historical towns. In Santa Cruz
de la Cañada, for example, one of the first four missions in the state,
destroyed by the rebellion of the Indians against Spanish rule in
1680, and rebuilt during the reconquest in 1695. A school in Glorieta
and Cañoncito, both situated at the entrance to Apache Canyon,
called the Front Door of the East, on the old Santa Fe trail leading
from Missouri to Santa Fe. At La Cueva (the cave); at La Joya (the
jewel); in Chimayo, where the famous old *Sanctuario* is located—a
place made famous by the purported appearance of the Blessed
Virgin.

As I have told you, my people are a simple people. There are no
complexities which harass us. We live—we love—we die. We laugh
in joy and weep in sadness. We are superficial? Indeed, no. But
there is an acceptance, a resignation, a logic, I might say, in our
attitude toward life and living. An instance of this last occurred
when I recently visited a home in Tesuque where a little child, one
of my school children, was very ill. The doctor and nurse had reported a severe illness. I went early the next morning to inquire
after the child, and the father met me at the door, not in grief, but
in complete resignation. I asked,

"How is Teresita to-day?"

"Señora, my little girl is well now. She no longer suffers. God
has taken her."

These and their kind then are the Spanish-American people of
New Mexico who have found peace and contentment in the canyons
and the mountain tops. A vigorous people with a background of
culture, of loyalty. A sensitive people with high ideals, loving the
solitude of the wilderness and fearing no danger. Whether it is in
defense of America or war with Spain, we respond. We are avowedly
citizens of the United States. There is no shirking of our suffrage
responsibility. In times of national and state elections we go eagerly

to the polls, for we love the political game. What, then, is to be the trend of education in New Mexico? Is it not a question of our gradual merging, of our assimilation, into this great nation, but at the same time of conserving our distinctive contribution through the preservation of the customs, traditions, the arts and crafts of the Spanish Southwest?

The Spanish era is probably the most colorful in the history of the United States, and I am wondering, as I write this, if this progressive and advanced republic has still time and patience for charm?

An appreciation of this charm in shown by the large and increasing number of *Anglos* who have come to New Mexico to live and who have learned to love it. I do not believe there is an *Anglo* who does not feel that unless he takes this country and the people to his heart—loving it, scars and all—that he is every happy among us. The moment he begins to resent any aspect of his life, we still remain foreign to him.

El sol va bajando sobre mi patria, pero ningun dia muere sin el mejor entendimiento de mi gente. (The sun is setting over my country, but no day dies without a better understanding of my people.)

RANCH
MEXICANS

[The cowboy is an American folk hero belonging to the post–Civil War "Wild West." But the first cowboys were Mexican *vaqueros*, riders of the Western range whose costume, equipment, and life style were taken over by the Anglo cowpunchers in the decades after the Mexican War. To a brief glimpse at the *vaquero*'s past, historian J. Frank Dobie appended a description of the twentieth-century Mexican-American ranch hand.]

The word "cowboy" is very old; in Merry England, far back in the Age of Innocence, the cowboy followed on foot the lowing herd winding slowly o'er the lea and was as gentle as the shepherds of pastoral romance. But the cowboy on a bucking bronco, the cowboy armored in leather and spurring with coiled *reata* after fierce longhorns through thickets of prickly pear and barbed *chaparral*, rounding up great herds over vast ranges and then trailing them for a thousand miles to far away markets and ranges—this cowboy is very modern. He dates only from about 1836.

In that year the Republic of Texas gained her independence from Mexico, and almost immediately after the surrender of the Mexican

From *Survey Graphic*, May 1, 1931.

armies, bands of Texans began raiding down on the cattle and
horses belonging to *rancheros* between the Nueces River and the
Rio Grande. They already knew a little about cattle raising but after
they had exchanged this captured stock in the Louisiana markets
for gold they realized as never before that what was valuable
enough to "lift" was also valuable enough to raise. Thus, broadly
speaking, the range industry of Texas, which within forty-five years
had spread to the Canadian Rockies and occupied almost the whole
virgin world west of the Missouri River, was born.

The English speaking men who carried this industry forward and
created a range tradition that yet flourishes learned nearly all they
knew about ranching from the *rancheros* and *vaqueros*. The mustang horses that they rode and the long-horned cattle that they lived
for and with were Spanish to the core. Cowboy saddle and other
paraphernalia, the cowboy manner of riding, the art of roping, the
rodeo (or roundup), the marking and branding of stock—the whole
business of the range industry was taken over from Spanish-Americans. No other industry, or occupation, in the United States, not
even mining, shows such a direct derivation from the Spanish influences. The very language of the range is Spanish: however corrupted some of the words may have become—*rancho, rodeo,
bronco, (mestaño),* and the rest, a language familiar to thousands of
booted riders who saw a Mexican *vaquero*. The very growth
of soil, the flora, all over the Southwest is popularly known only by
Spanish nomenclature, as *mesquite, nopál, chaparrál, ceniza, grama,
biznaga, huisache, retama,* etc.

The *vaquero*, then, was the first range rider of North America; his
brother in South America took the name of *gaucho*. In the present
limits of the United States the *vaquero*, as a precursor of the cowboy, rode two great ranges. He rode in California, where his cattle
were long killed for their hides and were then neglected in the mad
stampede for gold. He rode on the Rio Grande, on the lower reaches
of which the Texans learned from him, took even his name and
drove his cattle forth to stock an empire once occupied by only
buffaloes and Indians.

And the *vaquero* went with the Texans to serve them and teach
them. Pioneer ranchmen in the border region depended almost exclusively on Mexican *vaqueros* to do their work. Great domains like
the King and Kenedy ranch in southern Texas and Milton Favor's
ranch on the old Chihuahua Trail down the river from El Paso employed *vaqueros* by the score. In the spacious times of trail driving
that followed the Civil War *corridas* of Mexican *vaqueros* drove
herds to Kansas and Wyoming and over the Pecos Trail to meet
thirst and Apaches.

But unlike the "white" hand, many of whom remained in the
Farwest and the Northwest to establish the traditions of the Texas
cowboy, the trailing *vaqueros* generally came back to the border

ranges. As time went on, however, they worked farther and farther out from the international line.

Just here it is necessary to refute a popular misconception—the idea that ranching has become a thing of the past. Over millions of acres in the Southwest and West the ranching industry still obtains. The methods of the industry have, thanks to barbed wire, windmills, improved breeds, and higher prices, changed, but the industry itself has not been supplanted. The ranch hands must often work on foot, building fences and tanks, repairing windmills, even cultivating feed stuffs, but the end of their work is to grow stock and when they work cattle they work on horseback.

In Texas, where within the last three decades the "dry" farmer has plowed under so much good grass, the amount of land devoted to grazing still amounts to more than is devoted to agriculture. The great coastal belt and immense stretches of post oak and piney woods land are yet grazed, though east of the San Antonio River ranch labor is performed by Negroes and some "whites." The ranches left in the Texas Panhandle and southward to the Texas and Pacific Railroad, which for half a thousand miles between Fort Worth and El Paso runs through ranch country, are worked mostly by "white" cowboys—the punchers. The brushy region lying between the Nueces and the Rio Grande has been called the "nursery" of American ranges; it is still, despite development, a cow nursery, the King ranch here comprising over 1,000,000 acres, the Bill Jones holdings amounting to 500,000 acres, and many other ranches embracing from 50,000 to 300,000 acres each. Mexican *vaqueros* are depended upon to work all this range; a considerable part in two or three border counties is owned by descendants of Spanish families who received grants from the Spanish crown. From San Antonio northwest to El Paso, nearly six hundred miles, the route lies almost wholly through arid grazing lands tended largely by Mexicans. In various parts of New Mexico, Arizona, and California *vaqueros* are extensively employed; they have penetrated Wyoming and Montana also. Nowhere else, however, are they depended upon so widely as in Texas.

The ranges of New Mexico and of other states to the north and west probably employ more *pastores* (shepherds) than they do *vaqueros*.

Today on many ranches of the Southwest, particularly of Texas, one may find Mexicans doing the work that twenty-five years ago and less "white" men were doing. The *vaquero* is supplanting the cowboy. He will work for less, expect less, and often do more—so the ranchmen who employ him say. He is more willing to stay away from town and less given to spurring up automobiles.

On the smaller ranches the *vaquero* is apt to be a kind of roustabout, handy at anything. He is apt to have a family, and his children may once in a while attend the community school. On the larger

ranches the *vaqueros* are still a part of something like feudal domain, getting their supplies largely from the ranch commissary,
which does not overcharge, depending on other Mexicans of the
ranch for human association, voting as the *mayordomo* advises, and
very often regarding the ranch, in the manner that other people
regard a town or a county, as a unit of citizenship. For instance, a
King ranch Mexican calls himself a *Kineño*. Here on these larger
ranches the *vaqueros* spend several months each year in camp,
working cattle, building and repairing fences, scraping out tanks,
in times of extreme drouth singeing the thorns off prickly pear so
that cattle can eat it or cutting *sotol* for the same purpose.

If the ranch owner lives away, he has a "white" man for manager. The *caporál*, or foreman, under the manager may be either a
Mexican or a "white" man. Frequently "white" hands work along
with the Mexicans, particularly in handling cattle; in such cases,
however, the *caporál* is nearly always "white" also.

Some of the *vaqueros* live with their families about the "home
ranch"; some of them live far separated in remote pastures. The
pastero, or pasture tender, leads an isolated existence, riding his
fences and watching the waterings day after day, his wife sometimes
going for months without seeing another woman.

The pay of the vaquero averages $25 or $30 a month, "grub" furnished; about $10 a month more if he furnishes himself. "White"
hands receive around $10 a month more than the Mexicans. The
cocinero (cook) draws $5 more than the *vaquero*. A *jinete* (horse
breaker) also draws a premium. The best way to keep ranch Mexicans satisfied is to give them plenty of meat, whether beef or *cabra*
(goat). Many ranches in southwest Texas keep herds of common
Mexican goats for the purpose of supplying meat.

A Mexican will leave a $35 job on a small ranch where meat and
company are scarce to work for $25 a month on a big ranch where
he can be with a "crowd" and get plenty of meat.

In the land of the *vaquero* there is still, comparatively speaking,
remoteness; there is still a kind of primitive simplicity in the ways
of living and thinking. Hence the *vaquero* and *pastor* of today retain perhaps more than any other class of laborers the characteristic
traits of their simple-lived forefathers. Life for them is almost as
free of complexities as it was before the automobile, the radio, and
labor unions were invented. Many of the young people of these pastoral families drift away, but those who remain on the ranch accept
pretty much without question the stark simplicities that a life of
hard labor to the soil requires—and rewards. True, the ranch Mexican now buys ready-made many of the things he used to make for
himself; but the arts of weaving cinches out of horse mane, of fash-
ioning *reatas* out of rawhide, of tanning buckskin, and of plaiting
quirts and cow whips are not yet lost arts. He no longer burns cow
chips to make soda, but he brews tea of the *ceniza* (a kind of sage)
to cure inflammation of the chest, and tea of the San Nicolás herb

affords a beverage as delectable to him as that of the Chinese herb
is to any four-o'clock Englishman. He wants to sleep under a shingle
roof and has become awkward at thatching with bear-grass, but he
can trail a cow or any wild animal as unerringly as Comanche warrior ever trailed.

He may or may not speak English. The nearer he is to the Border
and the bigger the ranch he works on the less English he hears, for
the *Americanos* of the border ranches almost without exception
talk Spanish, often interlarding their own language with racy Mexican idioms. These *Americanos*, being to the manner born, have,
incidentally, few of the labor problems that bother newly-come
farmers and tradesmen. The majority of ranch Mexicans—that is to
say the men—can spell out simple print, but one who subscribes for
even a weekly paper is a rare exception, and the *amo* (master) is
frequently called upon to write letters for his dependents. The ranch
Mexican's library is likely to be confined to an almanac, a book of
dreams, and a pamphlet of testimonials and directions found
wrapped around some bottle of patent medicine.

He may possess a cheap phonograph and a few records, but the
best music he hears is what he and his *compañeros* make while
singing in camp at night to the accompaniment of wailing coyotes.
I wish I could describe the song of the *vaquero*. I cannot. It is a
wail; it is, no matter what its theme, a note of sorrow, of something
far, far away. It seems to go quivering up to the stars; it is wild; it
is barbaric. It may be about a *ladino* (outlaw) steer roped out in
the brush; it may be about a *caballo fragado* (broken down horse)
that some *vaquero* has had to lead in; it may be the old and haunt-
ing *Golondrina* or the sad ballad of the *Cuatra Milpas*. Often it concerns itself with such heros as Pancho Villa or some daring border
smuggler killed by Texas rangers. The *vaquero* sings best after a
big supper of fresh beef. Well filled with good meat, he must sing
or bust.

He is full of stories about buried treasures, which priests and
gachupines are usually somehow connected with and which are
guarded by white *bultos*, clanking chains, eerie lights and other
mysteries. If he does not know a witch, he knows of one. If he does
not fear the evil eye, he respects it. If he or any of his family become very ill, he wants a doctor, but at the same time he yearns for
a *curandéro* (a kind of quack that a whole essay would be required
to picture forth). He is familiar with the habits of every creature
of his soil. For him every hill and hollow has a personality and a
name. He regards the stars; he watches the phases of the moon.
He knows the name and virtue of every bush and herb. He is a child
of nature; he is truly *un hombre del campo*.

GETTING RID
OF THE MEXICAN

[During the decade
from 1920 to 1929, more than half a million immigrants entered the
United States from Mexico on permanent visas, and the illegal or
"wetback" immigration was proportionally large. But the Great
Depression cut down the number of arrivals drastically. And, as
unemployment increased and the welfare rolls grew longer, some
states hit upon the idea of sending Mexicans back to Mexico or
forcing them to return. Unfortunately, once such a policy was
adopted, it was often applied indiscriminately, and many (actually
more than half) who were "repatriated" were native-born Americans. The obvious illegality—to say nothing of the injustice—of such
action did not seem to bother the states concerned, for the important thing was to cut down on "unnecessary" welfare payments.
Early in the Depression, of course, the federal government was
doing nothing for the relief of the unemployed, and the burden on
the states grew suddenly and alarmingly. Carey McWilliams, long-
time specialist in Mexican-American affairs, described California's
dealings with the Mexican population from 1930 through 1932.]

In 1930 a fact-finding committee reported to the Governor of California that, as a result of the passage of the Immigration Acts of

From *American Mercury*, March 1933.

1921 and 1924, Mexicans were being used on a large scale in the Southwest to replace the supply of cheap labor that had been formerly recruited in Southeastern Europe. The report revealed a concentration of this new immigration in Texas, Arizona, and California, with an ever increasing number of Mexicans giving California as the State of their "intended future permanent residence." It was also discovered that, within the State, this new population was concentrated in ten southern counties.

For a long time Mexicans had regarded Southern California, more particularly Los Angeles, with favor, and during the decade from 1919 to 1929 the facts justified this view. At that time there was a scarcity of cheap labor in the region, and Mexicans were made welcome. When cautious observers pointed out some of the consequences that might reasonably be expected to follow from a rash encouragement of this immigration, they were shouted down by the wise men of the Chamber of Commerce. Mexican labor was eulogized as cheap, plentiful, and docile. Even so late as 1930 little effort had been made to unionize it. The Los Angeles shopkeepers joined with the industrialists in denouncing, as a union labor conspiracy, the agitation to place Mexican immigration on a quota basis. Dr. Paul S. Taylor quotes this typical utterance from a merchant:

> Mexican business is for cash. They don't criticize prices. You can sell them higher priced articles than they intended to purchase when they came in. They spend every cent they make. Nothing is too good for a Mexican if he has the money. They spend their entire pay-check. If they come into your store first, you get it. If they go to the other fellow's store first, he gets it.

During this period, academic circles in Southern California exuded a wondrous solicitude for the Mexican immigrant. Teachers of sociology, social service workers, and other subsidized sympathizers were deeply concerned about his welfare. Was he capable of assimilating American idealism? What anti-social traits did he possess? Wasn't he made morose by his native diet? What could be done to make him relish spinach and Brussels sprouts? What was the percentage of this and that disease, or this and that crime, in the Mexican population of Los Angeles? How many Mexican mothers fed their youngsters according to the diet schedules promulgated by manufacturers of American infant foods? In short, the do-gooders subjected the Mexican population to a relentless barrage of surveys, investigations, and clinical conferences.

But a marked change has occurred since 1930. When it became apparent last year that the programme for the relief of the unemployed would assume huge proportions in the Mexican quarter, the community swung to a determination to oust the Mexicans. Thanks to the rapacity of his overlords, he had not been able to accumulate any savings. He was in default in his rent. He was a burden to the taxpayer. At this juncture, an ingenious social worker suggested the desirability of a wholesale deportation. But when the Federal authorities were consulted they could promise but slight assistance, since many of the younger Mexicans in Southern California were American citizens, being the American-born children of immigrants. Moreover, the Federal officials insisted, in cases of illegal entry, upon a public hearing and a formal order of deportation. This procedure involved delay and expense, and, moreover, it could not be used to advantage in ousting any large number.

A better scheme was soon devised. Social workers reported that many of the Mexicans who were receiving charity had signified their "willingness" to return to Mexico. Negotiations were at once opened with the social-minded officials of the Southern Pacific Railroad. It was discovered that, in wholesale lots, the Mexicans could be shipped to Mexico City for $14.70 *per capita*. This sum represented less than the cost of a week's board and lodging. And so, about February, 1931, the first trainload was dispatched, and shipments at the rate of about one a month have continued ever since. A shipment, consisting of three special trains left Los Angeles on December 8. The loading commenced at about six o'clock in the morning and continued for hours. More than twenty-five such special trains had left the Southern Pacific station before last April.

No one seems to know precisely how many Mexicans have been "repatriated" in this manner to date. The Los Angeles *Times* of November 18 gave an estimate of 11,000 for the year 1932. The monthly shipments of late have ranged from 1,300 to 6,000. The *Times* reported last April that altogether more than 200,000 *repatriados* had left the United States in the twelve months immediately preceding, of which it estimated that from 50,000 to 75,000 were from California, and over 35,000 from Los Angeles county. Of those from Los Angeles county, a large number were charity deportations.

The repatriation programme is regarded locally as a piece of consummate statescraft. The average per family cost of executing it is $71.14, including food and transportation. It cost Los Angeles county $77,249.29 to repatriate one shipment of 6,024. It would have cost $424,933.70 to provide this number with such charitable assistance as they would have been entitled to had they remained—a saving of $347,468.41.

One wonders what has happened to all the Americanization programmes of yesteryear. The Chamber of Commerce has been forced to issue a statement assuring the Mexican authorities that the community is in no sense unfriendly to Mexican labor and that repatriation is a policy designed solely for the relief of the destitute—even, presumably, in cases where invalids are removed from the County Hospital in Los Angeles and carted across the line. But those who once agitated for Mexican exclusion are no longer regarded as the puppets of union labor.

What of the Mexican himself? The repatriation programme, apparently, is a matter of indifference to this amiable ex-American. He never objected to exploitation while he was welcome, and now he acquiesces in repatriation. He doubtless enjoys the free train ride home. Probably he has had his fill of bootleg liquor and of the mirage created by pay-checks that never seemed to buy as much as they should. Considering the anti-social character commonly attributed to him by the sociological myth-makers, he has coöperated nicely with the authorities. Thousands have departed of their own volition. In battered Fords, carrying two and three families and all their worldly possessions, they are drifting back to *el terenaso*—the big land. They have been shunted back and forth across the border for so many years by war, revolution, and the law of supply and demand, that it would seem that neither expatriation or repatriation held any more terror for them.

The Los Angeles industrialists confidently predict that the Mexican can be lured back, "whenever we need him." But I am not so sure of this. He may be placed on a quota basis in the meantime, or possibly he will no longer look north to Los Angeles as the goal of his dreams. At present he is probably delighted to abandon an empty paradise. But it is difficult for his children. A friend of mine, who was recently in Mazatlan, found a young Mexican girl on one of the southbound trains crying because she had to leave Belmont High-School. Such an abrupt severance of the Americanization programme is a contingency that the professors of sociology did not anticipate.

Part Five

TRAVAILS OF LA RAZA, 1940-70

Since World War II, La Raza has gradually emerged as a recognized entity on the American scene. Whereas Professor George Sanchez could describe the Mexican Americans of 1940 as forgotten Americans—and indeed they had been just that for ninety years—by 1970 they were anything but forgotten. It is true that the revitalization of ethnic consciousness among Mexican Americans has taken place largely in the shadow of the civil rights movement and the "black revolution," as have similar stirrings among Indians and Puerto Ricans. But the awakening of La Raza also has a life of its own, just as La Raza has unique areas of grievance against the Anglo majority that are not shared by other groups.

The resurgence of ethnic-cultural consciousness is both a positive and a negative factor for any group in which it occurs. It is positive in what it emphasizes about the people concerned—their language, heritage, cultural and social contributions, and ethnic characteristics. The appeals to nationalism delivered by some leaders are calls to unity and action through which grievances may be resolved. Yet there is a negative aspect to ethnic-nationalistic self-awareness, for great emphasis on it highlights the very dilemma of the group—its exclusion from full participation in the majority society and the discrimination that is the mark of such exclusion. Had all the patterns of social, economic, and political discrimination against La Raza been erased in past decades, so that Mexican Americans could share as fully as they wanted to in the national life, much of the cultural-ethnic-nationalistic baggage that they now carry would have been left behind, as has happened with most immigrant groups. Others—Swedes, Poles, or Italians, for instance—preserve as much of their cultural heritage as seems to them necessary, while otherwise thoroughly accommodating themselves to "the American way of life." But the Mexican Americans (as well as the blacks, Puerto Ricans, and Indians) have not been allowed this luxury. They have therefore had to cleave to their pride in La Raza, with all that it entails.

La Raza, then, is reacting to its own position in American life and to the inequality of opportunities in education, housing, and work its members have experienced. One writer on the sociology of Mexican Americans wisely notes that the relative failure of La Raza to participate in the nation's life cannot be simply ascribed to racism (Nancie L. González in *The Spanish-Americans of New Mexico*). Racism has been all too evident in the relationships between Anglos and Mexican Americans. But between the two groups there has also persisted a contrast of cultures and social values that has worked to the disadvantage of the Hispanos while favoring the Anglos. It is the Anglo community that decides which language shall be spoken, what the schools shall teach, and which social values shall be commended and rewarded. Thus La Raza has recently found itself in the dilemma of seeking an accommodation with many of the ways of Anglo-America in order to obtain the benefits thereof, while promoting (at least in part) forms of cultural nationalism or separatism within which long-range solutions are not likely to be found.

The revived self-awareness of La Raza has been reinforced by two external circumstances. One is the continuing immigration from Mexico. This has meant both a numerical increase in the Mexican-American population and a renewed involvement with the customs and traditions of Old Mexico. In addition, there has been a growing identification, particularly among the poorer and more militant Mexican Americans, with the so-called Third World, especially the "Brown Continent" (Central and South America), the nations of which are felt to be members of the brotherhood of exploited peoples, or, in Frantz Fanon's phrase, "the wretched of the earth."

But, even today, in this era of self-realization, La Raza is not united. It is as diversified within itself as the communities of black Americans have been. Ethnicity and cultural heritage are frequently eclipsed by other issues, such as economic and social status or professional attainment. The militant *Chicanos* (and not all Mexican Americans embrace that term) accuse others of La Raza of being coconuts (brown outside, white inside) or *Vendidos* (sellouts); and the more affluent, "gringoized" middle-class Hispanos denounce militancy because they feel it will bring repression instead of social gains. Nor is the leadership of La Raza united in its goals or tactics, although it is the latter that causes the most difficulty. There is general agreement that Mexican Americans want specific social and economic benefits that they see other Americans enjoying; the degree to which La Raza should accommodate itself to the Anglo society creates differences of opinion. But the matter of means—militant versus nonmilitant, for instance—causes deep divisions. As of 1970, it seemed that the Mexican Americans were taking a cue from the black community and, while maintaining a strident posture in terms of demands were generally shunning violence as a means of gaining results.

One specific social change among Mexican Americans since 1940 has made practicable an increased sense of community. In those thirty years, the Mexican Americans shifted from a largely rural to an overwhelmingly urban life. By the late 1960's, about 80 per cent of them could be found in cities. Most of the Mexican Americans still reside in the Southwest and a majority of these are in California and Texas. The Long Beach–Los Angeles area has, after Mexico City, the most Mexicans of any city in the western hemisphere. There are also sizable communities in the industrial centers of the North: Chicago, New York, Detroit, and Kansas City. This urbanization of La Raza, coinciding with the great increase in affluence following World War II, bred a dissatisfaction with their condition induced by proximity with Anglo neighborhoods. In a word, they became more conscious of their second-class citizenship. Their feelings of alienation were often increased by governmental actions, such as the bracero program, which tended to work against their interests.

As an urban minority, the Mexican Americans in the last third of the twentieth century share most of the problems of the poor in cities: inferior education, segregated housing patterns, higher prices for commodities, lower-paying jobs, and cultural deprivation. To these is added the matter of language difference, frequently regarded as the main barrier to economic and social advance. But the foremost problem of La Raza is really not theirs at all. It is the problem and the challenge faced by America itself—the need to create a society in which justice and equality prevail for all citizens, not just the fortunate majority.

THE NEW MEXICAN IN 1940

[When Professor George I. Sanchez wrote *Forgotten People*, the book from which this selection is taken, more than half of New Mexico's population were Indo-Hispanic. They were primarily rural, with little of their life style oriented toward the values of the Anglo-American community. Some, of course, had obtained the education necessary to enter the professions, and there was a small, though growing, middle class. But the majority were poor and, in many cases, were made poorer over the years as the federal government expropriated their grazing lands for national forests. The coming of mechanized farming also tended to make the old ways no longer viable. Many began, early in this century, to turn to wage-earning jobs and away from trying to make a living off of a small plot of ground. But the Depression hit the region very hard and nearly eliminated the supply of available jobs. During the hard years of the 1930's, a majority of the Spanish Americans of New Mexico became dependent on the federal government's relief programs. During the 1930's, also, hundreds of families lost their land through foreclosures and tax sales. Thus, the 1930s ended with the beginning of a Hispano movement to the cities.]

From George I. Sanchez, *Forgotten People: A Study of New Mexico.* Albuquerque, 1940. Chapter 3.

The descendants of the Spanish colonists of New Mexico are to be found in every walk of life. The conditions arising out of the adjustments which resulted from the development of the region within the last ninety years have had varying effects upon the populace. Some managed to retain their land holdings and are in comfortable circumstances as farmers and as ranchers. Some have taken advantage of new economic opportunities and have proven successful in business. A few have seized upon educational advantages and are to be found in the professions and in government. Many make their living as clerks and as skilled workers.

While due recognition must be made of the successful manner in which some members of the group have adapted themselves to the new environment, it is to be observed that the great masses of the people constitute a severely handicapped social and economic minority. Generally speaking, their status is one of privation and want, of cultural inadequacy and of bewilderment. Neglected for more than two hundred years as Spanish colonials and Mexicans, their cultural situation was not greatly improved by the territorial regime. In fact, the little improvement that took place through the limited educational efforts that were made in their behalf was more than offset by the social and economic decline that resulted from the influx of new peoples and of a new economic order.

The evidence of decline and deterioration is best observed in situations faced by those rural sections of the state where New Mexicans represent a substantial sector of the population, though such evidence is not lacking in the towns and cities. Almost a hundred years after becoming American citizens, a broad gap still separates them from the culture which surrounds them. In lieu of adequate instruction, they have clung to their language, their customs, their agricultural practices. Though no fault can be found with a society because it seeks to perpetuate worthy elements of its culture, it is to be regretted that, in this instance, the process has not been accompanied by suitable adaptations.

The New Mexican often carries on inferior and obsolete practices and beliefs because he has been permitted, and forced to remain in isolation. Of necessity, he has persisted in a traditional way of life that is below current standards. His language has suffered by disuse, yet he has had little chance to learn to use English effectively. His social status reflects his economic insufficiency. His lack of education handicaps him in the exercise of his political power. That same lack makes him a public charge once he has lost his land, his traditional source of livelihood. Midst the wreckage of his economy and his culture, and unprepared for the new order of things, he is pathetic in his helplessness—a stranger in his own home.

The task of portraying the present status of the citizens of Spanish descent in New Mexico is one that exceeds the bounds of this limited report. Those who are familiar with the area and its people recognize that the task is a difficult and a highly complicated one. There are many ramifications of the questions involved, and issues

arising from those questions present perplexing social and economic problems. It needs to be pointed out that no organized effort
has ever been made to compile and present information with reference to these questions. Isolated agencies and individuals have
made researches and, on occasion, have inaugurated action programs of limited scope. At no time, however, have these efforts been
coördinated nor has joint study ever been given to the various
phases of the minority problem of the area by those who have devoted time and effort to its study.

In each of fifteen (of the thirty-one) counties this element comprises 50 per cent or more of the population. These fifteen counties
have almost three-fifths of all the people in the state. In each of
seven counties, (Taos, Rio Arriba, Mora, San Miguel, Valencia, Sandoval, and Socorro) the Spanish-speaking people constitute more
than 80 per cent of the population. In the light of the observations
made above, these figures suggest the severity of the situation faced
in these areas. A brief survey of readily available facts will illustrate
the nature of this situation.

The United States census of 1930 revealed that 13.3 per cent of
the people in New Mexico were illiterate. When compared with
other states, New Mexico ranks third from the lowest in literacy.
Though sparsely populated, the state is twenty-second in number
of illiterates. As might be expected, the counties with the highest
proportions of Spanish-speaking people also tend to have the highest
illiteracy rates. This is true even when illiteracy rates are corrected
for the Indian population.

New Mexico has more than fourteen people for each daily news-
paper, giving her a rank of forty-seventh among the states. The state
has about one-sixth-of-a-volume-in-public-libraries per capita, in
which item New Mexico has a rank of thirty-eight, though her rank
is still lower when the circulation of such volumes is taken into
consideration. There is an almost total absence of literature in
rural areas. The people of those areas are also the least able to
afford radios, have fewer means and opportunities for social contacts, and are served by the poorest schools. In addition, the rural
New Mexican has had the least contact with English and with the
culture represented by that language. And so on almost endlessly,
the inherent inertia of the situation breaking down with exasperat-
ing slowness. . . .

The special nature of the problem of educating this cultural
minority has never been properly recognized by federal and state
governments. Educational practices in New Mexico have been pat-
terned after those developed in the Middle West and in the East
for peoples and conditions vastly different from those obtaining
here. The selection of educational officials by popular election is a
practice that is particularly incongruous in this situation. So is the
district system. The use of standard curricula, books, and materials
among these children is a ridiculous procedure.

The language problem illustrates the inadequacy of current in-

structional practices. Imagine the Spanish-speaking child's introduction to American education! He comes to school, not only without a word of English but without the environmental experience
upon which school life is based. He cannot speak to the teacher and
is unable to understand what goes on about him in the classroom.
He finally submits to rote learning, parroting words and processes
in self-defense. To him, school life is artificial. He submits to it during class hours, only partially digesting the information which the
teacher has tried to impart. Of course he learns English and the
school subjects imperfectly! The school program is based on the
fallacious assumption that the children come from English-speaking
homes—homes that reflect American cultural standards and traditions.

The unresponsiveness of the school to the environment of New
Mexican children tends to force them out of school. Most of these
children leave school before they have learned enough to help them
become effective in improving their environmental conditions. They
leave school not only without an adequate knowledge of English
but without the rudiments of education in health and work habits,
in social practices and personal duties. It is conceivable that, with
superior teachers and instructional materials, considerable improvement can be brought about even under the handicap of present
administrative and curricular defects. However, superior teachers
cost money and these people are poor. The counties with the largest
Spanish-speaking population are also the poorest counties in the
state—the higher the percentage of Spanish-speaking people in a
county, the lower the per capita assessed valuation. Not only that,
but the distribution of state school revenues tends to accentuate
rather than to reduce this handicap. . . .

The inadequacy of the provisions made for the support and administration of public education is illustrative of the failure of government to meet the problems presented by the New Mexican. This
inadequacy is apparent in all fields of public service. Vital statistics
are of particular significance in this connection. Whereas the infant mortality rate for the nation is 51 for every 1,000 live births,
the rate in New Mexico is 125.9. Thirteen of the counties have an
infant mortality rate of less than 100, eighteen counties have rates
ranging from 104.8 to 167! It is significant to note that the ten
counties that have the highest infant mortality rates in the state
are counties where more than half of the population is Spanish-
speaking.

New Mexico, with a death rate of 13.8, has almost three more
deaths per 1,000 of population than the nation at large. All of the
ten counties, except one, having the highest death rates (from 14.7
to 22.1 per thousand) are counties where the people of Spanish
descent constitute more than half of the population. The lack of
health services in these counties is made evident by the fact that
in Mora County almost 80 per cent of the deaths were from *unknown* causes! In Taos and Sandoval this percentage was sixty-nine.

The rank of the counties of the state on percentage of deaths from unknown causes corresponds very closely to their rank on percentage of population of Spanish extraction!

These facts serve merely to emphasize the general observation that the descendants of the colonizers of New Mexico constitute an underprivileged socio-economic minority in the state. As the common day laborer and subsistence farmer, the economic status of the native New Mexican puts him at the disadvantage felt by similar classes elsewhere in the country. In addition, it is quite apparent that, in New Mexico, this group suffers additional handicaps that are products of the cultural gap that separates the New Mexican from other Americans.

Health practices are often guided by medieval traditions and superstitions. These beliefs range from such matters as credence in the Evil Eye to faith in incompetent midwives and *curanderos* (herb doctors)—to say nothing of homely remedies, patent medicines, and general ignorance of modern health practices. Many of these people still live in the seventeenth century, in so far as matters of health are concerned. It is easy to understand why this is so. Modern health standards were developed in Western civilization *after* these people went into isolation. When the Spaniards came into New Mexico in the sixteenth and seventeenth centuries they came with the beliefs and standards of that time. Since then they have had no opportunity to learn of new developments in that field. They have, perforce, continued practicing the only standards they know. It is not at all remarkable that, being so far behind the times in health knowledge, these people should lag behind current trends in health status. Indeed, it would be remarkable if they did not. What is startling is that so little has been done to improve these conditions.

What has been said about the cultural handicap in the field of health applies to civic activities and to other social practices as well. It is not a matter of wonder that, lacking the leadership and the instruments of progress, a society should not be progressive. The persistence of outmoded practices and beliefs among a people is remarkable when those practices and beliefs are, in truth, outmoded. As has been suggested before, the incorporation into the American fold of the people adopted by the United States through the Treaty of Guadalupe Hidalgo has been left largely up to them. Through trial and error, by casual contacts with other Americans, and with their coöperation, some progress has been achieved, notably within the last two decades. Even so, as indicated by the figures cited in the matters of education and health, the American of Spanish descent in New Mexico is still behind the times. Left largely to his own resources, he has, of course, been unable to outmode his own standards and traditions. . . .

Citizenship and suffrage for the New Mexican did not constitute the means for his self-regeneration. He did not, and still does not, know the nature of his problems nor the techniques for their solution. The value of his vote as an instrument of reform is decreased by his lack of understanding of issues and goals, of political tactics, and of party politics. Because of this he has proven ineffective in bringing about necessary governmental changes even though he is politically powerful from the standpoint of numbers. More often than not he sees little connection between candidates for office and his own welfare. Elections are disassociated from the vital factors of making a living, from education, from health. As a consequence, political leaders and office-holders show an amazing indifference to the major needs of these people. Too often it appears that these leaders feel that they have discharged their obligation to the New Mexican when they have graded a road in his county or when they have hired some of his friends as clerks and laborers at his expense.

This has been the tenor of self-government in New Mexico. The progress that has been made has been haphazard and slow in its development. Only as popular education has spread have reforms been instituted. Bossism and machine politics based on the spoils system on a crude scale is still the rule, however. The time for a major attack through government upon the social and economic ills facing the New Mexican is yet in the future. An educated electorate and a conscientious leadership are the prerequisites.

Too often the problem presented by these people today is regarded simply as a "bi-lingual problem—one wherein language differences are of primary importance. It is much more than that. The problem is one of culture contacts and conflicts—one wherein traditional cultural and geographic isolation accentuate the normal problems presented by incorporation and aggravate the deficiencies of an undeveloped economy and of a frontier social structure.

Without minimizing the importance of the problems presented by native New Mexicans in cosmopolitan centers, rather assuming that the rural field offers a valuable approach to those problems, the rural New Mexican constitutes the major issue in acculturation in this area. In migratory labor communities, or in permanent rural settlements which are predominately Spanish-speaking, his social and economic situation offers the most serious obstacles to incorporation. Living in isolation, he is not only removed from the normal social contacts which would tend to improve his condition, but he is highly inaccessible, physically and culturally, to the public agencies of incorporation. In the one case, he lives in the home of his colonial ancestors, unprepared to participate successfully in current affairs and unresponsive to the goals and values of his fellow Americans. In the other case, he labors in the sheep camps, in the vegetable and cotton fields, and in the fruit groves—a piecework cropper with no permanent roots in the community and, because of his condition, offering little opportunity to the normal public service organizations. In either case, these people are society's stepchildren —forgotten people on the "other side of the railroad tracks." . . .

The very nature of state and county government in New Mexico militates against an adequate approach to the problems herein suggested. The New Mexican's needs are great, yet he is least able to afford the services that will meet those needs. In addition, his cultural status makes him less effective in voicing his needs before county, state, and federal governments than is the case with any other large group in the state. This ineffectiveness is evidenced in the officials he selects for both state and county offices and in their after-election indifference to his vital problems.

In summarizing the viewpoint herein presented, it needs to be said that the generally inferior status held by the native New Mexican today is, in large measure, a result of the failure of the United States to recognize the special character of the social responsibility it assumed when it brought these people forcibly into the American society. Granting them technical citizenship did not discharge that responsibility. The legal right to "life, liberty, and the pursuit of happiness" is an empty privilege when the bare essentials of Americanism and of social welfare are wanting.

MEXICANS TO MICHIGAN

[Most of the Mexican immigrants went to Texas, Arizona, New Mexico, and California—the states contiguous to Mexico. But, as labor shortages, especially in seasonal agriculture, became known farther to the north and east, teams or families of migrant workers headed in the direction of the jobs. It was not only immigrants who went searching for work, however. Many native-born Mexican Americans, who suffered from the competition of cheaper labor coming from south of the Rio Grande, gradually ranged farther afield themselves in search of higher-paying work. Thus, many families who had lived long in one place were uprooted to join the ever growing throng of migrants. Between 1910 and 1920, the number of Mexicans going to Michigan increased twentyfold, and this figure does not include the Mexican Americans who went there for seasonal labor. In the following article, published in 1941, Carey McWilliams describes the traffic of Mexican workers between Texas and Michigan.]

The Mexican *barrio* of San Antonio is an indolent and rather attractive quarter. Unpainted shacks, in a state of perpetual ill-repair, rest on stilts and lean precariously in all directions; dogs bark, children yell, and radios blare in every hovel. But the windows are decorated

From *Common Ground*, Autumn 1941.

with plants, feeble shrubs sprout in the dirt yards, and morning-glories climb the fence posts. Every corner has its grocery store and beer hall (and above the beer hall the *bagnio*). Thousands of Mexicans, constituting perhaps 40 per cent of the population of San Antonio, live in the quarter. It is the hunting ground of labor contractors: the capital of the Mexico that lies within the United States.

Here, on El Paso Street—the "skid row"—are the headquarters of Mr. Frank Cortez. A versatile citizen, Mr. Cortez is the principal emigrant agent or labor contractor in Texas, and also the operator of several stores, cafes, and a funeral parlor in the *barrio*. Young, snappily-dressed, affable, Mr. Cortez was once a migrant worker himself. One year in the service of a Pennsylvania steel mill as a contract-employee was enough, however, to convince him he should seek another vocation. He returned to San Antonio and opened a funeral parlor—a happy decision, for the death rate among the Mexican population is high, the Mexicans like ornate funerals, and most of them carry burial insurance.

A few years ago, Mr. Cortez became a licensed emigrant agent, authorized by the State of Texas to recruit labor for employment beyond its borders. From mid-March until May each year, he is busy signing up Mexican sugar-beet workers at the funeral parlor for his good friend, Mr. Max Henderson of the Michigan Beet Growers Employment Committee. Each year he recruits 6,000 workers for the Committee, for whom he is paid $1 a head.

"There isn't much expense, and I make $6,000 for about three weeks work. It's a nice business," says Mr. Cortez.

Of the northern sugar-beet areas in the Middle West, Michigan imports, by a considerable margin, the most Mexican labor. The average planting, about 140,000 acres, necessitates the employment of nearly 20,000 field workers. Ninety-five per cent of this acreage is handled by contract-labor (that is, labor performed not by the growers but by field labor under contract), and two-thirds of it comes from Texas. At least 10,000, and perhaps 15,000, field workers make the trip to Michigan every season. Originally the sugar-beet companies imported Polish, Belgian, and Hungarian immigrant families, who were settled on small acreage allotments in the immediate vicinity of the 13 sugar-beet districts in the State. But now that the first generation of these families is rapidly disappearing and succeeding generations have drifted to the cities for industrial employment, Mexican labor has almost completely supplanted the original immigrant groups. The transition began to be effected, on a large scale, immediately after the passage of the Immigration Act of 1924, which cut off the supply of European hands, but was also accelerated by the formation, on the part of the remnants of the early immigrant families, of an A.F. of L. Agricultural Workers Union, which, in May, 1935, struck for higher wages at Blissfield, Michigan.

Prior to this strike, out-of-state Mexican labor had been recruited in a haphazard, informal manner, with each grower obtaining his own. To streamline the process, on April 7, 1938, the Beet Growers Employment Committee was formed to recruit workers for growers who raised beets for the Michigan Sugar Company. While the companies never contract with workers directly, and invariably disclaim responsibility for their welfare, they have, nevertheless, an active interest in maintaining a cheap labor supply. If wage rates increase, growers will demand more for their beets.

The companies are particular: they want rural Mexican families, not the urbanized proletariat—the pecan shellers, street cleaners, dish washers, and common laborers of San Antonio. Of the workers recruited by Mr. Cortez, at least two-thirds come from rural areas outside the city—from El Paso, Brownsville, Corpus Christi, Crystal City—and many travel great distances. . . .

Traveling from Texas to Michigan by truck is a nightmare. Most of the trucks are the open stake kind, never intended for passenger transportation. Old models, seldom in a state of good repair, they are used during the season to haul sugar beets from field to factory. Before starting out, the driver is careful to substitute Michigan license plates (which have been forwarded to him) for his Texas plates, so he will not catch the eye of a wary highway patrolman in Michigan. Planks or benches are then placed on the truck, and it is loaded with passengers and equipment. Frequently 60 and 65 are huddled together. Although some companies have issued instructions that not more than 25 passengers be carried on a truck (quite a load in itself), the average carries about 50 people, their bedding and equipment and food for the trip. Once the Mexicans have crowded into the back, a heavy tarpaulin is thrown over them and fastened down around the edges so they are concealed. Outwardly the truck looks as though it were loaded with a cargo of potatoes. Before climbing into the driver's seat, the trucker tosses a couple of coffee cans into the back to be used as urinals during the journey. Then, usually around midnight, the truck rolls out of El Paso Street for the long trip north.

Afraid of being arrested for violating the Emigrant Agent Law, fearful of being charged with breaking the motor vehicle regulations of the states along the line of march, usually apprehensive that the truck itself will be picked up by a finance company, the truckers drive like devils. With a relief driver in the cab, they go straight through to Michigan, stopping only for gas and oil. By driving night and day, they can make the trip in from 45 to 48 hours. Paid $10 a head to deliver Mexicans in Michigan (ultimately charged to the workers), some truckers make $3,000 a year. Naturally they are in a hurry: they want to make two or three trips. Instead of traveling the main highways, however, they pursue a zigzag course, making many detours zooming along country roads and minor highways to avoid patrolmen. As a rule they are as arrogant as captains on a slave-galley. They pay little heed to their passengers, drink to stay awake, and drive against time. Notoriously bad drivers, and traveling under these circumstances, they have many accidents every season. On March 14, 1940, one such truck, with wooden sides and a tarpaulin covering 44 workers, was struck by a train while crossing a railroad grading near McAllen, Texas; 29 were killed, eleven of them children under 16. . . .

Those who travel in their own cars have a somewhat easier trip. Most of them leave San Antonio, however, without a cent; advances frequently have to be made to enable them to buy their gasoline and oil. Their cars are old and broken-down; they often have to stop for repairs and wire ahead for further advances to get their cars out of hock. Fines for traffic violations are, of course, major calamities. . . .

Workers arrive in Michigan from April 15th to June 1st. The first labor operation—blocking, thinning, and cultivating the beets—consumes about 30 days. After an interval of several weeks, there is a second hoeing and weeding operation which takes about 15 days. Once this is concluded, there is nothing to be done until the harvest, which starts around October 15th and is usually over by December 1st. Although workers may be in Michigan in fulfillment of their contracts for seven or eight months, they may actually be working in sugar beets for only 75 or 80 days. During the period they are not working in beets, they can pick up some non-contract work in such crops as pickles, string beans, cherries, tomatoes, chicory, onions, and mint. But they cannot migrate far from the beet fields, for, by the terms of their contract, they are held to the crop. There is usually a provision in the agreement that requires them to be constantly available. Also, a hold-back payment of $2 an acre forces compliance with the contract under penalty of forfeiting a major part of the compensation. . . .

Gradually, as more families are stranded, Mexican colonies have developed. In Minnesota a residual group of non-resident beet workers, now exceeding 6,000 in number, presents a serious welfare problem. Similarly, Mexican colonies are growing in the sugar-beet areas in Michigan. Some of the young men, in particular, stay over after the season, marry the local girls, and become residents. To date the winter relief problem in Michigan has not been serious, but the number of stranded families is likely to increase. Mechanical cultivating and blocking of beets and the use of tractors instead of horses to haul them to the factory have already replaced many hand laborers. Although the average yield per acre has increased 10 per cent, man-hours required to produce it have dropped from 112 in 1920-24 to 94 in 1933-36, and the harvest itself is now in the process of being mechanized. . . .

During the years that Mexican labor has been imported to Michigan, there has, at all times, been an adequate supply of resident local labor. On June 3, 1938, the A. F. of L. reported there were "hundreds of Michigan workers, many of them unemployed members of the Agricultural Workers Union, who are anxious for employment, while these Mexican families are brought in from a distance of 2,000 miles." On June 24, 1938, the Bay City newspapers commented that "if those 1,000 jobs in the fields had been given to unemployed men here, the relief question would be answered and there would be no unemployment in the county." "These Mexican workers were brought to Michigan to break the union of beet workers at Blissfield," said the press on May 20, 1938. "There is a colony of 'old beet workers' living near Blissfield on relief. They are Hungarians, Bulgarians, and Polish people who came years ago and have been working in the beets ever since. Last year they organized an A. F. of L. Agricultural Workers Union and got their wages up to $21 an acre, which is only $2 less than the wage that prevailed in the low-wage era before the [First] World War. This year the company is permitting them to remain idle on relief, while it imports hundreds of Mexican families to tend the beets at $18 an acre." . . .

Mexicans arrive in Texas, as they left, with scarcely any money. The report of the WPA in San Antonio for November, 1939, states that "Mexicans are returning in a much worse state than when they left. Of all these people re-interviewed, not one has started his children to school this term. They state that they barely manage to buy food enough to exist and can buy no clothes at all." While some families fare much better than others, it is debatable if the average family is able to accumulate as much as $200 for eight months employment in Michigan; yet earnings there are higher than for field work in Texas, where the migratory labor problem is even greater and more complex—"the worst in the nation," in the words of the Farm Security Administration. In spite of this siphoning off of workers to the Michigan sugar-beet fields, to Colorado, Minnesota, and Montana, some 400,000 Mexicans—75 per cent of all the migratory workers in Texas—remain to follow the crops within its boundaries. Bad as wages and conditions in Michigan are, they are relatively better than the workers would have known had they stayed in Texas.

When they arrive in San Antonio, they spend a few weeks visiting friends and relatives in the *barrio*, and then disperse to their "homes"—in El Paso, Laredo, Crystal City, Robstown, and other communities.

The great march is over; the army is disbanded. But when spring rolls round again, they will be back in front of Mr. Cortez' funeral parlor on El Paso Street. They are a brave army, an army capable of almost incredible endurance. They are also an amazingly patient army; they make few complaints . . . which usually go unheard.

PACHUCOS IN THE MAKING

[World War II
ushered in an era of prosperity that brought affluence to some
Americans for the first time. Among these were the Mexican Americans in Los Angeles neighborhoods, or *barrios*. Along with the new
affluence came a revitalized ethnic pride and self-awareness and,
conversely, some indication of what had been missed in American
life that others had enjoyed, a new consciousness of discrimination
and prejudice. One of the social outgrowths of this situation was
the formation of youth gangs in the *barrios*. The name they most
commonly used to describe themselves was *Pachuco*, borrowed
probably from the town of the same name in Mexico. Many of the
youths, as an evidence of their "making it," adopted in their dress
the briefly fashionable and rather outlandish "zoot suit." The
Pachucos were, in an unsophisticated way, precursors of more recent young and militant Mexican-Americans—or, as they prefer it,
Chicano—groups such as the Brown Berets. The *Pachucos* might
have remained only one more social anomaly in Southern California,
had it not been for the infamous "Zoot Suit Riots" of June, 1943, in
Los Angeles. Amidst already uneasy racial tensions, a fight took
place between Chicano youths and U.S. sailors. For nights afterwards, gangs of sailors in cars drove through the *barrios* seeking
"revenge" by attacking Chicano youths, while the police department
looked the other way. The youths, mostly *Pachuco* gang members,
regarded themselves as a *barrio* self-defense organization against
the depredations of the sailors and partiality of the police. In the
article reprinted here, George I. Sanchez describes the social background out of which the *Pachuco* movement grew. His article was
published a few months after the riots.]

From *Common Ground*, Autumn 1943.

Widespread attention has been drawn to the Los Angeles, California, gangs of zoot-suited, socially maladjusted, "Mexican" youngsters known as "pachucos." Mixed with the intelligent efforts and genuine concern of some public officials and laymen over the disgraceful situation which has been allowed to develop in the Los Angeles area, there is also much sanctimonious "locking of barn doors after the horses have been stolen" sort of expression and action by those whose past lack of interest and whose official negligence bred the juvenile delinquency which now plagues that city's officialdom, hinders the program of the armed forces, and embarrasses the United States before Latin America and the world.

The seed for the pachucos was sown a decade or more ago by unintelligent educational measures, by discriminatory social and economic practices, by provincial smugness and self-assigned "racial" superiority. Today we reap the whirlwind in youth whose greatest crime was to be born into an environment which, through various kinds and degrees of social ostracism and prejudicial economic subjugation, made them a caste apart, fair prey to the cancer of gangsterism. The crimes of these youths should be appropriately punished, yes. But what of the society which is an accessory before and after the fact?

Almost ten years ago, I raised this issue in an article in the Journal of Applied Psychology: "The frequent prostitution of democratic ideals to the cause of expediency, politics, vested interests, ignorance, class and 'race' prejudice, and to indifference and inefficiency is a sad commentary on the intelligence and justice of a society that makes claims to those very progressive democratic ideals. The dual system of education presented in 'Mexican' and 'white' schools, the family system of contract labor, social and economic discrimination, educational negligence on the part of local and state authorities, 'homogeneous grouping' to mask professional inefficiency—all point to the need for greater insight into a problem which is inherent in a 'melting pot' society. The progress of our country is dependent upon the most efficient utilization of the heterogeneous masses which constitute its population—the degree to which the 2,000,000 or more Spanish-speaking people, and their increment, are permitted to develop is the extent to which the nation should expect returns from that section of its public."

When the pachuco "crime wave" broke last year, I communicated with the Office of War Information: "I understand that a grand jury is looking into the 'Mexican' problem in Los Angeles and that there seems to be considerable misunderstanding as to the causes of the gang activities of Mexican youth in that area. I hear also that much ado is being made about 'Aztec forebears,' 'blood lust,' and similar claptrap in interpreting the behavior of these citizens. It would be indeed unfortunate if this grand jury investigation were to go off on a tangent, witchhunting in anthropological antecedents for causes which, in reality, lie right under the noses of the public service agencies in Los Angeles County."

Subsequent developments have borne out the fears implied above. And still, in June of this year, the Los Angeles City Council could think of no better answer to the deep-rooted negligence of public service agencies than to deliberate over an ordinance outlawing zoot suits! The segregatory attitudes and practices, and the vicious economic exploitation directed against the "Mexican" in California in the past—not zoot suits—are responsible for the pachucos of today.

The pseudo-science of the Los Angeles official who is quoted as reporting to the Grand Jury on the Sleepy Lagoon murder case that "Mexican" youths are motivated to crime by certain biological or "racial" characteristics would be laughable if it were not so tragic, so dangerous, and, worse still, so typical of biased attitudes and misguided thinking which are reflected in the practices not only of California communities but also elsewhere in this country.

The genesis of pachuquismo is an open book to those who care to look into the situations facing Spanish-speaking people in many parts of the Southwest. Arizona, Colorado, Texas, and, to a much lesser degree, even New Mexico have conditions analogous to those which have nurtured the California riots. In some communities in each of these states, "Mexican" is a term of opprobrium applied to anyone with a Spanish name—citizen and alien alike, of mestizo blood or of "pure white" Spanish colonial antecedents. In many places these people are denied service in restaurants, barber shops, and stores. Public parks and swimming pools, some of which were built by federal funds, are often closed to them. Some churches, court houses, and public hospitals have been known to segregate them from "whites." Separate, and usually shockingly inferior, segregated "Mexican" schools have been set up for their children. Discriminatory employment practices and wage scales, even in war industries (the President's Executive Order 8802 and his Committee on Fair Employment Practice to the contrary notwithstanding), are still used to "keep the 'Mexican' in his place." . . .

A pathetic letter from a descendant of the colonial settlers of Texas states: "Do you think there is any hope of getting our problems solved? We wish you would do something to help us. We are being mistreated here every time we turn around. We are not allowed in cafes, movies, restaurants. Even Latin Americans in United

States Army uniforms are sometimes told they can't see a show because the Mexican side is full. In the public schools our children are segregated. They are given only half a day's school because of the teacher shortage, while the others have full-time classes. There is no teacher shortage for them. Please tell us if there is anything to do about it. We wrote a letter to the Office of Civilian Defense, Washington, D.C. But we haven't heard from them. We don't know if that is the right place to write to or not." . . .

Many communities provide a separate school for children of Spanish name. These "Mexican schools," are established ostensibly for "pedagogical reasons," thinly veiled excuses which do not conform with either the science of education or the facts in the case. Judging from current practice, these pseudo-pedagogical reasons call for short school terms, ramshackle school buildings, poorly paid and untrained teachers, and all varieties of prejudicial discrimination. The "language handicap" reason, so glibly advanced as the chief pedagogical excuse for the segregation of these school children, is extended to apply to all Spanish-name youngsters regardless of the fact that some of them know more English and more about other school subjects than the children from whom they are segregated. In addition some of these Spanish-name children know no Spanish whatsoever, coming from homes where only English has been spoken for two generations or more. . . .

On July 12, 1941, before the pachuco question had become a matter of general interest, a Spanish American from California summarized the situation this way: "The so-called 'Mexican Problem' is not in fact a Mexican problem. It is a problem foisted by American mercenary interests upon the American people. It is an American problem made in the U.S.A." He was protesting the movement then on foot to permit the indiscriminate and wholesale importation of laborers from Mexico. In response to such protests steps were taken by the governments of the United States and Mexico to protect both the imported alien and the residents of this area from the evils inherent in such letting down of the bars, evils of whch ample evidence was furnished during World War I under similar circumstances. Today, however, the pressure of vested interests is finding loopholes in that enlightened policy and, again, the bars are rapidly being let down.

Si Casady of McAllen, Texas, in an editorial in the Valley Evening Monitor hits the nail on the head when he says: ". . . there is a type of individual who does not understand and appreciate the very real dangers inherent in racial discrimination. This type of individual does not understand that his own right to enjoy life, his own liberty, the very existence of this nation and all the other free nations of the world depend utterly and completely on the fundamental principle that no man, because of race, has any right to put his foot upon the neck of any other man. The racial discrimination problem has been daintily out of sight for so long in the [Rio Grande] Valley that it cannot now be solved overnight. Instead of dragging it out into the sunlight where it could be left lying until all the nauseous fumes of hypocrisy and bigotry had dissipated, we have shoved the problem down into the cellar like an idiot child, hoping the neighbors would not notice its existence." . . .

The establishment of segregated schools for "Mexicans" lays the foundation for most of the prejudice and discrimination. Local and state educational authorities have the power to institute satisfactory remedies. There is no legal requirement in any state calling for the organization of such schools. There are all sorts of legal mandates to the contrary. Forthright action by school authorities could remove these blots on American education in a very brief period of time. As an illustration of how this may be done in Texas, consider this provision adopted by the State Legislature in 1943: "The State Board of Education with the approval of the State Superintendent of Public Instruction shall have the authority to withhold the per capita apportionment to any school district at any time that a discrimination between groups of white scholastics exists."

The exclusion of "Mexicans" from public places, solely on the basis of "race" (legally, they are "white"), can be stopped through the enforcement of such provisions as that embodied in the legislative Concurrent Resolution adopted in Texas a few months ago: "1. All persons of the Caucasian Race within the jurisdiction of this State are entitled to the full and equal accommodations, advantages, facilities, and privileges of all public places of business or amusement, subject only to the conditions and limitations established by law, and rules and regulations applicable alike to all persons of the Caucasian Race. 2. Whoever denies to any person the full advantages, facilities, and privileges enumerated in the preceding paragraph or who aids or incites such denial or whoever makes any discrimination, distinction, or restriction except for good cause applicable alike to all persons of the Caucasian Race, respecting accommodations, advantages, facilities, and privileges of all public places of business, or whoever aids or incites such discrimination, distinction, or restriction shall be considered as violating the good neighbor policy of our State." Vigorous action by public officials in enforcing this mandate in Texas, and similar legal provisions in other states, would go far in solving this fundamental phase of the whole "Mexican" question.

These illustrations of specific remedial action could be multiplied by reference to legal mandates as to suffrage, jury service, practices in war industries, etc. Public officials—local, state, and federal— have in their hands the power to correct the discriminatory practices which lie at the root of prejudicial attitudes and actions on the part of some sectors of the public. I have the fullest confidence that the great majority of Americans would applaud the enforcement of those legal mandates.

The Spanish-speaking people of the United States need to be incorporated into, and made fully participating members of, the American way of life. The "Mexican" needs education, he needs vocational training and placement in American industry on an American basis, he needs active encouragement to participate in civic affairs and to discharge his civic obligations, and he needs constant protection by public officials from the pitfalls into which his cultural differences may lead him or into which he may be forced by unthinking sectors of the public.

STEPCHILDREN OF A NATION

[This selection is taken from a short study prepared by Isabel Gonzalez of Denver, Colorado, for the Panel on Discrimination of the National Conference for the Protection of the Foreign-Born held in Cleveland in October, 1947. In touching upon the exploitation of labor, the author focuses on a situation that has been endemic among the poorer Mexican-American wage-earner and his brother from across the border. Especially unfortunate have been the migrant workers, who, precisely because they are migrant, are never able to establish the kind of economic or social base from which to make their needs felt in any community.]

Economic Exploitation

History has made economic exploitation by American interests the lot of the Mexican people both north and south of the border. Powerful interests, like the Great Western Sugar Company, the greatest importer of Mexican labor, the railroads, the mining and lumbering industries, the cotton and fruit growers, and the cattle and sheep industries have succeeded in keeping the Mexican the most under-

From Isabel Gonzalez, *Step-Children of a Nation.* New York, n.d. Pages 9–13.

paid and most oppressed worker so that they will always have a surplus of cheap labor. This is amply demonstrated by the constant demand for importation of Mexican nationals by the sugar industries and the railways, supported by the powerful lobbies maintained by these interests in Washington.

The demand for importation of Mexican labor is based on the theory that the native American worker would not "work for the wages paid to the Mexicans." In this way not only is cheap labor obtained, but, equally as important, the standard of living of the native worker is dragged down. And so we find our government acting as procuror and solicitor for the big sugar, cotton and the rest of the interests mentioned, exploiting our neighbors and breaking the standard of living in our own country. A Texan testifying before the House Committee on Immigration and Naturalization in 1926 is quoted by Carey McWilliams in ILL FARES THE LAND as saying:

> Mr. Chairman, here is the whole situation in a nutshell. Farming is not a profitable industry in this country, and in order to make money out of it, you have to have cheap labor. In order to allow landowners now to make a profit off their farms, they want to get the cheapest labor they can find, and if they get the Mexican labor, it enables them to make a profit. That is the way it is along the border, and I imagine that is the way it is anywhere else.

What does this mean in round figures for the Mexican worker? Pauline Kibbe in her book, "Latin Americans in Texas," gives the following figures which she takes from a study made by the Children's Bureau on agricultural workers in Hidalgo County, Texas: ". . . . the weekly family income for two-thirds of the 342 families was $7.69; the median earnings per week were only $6.54; and one out of every eight families earned less than $3.85 per week in 1940." Carey McWilliams found that seasonal agricultural workers in Arizona earn about $6.00 per week and their annual earnings per family do not exceed an average of $250. He also found that a Mexican family of 5.6 members working in the beet fields of Colorado, Montana, Wyoming or Nebraska, the domain of the Great Western Sugar Company, earns an average of $259 per year from their labors.

In Texas, Pauline Kibbe says: "The fable that migrants 'get rich' in the beet fields is effectively exploded by the earnings reported by the Crystal City laborers. Of the total of 188 families who engaged in beet work, 13 per cent earned less than $200.00 per family; 23 per cent earned less than $300.00 per family; while only 9 per cent earned $1,000.00 or more. For individual workers, weekly earnings during the seven-months period averaged $6.33 for forty-nine hours of work per week."

Mexican cotton pickers in Texas have been known to earn an average of 80 cents per day and other agricultural or truck farm workers to make 60 cents per day. Entire families of pecan shellers have averaged 75 to 90 cents per day per family. In California in the late 30's migratory Mexican families earned an average of $254 per year.

You might feel that these figures do not reflect the complete wage picture for the Mexican worker because they are only for agricultural work. The fact remains that a very small portion of Mexicans are employed in industry, and that no matter what field of employment you choose, you still find them in the lowest paid jobs with little or no chance of promotion or up-grading. In petroleum, the biggest industry in Texas, only three per cent of those hired during the war were Mexicans, and then they received 91 cents per hour, while the Anglo worker got $1.06 for the same kind of work. The wage pattern for Mexicans is the same everywhere, even in the states of Michigan, Wisconsin and Minnesota.

You might ask how these special interests have been successful in keeping such a large mass of workers in a constant state of impoverishment, hunger and misery. Obviously, such a condition is not voluntarily agreed to by the Mexican people. The answer is: only through terror and oppression. One of their chief weapons has been and still is the threat of deportation and the refusal to grant to the Mexican people the citizenship which they so richly deserve. This can be understood if we get a picture of the conditions of immigration.

Immigration from Mexico

Immigration quotas do not apply to Mexicans. They are permitted to enter this country either upon being recruited by American commercial interests, or upon the whim of American consular officials. It is next to impossible for a Mexican to enter this country to stay and become a citizen.

Most of the Mexicans living in this country entered from 1910 to 1930. Up until 1910 immigration from Mexico had been a mere trickle, compared to that coming from Europe. For most of these Mexicans, even though they have lived in this country many years, it is very difficult to establish proof of legal residence. Either they have lost their papers or are incapable of wading through all the red tape necessary because of their inadequate command of the English language. In fact, for the Mexican immigrant who entered the U. S. prior to 1924, the process of proving that he ever got here at all is complicated, expensive and loaded with potential danger. He may very well succeed in proving only that he was an illegal entrant and find himself holding, instead of first papers, a one-way deportee's ticket to the border. It is a recurring nightmare for him every time he has to fill out an application for public assistance, a job, as well as for citizenship. Even when he decides to steel himself to the possibility of being deported, the process of proving continuous residence in the United States since he entered, and/or the legal nature of any subsequent return and re-entry, no matter how brief, is a herculean undertaking. For persons who have been excessively migrant, as most of the agricultural workers have been of necessity, or for those who were brought to the U. S. at an early age by their parents, proof may be simply impossible. At best, it is likely to involve fees for expert assistance running as high as several hundred dollars.

Naturalization Difficulties

Anyone who has tried to assist a Mexican immigrant in the preliminaries to citizenship is well aware of the difficulties involved. It is no accident that the bulk of naturalized citizens in the U. S. are those who entered after 1924, when regulations for entry were enforced and some sort of orderly accounting maintained. A large number of quasi-immigrants who remain unnaturalized, even though they have spent their lives in the U. S., and speak perfect English, quite frankly admit that they remain aliens because they have neither the finances nor the courage to tackle the job of proving that they entered legally. Even the older immigrant, after he has given you all the customary reasons about having a "hard head" for the learning of English and history, is likely to settle on the difficulty of proving entry as the main deterrent. They often remember some "paisano" who tried to become a citizen and will tell you: "Look at Juan Martinez. He was going to be a citizen. And where is he now? Back in Juarez and his wife and children starving here."

In view of the fact that slipshod entry was largely the result of American greed for cheap labor, it might seem as though some of the unholy punctiliousness after the act might be relaxed. A reasonable construing of facts of entry prior to 1924, combined with some conveniently located and resourcefully taught adult education classes might result in a veritable rush of Mexican applicants for citizenship. As it is now, even the inducement of old age pensions, so desperately needed by the older folks, are insufficient to entice them into the perilous and costly business of applying for citizenship. Besides, as a number of them rightfully ask, "What added status or privileges can citizenship confer on me, as long as the tenet is held by the dominant group that 'once a Mexcan, always a Mexican'?" He knows that the position of the naturalized citizen is little different from that of his alien neighbor. In some respects, it may be worse, because the protection of the consulate is thereby withdrawn.

SEGREGATION OF MEXICAN-AMERICAN SCHOOL CHILDREN

[The Southwest has seen, for more than a century, the coming together of two cultures, the Indo-Hispanic and the Anglo-American; and the latter has not been reluctant to impose its values and language on the former. The public school systems set up in the Southwestern states are guided by educational criteria generally prevailing throughout the United States. The same guidelines have been used for Spanish-speaking children as are applied to Anglo pupils. Basic to the educational principles has been the insistence on the use of English in teaching all subjects and the denigration of the Spanish language. To many Mexican Americans, this educational policy, especially where children are intimidated or corporally punished for speaking Spanish, looks like a systematic attempt to eradicate their heritage and replace it entirely with Anglo values. Yet there is also a persistent recognition of the need for facility in English to attain success in the complex society of the present. In the past few years, there has been in some areas a recognition of the value of bilingual education, but, as recently as the 1950's, the difference in languages still served as an excuse to operate segregated schools. Instances of such a policy were detailed in 1948 in an article by W. Henry Cooke, sections of which are reprinted here.]

From "The Segregation of Mexican-American School Children in Southern California," by W. Henry Cooke, in: *School and Society*, June 5, 1948.

Schools for "Mexicans" and schools for "Americans" have been the custom in many a Southern California city. It mattered not that the "Mexicans" were born in the United States and that great numbers of them were sons and daughters of United States citizens. It has been the custom that they be segregated at least until they could use English well enough to keep up with English-speaking children. Neither did it matter that many of them had a command of English nor that there was no legal basis for their segregation. Under a law, enacted in 1885 and amended in 1893, it has been possible to segregate Indians and Mongolians in California's public schools. To many an administrator this included "Mexicans." This pattern was followed principally because the majority groups in the local communities wanted it done that way. Since the spring of 1947, a new legal situation has maintained: it is not now legal in California to segregate any ethnic group. And yet the practice still continues in many cities. This fact needs explanation. But first, just what is meant by "racial segregation" as applied to schools?

Segregation as a school policy does not come about by accident. If it exists, there must be intent to separate children between schools or into school groups on the basis of race, national origin, or religion. This sometimes takes the form of an action by a school board providing that all students of a named ethnic group be registered in a given school. In other instances a school board approves the drawing of zone boundaries in such a way as to throw all families of a certain ethnic group into homogeneous areas. When neither of these two methods seems feasible, a policy of transfer of students from zone to zone brings about the same result. Few, if any, cases of segregation of Mexican-Americans have been absolute in nature, for the parents who have had sufficient influence could usually have an exception made for their children. Once made for an elder child, it usually held for all of the succeeding children of the family. Thus it is that the question of privilege raised its head—privilege as between Mexican and Mexican, as well as between Mexican and "Anglo." . . .

The Mexican people came to the United States as agricultural laborers, their wages were traditionally low as compared with American standards, although not with Mexican levels. They found habitat in the edges of California towns where land was cheap, and they built simple and inadequate buildings. Often there would be no sewers in the section they chose and few taps for running water were opened. Many people lived upon small pieces of property that should have housed but one family each. Two decades ago they were hesitant about investing more of their earnings in residences because they harbored the idea that they would soon go back across the border. The fact is that they have stayed in very large numbers, and relatively few of them have left their "colonies" to live in better conditions, although the numbers have been increasing in recent years.

The characteristics of all Mexican-Americans have been set in the minds of most citizens by the descriptions of these early peasants who spoke a foreign tongue and lived unto themselves in ways that seemed uninviting or even squalid. It did not look like discrimination twenty-five years ago to furnish these people with a school and a teacher or two. The building did not have to be much to be better than their homes. The teacher might have been just anybody who would go "down there"; no results were to be expected. Mexican people were roving workers who were a charge upon any school district.

Today these conditions have changed in that the Mexican-Americans have become established as permanent residents in very large numbers. A third generation is now growing up in the once temporary shacks. New houses have been built that would do credit to any worker family. A sizable percentage of Mexican-American young people have become educated, have been around the world with the American armed forces, and want to be accepted in the larger community. Many of the first-generation people and virtually all of the second and third generation speak English. Organizations for their own improvement and integration exist among them. They are now in large numbers "Americans" in every sense of the word. In addition, the whole country is awakening to the injustices under which many backward and colonial peoples have lived. We are more conscious of civil rights for all members of society than we once were. What was once winked at in California can now justly be called discrimination.

That an "Anglo" who was young and intelligent as a business man should be driven out of his new home in a Southern California city because his wife was of Mexican ancestry, although born in that same city and educated in its high school, is an evidence of discrimination. The neighbors waited upon him and he had to sell his home. That a schoolteacher who took her class to a motion picture theater had to divide them so that the "whites" sat in their proper sections and the "Mexicans" in theirs, is evidence of discrimination. When a probation officer finds on his hands a Mexican-American boy who is so brilliant that he gets ahead of his classes and gets into trouble and when this officer tries to place the boy in employment and finds the jobs that are suited to his caliber closed to him because he is a Mexican, there is evidence of discrimination. When a vice-principal of a high school admits that he does not urge Mexican boys to seek varied employment as other boys do because he knows that they cannot do anything more than work in the groves, there is discrimination. When a city council refuses to let Mexican-American boys and girls swim in the public plunge and when it places at the entrance of the bathhouse a red sign reading FOR WHITE RACE ONLY and when it admits through its city clerk that this is for the purpose of keeping out "Mexican" children, it is both ignorance and discrimination.

Many instances of this kind could be cited from California. And yet this state is better than some of its neighbors in that it has adequate laws that prohibit these practices. They continue because communities demand them. The point of this article is not to review the whole field of discrimination, but to study this phenomenon within the public schools—the place above all others where it should not exist.

On the brighter side of the picture several facts can be set forth. The large city school systems of the state have all abolished the segregation of Mexican-Americans and, with the exception of a few vestiges of segregation by zoning or transfer, the segregation of all ethnic groups. Some of these cities have staff members detailed to work upon a better integration and understanding throughout all their schools. This does not mean that all teachers are yet convinced of the values of mixing all students in the schools, but it does reveal an administrative policy that will in time have its effect. In these cities teachers of Negro, Mexican, or Chinese backgrounds are finding their places upon teaching staffs. One large city has five Negro building principals and another has a director of intercultural education. Other cities have committees working on intergroup relationships. In a number of smaller cities where the segregation of Mexican-Americans has been a tradition, the school boards have definitely abolished the policy and practice. In most cases they aroused a clamer of opposition from parents of the majority group, but by tactful handling this has subsided. Some parents sent their children outside of these progressive districts for their schooling in order to avoid having their children sent to the "Mexican school" or to avoid intermingling of their offspring with Mexican-Americans. A number of these changes came about because the administrators realized that segregation was good for neither the English- nor the Spanish-speaking children and that the best type of community could come from having all students learn and play together. Other administrators persuaded their school boards to change to integration because of the danger of lawsuits against them such as four districts in Orange County had had to fight. Certain county superintendents of schools have been working to educate school boards in their jurisdiction to the values of integration and to the dangers of continued segregation. The work of supervisors and the influence of county meetings and institutes have begun to show results in counties that could be named. In other counties changes are overdue.

MEXICANS IN MINNESOTA

[The following selection is a chapter of a report prepared by the Governor's Interracial Commission of Minnesota for Governor Luther W. Youngdahl and delivered to him in August, 1948. Following World War II, thousands of Mexican immigrants were encouraged to come to Minnesota as farm laborers, and many hundreds of them decided to remain. The commission inquired into their status to learn what problems they were having, how they were being treated by other residents, what kind of housing they had, and whether their children were readily accepted in the schools. Unfortunately, the report makes no apparent attempt to distinguish between Mexican Americans and Mexican immigrants, and, since only the term "Mexican" is used throughout, it must be presumed that only immigrants are meant. It is hard to believe, however, that native-born Mexican Americans did not also find their way north following the war.]

The Process of Assimilation

The success with which a new populational element achieves integration in a previously settled society is measured by the effectiveness of the two-way process which such a merger inexorably de-

From *The Mexican in Minnesota*, a Report to Governor Luther W. Youngdahl of Minnesota. August 15, 1948.

mands. Plan and effort must exist on both sides, as well as the knowledge of underlying differences and similarities. Generally speaking, the burden of proof of failure rests upon the majority group, since it commands the greater strength and resource.

When we consider that 4,000 Mexicans living in Minnesota make but a fraction of our total population of 2,792,300 (1940 census figure) absorption would seem fairly simple, numerically at least. It is pertinent to remember, too, that most Mexicans are a blend of Spanish and Indian blood representing two ancient and highly developed cultures recognized by scholars as having rich contributions to make to our own.

But in many instances the important heritage of the immigrant Mexican is offset, and often nullified, by the conditions of life he sought to escape in coming to the United States. A caste system set up by the Spanish conquerors of Latin-America centuries ago has made the growth of democracy as we know it almost impossible. This system limits opportunities for development of whole sections of the Mexican population.

The language barrier prevents rapid integration of the Mexican into Minnesota social and civic life. Even the considerable percentage of the Minnesota community composed of persons born in the United States and thus possessed of American citizenship before coming here, cannot speak English fluently. The Mexicans have lived for the most part in districts where only Spanish is spoken. To some extent residential restrictions limit the Mexican to his own group but these are not so often imposed by the community as sought by the Mexican himself. It is habituary for new-comers to settle in an already established Mexican district for protection, understanding, and companionship.

Facts and figures indicate, however, that the movement toward integration of the Mexican into Minnesota life, while it may be slow, is a steady one. Most significant of all is the educational record. Less than five years ago it was remarkable to find a Mexican child remaining in school after he had reached the ninth grade. After that he was considered by his people to have had enough of book learning and to be ready to contribute toward the economic support of his household, or to prepare himself for a trade.

Today, 75 Mexican boys and girls from St. Paul are attending high school and two have gone to college. This indicates that parents are becoming interested in having their children seek higher education and that difficulties of language and other bars to adjustment in school, difficulties very real to newcomers, are growing less. On the basis of this record it seems fair to predict that an increasing number of Mexicans will seek greater educational opportunities.

There is no doubt that Mexicans have much of value to offer their new home in the field of talent in the arts. Students of music note how richly it has flourished in lands where Spanish blood has fused with that of other races. In the Philippines, the Caribbean, and the South and Central American countries universally practiced folk-song and folk-dance have given opportunity and encouragement. From these roots phases of high advancement and sophistication have grown. Produced from these same sources are strikingly gifted practitioners of the graphic arts and highly developed handicrafts. Given an opportunity for expression in a sympathetic environment, all of these assets can become valuable to American culture.

Whether or not the population at large in America can be a beneficiary of the important contributions which Mexicans have to offer depends largely on the extent to which white Americans meet the problems of racial discrimination.

Many Minnesota Mexicans are of pure, or nearly pure, Indian descent, and very dark in color. Those with proportionately greater percentage of Spanish blood are usually readily recognizable, a fact which sometimes makes it easy for the unthinking to indulge in labels of distinction. Any type of discriminatory practice always results in an artificial slowing-up of a normal assimilative process.

Alleged Discriminations

In spite of the fact of color and other easily discernable physical characteristics, the Mexican does not seem to encounter within Minnesota, extensive discrimination based upon skin color. Definitely they are free from many discriminatory practices which they encounter in the South-western part of the United States.

Possibly they may be the beneficiaries both of the spirit of brotherhood which usually accompanies a war and also of the extensive interracial programs conducted across the state during the past five years.

Data presented earlier in this report does not provide evidence that Mexican children have been denied entrance to the public schools of Minnesota. In the rural schools there have been some acts which might arouse suspicion of discrimination but there the objection to Mexicans is not on the basis of race or color, but rather because of their irregular attendance.

Facts given earlier in this study would indicate that a variety of employment was offered the Mexican within the Twin Cities. It may be that Mexicans of light skin are upgraded but the Commission has no evidence for this assertion.

Since the Mexicans were the last group to come to Minnesota, they acquired the poorest houses. Because they spoke another tongue, they congregated for social purposes. Some, as their economic position improved, have moved into better residential districts and encountered little opposition.

In the rural areas there are some cases reported where Mexicans have been refused service in restaurants. They encounter signs reading, "No Mexicans may eat here." The basis of opposition seems to be a point of hygiene.

In the cities, the Commission has received no report of Mexicans being denied service. Possibly, as the Mexican acquires greater familiarity with English and consequently greater mobility, he may meet discrimination.

Minnesota's Need of the Mexican

No one racial or national group have a monopoly on all culture and knowledge and art. The people of Minnesota are not an exception. From the Mexican they have much to learn. The larger the number of Mexicans assimilated into the population of the state, the higher may be the status of culture, the arts and learning. Culturally Minnesota needs the Mexican.

Economically Minnesota needs the Mexican. For many decades now intermittent efforts have been made to bring them here to work in the beet fields and about the canneries. The growth of those industries in part will depend upon increased migration of Mexicans into the state.

Demographically Minnesota may need the Mexican. An increase in number is usually a sign that a group is growing and that the economy is a healthy one. Unfortunately there are some rather disturbing trends. The United States Bureau of Statistics shows that the Minnesota population declined from 2,792,300 in 1940 to 2,497,486 in 1945. Much of the decrease was due to people moving away from the state. It is true that the birth rate jumped from 54,462 in 1941 to 58,902 in 1942. But this rise was reversed in 1943 and by 1945 the rate had dropped to 54,154. An increase by migration of an industrious people would be an asset to Minnesota. The Mexicans are in that category and what is more they are a youthful group.

A Program for Retaining Mexicans

There is already on the statute books some legislation which might be invoked to protect the Mexican if racial discriminations against him should increase. Since 1885 Minnesota has had an equal rights law which prohibits discrimination in hotels, restaurants and other public places. The recent decision of the United States Supreme Court will give some protection against restrictive covenants. If the Legislature deems it wise to enact a state Fair Employment Statute the Mexican will be a beneficiary of that law.

But in addition to the existing law the Commission is of the opinion that a program of six objectives should be recognized and accepted both by the people and the officials of various political units within the state.

1—All schools throughout the state should place greater emphasis upon the values of Latin American civilization.
2—Private organizations such as women's clubs and service organizations might have informational programs treating of the state's need and use of the Mexican.

3—The State Department of Education should assume the initiative in examining the possibility of developing summer schools for the children of Mexicans who work in the beet fields and about the canneries.

4—The Chambers of Commerce and other industrial groups possibly with the assistance of the proper state officials should give thought to the development of such seasonal industries that the Mexicans who work in the beet fields during the summer would have employment in the state during the winter months.

5—When the construction of public housing units is started in the Twin Cities, care should be taken by the officials that Mexicans have access to them, since they now occupy probably the worst houses.

6—The present statutory provisions covering residence, settlement, and the giving of assistance to needy non-resident migratory workers should be amended to the end that such workers that are brought into the state to perform specific tasks required by our agricultural economy may receive the same treatment and care as the state's other residents. The memory of the deportation of the thirties is still a bitter memory in the Mexican community.

THE MEXICAN AMERICAN AS A NATIONAL CONCERN

[Ernesto Galarza, author of this article on the problems of the Mexican-American minority, came to the United States with his family in 1911. He did his college work in California and took a doctor's degree from Columbia University. In 1949, at the time he wrote this selection, Galarza was director of research and education for the National Farm Labor Union of the American Federation of Labor.]

The conditions of life and work of the Spanish-speaking minority in the United States are no longer a problem only of the borderlands. A historical process has been at work lifting this problem above local and sectional concern. It now involves communities as distant from the United States-Mexican border as Chicago, New York, and Detroit. It shows up in the rural slums that lie on an arc stretching from Arkansas to northern California. It is documented in federal reports on employment and in community conferences on human relations in the urban industrial East as well as in the rural agri-

From "Program for Action," by Ernesto Galarza, in: *Common Ground*, Summer 1949.

cultural Southwest. It has become a skeleton in the closet of our Latin American policy.

The Mexican agricultural migrant and itinerant railway maintenance worker have been the primary agents in this process. Over the past fifty years they have moved into practically every state of the Union. Today, while the bulk of over 2,500,000 of this minority is still anchored in California, Texas, Arizona, and New Mexico, thousands can be found in Illinois, Michigan, Ohio, Pennsylvania, and Kansas.

Within the group, the inferiority complex has been disappearing. From the uncomplaining ranks of Mexican "stoop labor" have emerged trained men and women to spoil the myth of the innate servility and incompetence attached to this group, with some romantic concessions, by the finance farmers and railway corporations that long have exploited them. Two world wars proved the courage, tested the loyalty, broadened the experience, and tempered the will of young men born and bred in a no-man's-land of social rejection and lack of civic opportunity for adult citizenship. . . .

In the living and working conditions of this group certain problems have been isolated, defined, studied, and analyzed. Now they must be resolved. Which are most urgent?

Wages and income. The Mexican agricultural workers, as well as those who work in the manufacturing, transport, and service industries, fall into the lowest income class. The purchasing power of semi-stable agricultural workers in California and Texas is comparable to that of the sharecroppers of Arkansas and Mississippi. As a group the Mexican workers have not been able to shake off the tradition of "cheap labor." Wage discrimination based on race has been uncovered by federal investigators even in the mining industry. In the absence of adequate wage and income studies of the group, the economic status of the Mexicans can be verified by simple observation of their community life. Slum housing, child labor, inadequate food, school absenteeism, indebtedness, unpaved streets, and the almost total absence of decent recreation facilities for the whole family immediately type the average Mexican community.

Employment. In the urban centers, the Mexican still finds barriers to the better-paid jobs. In industry individual skill is not infrequently discounted because of color. Employers in the service industries, where "the customer is always right," yield to prejudice and close certain avenues of economic advancement to dark-skinned citizens of Mexican ancestry. In agriculture the employment situation is somewhat less subtly arranged. The Mexican field workers, by and large, are dependent on contractors, whose controls of the total social life of the group are all-pervading. These contractors are the bridge improvised by the boss-culture of the employers and the servant-culture of the workers. The labor power that passes back and forth over that bridge pays a heavy toll in the form of petty larceny, short-weighing, usuary, wage competition, rent gouging, company-store profits, alcoholism, and other types of catering to starved human needs. Even where the contractor happens to be a decent fellow, or where the corporation ranchers go into the labor market themselves, the Mexican farm worker fares little better. He may expect, as he has found in California, that the corporate interests will move into the machinery of farm-employment placement, through which, in part, the labor market can be kept in a profitable state of over-supply.

Foreign labor. Since 1942 a new element has been added to the wage and employment situation of the Mexican farm workers in the United States. This is the recruitment of *braceros* or Mexican Nationals, through agreements between the government of Mexico and the United States. These agreements were originally signed as a wartime measure, but they have been continued under the insistent pressure of the agricultural employers' associations who were looking for a counterpoise to the wage demands of Mexican workers long resident in this country.

Stripped of technicalities, the recruitment of Nationals is a new phase of the old quest for sources of low-cost, inexperienced, unorganized mass labor power. The original intention of the agreements as understood by some of their early advocates—the protection of wage and living standards as well as civil rights of imported workers and domestic labor in time of great national stress—has been sidetracked. Instead, there is now the concept of "task forces" of Mexican Nationals, maneuvered in divisions of 5,000 or more, and assigned to duty in any state of the Union where local Mexicans, Negroes, Filipinos, and Anglo-American whites threaten to organize or ask for higher wages.

The negotiation of these agreements, practically behind closed doors, and the determination of the conditions of such employment by self-appointed arbiters in Washington and Mexico City, establish a form of international economic government practiced without the consent of the governed—in this case the millions of agricultural workers whose wages and standards are immediately affected by such agreements. Relief from this kind of misgovernment has not yet been found by the Mexican workers in the United States, either through Washington officialdom or through the present administration in Mexico City.

Inter-American standards. Since the wartime *bracero* agreements have been repeatedly hailed as a shining example of the Good Neighbor policy in action, their essential function and results in peacetime must be pointed out to be a glaring violation of the spirit of that policy. This is indeed the opinion of the former Secretary of Foreign Affairs of Mexico, Jaime Torres Bodet, stated publicly in October 1948.

By all the standards for decent living and working conditions laid down in the Chapultepec Conference and later in the Inter-American Conference of Bogotá, the agreements have been an economic Trojan horse, an administrative subterfuge, and a long-run political boomerang. Here was an area in which the Inter-

American System, through the Pan American Union, could have taken over administrative responsibility on a truly multilateral, representative basis. These agreements could have been drawn up with the participation of legitimate trade union representatives. They could have been administered without yielding to special interests or political expediency. But, as it has turned out, the Pan American Union, which the workers support directly through public funds appropriated from taxes, has proved an utterly useless instrument for the maintenance of inter-American standards of work and living. In public affairs the misuse of a symbol must be challenged as promptly and as decisively as the subversion of a human right or a constitutional liberty. In this case, the kidnapping of the Good Neighbor symbolism by those who have shut the door of the House of the Americas on the workers is something to which the organized Mexican workers in the United States will have to give special attention.

Illegal labor. There is also the wide-spread exploitation of Mexican workers brought to this country illegally. These so-called wetbacks number probably not less than 60,000 in southern Texas alone. In some border areas—Imperial Valley, Brownsville, El Paso—the bulk of the unskilled farm labor is done by these people. In the San Joaquin Valley between Bakersfield and Modesto there are probably not less than 20,000 illegals. People who talk about labor pools could well describe these reservoirs of bootleg manpower as labor quicksands, for in them all efforts to raise income for the agricultural worker flounder.

Up to the present, the burden of blame and punishment for violation of the immigration laws of the United States falls on the wetback himself. He pays the penalty in the low wages he must accept, the mistreatment he must put up with, the constant fear of arrest, the loss of wages if he is picked up, and the hostility of the local Mexican community. That he is a symptom of a basic maladjustment in the economies of the two countries and a victim of the feebleness of inter-American standards is not generally recognized. Moreover, it is not only the bootleg contractor and the grapevine headhunter who paves the way for the wetback. In a sense he is forced to seek better conditions north of the border by the slow but relentless pressure of United States' agricultural, financial, and oil corporate interests on the entire economic and social evolution of the Mexican nation. Inflation, rising utility rates, the agrarian stalemate, and the flank attack on oil expropriation are some of the major causes of the persistent exodus of Mexican workers.

Racial tension. The Mexicans, by tradition and custom, are a racially tolerant group. The acute sense of personal dignity, a Spanish legacy, strengthens the notion that no man should be judged according to his color or his race. Normally, Mexican communities in the United States have preserved remarkably well this valuable cultural trait.

But the operation of the present wage system of contracting and employment and the strategic use by corporation agriculture of race blocs to maintain and encourage racial jealousies as a means to competitive wage bidding, is injecting bad blood into normal racial tolerance. Today there is emotional dynamite lying around loose between Mexican local workers and Mexican Nationals, between Mexican Nationals and Mexican illegals—not to mention the possibilities for racial misunderstanding between Mexicans on the one hand and Filipinos, Negroes, and white Anglo-Americans on the other. Fortunately, this encouragement of racial antagonism is being held in check by the responsible leaders of all these racial groups. But for how long? Will their influence be strong enough to counteract the effects of prolonged unemployment?

Discrimination. In many communities Mexicans are still excluded from parks, from motion picture theatres, from swimming pools, and from other public places. Certain neighborhoods exclude Mexicans, however acceptable they may be culturally and professionally. There are still schools for Mexican children separate from those maintained for "white" children. In some important towns Mexicans do not patronize certain barber shops or stores. There are no "Keep out" signs, but instead of having a pleasant greeting for Mexican customers "they make one a bad face," as the saying goes. This type of social exclusion has been responsible for a good deal of the northward migration of Mexican workers and their families. Like the Negroes of the Deep South, the Mexicans have sought the more friendly towns and cities of central and northern California, Colorado, Wyoming, Indiana, and Ohio, where prejudice does not make a specific target out of them.

Closely tied to this problem is that of segregation. The location of the hundreds of Mexican colonies—invariably marked by the railroad tracks, cactus patch, city dump, and employment bureau signs —is in itself one huge, ubiquitous case of segregation.

Housing. This leads directly to the problem of housing, typically resolved by the Mexican workers in their patchwork neighborhoods commonly called *colonias.* Usually lying outside the corporate limits of the towns and cities to which they are attached, these neighborhoods cling to the surrounding countryside like gray desiccated barnacles, from which some unseen inexorable hand constantly squeezes the vital humors and amenities of community living.

A trip through one of these *colonias* is easy to make. Any motorist traveling along US 99—California's Main Street, as it has been called —can see these typical California rural slums from the windows of his car. From the upper stories of the better hotels in Fresno, Modesto, Sacramento, or Bakersfield, good views can be obtained of shack rows, tent settlements, and privy subdivisions occupied by Mexican families. In the Shafter colony of Mexican agricultural workers the stench from backyard toilets in summer is intolerable. In the heart of the Mexican colony of Bakersfield, young children play barefoot in sewer water backed up by winter rains. The

Mexican Laborers Working in the Fields

Between 1849 and 1910, Mexican Americans became a "forgotten people." As thousands of Anglos and immigrants poured into the Southwest, Mexican Americans found themselves an often exploited minority in their own homeland. Between 1910 and 1939, many Mexicans emigrated from south of the border to work as seasonal agricultural laborers. Because they would work for lower wages than native-born Americans, they were in direct competition with many Mexican Americans in the Southwest, who in turn began moving to industrial and agricultural regions in the North, where jobs were plentiful and wages higher.

Wide World Photos

Young Mexican Americans Herding Sheep in New Mexico

Many Mexican Americans remained in the Southwest, hoping to find a future in farming and sheepherding.

"Zoot Suit" Riots of 1943

During World War II, many Mexican Americans experienced a certain measure of affluence for the first time. With this affluence came a new sense of racial pride and a new consciousness of discrimination and prejudice. Youth gangs were formed, especially in the barrio of Los Angeles, to protect the residents against servicemen and the police, and the fashionable "zoot suit" was adopted as a sort of uniform and a sign of prosperity. In June, 1943, a fight between Mexican-American youths and U.S. sailors led to the "Zoot Suit Riots" in Los Angeles.

Wide World Photos

"Zoot-Suiters" Flying Flags of Truce

Mexican-American Teenagers Working
in a Neighborhood Project in Los Angeles

The new awareness that has taken place among Mexican Americans since 1940 has led to a heightened sense of community and general agreement that Mexican Americans want to share in all the social and economic benefits that other Americans enjoy. But, as with other minorities, the means of achieving these aims have taken many forms. Among the young, especially, there has been increasing concern for the problems of the poor.

Wide World Photos

A Young Mexican American Tutoring in
a Neighborhood in Which She Grew Up

A Migrant Camp in Florida

The plight of Mexican Americans and immigrants from Mexico who work as migrant farm laborers began to arouse attention early in the 1960's. In many migrant camps, children were often left alone or locked in a car next to a field while their parents worked. With local help, a young Mexican-American minister established a day-care center for workers in Florida camps. Each day, after two hours of bouncing from one camp to another in a bus or van, the children are delivered to the center.

Religious News Service Photos

Loading the Bus for
the Day-Care Center

Here, the young Mexican-American minister loads pre-schoolers, including infants, into a van for their trip to a day-care center in the strawberry-growing area south of Miami.

Grape Pickers Marching Through California's San Joaquin Valley

Mexican-American migrant workers have long been among the most exploited people on the labor market. But it was not until 1965, when the grape pickers, under Cesar Chavez's leadership, began their strike against the growers in Delano, California, that they received nationwide attention. Early in the strike, some major wine-grape growers did meet the migrants' demands for higher pay, paid vaca-tions, and other benefits. But the table-grape growers refused. In 1968, Cesar Chavez received national support in a boycott of all California table grapes, and, as the strike wore on, it developed into *la causa*, the cause, or the demand of Mexican Americans for justice and equality in all areas of American society.

Religious News Service Photo

Cesar Chavez

Cesar Chavez, the leader of the grape pickers' strike, was the son of poor Mexican Americans and spent his early life in various migrant camps.

Rodolfo Gonzalez and Supporters in Denver

Rodolfo "Corky" Gonzalez founded the Crusade for Justice in Denver, Colorado, in 1965 to further Mexican-American demands for jobs, better housing, and land reform.

Wide World Photos

Arrest of Tijerina and His Wife

Reies López Tijerina founded the Alliance of Free-States, whose purpose was to reopen the question of Spanish and Mexican land grants. In June, 1969, he and his wife were arrested in Coyote, New Mexico, for activities connected with their organization.

Cesar Chavez Signing the Pact that Ended the Strike

An important milestone in the history of Mexican Americans was reached on July 29, 1970, when the United Farm Workers Organizing Committee signed a contract ending their five-year-long grape pickers' strike. The "forgotten people" won, if not a battle, a major skirmish in their struggle for recognition and full participation in American life.

Religious News Service Photo

colonias rarely are taken into account in public-housing projects. They have become normal sights. But public agencies and social workers know that these areas are foci of disease. On the tuberculosis maps the black dots are heaviest in the Mexican colony.

Education. The educational problems of the Mexican minority are of two basic types—the extension of educational opportunities to the young, and the creation of adult education programs adapted to the needs of these communities. So far as the children are concerned, education and child labor are waging, now as in past years, a bitter struggle for the young mind. The tent schools of San Luis Obispo County in California are better than what most counties in that state provide for the children of wandering Mexican pickers. But they are also mute reminders of the inability of local, county, state, and federal authorities to provide these young American citizens with decent facilities for learning.

The adolescent and college-age Mexicans today represent a reservoir of possibilities for leadership that has not been recognized. Hundreds of young men and women who have somehow survived the attrition of the crops and the economic pressure on the home and have finished high school can go no further. They represent what the American way of life can do at its best, even against the underlying resistance of finance farming, the international traffic in low living standards, and the other complexities of the boss culture.

Civil liberties. The degree of enjoyment of civil liberties and constitutional rights varies with the nature of sub-groups within the Mexican minority. Lowest in the scale are the wetbacks, the illegals, for whom there are no rights. Next come the Nationals, whose rights are defined by contract and occasionally enforced by a weak bureaucracy of United States and Mexican officials. Then there are the long-resident Mexicans who have never become citizens. They are reluctant to demand protection or to insist on their constitutional prerogatives because their status, too, is vulnerable.

The Mexicans have probably not missed any of the forms of mistreatment and violation of civil liberties that have been visited on the other minority groups in American life. Thus far, however, they have failed to develop strong institutional resistence to such invasions.

Community relations. The relationship between the Mexican minority and the dominant elements has generally been a punitive-inquisitorial one on the part of the latter. It is interesting to note how the Mexicans shrink from contact with even those agencies of the dominant group that are intended to "do good." These agencies too often approach the Mexican client with a questionnaire in hand. Being questioned, for the Mexican worker, has too often been but the first step toward being arrested. Hence the reluctance of the Mexicans to ask for relief, to apply for medical assistance, or to have any truck with the formidable apparatus of any federal agency. The machinery of government, to the Mexican, has been something to avoid. It must be met only when it comes at one aggressively in the war dress of a cop. What lies across the railroad tracks can be left well enough alone.

But the dominant community is there. And so is the Mexican *colonia*. What adjustment there is has been worked out by the contractors on the economic level, by the survival of patriotic and cultural traditions that have worn thin, and by a silent skepticism toward the questionnaire-state that lies across the tracks and runs the show.

Rural and urban relations. Many important Mexican communities lie in the heart of metropolitan areas. In Los Angeles, Chicago, and San Antonio they have often been engulfed, sometimes bull-dozed out of old quarters to make way for swank subdivisions or modern highways. Mexican centers of this type play a multiple role. They are winter havens for the migrant workers that criss-cross the land in spring and summer. They provide a stepping-stone from farm to industrial employment. They bring the young people into closer and more intense contact with the dominant culture. Here the rural attitude dissolves into an urban resentment and a mental confusion created by the economic and social conditions which face all city workers. One result, for the Mexicans, has been the separation of the urban from the rural groups, so that the full force of the Mexican community has never been brought to bear on the problems they have in common. The urban Mexican has never reached, as has the urban Negro, toward the rural Mexican so that both could improve their status. This gap is one that has not been sufficiently noticed by Mexicans themselves or by non-Mexicans who have attempted to work with the group.

Political impotence. From what has been said, it is not surprising to find that the Mexicans are a political nonentity in the United States. Though many thousands of them are citizens by birth or naturalization, they keep clear of political obligations and therefore do not take advantage of political opportunities. There are counties in the Southwest where the Mexicans could theoretically swing the results of an election if they registered and voted. But too often they do not. This in turn means that state and federal legislation rarely takes them into account. Even in municipal affairs it is uncommon to find spokesmen for the Mexican. Therefore all pleas to the state governor, the President of the United States, the legislature, or Congress must be based on considerations of high human sentiment. In the American political system, however, such sentiments have always been found to fare much better when supported by precinct organization and votes in the ballet box.

Trade-union organization. Perhaps the most serious weakness, and by no means the least important of the problems of the Mexicans in the United States, is their lack of economic organization.

The Mexican workers, both in industry and agriculture, have given sufficient proof of their understanding of solidarity among workers. They have shown that they can take every form of violence which vigilantism in this country has been able to devise. Mexican workers in Imperial, Salinas, and Orange have sustained industrial disputes single-handed against the combined police, political, and propaganda resources of finance-farming and corporation ranching. But as yet they have not solved the problem of union organization. The attempt to set up separate unions on racial lines has been disastrous. There is a language barrier. The labor movement itself until recently has taken a somewhat benevolent interest rather than an active organizational concern in Mexican workers.

In the field of agriculture, there are still other difficulties. There is the myth that farm workers are unorganizable and Mexican farm workers twice so. Farm wages are so low that the monthly union dues seem a heavy tax on the workers. There are long periods of unemployment when union obligations can be met only at considerable sacrifice. A trade-union of farm workers must face and meet assaults on its security ranging from local irritation, through state legislative attacks, and up to international maneuvers to swamp local living and working standards.

Nevertheless, the problem of union organization must be solved. The economic education of the Mexican worker is much more advanced than his cultural assimilation or his political experience. The union is his most vital point of contact with the larger community.

Here, broadly speaking, is the situation. Left to themselves, the Mexicans in the United States will undoubtedly continue to devise their own defenses against pressures of the kind I have described.

But what distinguishes the present moment is the growing feeling, in and out of the Mexican group, that future adjustment does not have to be left to laissez-faire, that it can be accomplished much more intelligently through widespread information about the group among Americans generally, through mutual counsel, planning, and concerted democratic action on the part of all those concerned with bringing all elements of the American population into participating partnership in American life.

THE GRAPES OF WRATH– VINTAGE 1961

[Public Law 78 was enacted by Congress in 1951 as a "temporary" measure designed to afford a controlled annual importation of farm workers, or braceros, as they are commonly called, from Mexico. The legislation was immensely popular with the large agricultural enterprises of the Southwest and was kept on the books for several years to allow hundreds of thousands of braceros to be brought into the country. It was highly advantageous to large-scale agriculture to have an inexhaustible supply of cheap, nonunion labor available every year. But, during the 1950's, pressures began to mount for the repeal of Public Law 78. As this article by Arnold Mayer indicates, repeal was not forthcoming immediately. In February, 1962, the braceros became subject to minimum wage provisions, and, in 1965, the importing of workers under the bracero program was ended.]

At eleven o'clock on the hot August night that proved to be the last of the Eighty-sixth Congress, Arizona's eighty-three-year-old Carl Hayden was on the Senate floor pleading for a six-month extension of the Mexican farm-labor importation law.

From *The Reporter*, February 2, 1961.

The Hayden speech marked the first defeat ever experienced by the grower organizations of this country on a farm-labor issue. Up to then, the growers' Congressional supporters had been able to extend this nine-year-old law for two years at a time.

Now that the Eighty-seventh Congress has convened, we can expect the battle over the program incorporated in Public Law 78 to resume, with church, labor, small-farm, and civic groups—who believe that P.L. 78 is an abomination—pitted against the grower organizations—who believe it provides a necessary source of labor.

The fight promises to be bitter. Both sides recognize that in this battle lies the key to whether America's 2,300,000 farm workers—probably the most poverty-stricken, depressed, and exploited group in our country—can get the kind of protection from which other Americans have long benefited.

Under P.L. 78, a total of 437,600 Mexican farm workers, known as braceros, were imported for seasonal work in 1959, mostly by growers of cotton, vegetables, fruits, and sugar beets. These growers represent less than two per cent of America's farmers and are chiefly concentrated in California, Texas, Arizona, New Mexico, and Arkansas. But their farms, mainly large-scale operations, provided a disproportionate source of agricultural employment in the United States.

The huge influx of braceros has made it possible for these growers to keep wages down. (American farm workers earned an average of only $829 and got an average of only 138 days of work in 1959.) If domestic farm workers refuse the wage rate offered, the grower need not raise it. He tells the Federal government that he is unable to get workers (true, at his wage scale), and he then gets a group of braceros.

The effect on farm-labor income has been disastrous. Wages for field labor in most of Texas have stayed at the same level for nearly a decade—about fifty cents an hour. Wages for cotton harvesting— cotton is the chief crop on which braceros are used—have even dropped in recent years, and cotton chopping pays as low as thirty cents an hour in many areas of Arkansas.

More than 60,000 farm workers migrate from their homes in Texas to harvest crops in other states at the same time some 180,000 braceros are imported to harvest the crops in Texas. The growers say Americans will not perform "stoop labor." But the same growers use tens of thousands of braceros in a number of skilled jobs.

The bracero also gets some benefits denied the domestic farm worker. He receives a minimum wage of fifty cents an hour, while many U.S. migrants work for as little as thirty cents an hour. The braceros are guaranteed employment for at least three-quarters of their contract period; they also get free transportation to the job and various housing advantages. The domestic farm workers, however, have none of these guarantees. Amendments to P.L. 78 to provide American agricultural labor with the same benefits and guarantees as the braceros have been defeated in the House at least twice.

If braceros get better conditions than domestic farm workers, why does the grower prefer them? There are several important reasons. First, the bracero importation creates a surplus of labor that keeps all farm-labor wages low. Then, the braceros come alone instead of with their families, so that the grower saves money on housing. Also, the extreme poverty of rural Mexico brings prime bracero labor willing to work at fifty cents an hour. And, finally, the bracero is far more docile than the American migrant. The threat of being sent back to Mexico is enough to bring him into line if he complains too much about conditions.

A recent report prepared for the Senate Subcommittee on Migratory Labor puts the matter succinctly: "The foreign migrant is indentured to a particular farmer or farm association for the duration of his contract. One grower, speaking of the Mexican farm labor program, said that 'we used to own slaves, now we rent them from the government.'"

Some Mexican farm labor has been used in the United States, legally or illegally, on an organized or unorganized basis, for decades. When in the late 1940's the illegal border crossings by the so-called wetbacks became an increasing problem, the growers saw an opportunity to get an organized government-sponsored labor-importation program, such as they had during the Second World War. Arguing that "controlled importation" was the answer to the wetback problem and that a shortage of farm labor existed because of the Korean War, the growers secured the enactment of P.L. 78 in 1951. The so-called "temporary program," which legalized the wetback migrations, was renewed in 1954, 1956, and 1958.

The period between the third renewal in 1958 and the fourth renewal attempt in 1960 was a time of increased government and public concern about farm workers. Information reaching Secretary of Labor James P. Mitchell on the Mexican farm-labor program prompted an investigation. The investigation led to a shutdown of several bracero camps and improvements in others, and Mitchell began to take an increasing interest in farm-labor problems—more than any previous Secretary of Labor.

In 1959, he appointed four distinguished citizens to study P.L. 78 and its administration. Their unanimous report urged specific changes in the law. In essence, they recommended (1) real protection against the adverse effect on the employment and wages of domestic farm workers caused by the importation of Mexicans; (2) a guarantee of at least the same benefits for domestic workers as for braceros; and (3) limitation of the bracero program to unskilled seasonal jobs on nonsurplus crops.

While the consultants were working on their report, Secretary Mitchell established regulations for the recruitment of domestic farm workers by the U.S. Employment Service. These regulations dealt with wages, housing, and transportation. Their net effect was to prevent the USES, a tax-financed public agency, from being used to undercut prevailing area wages and other conditions for migrants. Weak as they were, these regulations brought loud howls of "socialism" and "government interference" from the growers and their supporters in Congress.

When the 1960 session of Congress opened, the growers struck the first blow. A number of Republican and Southern Democratic congressmen, including the chairman of the House Agriculture subcommittee, E. C. Gathings (D., Arkansas), introduced nearly identical bills to extend P.L. 78. Actually, the measures would have made conditions far worse for farm workers than they already are. As it turned out, this was a serious mistake on the growers' part: they overplayed their hand.

The groups hoping for improvements in P.L. 78 waited for the Labor Department to offer a reform bill on behalf of the Eisenhower administration. Their wait was in vain: the department's bill was shelved within the administration—thanks to the efforts of the defenders of corporation agriculture, led by Secretary of Agriculture Ezra Taft Benson and White House Administrative Assistant Jack Z. Anderson, himself a California grower who has made use of braceros.

With the hearings of the House Agriculture subcommittee only a week away, those who opposed P.L. 78 seemed at a hopeless disadvantage. They had no plan of action, no organized effort, and no bill to support. But the extreme provisions of the growers' bills and the unexpected failure of the Labor Department to introduce any bill shocked them into action. George McGovern (D., South Dakota), a young and able member of the House Agriculture Committee, agreed to introduce a reform measure.

The McGovern bill incorporated the four consultants' recommendations, some verbatim. And it provided for a gradual ending of P.L. 78, as had been suggested in a resolution by the general board of the National Council of the Churches of Christ in the United States.

It was an uphill fight. On occasions such as these the American Farm Bureau Federation, one of the most powerful lobbying groups in the capital, applies intense pressure. Industrialized agriculture joins with canners and processors to exert maximum influence on congressmen. By themselves, voteless farm workers are no match for such powerful forces, and this disparity is the major reason for the absence of protective legislation for agricultural labor.

But in the P.L. 78 fight of 1960 the growers, canners, and processors were opposed by a number of organizations that were working to give farm workers a better deal. They were religious groups, such as the National Council of the Churches of Christ and the National Catholic Welfare Conference. They were labor unions, led by the AFL-CIO and its Amalgamated Meat Cutters and Butcher Workmen. They were civic groups, such as the National Consumers League and Americans for Democratic Action. They were the small farmers, represented by the National Farmers Union. And they were the groups specifically and solely concerned with the plight of farm workers, such as the National Advisory Committee on Farm Labor and the National Sharecroppers Fund.

Within Congress, the growers were in a good position. Some very important Southerners and Republicans were ready to lead their battle. Their control of the Agriculture Committees, where the legislation had to originate, seemed unshakable. And they counted on being able to invoke the tremendous power of the Republican-Southern Democratic coalition when the going got rough.

On the liberal side of Congress, P.L. 78 reform had to compete with far more potent political issues for the attention and concern of legislators. Although sympathetic to the exploited farm workers, many of the embattled liberal congressmen felt they had better concentrate on the mass of social legislation that, unlike P.L. 78, would immediately affect the voters of their districts.

During the seven-month fight in 1960, the Congressional supporters of both the growers and the reform groups had to change their strategy and their objectives. It soon became apparent to the legislators seeking reform that they did not have the strength to pass the McGovern bill. Therefore they concentrated on blocking the growers' bill, planning to resume the fight for reform in 1961, when they hoped a new administration would support them in the battle.

The Eisenhower administration's "position" on P.L. 78 was a study in ineffectualness. A bitter fight continued within the administration after Mitchell was stopped from supporting the introduction of a reform bill: the Labor Department wanted administration support for P.L. 78 reforms, the Agriculture Department wanted support for the growers' bills.

The House hearings on P.L. 78 brought a showdown. A compromise was reached between the departments—and it provided against any action. The administration urged that consideration of P.L. 78 legislation be postponed until 1961. Mitchell also agreed that he would not push for an agricultural minimum wage or any other farm-labor legislation in 1960.

As it turned out, the administration could not stand firm on P.L. 78. When the reform groups sought to keep the growers' bill in the House Rules Committee—a way of assuring no action in 1960— the administration either would not or could not do anything. During the debate in the House of Representatives the White House was silent. Only a letter from Secretary Mitchell restated the view of the "administration and the Labor Department." But congressmen—especially the Republicans—knew that this was more the position of the Labor Department than of the administration. As a result, very few Republicans opposed the growers' renewal bill.

The growers' support in the two houses' Agriculture Committees was a huge stumbling block for the reform groups. Hearings were held before a House subcommittee strongly partisan to the growers' cause. Some subcommittee members competed with grower witnesses in lambasting "do-gooders" and "government bureaucrats."

Not suprisingly, the House Agriculture Committee approved the growers' bill, although three members—McGovern, Merwin Coad (D., Iowa), and Lester Johnson (D., Wisconsin)—submitted a devastating minority report.

"The moral implications of [the bill] are shocking," the three congressmen concluded. "It would literally increase the destitution, the underemployment, and the exploitation of 2,300,000 domestic farmworkers, who are the poorest of poor in our nation. It would put the family farm at a further competitive disadvantage. It would increase the stain Public Law 78 has already placed on our national values and prestige."

The Congressional supporters of reform were forced to fall back on delaying tactics. These, along with some fortuitous circumstances, held up action in the House of Representatives until nearly the end of the regular 1960 session. A bill providing for a two-year extension of P.L. 78 without any of the growers' changes was considered by the House in late June.

The reforms of the McGovern bill, offered by Representative John Fogarty (D., Rhode Island), were defeated by a 2-1 margin. Similarly trounced was an attempt by Representative Alfred Santangelo (D., New York) to deny braceros to cotton producers, the lowest-paying farmers and largest single users of foreign workers. The unamended two-year extension of P.L. 78 was finally passed by the House.

Then late in August, in the special session of Congress, the Senate Agriculture Committee suddenly and unexpectedly reported out a bill giving P.L. 78 a six-month extension, brushing aside the reform bill sponsored by Eugene McCarthy (D., Minnesota) and nine other senators. This happened after the growers' Senatorial supporters had summarily taken the House-passed bill from the subcommittee headed by Hubert Humphrey and, without hearings or previous announcements, brought it before the full Senate Agriculture Committee for consideration.

At this stage, the six-month bill was a possible trap. It seemed reasonable, but the liberals knew that Congressional procedures would give the growers ample opportunity to turn six months into two years again in the House-Senate conference committee. A bipartisan group decided to block the Agriculture Committee's bill with a Senate filibuster, if necessary, and made their intentions fully known. For all practical purposes, the bill seemed to be quite dead.

But strange things happen during the last days of a Congressional session. Senator Hayden's attempted face-saving action for the growers on the last evening was such an oddity. After a brief debate in which the reform forces showed that their surprise did not diminish their determination to block a two-year extension of P.L.

78, an agreement was reached. Senators Hayden and Allen Ellender of Louisiana, chairman of the Agriculture Committee, agreed that six months would be the limit of the extension. They further agreed that the abuses, reform, and extension of P.L. 78 would be considered in thorough hearings in 1961. In return, the liberals agreed not to block the six-month extension which carried P.L. 78 through the harvest season until December 31, 1961.

The maneuvering had ended in a definite if not complete victory for the anti-P.L. 78 forces. They had prevented the Farm Bureau from upsetting Secretary Mitchell's interstate recruitment regulations. They had prevented the growers from giving the Secretary of Agriculture joint administration over P.L. 78 with the Secretary of Labor. They had cut down the extension from two years to six months. But most important, they had shown that the growers' lobby was not invincible.

THE SPANISH LAND GRANT QUESTION IN NEW MEXICO

[When Mexico ceded its Southwestern territories to the United States, much of the land in New Mexico was part of land grants that had been given to settlers by Spain and Mexico between 1598 and 1846. The precise number and extent of the grants will probably never be known because of the destruction of the archives at Santa Fe between 1869 and 1871. The loss of many records, together with the fact that many of the titles were already unclear, opened up unique opportunities for chicanery. By the end of the century, more than four-fifths of the old Mexican and Spanish grants were lost to their claimants, notwithstanding the guarantees of protection of private property in the Treaty of Guadalupe Hidalgo. In 1891, a Court of Private Land Claims was established to deal with the land issue, but this amounted to nothing more than a fairly transparent means of justifying the expropriation of the old claims. What was true in New Mexico was also true in slightly differing circumstances in Texas and California. In addition to losses suffered through the machinations of private speculators and lawyers, the federal government has also unhesitatingly taken land from the native New Mexicans for national forests and preserves, thereby cutting down the available grazing land, forcing herds to be cut, and driving many into destitution and onto welfare rolls.

During the 1960's, the land grant question was reopened in New Mexico (if indeed it had ever been closed) by Reies Lopez Tijerina and his *Alianza Federal de Mercedes* (Federal Alliance of Land Grants), later renamed the *Alianza de los Pueblos Libres*—Alliance

From *The Spanish Land Grant Question Examined*, Albuquerque, 1966.

of Free City-States. The primary goal of the *Alianza* is the regaining of all of the land grants lost over the years, a goal regarded by most observers as impossible of fulfillment. In October, 1969, Tijerina resigned from the *Alianza* because of the nationalistic-militant turn it was taking. He was at the time in jail on a two-year sentence for assaulting forest rangers in 1966. This selection reprints the greater part of a small booklet, issued by the *Alianza* in 1966, on the history of the land grant problem.]

The question of the Spanish Land Grants is over a century old, and still not resolved. The reason for this is that these grants were not given adequate protection by the officials of the State of New Mexico, who were either corrupt, incompetent or did not care if justice was done or not to their neighbors. Out of this situation arose a melancholy one and it invites a particular examination in the light of actual facts. And all men who are responsible men, have a moral obligation to help right a grave wrong and injustice; which if not corrected soon, might take their rights and property away as well, through the lack of adequate protection being given by the officials of the State of New Mexico to property and property rights.

The inhabitants of New Mexico should consider that if New Mexico was worth fighting the Mexicans for, it is worth governing and caring for by decent and civilized methods. More than a century has passed since the United States of America invaded and occupied New Mexico, yet the question of Spanish Land Grants is still very much in the air. The apparent reason why this question has not been fully resolved is due to the Administration of the State of New Mexico being incapable of adequately enforcing the law for what the law really is, and being incapable of suppressing all frauds and perjuries, and corruptions in the courts. New Mexico has sunk into a morass of fraud, forgery and perjury.

Here on the Rio Grande, the Royal Laws of the Indies existed and still exists as the local law. For these royal laws have never been repealed or abrogated by any duly constituted authority. When the Empire of Mexico invaded and occupied New Mexico, the Royal Laws of the Indies remained in force. And when the United States of America invaded and occupied New Mexico, the Royal Laws of the Indies remained in force, except as changed by legislation; but such changes apply only to newly initiated rights and do not disturb prior vested rights, such as old royal grant rights. The Royal Laws of the Indies were continued in force, as the local laws and customs, and are the common-laws of the State of New Mexico, and not the English common-law, which is foreign to such old royal granted rights and concepts under the Laws of the Indies. And the old Royal Laws of the Indies is protected by the laws of nations as the local law of New Mexico.

The new-comers to New Mexico, the Anglos, have been endeavoring to ignore prior vested and paramount rights in New Mexico, but such ignoring of such old rights do not change the same. The Anglos, purporting to be the "conquerors" brought their own laws and doctrines (from English common-law sources) with them into this region, and, in the purported administration of the law, the Anglos have impinged upon rights and concepts of the inhabitants of New Mexico, and subjected them more or less to the doctrines of the "new-comers" in the land, which are foreign here and shall always remain so. A great deal of confusion has been created in New Mexico by these Anglos who have no respect for international law or local law, and, who have been and are endeavoring to foist upon the people of New Mexico English common-laws, in order to terrorize the owners and heirs of these Land Grants into not exercising their rights under these grants. . . .

Under the 1848 Treaty of Guadalupe Hidalgo, the United States of America undertook to protect all prior vested property rights in New Mexico, so that such later enacted laws of the United States of America and their political subdivisions could not impair such old vested rights, and all aggressions by late comers would not have harmed such prior vested and paramount rights. And under this Treaty the U.S. Government undertook to complete and see that all inchoate titles to lands were perfected. For these imperfect titles to lands were contracts for perfect titles, which the United States contracted to honor and perfect. And one of the best evidences of title is that of long, open and continued possession and occupation of the lands under claim of title. The U. S. Government had no valid reason to deny any inchoate title to lands in New Mexico; and any such denial constitutes a breach of contract and a denial of justice. Such breach of contract and denial of justice, did not impair or deminish an inchoate title to lands, for the U. S. Government can be compelled to specifically perform its contracted obligations under the 1848 Treaty, to perfect these inchoate titles. An inchoate title is property, being in the nature of a contract for a perfect title to land. . . .

There are many trespassers on these Spanish Land Grants, which have through various and devious means seized these lands both contrary to law and the true owner's interest. The true owners of these lands have the legal right to use all the force necessary to oust these trespassers, without running into an Anglo controlled and orientated court for a "Quit Title Action" wherein title to the property is up for grabs. Whatever the source and origin of the title and rights of these trespassers to these lands might be, they cannot overcome prior vested and paramount rights and title. Not even a claim of adverse possession will do these trespassers for a defense. For although Law 20, Title 9, of the Third Partida of the laws of the Kingdoms of the Indies, states that "if a man possess a thing 30 years, even if he stole it or obtained it by violence and robbery," it was and became his. Such acquisition of ownership or title, is, in law, called prescription. But examining the ordinance further, the ordinance provided that "only such things as can be alienated are subject to prescription," and states that "public squares, streets, roads and other things belonging to communities and of which the inhabitants have the use; are not prescriptible." And Law 21, Title 12, Book 4, declares:

> If any private individuals shall have occupied lands of public places, small towns, and concejiles, lands of the cities, they must restore them, in conformity with the law of Toledo.

(See: Leyes de los Reynos de las Indias, Ordinance of Don Felipe III, April 26th, 1618.) And it is a well known and established fact that, the majority of these Spanish Land Grants were to pueblos (towns), that is, to municipal corporations. And under the Laws of the Indies, the pueblos had prior and paramount right to these grant lands and waters, and all other rights were and are subordinate to the pueblo's better rights. And the pueblo's rights were a trust created, imposed and recognized by the laws, orders and decrees of the Imperial Government of the Kingdoms of the Indies, that was duly recognized by the Government of the United States of America, in virtue of its decrees of confirmation of these grants. And we maintain that it was and is impossible for any official or body of officialdom of the State of New Mexico or of the United States of America, to give away or cancel or alienate any perpetual right held in trust by these pueblos. If any organization or official or body of officials of the State of New Mexico or of the United States of America violated these grants, the failure there, was in the official or officials, not the law, the law remained, and can be enforced to recover that what was erroneously, arbitrarily and corruptly given, to many persons who should have known better than to accept such gifts contrary to the general public's welfare.

The majority of these Spanish Land Grants were to pueblos, that is, to towns. The term PUEBLO answers to that of the English word TOWN, in all its vagueness, and in all its precision. As the word town in English generally embraces every kind of population from the Village to the City, and also, used specifically, signifies a town 'corporate and politic,' so the word 'pueblo' in Spanish, ranges from the hamlet to the city, but, used emphatically, signifies a town 'corporate and politic.' The Spaniards in Spain prefer the word 'LUGAR' to that of 'PUEBLO.' The Spanish-Americans commonly used the word pueblo, because the American pueblos differed so much

from the European Spanish lugares, the variation in the terms denoted the specific varieties of members of the same general family,
and the word pueblo as used in the Spanish Indies, denoted one of
the emancipated, homogeneous, American pueblos which owed their
existence to the experience, wisdom, piety, and bounty of the Kings
of the Eastern and Western Indies and of the Spains. Sometimes,
American pueblos were commonly called a lugar, a puesto, a pobla-
zon or a sitio. But, without some further distinctions, we shall mis-
lead ourselves. A pueblo manifested itself in various ways. It had a
political jurisdiction, embracing all the legal voters, within a certain territory." It had a judicial jurisdiction: 'termino Jurisdic-
cional', jurisdiction—partido or distrito—is understood all that is
comprised within the limits to which the jurisdiction of the Alcalde
or Judge of the pueblo extends. It had also a proprietary existence,
embraced in the phrase 'termino municipal', 'fundo legal', 'the lands
owned by the corporation': 'that land which has been assigned to
the pueblos for the relief of their herds, within which neither the
cattle nor inhabitants of neighboring pueblos can enter, for the
purpose of grazing or cutting wood, without being denounced and
brought to condign punishment, unless they had some charter of
commonalty'. The pueblos were closed corporations, with member-
ship restricted to the descendents and heirs of the founding fathers
and mothers, and to those granted a charter of commonalty. The
pueblos were commonwealths, republics, that is, feudatory city-
states: See: Law 3, Title 12, Book 4, Leyes de los Reynos de las Indias, Tomo II, Ordenanza 107, whose citation recites, to-wit:

> Los que aceptaren asiento de caballerias y peonias, se obliguen
> de tener edificados los solares, poblada la casa, hechas y repar-
> tidas las hojas de tierras de labor, y haberlas labrador, puesto
> de plantas, y poblado de ganados las que fueren de pasto, den-
> tro de tiempo limitado, repartido por sus plazos, y declarando
> lo que en cada uno ha de estar hecho, pena de que pierdan el
> repartimiento de solares, y tierras, y mas cierta cantidad de
> maravedis para la Republica, con obligacion en public forma,
> y fianza llana y abonda. [Those who accept lands, knights or
> soldiers, have the obligation to build houses and to dwell in
> them, to cultivate the land or to breed cattle, if it were grass-
> land, in the time specified by the terms of distribution; and they
> have to declare what they have done, or risk losing the rights
> to the grant, in addition to a certain amount of maravedis
> (money) for the Republic, with bond in public form and with a
> sufficient and nonnegotiable bail.]

There were two methods for establishing pueblos, one by the
government, and two, by virtue of a capitulation or agreement entered into between a given person and the government, whereby
the contractor was to establish a town upon conditions established
by law, that is, in accordance with Ordinances 88 and 89 of Don

Felipe II, which are embodied in Law 6, Title 5, Book 4, of the Laws of the Indies; but Ordinance 100 of Don Felipe II, which is Law 7, Title 5, Book 4, modifies the forgoing by permitting the contractor to furnish not less than ten (10) inhabitants. And the powers of the Contractor according to Ordinance 95, which is Law 11 of Book 4, Title 5, was civil and criminal jurisdiction of the first instance, during his life, and also one son or heir had the same. He could appoint councilmen and other officers of the council. Appeals could be taken to the town-council or to the Alcalde Mayor of the province or to the Audiencia in the district wherein the pueblo was situated . . . in the case of the Province of Nuevo Mexico, the Audiencia in the Kingdom of Nueva Galicia in Guadalajara was the appellate court (see, Law 1, Title 3, Book 5, of the Laws of the Indies). This is the equivalent to the pueblo court being a district court, with right of appeal direct to the State Supreme Court. This right of these pueblos to have such courts of the first instance have never been taken away from them by any competent authority, but has been guaranteed to them by the 1848 Treaty of Guadalupe Hidalgo, and by Article II, Section 5, and by Article XXII, Section 4, of the Constitution of the State of New Mexico, whose citation recites, to wit:

> The rights, privileges, and immunities, civil, political and religious, guaranteed to the people of New Mexico by the treaty of Guadalupe Hidalgo, shall be preserved inviolate.
> ARTICLE II, Section 5,
> Constitution of the State of New Mexico.

> All laws of the Territory of New Mexico in force at the time of its admission into the Union as a state, not inconsistent with this constitution, shall be and remain in force as the laws of the state until they expire by their limitation, or are altered or repealed; and all rights, actions, claims, contracts, liabilities and obligations, shall continue and remain unaffected by the change in the form of government.
> ARTICLE XXII, Section 4,
> Constitution of the State of New Mexico.

Generally, the pueblos were governed by regidores, or councilmen, and alcaldes, or judges. Large pueblos had twelve regidores and small ones had six. (See: Law 2, Title 7, Book 4, Laws of the Indies, Ordinance No. 43 of Don Felipe II.)

In addition to political jurisdiction for the purpose of administering governmental activities, pueblos were allowed to own property. A pueblo could own property both within and outside its political boundaries. The interest that the pueblo has in property as an owner is distinguished from its governmental interest over property. The pueblo's owner interest in property is proprietary. The Surveyor General Decreed July 15th, 1859, that,

The instructions of this office provide that the existence of a town when the United States took possession of the country being proven, is to be taken as prima facie evidence of a grant to said town; . . . and was recognized as a town by the Mexican Government, it is believed to be a good and valid grant, and the land claimed severed from the public domain.

It remains both a historic and legal fact that neither these pueblos nor their rights have been duly abolished by any competent authority. And consequently, these pueblos have all their rights intact and enforcible. And these pueblos have the right to exercise police power to support them in exercising their rights to their property, without complaint being made by any trespassers, or the criminal element in the State of New Mexico.

These pueblos were recognized by both the Government of the United States of America and by the Government of the State of New Mexico. And old records show the fact of this recognition of these pueblos and their rights by these governments. And this recognition has never been withdrawn for any reason whatsoever, and constitutes an estoppel upon these governments, from ever declaring that these pueblos never legally existed in fact. Yet we find the Government of the State of New Mexico attempting to provide a civil administration for these pueblos, in wanton violation of their rights and liberties. We discover in many of these pueblos certain purported corporations entitled "Boards of Trustees" attempting to administer the pueblo and dispose of its property without consulting the pueblo if it can do these things to it and its property. It is well settled that there cannot be at the same time within the same territory, two distinct corporations exercising the same powers, jurisdiction and privileges. This rule is based upon the practical consideration that intolerable confusion instead of good government almost inevitably would obtain in a territory in which two corporations of like kind and powers attempted to function coincidentally. This is bad government; . . . away with bad government.

The Laws of the Indies provides for the de jure civil administration of these pueblos. Yet the Government of the State of New Mexico interfered into the internal affairs of these pueblos when it created and established these co-called corporations known as "Boards of Trustees" and gave them aid and comfort in infringing upon the rights of the lawful de jure government of these pueblos, as guaranteed to them by the 1848 Treaty of Guadalupe Hidalgo. This usurpation must cease once and for all, as must this chaos created by corrupt government. . . .

The Anglos should realize that the Spanish people of New Mexico are no longer a disunited people, but are uniting for the first time to recover and preserve their birthright and cultural heritage, and that each day they are getting stronger and more confidence in themselves. The days of hopelessness for the Spanish people of New Mexico are numbered. The Anglos should read this hand writing on the wall, and make allowances for it in their hearts and lives. For the justice and the just cause of the Spanish people, is their struggle to restore authority vested in the community, the natural unit of society, and down with all Anglo anarchists. All Anglos have a vested interest in and a moral obligation to help these pueblos and their townsmen to regain their ancient rights and heritage. For if this struggle of the Spanish people to restore their birthright to its proper place in the community is throttled, before it can be realized, why then the people will lack direction and see the futility of it all, and seek other roads to follow. The Anglos should not forget the "Mano Negra" movement in New Mexico earlier in the century. Vigilance Committees and venadetta movements are always terrible for both sides. The Alianza Federal de Mercedes has been endeavoring to guide the Spanish people into an enlightened course of action towards a solution of this century old problem of these pueblos. But if the Alianza loses the confidence of the Spanish people, and can no longer guide them upon a proper course of action within the law to recover their rights, then the Anglos should realize that the failure of the Alianza is their failure also.

The Spanish people do not want or seek to integrate with the Anglos. They want to be left alone. The Spanish people do not want new laws enacted; but rather they want to have the laws already enacted adequately enforced, so that all people can receive equal protection of the law for what the law really is; . . . so that all men may have dignity before the law and in the community. The Spanish people have great pride of race. They remember that they are the descendents of the Conquistadores and of the ancient pioneers of New Mexico. They remember the glory of the Spanish Monarchy, that was a world power for more than three hundred years (twice the length of time of the existence of the United States of America). They also remember how they were allies of the United States of America in their revolutionary war for independence. And they also remember how they were repaid by the Yanquis, by being made welfare charges and given powdered milk to silence their protests and objections of being robbed of their birthrights and heritage. Yet the Spanish people of New Mexico have great pride and self-respect even in their condition of poverty, for they are not humbled or debased by their poverty. The Spanish people of New Mexico are a noble people, and their nobility of person is guaranteed to them by Ordinance 99 of the Laws of the Indies, and by Article IX of the Constitution of the United States of America, and by the 1848 Treaty of Guadalupe Hidalgo.

The reason why the Alianza is not seeking at this time, court decisions relative to this Spanish Land Grant question, is due to the fact that the Supreme Council of the Federal Alliance of Land Grants, has passed a resolution of non-confidence in the Courts of the State of New Mexico and of the United States of America. The reason behind this resolution is the history of these courts, a history of a century of gross denials of justice and of arbitrarily misconstruing of the law, and the inability of these courts to overcome their own corruption, by always invoking their "stare decisis" doctrine as a defense to their frauds and as a denial to give just compensation for their arbitrary confiscation of property. Another reason for the action of the Supreme Council of Federal Alliance of Land Grants is the relative low standards of knowledge of law required of the judges of these courts. How many of the judges of these courts are required to possess knowledge of the laws of the Indies, which is the local law of New Mexico? The answer to that question is, that none of the judges are required to know any of the Laws of the Indies, the local law of the State of New Mexico. How can people have confidence in such courts, wherein the judges are not required to have even a rudimentary knowledge of the local laws? The resolution of the Supreme Council of the Federal Alliance of Land Grants is well taken by the Alianza Federal de Mercedes and by the Heirs. For why should these pueblos forsake exercising their rights to their property, while running into a corrupt court with an ignorant judge, to decide upon a thing of paramount importance to them which has already been decided by the Court of Private Land Claims and the United States Congress. The only reason why the pueblos would go into one of these courts would be to obtain damages for the injuries caused to them by these trespassers and their aiders and abettors, namely, the State of New Mexico and the United States of America.

AN ATTACK ON
CHICANO MILITANTS

[No ethnic group
is solidly bound together merely by ties of race, for there are numerous other interests that tend to pull the members of any group
in different directions. Financial status, social position, professional
qualifications, or any one of a number of other loyalties may take
precedence over, or at least shape, personal attitudes toward one's
place within a minority group. Even those minorities currently
striving for civil, economic, and social rights—whether black Americans, Indians, or Puerto Ricans—are divided among themselves
over both means and ends. Every group has its militant associations
as well as its less radical organizations that are more willing to
work patiently through established channels. The following portions of a speech in the House of Representatives by Henry B.
Gonzalez, member of Congress from Texas, reveal that such divisions exist as well within the Mexican-American communities of
the United States. His remarks were made on April 22, 1969.]

An ethnic minority is in a peculiar position. I happen to be an
American of Spanish surname and of Mexican descent. As it happens my parents were born in Mexico and came to this country
seeking safety from a violent revolution. It follows that I, and

From *Congressional Record*, 91 Congress, 1 Session. April 22, 1969.

many other residents of my part of Texas and other Southwestern States—happen to be what is commonly referred to as a Mexican American. That label sums up most of the elements of a vast conflict affecting perhaps most of the 5 million southwestern citizens who happen to bear it. The individual finds himself in a conflict, sometimes with himself, sometimes with his family, sometimes with his whole world. What is he to be? Mexican? American? Both? How can he choose? Should he have pride and joy in his heritage, or bear it as a shame and sorrow? Should he live in one world or another, or attempt to bridge them both?

There is comfort in remaining in the closed walls of a minority society, but this means making certain sacrifices; but it sometimes seems disloyal to abandon old ideas and old friends; you never know whether you will be accepted or rejected in the larger world, or whether your old friends will despise you for making a wrong choice. For a member of this minority, like any other, life begins with making hard choices about personal identity. These lonely conflicts are magnified in the social crises so clearly evident all over the Southwest today. There are some groups who demand brown power, some who display a curious chauvinism, and some who affect the other extreme. There is furious debate about what one should be and what one should do. There is argument about what one's goals are, and how to accomplish them. I understand all this, but I am profoundly distressed by what I see happening today. I have said that I am against certain tactics, and against certain elements, and now I find yet more confusion. Mr. Speaker, the issue at hand in this minority group today is hate, and my purpose in addressing the House is to state where I stand: I am against hate and against the spreaders of hate; I am for justice, and for honest tactics in obtaining justice.

The question facing the Mexican-American people today is what do we want, and how do we get it?

What I want is justice. By justice I mean decent work at decent wages for all who want work; decent support for those who cannot support themselves; full and equal opportunity in employment, in education, in schools; I mean by justice the full, fair, and impartial protection of the law for every man; I mean by justice decent homes; adequate streets and public services; and I mean by justice no man being asked to do more than his fair share, but none being expected to do less. In short, I seek a justice that amounts to full, free, and equal opportunity for all; I believe in a justice that does not tolerate evil or evil doing; and I believe in a justice that is for all the people all the time.

I do not believe that justice comes only to those who want it; I am not so foolish as to believe that good will alone achieves good works. I believe that justice requires work and vigilance, and I am willing to do that work and maintain that vigilance.

I do not believe that it is possible to obtain justice by vague and empty gestures, or by high slogans uttered by orators who are present today and gone tomorrow. I do believe that justice can be obtained by those who know exactly what they seek, and know exactly how they plan to seek it. And I believe that justice can be obtained by those whose cause is just and whose means are honest.

It may well be that I agree with the goals stated by militants; but whether I agree or disagree, I do not now, nor have I ever believed that the end justifies the means, and I condemn those who do. I cannot accept the belief that racism in reverse is the answer for racism and discrimination; I cannot accept the belief that simple, blind, and stupid hatred is an adequate response to simple, blind, and stupid hatred; I cannot accept the belief that playing at revolution produces anything beyond an excited imagination; and I cannot accept the belief that imitation leadership is a substitute for the real thing. Developments over the past few months indicate that there are those who believe that the best answer for hate is hate in reverse, and that the best leadership is that which is loudest and most arrogant; but my observation is that arrogance is no cure for emptiness.

All over the Southwest new organizations are springing up; some promote pride in heritage, which is good, but others promote chauvinism, which is not; some promote community organization, which is good, but some promote race tension and hatred, which is not good; some seek redress of just grievances, which is good, but others seek only opportunities for self aggrandizement, which is not good.

All of these elements, good and bad, exist and all of them must be taken into account. The tragic thing is that in situations where people have honest grievances, dishonest tactics can prevent their obtaining redress; and where genuine problems exist careless or unthinking or consciously mean behavior can unloose forces that will create new problems that might require generations to solve. I want to go forward, not backward; I want the creation of trust, not fear; and I want to see Americans together, not apart. . . .

Unfortunately it seems that in the face of rising hopes and expectations among Mexican Americans there are more leaders with political ambitions at heart than there are with the interests of the poor at heart; they do not care what is accomplished in fact, as long as they can create and ride the winds of protest as far as possible. Thus we have those who play at revolution, those who make speeches but do not work, and those who imitate what they have seen others do, but lack the initiative and imagination to set forth actual programs for progress. . . .

Not long after the Southwest Council of La Raza opened for business, it gave $110,000 to the Mexican-American Unity Council of San Antonio; this group was apparently invented for the purpose of receiving the grant. Whatever the purposes of this group may be, thus far it has not given any assistance that I know of to bring anybody together; rather it has freely dispensed funds to people who promote the rather odd and I might say generally unaccepted and unpopular views of its directors. The Mexican-American Unity Council appears to specialize in creating still other organizations and equipping them with quarters, mimeograph machines and other essentials of life. Thus, the "unity council" has created a parents' association in a poor school district, a neighborhood council, a group known as the barrios unidos—or roughly, united neighborhoods—a committee on voter registration and has given funds to the militant Mexican-American Youth Organization—MAYO; it has also created a vague entity known as the "Universidad de los Barrios" which is a local gang operation. Now assuredly all these efforts may be well intended; however it is questionable to my mind that a very young and inexperienced man can prescribe the social and political organizations of a complex and troubled community; there is no reason whatever to believe that for all the money this group has spent, there is any understanding of what it is actually being spent for, except to employ friends of the director and advance his preconceived notions. The people who are to be united apparently don't get much say in what the "unity council" is up to.

As an example, the president of MAYO is not on the Unity Council payroll; but he is on the payroll of another Ford Foundation group, the Mexican-American Legal Defense Fund. He is an investigator but appears to spend his time on projects not related to his defense fund work. This handy device enables him to appear independent of Foundation activities and still make a living from the Foundation. Of course, his MAYO speeches denigrating the "gringos" and calling for their elimination by "killing them if all else fails" do little for unity, and nothing for law, but that bothers neither him nor his associates.

As another example, the "Universidad de los Barrios" is operated by a college junior and two others. The "universidad" has no curriculum and offers no courses, and the young toughs it works with have become what some neighbors believe to be a threat to safety and even life itself. After a murder took place on the doorstep of this place in January, witnesses described the place as a "trouble spot." Neighbors told me that they were terrified of the young men who hung around there, that their children had been threatened and that they were afraid to call the police. After the murder, the "dean" of this "university" said that he could not be there all the time and was not responsible for what happened while he was away. This might be true, but the general fear of the neighbors indicates that the "university" is not under reliable guidance at any time. I note that since I have made criticisms of this operation its leader says it is ready to enter a "second phase." I hope so.

Militant groups like MAYO regularly distribute literature that I can only describe as hate sheets, designed to inflame passions and reinforce old wounds or open new ones; these sheets spew forth racism and hatred designed to do no man good. The practice is defended as one that will build race pride, but I never heard of pride being built on spleen. There is no way to adequately describe the damage that such sheets can do; and there is no way to assess how minds that distribute this tripe operate. But, Mr. Speaker, I say that those who believe the wellsprings of hate can be closed as easily as they are opened make a fearful mistake; they who lay out poison cannot be certain that it will kill no one, or make no one ill, or harm no innocent bystander.

I have no way of knowing whether foundation money goes into the publication of these hate sheets, but I cannot see why the foundation would permit its money to support groups that published these sheets either, and I cannot see how good can come from the building of passions that have throughout the history of mankind brought about only distrust, fear, hate, and violence.

I fear very much that the Ford Foundation miscalculated in choosing those who have charge over their grant money.

We see a strange thing in San Antonio today; we have those who play at revolution and those who imitate the militance of others. We have a situation in Denver where the local leader said, "This is our Selma," and not a week later a situation in Del Rio where the local leader said, "This is our Selma." But try as they might, Selma was neither in Denver nor in Del Rio. We have those who cry "brown power" only because they have heard "black power" and we have those who yell "oink" or "pig" at police, only because they have heard others use the term. We have those who wear beards and berets, not because they attach any meaning to it, but because they have seen it done elsewhere. But neither fervor nor fashion alone will bring justice. Those who cry for justice, but hold it in contempt cannot win it for themselves or for anyone else. Those who prize power for its own sake will never be able to use it for any benefit but their own; and those who can only follow the fashions of protest will never understand what true protest is.

I believe that a just and decent cause demands a just and decent program of action. I believe that a just and decent cause can be undermined by those who believe that there is no decency, and who demand for themselves what they would deny others. I have stood against racists before, and I will do it again; and I have stood against blind passion before and I will gladly do so again. I pray that the day will come when all men know justice; and I pray that that day has not been put further away by the architects of discord, the prophets of violence. I pray that these great tasks that face us in the quest for justice and progress will be taken up by all men; and I know that when all is said and done and the tumult and shouting die down those who only spoke with passion cast aside, and those who spoke with conviction and integrity will still be around. I am willing to let time be my judge.

DELANO GRAPE WORKERS' BOYCOTT DAY PROCLAMATION

[Large-scale agriculture in the Southwest has been dependent for decades on migrant workers, great numbers of whom have been Mexican Americans or immigrants from Mexico. Poorly paid, badly housed and fed, and ill-educated, the migrants were among the most exploitable elements in the American labor market. Moving about as they did, they had no social or economic base on which to build remedies for their woes. Nor had they any political "pull" with which to seek relief. Of organizational strength they had little or none. Beginning in 1912 with the efforts of the Industrial Workers of the World to organize them, they have known mostly broken strikes, defeated unions, violence, and the unceasing cycle of their working days. Early in the 1960's, an apparent beginning was made toward a permanent organization among California's farm workers. In 1963, the National Farm Workers Association was founded—since transposed into the United Farm Workers Organizing Committee of the AFL-CIO. Of its leaders, the one who has gained nationwide attention is Cesar Chavez. In September, 1965, at Delano, California, the grape workers, under the aegis of the NFWA, went on strike for a higher wage. Arrayed against the grape workers were the giant corporate farming enterprises of the state. The AFL-CIO came in on the side of the farm workers. As the strike wore on, the grape workers sought to elicit national support by calling for a consumer boycott of grapes. As the strike went into its sixth year, some of the smaller growers signed contracts with the unions, but the larger corporations still held back until July, 1970, when contracts were finally signed with them. The corporations benefited from several factors: the great

From "Proclamation of the Delano Grape Workers for International Boycott Day, May 10, 1969," in: *El Malcriado*, April 15-30, 1969.

majority of farm workers are not yet union members; the federal government awards huge subsidies to the growers; and the U.S. Defense Department has increased purchases of grapes enormously in an effort to offset the effects of the consumer boycott. The selection reprinted below is the Boycott Day Proclamation issued by the grape workers for May 10, 1969.]

We, the striking grape workers of California, join on this International Boycott Day with the consumers across the continent in planning the steps that lie ahead on the road to our liberation. As we plan, we recall the footsteps that brought us to this day and the events of this day. The historic road of our pilgrimmage to Sacramento later branched out, spreading like the unpruned vines in struck fields, until it led us to willing exile in cities across this land. There, far from the earth we tilled for generations, we have cultivated the strange soil of public understanding, sowing the seed of our truth and our cause in the minds and hearts of men.

We have been farm workers for hundreds of years and pioneers for seven. Mexicans, Filipinos, Africans and others, our ancestors were among those who founded this land and tamed its natural wilderness. But we are still pilgrims on this land, and we are pioneers who blaze a trail out of the wilderness of hunger and deprivation that we have suffered even as our ancestors did. We are conscious today of the significance of our present quest. If this road we chart leads to the rights and reforms we demand, if it leads to just wages, humane working conditions, protection from the misuse of pesticides, and to the fundamental right of collective bargaining, if it changes the social order that relegates us to the bottom reaches of society, then in our wake will follow thousands of American farm workers. Our example will make them free. But if our road does not bring us to victory and social change, it will not be because our direction is mistaken or our resolve too weak, but only because our bodies are mortal and our journey hard. For we are in the midst of a great social movement, and we will not stop struggling 'til we die, or win!

We have been farm workers for hundreds of years and strikers for four. It was four years ago that we threw down our plowshares and pruning hooks. These Biblical symbols of peace and tranquility to us represent too many lifetimes of unprotesting submission to a degrading social system that allows us no dignity, no comfort, no peace. We mean to have our peace, and to win it without violence, for it is violence we would overcome—the subtle spiritual and mental violence of oppression, the violence subhuman toil does to the human body. So we went and stood tall outside the vineyards where we had stooped for years. But the tailors of national labor legislation had left us naked. Thus exposed, our picket lines were crippled by injunctions and harrassed by growers; our strike was broken by imported scabs; our overtures to our employers were ignored. Yet we knew the day must come when they would talk to us, *as equals.*

We have been farm workers for hundreds of years and boycotters for two. We did not choose the grape boycott, but we *had* chosen to leave our peonage, poverty and despair behind. Though our first bid for freedom, the strike, was weakened, we would not turn back. The boycott was the only way forward the growers left to us. We called upon our fellow men and were answered by consumers who said—as all men of conscience must—that they would no longer allow their tables to be subsidized by our sweat and our sorrow: They shunned the grapes, fruit of our affliction.

We marched alone at the beginning, but today we count men of all creeds, nationalities, and occupations in our number. Between us and the justice we seek now stand the large and powerful grocers who, in continuing to buy table grapes, betray the boycott their own customers have built. These stores treat their patrons' demands to remove the grapes the same way the growers treat our demands for union recognition—by ignoring them. The consumers who rally behind our cause are responding as we do to such treatment—with a boycott! They pledge to withhold their patronage from stores that handle grapes during the boycott, just as we withhold our labor from the growers until our dispute is resolved.

Grapes must remain an unenjoyed luxury for all as long as the barest human needs and basic human rights are still luxuries for farm workers. The grapes grow sweet and heavy on the vines, but they will have to wait while we reach out first for our freedom. The time is ripe for our liberation.

BILINGUAL EDUCATION FOR LA RAZA

[Ethnic groups that are for any reason cut off from full participation in the life of the nation usually, by way of compensation, fall back upon an almost nativistic emphasis on their racial and cultural heritage. This has been true of Indians, black Americans, and Puerto Ricans in recent years, as it was true of several immigrant groups earlier in the century. If this quest for dignity through self-awareness and ethnic pride is also foreclosed, a frustrating situation develops that is psychologically damaging to the group affected. Many Mexican-American communities of the Southwest have inherited just such a frustration through their local public school systems. While in the larger society full economic and social participation has been either difficult or openly denied, the heritage through which group pride and cohesiveness is passed from one generation to another has been ignored or despised in the schools that Mexican American children attend. The rule has been: the same education for all; and that education has been Anglo-devised and -oriented. The results for Mexican Americans have frequently been miseducation, hostility toward American society in general, high dropout rates, and a consequent failure to acquire the skills necessary to make a good living in a complex economy. To remedy the situation in the schools, a bilingual curriculum has been suggested. This article by Texas state senator and former teacher Joe Bernal illustrates some of the problems connected with the traditional approaches and points out the advantages of bilingualism.]

From "I Am Mexican-American," by Joe Bernal, in: *National Education Association Journal*, May 1969.

The average Mexican-American drops out of school by the seventh grade. In Texas, almost 80 percent of students with Spanish surnames drop out before completing high school. In California, 73.5 percent of the state's Mexican-American students do not complete high school.

Some incidents that took place in a Texas high school where 98 percent of the students are Mexican-American may help to explain the high dropout rate.

"I don't know what the fuss is all about," the teacher said to her senior civics class. The "fuss" the teacher referred to was a potential walkout by 300 to 500 students who had made certain demands on their school personnel.

Their demands were simple. They wanted to select the nominees to the student council instead of having school officials name the candidates. Because some students were interested in going to college, they wanted chemistry and trigonometry and sociology taught in their school and they wanted to be counseled about available college grants, scholarships, and work-study assistance. Finally, they wanted to be taught about the contributions their ancestors had made to the state of Texas.

The civics teacher could see no reason for their demands, particularly the last one. "After all," she said, "you're all Americans."

Anita, one of the school cheerleaders, stood up and disagreed. "I'm not American. I'm Mexican-American. You're white and I'm brown."

Anita sat down, sobbing. She had never spoken up to a teacher before. But she was on sure ground, she felt. In spite of her tears, she felt glad that she had said what she had. She *was* Mexican-American.

Like many other Mexican-American girls, Anita had been taught at home to regard her bronze color as a matter for pride. After all, Anita told herself, the appearance of the Virgin of Guadalupe to the lowly Indian, Juan Diego, showed without any doubt that the Virgin, *La Virgen Morena*, had Anita's Mexican-American coloring. But Mrs. Smith wouldn't know that.

Color, of course, has been only one source of misunderstanding between Mexican-American students and many of their Anglo teachers.

The Mexican-American has maintained his mother tongue longer than has any other minority group. Whereas most immigrants largely replaced their mother tongues with English in one or two generations, the Mexican-American has clung to Spanish for three, four, and five generations. This is due primarily to the proximity of the Mexican border. Spanish language TV, newspapers, radios, and movies are commonplace in the barrios.

Many unfortunate classroom situations have arisen because schools and teachers have refused to recognize that Spanish is the social language of their Mexican-American students.

"¿Traes un lapiz?" Ector had leaned over to Juan for a pencil.

"I've warned you about speaking Spanish in my class," the teacher said sharply. "Go see the vice-principal right now, Ector. I can't have any more of that murmuring in Spanish."

Mrs. Jones was irritated. Too many of her students kept lapsing into Spanish. There was a school policy against the use of Spanish and she had a vague idea that there was a law against speaking Spanish in the schools of Texas.

Ector, a six-foot varsity tackle, was active in all school activities and popular with his peers.

I didn't do anything wrong, Ector kept repeating to himself as he made his way to the office. I get A's in Spanish class but when I use Spanish to whisper to a friend in Mrs. Jones' room, I get sent to the office.

Ector arrived at the vice-principal's office. After explaining why he was there, Ector sat through a 15-minute lecture on why it is very American to speak English.

Mr. Neill's lecture, which he had often delivered before, mentioned the vague law that prohibited the use of the Spanish language in the schools.

"Well, Ector, you can take three licks and go back to class or go home and bring your parents," Mr. Neill stated after the lecture.

I know I'm as good an American as he is, Ector thought to himself. My brother is in Vietnam and I'll probably be going, too. Why does Mr. Neill have to tell me about speaking English and being an American? I can speak it, and I was born in the United States. Mr. Neill wants to whip me! He's worse than Mrs. Jones. My father hasn't given me a licking since I was eight. Now he will have to miss work to come to school because my mother can't speak English. He's going to be mad.

"Well, Ector, will it be three licks or your parents?" Mr. Neill asked.

"The three licks."

The school district has now changed its policy and Spanish can be used whenever it enhances a teaching situation. High schools there offer courses in sociology, chemistry, and many other college preparatory subjects formerly considered too difficult for "Mexican" children. The high school where the incidents took place has had a change of administration and the new principal, Mexican-American, is well aware that frequently schools have not been able to work successfully with Mexican-American students.

It is important for schools to recognize the advantages of being truly bilingual. The so-called language-educated person is skilled in reading, writing, listening, and speaking. Generally, the Mexican-American's Spanish language skill is limited to listening and speaking, sometimes to listening only. And yet the skill he has developed in speaking and/or understanding Spanish impairs his ability to become skilled in speaking and/or understanding English. Much of this can be traced to conflicting attitudes on the part of school people. His two languages are placed in constant conflict and it is difficult for him to achieve true proficiency in either.

In the classroom, much can be done to help Mexican-American students overcome this language conflict. The use of Spanish in the education process will help. In some cases Spanish can be used as the teaching language. For instance, bilinguists can be taught mathematics in Spanish. Admittedly, this will not improve their abilities in English, but at least their mathematical learning will not be held back because of their deficiency in English.

Intelligence tests, if they are to be regarded as such, that are not as heavily weighted on verbal ability should be developed, and until they are, teachers and counselors may inadvertently classify bright bilingual children as slow learners.

The schools need to consider the cultural and economic environment that surrounds the lower four-fifths of Mexican-American citizens. Having become a minority in the land that belonged to their ancestors, these people have existed in a system dominated by Anglo institutions—governmental, educational, and economic. They have expressed their rebellion against foreign institutions by withdrawing from the culture and clinging to their own Mexican-American traditions.

It is important that teachers show respect for the language and the culture their Mexican-American students cherish. Even if the teacher does not speak English and the class is being conducted in English, he should allow a child to express himself in Spanish when he becomes stuck for words. When the teacher wants to encourage students to speak English to one another, he should not put it on the basis of "You're American. Speak American." Instead, he should say something like, "Yes, Spanish is a great language—even Thomas Jefferson said so. You need English, though, to live and work in the United States."

Mexican-Americans have a proud heritage and they deserve to learn about it in school. They should study histories of Latin America. United States history ought to emphasize Mexican contributions. School libraries should make available biographies of Spanish-speaking leaders.

Students need to have the opportunity to learn about contemporary Mexican-Americans who are contributing to the American scene. Successful Spanish-speaking community leaders and college students should be brought into high schools to discuss career attainment. (Similarly, successful Mexican-American high school students should be urged to speak to elementary and junior high students to point out the advantages of remaining in school.)

Particularly helpful in adapting the schools to the needs of Mexican-American students will be for the teachers of these students to have special training—courses dealing with the education of the culturally different and economically deprived.

MEXICAN-AMERICAN CASUALTIES IN VIETNAM

[The war in Vietnam has taken a high toll among soldiers from low-income backgrounds. The cause has usually been traced to the exemptions built into the Selective Service System, exemptions that seem to favor the sons of middle- and upper-income families. Even when, in April, 1970, the President announced that most deferments would be ended, there was conjecture that this would have the effect of increasing the number of enlistments, particularly among those who wanted to take advantage of educational opportunities in the service, as well as of the prerogative of having more to say about where they would spend their service time and what they would do. At any rate, it seemed certain that the brunt of the fighting in American wars in Southeast Asia would continue to be borne by blacks, poor whites, Mexican Americans, and other minorities. This article by Professor Ralph Guzman of the University of California at Santa Cruz examines the casualty rate among Mexican-American soldiers for the first eight years of the Vietnam war.]

From *Congressional Record*, 91 Congress, 1 Session, October 8, 1969.

Mexican American military personnel have a higher death rate in Vietnam than all other servicemen. Analysis of casualty reports for two periods of time: one between January, 1961 and February, 1967 and the other between December, 1967 and March, 1969, reveals that a disproportionate number of young men with distinctive Spanish names do not return from the Southeast Asia theatre of war. Investigation also reveals that a substantial number of them are involved in high-risk branches of the service such as the U.S. Marine Corps.

In the southwest, where the majority of the people of Mexican American descent reside, Spanish named casualties remain consistently high in both periods. During the first period (January, 1961 to February, 1967) casualties with home addresses in the states of Arizona, California, Colorado, New Mexico, and Texas, totalled 1,631 deaths from all causes. Of these, 19.4 percent had distinctive Spanish names. In the second period (December, 1967, to March, 1969) there were 6,385 deaths. Casualties with distinctive Spanish names represented 19.0 percent of the total.

Casualty figures for each period are high when compared with the total Spanish surnamed population living in the southwestern United States. According to the 1960 report of the U.S. Bureau of the Census 11.8 percent of the total southwestern population had distinctive Spanish surnames and were, therefore, presumably Mexican American. The figures remain high when the comparison is based only on males of military age, meaning, individuals between age 17 and 36 years. Mexican Americans are estimated to represent 13.8 percent of this age group.

While these figures are estimates, they are sufficient to indicate others of magnitude. If one were to project birthrate, immigration, natural death and other factors, the statistical relationship would not be substantially different. It is probable that Spanish surnamed individuals would be slightly more numerous. It is significant that the percentages of Spanish named casualties for each period remains nearly constant at 19.0 percent.

War deaths by branch of service indicate that a great number of Mexican Americans choose high-risk duty. For example, during the first period, 23.3 percent of all southwest Marine Corps casualties had distinctive Spanish surnames. The Army, also supplies an important number of ground troops, 19.4 percent of the casualties reported between January, 1961, and February, 1967, had Spanish surnames and were presumably of Mexican parentage. In the later period, between December, 1967, and March, 1969, Spanish surnames represented 17.5 percent of all southwestern Army casualties.

When these figures are analyzed by state, California shows both the greatest number of total deaths from all causes and the greatest number of Mexican American casualties. During the first period 821 servicemen from California were killed. Of these, 15.0 percent had Spanish surnames, which is well above the 10.0 percent estimate of Spanish surnames in the total population of the state. During the second period 3,543 servicemen from California were reported as casualties in Vietnam, 14.8 percent had Spanish surnames. The State of Texas ranks second in total deaths and in Mexican American casualties. During the first period 554 Texans died in the war. Of these, 22.4 percent were presumably Mexican American. In the more recent periods, between December, 1967, and March, 1969, there were 1,921 deaths with home addresses in Texas. Casualties from Texas with Spanish surnames represented 25.2 percent of the total. In both California and Texas, Mexican American deaths are consistently high and disproportionate to the size of this minority group.

An adequate interpretation of the data is impossible without more information from official sources. For example, there is a gap between February, 1967 and December, 1967. Data were not available when this report was written. In a different sense, Spanish-surnamed servicemen may be over-represented in the Vietnam reports because they are over-represented among those who are drafted for military service and those who volunteer.

Historically, Mexican Americans have been a suspect, "foreign," minority. Like the Japanese Americans during World War II they have been under great pressure to prove loyalty to the United States. However, there are other reasons why Mexican Americans join the military. The reasons are several. One is the desire for status that the military life offers. Another is economic. Mexican Americans, particularly those from extremely poor families, help their families with their service allotments. Still others wish to prove their Americanism. Organizations like the American G.I. Forum, composed of ex-GI's of Mexican American identity, have long proclaimed the sizeable military contributions of the Mexican American soldier. According to the American G.I. Forum and other Mexican American groups, members of this minority have an impressive record of heroism in time of war. There is a concomitant number of casualties attending this Mexican American patriotic investment.

Only a relatively small number of Mexican Americans have been able to circumvent obligatory military service by attending college. Student deferments for residents of our southwestern *barrios* are scarce. The reason, of course, is the under-representation of Mexican Americans in institutions of higher learning. At the University of California, Mexican American students number less than one percent (1%) of the total student population of 97,000.

There are other factors that motivate Mexican Americans to join the Armed Forces, some may be rooted in the inherited culture of these people while others may be more deeply imbedded in poverty and social disillusion. Whatever the real explanation, we do know with a high degree of certainty that Mexican Americans are over-represented in the casualty reports from Vietnam and under-represented in the graduating classes of our institutions of higher learning.

REIES TIJERINA'S LETTER FROM THE SANTA FE JAIL

[Reies Lopez Tijerina was the founder and, until October, 1969, the director of the *Alianza de los Pueblos Libres* (Alliance of Free City-States), organized to open up the question of the old Spanish and Mexican land grants. During his rather flamboyant career in New Mexico, Tijerina had several encounters with the law. The most famous of these was the "courthouse raid" at Tierra Amarilla on June 5, 1967, to make a citizen's arrest of the state district attorney. Charges of kidnapping and assault to commit murder were brought against him, but, in the fall of 1968, a jury found him innocent. In June, 1969, he was arrested on charges of destruction of federal property and assaulting two officials. He was tried and convicted of the assault charges and subsequently sentenced to jail. His followers contend that frequent brushes with the police are not because of lawbreaking by members of the *Alianza* but are the result of a conspiracy by public officials and law-enforcement agencies to get Tijerina out of the public eye and to destroy the *Alianza*. On August 15–17, 1969, while Tijerina was in jail awaiting trial to begin on September 22, he wrote a long open letter to his followers, part of which is reprinted here.]

From *El Grito Del Norte*, September 26, 1969.

From my cell block in this jail I am writing these reflections. I write them to my people, the Indo-Hispanos, to my friends among the Anglos, to the agents of the federal government, the state of New Mexico, the Southwest, and the entire Indo-Hispano world— "Latin America."

I write to you as one of the clearest victims of the madness and racism in the hearts of our present-day politicians and rulers.

At this time, August 17, I have been in jail for 65 days—since June 11, 1969, when my appeal bond from another case was revoked by a federal judge. I am here today because I resisted an assassination attempt led by an agent of the federal government—an agent of all those who do not want anybody to speak out for the poor, all those who do not want Reies Lopez Tijerina to stand in their way as they continue to rob the poor people, all those many rich people from outside the state with their summer homes and ranches here whose pursuit of happiness depends on theivery, all those who have robbed the people of their land and culture for 120 years. . . .

What is my real crime? As I and the poor people see it, especially the Indo-Hispanos, my only crime is UPHOLDING OUR RIGHTS AS PROTECTED BY THE TREATY OF GUADALUPE HIDALGO which ended the so-called Mexican-American War of 1846–48. My only crime is demanding the respect and protection of our property, which has been confiscated illegally by the federal government. Ever since the treaty was signed in 1848, our people have been asking every elected president of the United States for a redress of grievances. Like the Black people, we too have been criminally ignored. Our right to the Spanish land grant pueblos is the real reason why I am in prison at this moment.

Our cause and our claim and our methods are legitimate. Yet even after a jury in a court of law acquitted me last December, they still call me a violent man. But the right to make a citizens arrest, as I attempted to make that day on Evans, is not a violent right. On the contrary, it is law and order—unless the arrested person resists or flees to avoid prosecution. No honest citizen should avoid a citizen's arrest.

This truth is denied by the conspirators against the poor and by the press which they control. There are also the Silent Contributors. The Jewish people accused the Pope of Rome for keeping silent while Hitler and his machine persecuted the Jews in Germany and other countries. I support the Jews in their right to accuse those who contributed to Hitler's acts by their SILENCE. By the same token, I denounce those in New Mexico who have never opened their mouths at any time to defend or support the thousands who have been killed, robbed, raped of their culture. I don't know of any church or Establishment organization or group of elite intellectuals that has stood up for the Treaty of Guadalupe-Hidalgo. We condemn the silence of these groups and individuals and I am sure that, like the Jewish people, the poor of New Mexico are keeping a record of the Silence which contributes to the criminal conspiracy against the Indo-Hispano in New Mexico.

As I sit in my jail cell in Santa Fe, capitol of New Mexico, I pray that all the poor people will unite to bring justice to New Mexico. My cell block has no day light, no ventilation of any kind, no light of any kind. After 9 P.M., we are left in a dungeon of total darkness. Visiting rules allow only 15 minutes per week on Thursdays from 1 to 4 P.M. so that parents who work cannot visit their sons in jail. Yesterday a 22-year-old boy cut his throat. Today, Aug. 17, two young boys cut their wrists with razor blades and were taken unconscious to the hospital. My cell is dirty and there is nothing to clean it with. The whole cell block is hot and suffocating. All my prison mates complain and show a daily state of anger. But these uncomfortable conditions do not bother me, for I have a divine dream to give me strength: the happiness of my people.

I pray to God that all the Indo-Hispano people will awake to the need for unity, and to our heavenly and constitutional responsibility for fighting peacefully to win our rights. Already the rest of the Indo-Hispano world—Latin America—knows of our struggle. It is too late to keep the story of our land struggle from reaching the ears of the Indo-Hispano world. All the universities of Latin America knew about our problems when Rockefeller went there last summer. Will Latin America ignore our cry from here in New Mexico and the Southwest? Times have changed and the spirit of the blood is no longer limited by national or continental boundaries.

The Indo-Hispano world will never trust the United States as long as this government occupies our land illegally. The honest policy of the United States will have to begin at home, before Rockefeller can go to Latin America again to sell good relations and friendship. Our property, freedom and culture must be respected in New Mexico, in the whole Southwest, before the Anglo can expect to be trusted in South America, Mexico and Canada.

This government must show its good faith to the Indo-Hispano in respect to the Treaty of Guadalupe-Hidalgo and the land question by forming a presidential committee to investigate and hold open hearings on the land question in the northern part of New Mexico. We challenge our own government to bring forth and put all the facts on the conference table. We have the evidence to prove our claims to property as well as to the cultural rights of which we have been deprived. WE ARE RIGHT—and therefore ready and willing to discuss our problems and rights under the Treaty with the Anglo federal government in New Mexico or Washington, D.C., directly or through agents.

This government must also reform the whole educational structure in the Southwest before it is too late. It should begin in the northern part of New Mexico, where 80% of the population are Indo-Hispanos, as a pilot center. If it works here, then a plan can be developed based on that experience in the rest of the state and wherever the Indo-Hispano population requires it.

Because I know WE ARE RIGHT, I have no regrets as I sit in my jail cell. I feel very, very proud and happy to be in jail for the reason that I am. June 8 in Coyote could have been my last day on earth. My life was spared by God, and to be honored by that miracle at Coyote will keep me happy for many years to come. I am sure that not one of my prison days is lost. Not one day has been in vain. While others are free, building their personal empires, I am in jail for defending and fighting for the rights of my people. Only my Indo-Hispano people have influenced me to be what I am. I am what I am, for my brothers.

CHICANO NATIONALISM: THE KEY TO UNITY FOR LA RAZA

[Rodolfo "Corky" Gonzales is one of the leaders of the Chicano movement in the West and a strong proponent of nationalism for La Raza. During the 1960's, while working to better the economic conditions of Mexican Americans, he moved gradually from a moderate to a revolutionary position on social issues as a result of the endless frustrations that came from trying to work "within the system." Now he speaks freely of self-determination, nationalism, *machismo*, and the need to "use more forceful methods" to gain La Raza's goals. In 1965, he founded the *Crusade for Justice* in Denver as a medium through which the demands of the Chicano movement could be articulated. Their demands, including better housing, educational opportunities, jobs, and land reform, are similar to the demands made by all civil rights groups, militant and nonmilitant. For Gonzales, the key to attaining these goals is in the laying of an adequate power base, and he has come to put heavy reliance on nationalism and political separatism among the Chicanos. His point of view was well enunciated during a symposium on "Chicano liberation" at Hayward, California, on November 13 and 14, 1969.]

From "What Political Road for the Chicano Movement?" in: *The Militant*, March 30, 1970.

What are the common denominators that unite the people? The key common denominator is nationalism. When I talk about nationalism, some people run around in their intellectual bags, and they say this is reverse racism. The reverse of a racist is a humanitarian. I specifically mentioned what I felt nationalism was. Nationalism becomes *la familia*. Nationalism comes first out of the family, then into tribalism, and then into the alliances that are necessary to lift the burden of all suppressed humanity.

Now, if you try to climb up a stairway, you have to start with the first step. You can't jump from the bottom of this floor to the top of those bleachers. If you can, then you must be "super-*macho*." (I don't talk about super-man.) But, you can't, so you start using those tools that are necessary to get from the bottom to the top. One of these tools is nationalism. You realize that if Chavez, or any popular figure in the Mexicano scene decides to run, and if he ran for any party, as popular as he is, then out of nationalism we would even vote for an idiot. If his name was Sanchez, if his name was Gonzalez, you would walk in and vote for him, whether you know him or not, because you are nationalistic. And we have elected too many idiots in the past out of nationalism, right?

Now, let's take that common denominator, that same organizing tool of nationalism, and utilize it to work against the system. Let's use it to work against the two parties that I say are like an animal with two heads eating out of the same trough, that sits on the same boards of directors of the banks and corporations, that shares in the same industries that make dollars and profits off wars. To fight this thing, you look for the tools.

Now, if Tony is a socialist, if my brother here is an independent, if my sister is a Republican—she might hit me later—if one of the others is a Democrat and one is a communist, and one from the Socialist Labor Party, what do we have in common politically? Nothing. We've been fighting over parties across the kitchen table, wives are Republicans and husbands are Democrats, sometimes, and we argue over a bunch of garbage. And the same Republicans and Democrats are having cocktails together at the same bar and playing golf together and kissing each other behind the scenes.

So you tell me then, what is the common denominator that will touch the *barrio*, the *campos* and the *ranchitos*? Are we going to go down there with some tremendous words of intellectualism which they cannot relate to, when they relate on the level of, "We need food. We need health care for our children. I need someone to go down to juvenile court with my son. There is no job for my husband." And the revolution of 15 or 20 years from now is not going to feed a hungry child today. . . .

All right, how do we start this? We start it and call it an independent Chicano political organization. We can use it as Tony mentioned also, under the FCC code, we can use it as a forum to preach and teach. We can gain the same amount of radio and TV time as any phony candidate. We proved it in Colorado. I ran for mayor as an independent, and I campaigned two weeks. Two weeks, because we were busy directing a play and busy in civil rights actions. But, we had the same amount of time on TV as anybody else, and on radio. We were able to start to politicize people. We were able to start to tell about an idea. We were able, even, to sue the mayor and the top candidates for violating the city charter, for spending more money than the city provided for under its constitution. We had that mayor and the most powerful Republicans and Democrats sitting on their asses down in the courtroom. Our method was to take them to court, to take them to task, to show the public that they were corrupt. And we proved that they were liars, over and over again.

We must start off by creating the structure—the *concilio*—by calling a congress sometime this spring, bringing together all those people that believe that it can be done. We understand that when we organize in an area where we are a majority, we can control. Where we are a minority, we will be a pressure group. And we will be a threat.

We understand the need to take action in the educational system. We understand that we need actions such as the "blow-outs," because the youth are not afraid of anything. Because the youth are ready to move. The whole party will be based on the actions of the young, and the support of the old.

Secondly, in the communities where we are a majority, we can then control and start to reassess taxes, to start charging the exploiters for what they have made off our people in the past. You can also incorporate the community to drive out the exploiters, to make them pay the freight for coming into the community, and sign your own franchises. You can de-annex a community as easily as they annex a *barrio* and incorporate it. You can create your own security groups, and place a gun here to protect the people, not to harass them, but to protect them from the Man who is going to come in from the outside. You can also create your own economic base by starting to understand that we can share instead of cut each others' throats.

Now what are the tools? We said nationalism, which means that we have to be able to identify with our past, and understand our past, in order that we can dedicate ourselves to the future, dedicate ourselves to change. And we have to understand what humanism really is. We can tie the cultural thing into it, but we also have to tie in the political and the economic. We tie these things together, and we start to use the common denominator of nationalism.

Now for those Anglo supporters, don't get up-tight. For the Black brothers, they are practicing the same thing right now. And we understand it and respect it. And we are for meaningful coalitions with organized groups.

We have to start to consider ourselves as a nation. We can create a congress or a *concilio*. We can understand that we are a nation of *Aztlan*. We can understand and identify with Puerto Rican liberation. We understand and identify with Black liberation. We can understand and identify with white liberation from this oppressing system once we organize around ourselves.

Where they have incorporated themselves to keep us from moving into their neighborhoods, we can also incorporate ourselves to keep them from controlling our neighborhoods. We have to also understand economic revolution, of driving the exploiter out. We have to understand political change. And we have to understand principle. And the man who says we can do it within the system—who says, "Honest, you can, look at me, I have a $20,000-a-year job"—he's the man who was last year's militant and this year's OEO employee [Office of Economic Opportunity]. And now he's keeping his mouth shut and he ain't marching any more. We have to understand that he is not a revolutionary, that he's a counter-revolutionary. He's not an ally, he becomes an enemy because he's contaminated.

You can't walk into a house full of disease with a bottle full of mercurochrome and cure the disease without getting sick yourself. That's what we say about the lesser of the two evils. If four grains of arsenic kill you, and eight grains of arsenic kill you, which is the lesser of two evils? You're dead either way.

We have to understand that liberation comes from self-determination, and to start to use the tools of nationalism to win over our *barrio* brothers, to win over the brothers who are still believing that *machismo* means getting a gun and going to kill a communist in Vietnam because they've been jived about the fact that they will be accepted as long as they go get themselves killed for the *gringo* captain; who still think that welfare is giving them something and don't understand that the one who is administering the welfare is the one that's on welfare, because, about 90 percent of the welfare goes into administration; and who still do not understand that the war on poverty is against the poor, to keep them from reacting.

We have to win these brothers over, and we have to do it by action. Whether it be around police brutality, the educational system, whether it be against oppression of any kind—you create an action, you create a blow-out, and you see how fast those kids get politicized. Watch how fast they learn the need to start to take over our own communities. And watch how fast they learn to identify with ourselves, and to understand that we need to create a nation.

We can create a thought, an idea, and we can create our own economy. You don't hear of any "yellow power" running around anywhere. Because they base their power around their church, their house, their community. They sell Coca Cola, but their profits go to their own people, you see, so that they have an economic base. We are strangers in our own church. We have got *gachupin* [traditional term of contempt for Spaniards who ruled Mexico for 400 years] priests from Spain in our communities, telling us *vamos a hechar unos quatros pesos en la canasta* [let's throw four pesos in the collection dish]. And then he tells you, "I'm your religious leader," and he tries to tell you how to eat, where to go, who to sleep with and how to do it right—while he's copping everything else out. You know, we're tired of this kind of leadership.

You have to understand that we can take over the institutions within our community. We have to create the community of the Mexicano here in order to have any type of power. As much as the young ladies have created power in their own community. But they have to share it with the rest of us. They have to be able to bring it together. And we are glad when they sit down instead of retreating. It means that we're all one people. It means that we're all one *Raza* and that we will work together and we will walk out of here in a positive fashion.

WHO IS
LA RAZA?

[In a speech on bilingual education given at Chicago in February, 1970, Armando M. Rodriquez, director of the Office for Spanish-speaking American Affairs of the federal Department of Health, Education and Welfare, attempted to answer the question: "Who is La Raza?" One becomes aware, in reading his remarks, that La Raza is not wholly an ethnic grouping. It is also, at least partially, a matter of cultural heritage. Perhaps the term is rendered best, and most simply, as "my people"—the socio-ethnic community in which I have my roots. Certainly the concept of La Raza is in part a defense mechanism used by people who want very much just to be Americans, but in their own way and not according to all the prescriptions of the larger Anglo society. Members of La Raza accept that there are different patterns of culture, but they assert that there is nothing wrong with difference, either in language or life style. They assert the virtues of cultural pluralism instead of a "melting pot" in which all variety is blended into a homogeneous mass. The opening paragraphs of Rodriguez's speech are reprinted here.]

For nearly three years I have traveled back and forth across our country as a representative of our national government, spurring

From "Bilingual Education—Profile '70," by Armando M. Rodriguez, in: Congressional Record, 91 Congress, 2 Session, February 26, 1970.

both governmental and private agencies to direct some of their resources to the Spanish-speaking population. In doing so I have found our people—Puerto Ricans, Cubans, and Mexican-Americans —to be regarded in some communities as non-existent, in others with fear, in others with respect, and in others with suspicion. I also found that this population is referred to as Spanish-Americans, Latinos, Hispanos, Spanish-Speaking Americans, Spanish-Surnamed Americans, Americans of Spanish or Mexican Descent, Los Batos Locos and a number of other names I choose not to repeat here tonight. But whatever we are called, we are La Raza, a name that unites us linguistically and culturally.

I have also found out that there are approximately 10 million of us, that more than 80% of us live in urban communities like Chicago, and that more than 70% of us are in the three states of New York, Texas and California. I also found that the states of Michigan, Illinois, Indiana, New Jersey, Ohio, Wisconsin and Iowa are the fastest area for settlement of Spanish speakers in the country outside of New York, Texas and California. I also found that the Spanish speaking American population is the youngest in the country with more than 50% under age 20. I found that our educational attainment—based on 1960 census figures—is the lowest in the country for any distinctive ethnic or racial group (in Texas it barely reaches the 5th year of school); that the dropout rate of the Spanish speakers is the highest in the country, exceeding 50% in some of the high schools in New York, Chicago, Los Angeles and San Antonio. That more than 80% of the youngsters from Mexican American families starting school in Texas do not finish. That in California less than 1% of the students enrolled in the seven campuses of the University of California are Spanish-Surname—how many of those are Puerto Rican or Mexican American, we do not know. This is the higher education situation in a state where 14% of the public school enrollment is Spanish-Surnamed. A shocking statistic is that the Mexican-American enrollment at California State College in Los Angeles, located in the heart of East Los Angeles, a barrio of more than 400,000 Mexican Americans, dropped almost 50% last year. These are some frightening statistics that tell a little about the second largest minority in our country.

Who is La Raza when you strip away the educational and economic chains that bind him? For the most part, he is still an alien, unknown in his own land. This is true even in the Southwest, where the cultural heritage is a living reminder of the part that Spain and Mexico played in forming the character of this nation. The Mexican is pictured on the one hand as the peon, who, hat in hand, holds the reins for John Wayne in the movies, or is the Frito Bandito on T.V. On the other hand, he is the glamorous *hidalgo*, the ambassador of good will for the city of San Diego and a participant in the Rose Bowl Parade. Between the fanciful extremes of the peon and the hidalgo is La Raza. Probably the most telling observation ever to be printed about us came from the pages of *Newsweek* (May 23, 1966): "We're the best kept secret in America."

I would like to say here today that the secret is now out. We are fast becoming America's most promising human catalyst for the creation of a democratic society where cultural heritage and language assets are prime instruments in the acceptance of human diversity as major national goal. I refute that television report in April of last year that identified La Raza as "The Invisible Minority." If the producers could sense what I feel and see in my travels, La Raza would be identified as the "dynamic and responsible minority." The old image that the Puerto Rican or the Mexican American is neither Puerto Rican, Mexican nor American: he is suspended between two cultures, neither of which claims him, is rapidly disappearing. Tomorrow's Puerto Rican and Mexican American— those forceful, creative, bold youngsters under 25 will be the American citizens who successfully retain and cherish their cultural heritage and simultaneously participate fully in the larger cultural environment of our society. And I suggest that the frontier of this movement will be found in the urban areas of our cities throughout this country. Who is the Puerto Rican or the Mexican American? He is that unique individual who has suffered from cultural isolation, language rejection, economic and educational inequalities, but who has now begun to take those instruments of oppression and turn them into instruments of change. Bilingual and bicultural education in our public schools will be a reality very shortly. The national moral and legal commitment of our federal government for educational programs that reflect the culture and language of the students will be a common part of curriculums throughout the country. And to a great extent this sweeping movement must be credited to the patience and perseverance of our youth—cultural qualities that for so many years was termed, "passivity."

It is this sweeping movement, vigorously enunciated by the Youth Movement, that will destroy an environment now existing that says to us and particularly the youngster in school, that the only Americanism is that which permeates the textbooks with little or no reference to positive historical accomplishments unless achieved by the Anglo. Mexican American and Puerto Rican children can and will do well scholastically, but only in schools, including colleges, that not only emphasize the Anglo way of life, but also fosters pride in the Mexican American and Puerto Rican for his origin, history, culture, and bilingual background.

A high school girl from the barrio in East Los Angeles said: "We look for others like ourselves in these history books, for something to be proud of for being a Mexican, and all we see in books, magazines, films, and TV shows are stereotypes of a dark, dirty, smelly man with a tequila bottle in one hand, a dripping taco in the other, a serape wrapped around him, and a big sombrero."

This, my friends, is not the hispano here or anywhere in the country. I ask that all of you here join me in a fight to eradicate such stereotypes from every aspect of our media. The negative images of La Raza in advertising on TV is one of the most destructive forces now existing for the creation of a society where cultural and human diversity is an imperative thread in the strength of the total fabric. This fight must be won before freedom for all of us can be realized. I would like to quote from three different sources which reveal the deep feeling of pride, dignity and concern so important for all of us, not because it is good or true but because these feelings exist especially among our youth who fight for self-identity and positive image recognition.

"Who am I?" asks a young Mexican American high school student. "I am a product of myself. I am a product of you and my ancestors. We came to California long before the Pilgrims landed at Plymouth Rock. We settled California the Southwestern part of the United States including the states of Arizona, New Mexico, Colorado and Texas. We built the missions, we cultivated the ranches. We were at the Alamo in Texas, both inside and outside. You know we owned California—that is, until gold was found here. Who am I? I'm a human being. I have the same hopes that you do, the same fears, the same drives, same desires, same concerns, same abilities; and I want the same chance that you have to be an individual. Who am I? In reality I am who you want me to be."

This same concern for dignity and respect is found in the poetry of Alberto Alurista:

> "Mis ojos hinchados
>   flooded with lagrimas
> de bronce
> melting on the cheek bones
> of my concern
>   razgos indigenos
> the scars of history on my face
>   and the veins of my body
> that aches
>   vomito sangre
> y lloro libertad
>   I do not ask for freedom
> I am freedom"

And this freedom means education. And this freedom means a bigger share in the economic and political pot.

THE CHICANO MOVEMENT

[Militancy among Mexican Americans, as among other ethnic groups, is based on legitimate demands for participation in American life. Youth is generally in the vanguard of such movements. However, not only the young Mexican Americans but also the disadvantaged of every age are seeking access to the opportunities the majority of citizens take for granted. But the Chicano movement is more than an economic- and political-rights campaign. It is also an assertion by Mexican Americans that they are "somebody," that their language and heritage mean something, and that they have made a contribution to life in the United States. In this article, Ysidro Ramon Macias outlines the history and aims of "Chicanismo." Macias is editor of the Chicano magazine *El Pocho Che*, published in Oakland, California.]

Although no one has categorically determined how the term "Chicano" was born, it is generally accepted that the word came from northern Mexico. It is here that burritos originated, where menudo, mole, pozole, and many other foods prepared by Chicanos are made in a manner distinct from that of greater southern Mexico.

From "The Chicano Movement," by Ysidro Ramon Macias, in: *Wilson Library Bulletin*, March 1970.

It is also in northern Mexico, because of its proximity to the United States, that the language academically called "Calo" and locally named "Pocho" came into being. Perhaps the citizens of Chihuahua, a city and state of northern Mexico, took the "Chi" from Chihuahua and added the "cano" from Mexicano to arrive at Chicano.

Common in the United States from about the 1930s, the term was used by the Mexicans long before "Mexican-American" and was generally understood to be an intimate name recognizing a particular status not entirely Mexican nor entirely U.S. American.

The term is nothing new, as is popularly supposed. In fact, it commanded significant national attention during the so-called "zoot suit riots" in Los Angeles in the early 1940s. Its use was revived about 1965 at the beginning of the Delano strike and continues to increase, helping to build a definite civil rights movement and philosophy. Actually, the concept behind the Chicano movement goes farther than that of civil rights, since many Chicanos want either a complete revision of the United Sttaes political and economic system or separation from it.

Among the salient characteristics of the Chicano are his self-awareness and self-respect, and a language at least the equal if not superior to the Anglo's. He rejects the notion that he must subjugate his heritage in order to rise within American society. Instead he presents the Anglo with the alternative to accept him as an equal. If the Anglo refuses to allow him his self-respect, as is often the case, the Chicano now seeks to establish political and economic hegemony over his communities in order to control them and perpetuate his existence as a distinct entity.

The Chicano is becoming more isolated from Anglo society than ever before because of the Anglo's refusal to accept him. The Chicano asks himself: "Why should I try to prove myself to the Anglos? I will be my own man, respecting my heritage. If accepted as such, it's well; if not, that's all right too."

The Chicano is aware of the history of Mexican peoples in this country. He recognizes that Mexicans fought against Santa Ana at the Alamo; that twenty percent of the G.I.s on the front lines in Vietnam are Chicanos, who comprise but three percent of the total population of this country; that educationally, politically, and socially, gross injustices have been perpetrated against Chicano communities by the dominant Anglo society.

The spirit of "compadrazgo" [social ties between parents and god-parents] is part of the Mexican heritage. This sense of personal responsibility or personal commitment is another characteristic that distinguishes the Chicano. Rejecting the Puritan ethic of self-improvement above all else, the Chicano believes that just because he "makes" it, it does not make the system valid to all Chicanos. He recognizes that he is part of a brotherhood, that he has an obligation to work for the betterment of his people in whatever way he can.

Accordingly, he automatically devotes a portion of his lifetime energies to work exclusively for the Chicano communities.

The concept of "Chicanismo" has not yet been precisely defined, but it is based on self-awareness and compadrazgo, enriched by the peculiar qualities of the Chicano, or Mexican, heritage. Chicanos point out that they are heirs to a great mixture of cultures, the Indian and the Spanish; and added to this Mexican culture is the experience of living in an English-speaking country, which is continuously endeavoring to erase the Mexican heritage.

Chicanos now accept their unique character as positive and beautiful, no longer as inferior and vulgar forms of expression and behavior. Further, no longer does the color of a Chicano's skin determine his status within his community in the same manner as before. The lighter-skinned Mexican is no longer the favored son; quite the contrary, the darker Indian type is now idealized as are other characteristics and customs which derive from our Indian heritage.

The Chicano movement seeks to play educational roles in three areas: educating the people (Chicanos) regarding their political and economic status; educating Chicanos in their heritage, history, and customs, thereby increasing their self-awareness, pride, and effectiveness as individuals; and promoting institutionalized education within the communities, where little enthusiasm for education existed before.

Two further educational objectives of the movement should be mentioned in this context. The first is to promote the use of "Pocho" (a mixture of Spanish, English, and some unique elements) in literary circles. Chicano and Latino artists have now recognized Pocho, with its Pochismos (idioms of Pocho), as a truly artistic and expressive bastard tongue. Moreover, it expresses the Chicanos better than either Spanish or English and should be preserved and expanded. Accordingly, throughout the great Aztlan (U.S. Southwest), Chicanos express themselves daily in their native tongue, Pocho, and continually seek new ways of reviving, maintaining, and enriching the Chicano culture.

The second goal is that of actively seeking greater recognition for our Mexican culture, language, and traditions, and working for their preservation. This aim is most fundamental; within it one may find the basis for our actions, outlook on life, familial and societal relationships—everything that goes into making us what we are. It is our blood that makes us what we are, and any attempt to apply a tourniquet would be suicidal.

The problems that beset the Chicano community in education are enormous. With the exception of the native American, perhaps no other ethnic group has had such a poor record of achieving normal educational levels. Part of the difficulty may be that, among Mexicans, there appears to have been a general lack of family motivation toward education, especially higher education. When one learns that due to his economic condition the Chicano is not apt to think about education, but is concerned primarily with existing for the moment, and that his lineage from Mexico is predominantly from peasant stock with little or no education itself, it is not difficult to understand why the Chicano communities were not preoccupied with education. Fortunately, the movement has provided tremendous impetus for Chicanos to secure better and higher levels of education.

The language barrier has been and continues to be a nagging educational dilemma. As stated before, many Chicanos are comfortable when speaking Pocho. This tongue serves to identify the Chicano from the Anglo and the Mexican national. When the Pocho-speaking Chicano confronts the English-speaking situation in the schools, however, the result is usually anxiety, frustration, anger. One positive step in the direction of alleviating this condition is teaching English as a second language at the elementary level. Remedies of this kind will, in time, reduce the serious and unjust disparities in levels of education that persist. To cite one example, educational attainment in California for Chicanos is eight years of schooling, compared with ten years for Blacks and twelve years for Anglos.

Greater mobility upward into higher education is sorely needed by Chicanos and is definitely being sought by the movement. Although the means that our own and other Third World communities are employing to reach that end are not generally approved by white America, such mobility is being grudgingly yielded in an increasing number of instances. In order for Chicanos to attain this greater mobility, two basic needs must be satisfied; first, more funds to insure that our qualified brothers and sisters will be able to enroll in the schools in which they are accepted. The reactionary onslaughts launched by Reagan, Rafferty, and Co. in California, plus the decision to discontinue the Educational Opportunity Program, have created a critical situation with regard to the ability of our communities to support Chicano students. The second need is for a more valid and just method of determining intelligence, for the currently used IQ tests are geared to people of white middle-class backgrounds.

It is truly depressing and frustrating for the Chicano that low quality education, including inferior teachers, counselors, schools, and books, all find homes in the "barrio," the Latin neighborhood. These second-rate educational vehicles and personnel continue to strangle and hold back the Chicano communities.

A typical example of racism and segregation is the tracking system employed in California's high schools. Under this system—which features two levels: college preparatory and general curriculum—Chicanos and other minority students are usually placed in general curriculum, regardless of their grades. This program basically prepares the student to graduate from high school and secure manual employment. He is almost thoroughly discouraged from pursuing his studies at a college; instead he is told that he has "vocational aptitude."

In this manner, educational institutions and their curricula perpetuate the Anglo superiority myth; they program Chicanos into mediocre jobs or into dropping out before graduation and discourage college or other forms of higher education for them. Such schools do not deal effectively with the cultural differences of Chicanos, but instead insist on adoption of Anglo-Saxon mores and idiom.

There is certainly great need for a better understanding and consideration of our cultural differences by the dominant Anglo system. For too long it has been 'chic' in the United States to speak a different language or to display differing cultural patterns as long as neither the language nor the culture is Spanish or Spanish-derived. This racist and arrogant view must be eliminated.

In order to correct these injustices and shortcomings, some basic social changes are essential. The Chicano movement, in the manner of other minority movements in the United States, is forcing education to look closer at itself, to make important changes in the social sciences in order to relate more realistically and comprehensively to contemporary society. For too long the archaic, ivory-tower social sciences have been turning out "professionals" who in reality are nothing more than bookish robots with little or no understanding of minority community problems. Now, through political and social pressure, often producing either ethnic studies courses or changes in existing curricula, the social sciences are beginning to change for the better.

Chicano or La Raza Studies may appear in many forms ranging from high school to university levels. In addition to enabling, in fact compelling, the social sciences to relate to the minority communities, Chicano Studies perform an even more important function: teaching the Chicano student the story of Mexico and Mexicans in its true historical context, not as viewed through the eyes of a biased and racist Anglo historian, author, or teacher.

The movement has also given rise to Chicano newspapers, magazines, literature, and textbooks. It has endeavored to reach all levels of the community, including the non-English speaking, the *pintos* (convicts or ex-cons), *tecatos* (drug users, usually of hard drugs), and the *Vatos locos* ("street" persons).

Chicano student groups have initiated various programs in the barrios designed to bring the schools and the community closer together, such as courses in political science taught to the younger Chicanos. Probably the most important function of the Chicano student groups up to this time, however, has been simply to involve the community in meetings, programs and action.

As an educational vehicle, libraries are almost non-functional in our Chicano communities. At best, the barrio is served by a branch library which is almost always poorly stocked in books, magazines, and reference materials, and is unimaginative in general decor. Furthermore, these libraries are staffed by Anglo women, who may want to understand the needs of the barrio youth but cannot evoke any trust from them. Libraries are generally viewed by our communities as extensions of the local schools, and since the schools are a negative and uncomfortable experience, the same feeling is transferred to the library.

Branch libraries, in order to begin to be more effective, should employ Latino librarians and supporting staff. There should certainly be a good stock of books available on ethnic subjects. Without these two requirements, branch libraries located in the barrio will continue to be little used, if at all.

A final word must be said about the sacred cow, the IQ. Countless numbers of Chicanos have received inferior educations based on scores achieved in some IQ test taken when they were about eight years old, barely spoke English, and hardly knew "American" mannerisms. Such "intelligence" tests are biased and invalid. They channel Chicanos into special education classes or seriously undermine a youth's confidence when he is refused participation in classes or experiences because his IQ is not high enough.

Schools and school districts have also been suspected of consciously employing these farcical IQ tests in order to gain benefits for themselves. Currently, in one Southern California city, almost two-thirds of all the children in "mentally retarded" or special education classes are Chicanos. The federal government gives $5,000 to a school district for every child in a "mentally retarded" status. It is common knowledge that this particular school district is not using the $5,000 per child to improve the education of these so-called "mentally retarded" children but rather is channeling these funds to improve the predominantly white schools.

Recently, the Rural Legal Assistance Foundation filed suit in the San Francisco U.S. District Court on behalf of nine school children of Mexican background in Monterey County, charging that these youngsters are "wrongfully placed in classes for the educable mentally retarded because they get low scores in IQ tests given in English, a language they don't know well.

"The suit charges that when given the IQ tests in English, the children, ranging from eight to thirteen years, failed. But when they were retested by a bilingual tester in both English and Spanish, they scored an average gain on the test of fifteen points. The school district, the suit stated, refuses to accept the results of the second tests and refuses to re-test the children themselves

"Placement in classes for the mentally retarded, the suit adds, is 'tantamount to a life sentence of illiteracy and public dependency.' "

It is for reasons such as these that the Chicano movement is educating its own and others—educating them to effect a change in the entire system, a change that can come only through revolution!

RECOMMENDED READINGS

GENERAL

BECK, WARREN A. *New Mexico: A History of Four Centuries.* Norman, Oklahoma, 1962

CLENDENEN, CLARENCE C. *Blood on the Border: The United States Army and the Mexican Irregulars.* New York, 1969

FAULK, ODIE B. *Land of Many Frontiers: A History of the American Southwest.* New York, 1968

GALARZA, ERNESTO. *Merchants of Labor: The Mexican Bracero Story.* New York, 1964

GAMIO, MANUEL. *Mexican Immigration to the United States.* Chicago, 1930

GONZALEZ, NANCIE L. *The Spanish Americans of New Mexico: A Heritage Of Pride.* Albuquerque, New Mexico, 1969

HELLER, CELIA S. *Mexican American Youth: Forgotten Youth at the Crossroads.* New York, 1966

HORGAN, PAUL. *The Centuries of Santa Fe.* New York, 1956

——. *Great River: The Rio Grande in North American History.* New York, 1954

HUTCHINSON, C. ALAN. *Frontier Settlement in Mexican California.* New Haven, Connecticut, 1969

JONES, OAKAH L. *Pueblo Warriors and Spanish Conquest.* Norman, Oklahoma, 1966

McWILLIAMS, CAREY. *North From Mexico.* New York, 1949

MADSEN, WILLIAM. *Mexican Americans of South Texas.* New York, 1964

The Mexican American: Quest for Equality. Office of Education, Washington, D.C., 1968

NABOKOV, PETER. *Tijerina and the Courthouse Raid.* Albuquerque, New Mexico, 1969

PITT, LEONARD. *The Decline of the Californios: A Social History of the Spanish-Speaking Californians 1846–1890.* Berkeley, California, 1968

RIVERA, FELICIANO. *A Mexican American Sourcebook.* Menlo Park, California, 1970

SAMORA, JULIAN. *La Raza: Forgotten Americans.* South Bend, Indiana, 1966

STEINER, STAN. *La Raza: The Mexican Americans.* New York, 1970

WARNER, LOUIS H. *Archbishop Lamy: An Epoch Maker.* Santa Fe, New Mexico, 1936

WELLMAN, PAUL I. *Glory, God and Gold.* Garden City, New York, 1954

FICTION

BRIGHT, ROBERT. *The Life and Death of Little Jo.* Garden City, New York, 1944

CATHER, WILLA. *Death Comes to the Archbishop.* New York, 1927

COOLIDGE, DANE. *Gringo Gold.* New York, 1939

CRICHTON, KYLE. *The Proud People.* New York, 1944

FERGUSON, HARVEY. *The Conquest of Don Pedro.* New York, 1954

————. *Followers of the Sun: A Trilogy of the Santa Fe Trail.* New York, 1949

GARNER, CLAUDE. *Wetback.* New York, 1947

JESSEY, CORNELIA. *Teach the Angry Spirit.* New York, 1949

PEREZ, LUIS. *El Coyote the Rebel.* New York, 1947

SHULMAN, IRVING. *The Square Trap.* Boston, 1953

STEINBECK, JOHN. *Tortilla Flat.* New York, 1937

STILWELL, HART. *Border City.* New York, 1945

SUMMERS, RICHARD A. *The Devil's Highway.* New York, 1937

TAYLOR, ROBERT LOUIS. *Two Roads to Guadalupé.* New York, 1964

VASQUEZ, RICHARD. *Chicano.* New York, 1970

VILLARREAL, JOSE ANTONIO. *Poncho.* New York, 1959.

INDEX

DATE DUE

GAYLORD			PRINTED IN U.S.A